mommy issues.

Chase Freeman

This is for anyone who ever finds themselves struggling with toxic relationships and finding ways to get out of them. For those seeking the light on the other side

... and for the people who voted "no" to my social media poll about whether or not I could pull this project off.

DISCLAIMER

I feel as if I should go ahead and include this little warning about this book project that I have somehow thrown together. This book at many points will be featuring my perspective and the many emotions that I have felt throughout the course of my life and a great deal of information (some might argue too much information) relating to the experiences I have gone through. I know that this information may be hard to digest for a lot of people, but I told myself that I was going to put my everything into this project and that means being as genuine and transparent as possible. While I am fairly skilled at talking about situations in my life in a way that makes it seem like I am completely unbothered by things that have transpired, I understand that not everyone is able to "turn off" their emotional response to reading things that might trigger some unwanted emotions.

That being said, I'm not going to make this an X-rated literature project or feature any form of outlandish explicit material by any means, but I will go ahead and say that I have gone through a number of things that I have no choice but to feature within this project for a number of reasons. At the risk of revealing spoilers, the key themes of this book that I believe might be triggersome involve mental health and sexuality. However, if you are reading this and you happen to be offended or uncomfortable with something that I am writing about or expressing, just know that it's coming from a place inside that has felt exactly what I am writing about at that given point of time. I'm hoping that by expressing these deep parts of myself and my journey, it might reach at least one person who may have been feeling a similar way at some point or another and that it helps that person in some way. If you haven't gone through any similar situations or find any profound clarity from my words, then I hope that you will at least be a little bit inspired and/or entertained throughout the duration of this ride and all of its twists and turns.

If you happen to be a family member that is reading this, just know that it wasn't easy putting my life (so far) onto paper. I hope that nothing that you read throughout this book makes you change your perception of me from positive to negative, but if that happens to be the case, I wish I could say that I was sorry. These are my stories about my life so far and I refuse to skew it with any lies or hold back from telling how things appeared from my perspective just for the sake of hoping to maintain good graces. But after everything that I have gone through, I know that the friends and family that I need to have my back are going to remain supportive of me and that's all that matters to me. Also, I have changed any and all names that may be used within this book as a way to protect everyone's privacy and, most importantly, keep the spotlight on myself.

Prologue

How the hell did I end up here? I stared down at the little desk in front of me in this small-town courtroom, attempting to wrap my mind around the last 13 or 14 months of my life. I looked up for a moment to make eye contact with my mother on the other side of the courtroom, her gaze smoldering with rage. We weren't physically (or emotionally) close enough to speak to each other, thankfully. However, I already knew everything that she would be saying to me if that were the case. I was a spoiled little brat. I hated her and my sister. I didn't want anything good for her. I betrayed the family. I teamed up with the evil enemy. I had better get my shit together if I wanted anything to do with her and my sister ever again. I was the evil one. I was a horrible person and a horrible son and a horrible brother. Nana would be so disappointed in me. I'm never going to have a future or a career after this. I was the son that no mother could ever

The doors suddenly opened and the judge for the day's proceedings stepped up to his seat at the front of the courtroom. I stood up beside my attorney and anxiously played through the various scenarios that I had already created in my head for how today may or may not turn out. One featured absolutely no change to the status of anything and yet another future court date to begin dreading. One featured him buying into my mother's story of betrayal and somehow undoing all the progress we had made the last year. Another somehow resulted in me being escorted behind those doors in handcuffs after it was all said and done. Before my mind could process many more of these randomized imaginary experiences we were told to be seated and prepare for the day to begin. I looked over at my attorney, who could probably tell that I was on the verge of a panic attack, and he gave me a reassuring soft smile. The judge was then handed a folder full of files belonging to the cases for everyone in the room this morning.

Our case number was called as we respectfully rose to be addressed by the man who would be determining our fate today. What seemed like a simple rise from my chair was made more difficult as I felt the entire weight of the last year resting on my shoulders. We adjusted back into our seats as he started reading over the various details of this case, from the many times we had already all met in court to the various demands laid out in painful detail. I couldn't help but feel like a microscopic dot on his radar as he skimmed over the pages that each represented about three or four months of my life since this warfare began. Three to four months of life each that were just another decision in a pool of others that he was burdened with making today. Warfare that had dominated the majority of my life for so much time was just another casual morning for this man that I had never met before. A man that was about to probably make one of the most important decisions of my life. He had zero knowledge of who I was or who my mother was or everything that had transpired before today's court hearing yet he was the ultimate deciding factor.

He took a deep breath and began addressing my mother, who had already taken it upon herself to stand up and shout her complaints for the entire state to hear. I watched her, voice rising with anger as she laid out everything as it existed in her mind. I kept my composure as this behavior was something I was painfully familiar with by now, even as she approached the level of growling in the courtroom and pointing towards where I was seated. A small part of me almost started to feel bad for the desperation in her tone and I wondered if I was the only one in the room that knew her well enough to hear it. But that quickly diminished as I started to reflect on the experiences, both small and enormous in significance, that landed us in a courtroom and sitting on opposite sides of an invisible dividing line. A line that showed no sign or possibility of being repaired after today, no matter what the outcome happened to be.

The room almost started to feel like it was being played in slow-motion as my mother stood and gave her best attempt at playing the scorned woman. I knew she was speaking but I wasn't hearing the words coming out of her mouth anymore. I stared at her with disbelief that she was the same woman that I had spent my entire childhood with. The woman who had given birth to me. The woman I would run to if I had fallen down and scraped a knee. The one person who was supposed to love and support you in this world no matter what. Yet here I sat on the other side of her in a courtroom. Here I sat listening to how evil I was and how much I was ruining her life. While some of my friends had mothers that showed up to every single game or every single school play, I was given one that attended every court hearing. One that would tell a judge that I was evil. One that left me voicemails saying that she would ruin my chances of a future if I didn't cave to her demands. But the worst part of all of this sudden analysis was that it wasn't always like this by any means. In fact, everything used to be quite the opposite of what I was seeing today. I looked down at my briefcase and started thinking back on my entire 22 years of life and everything leading up to this monumental morning...

Table of Contents

Chapter One

Remember When Everything Was Normal?

My eyes opened quickly from whatever dream I was having and my bedroom slowly came into view once I realized I was awake and back on Earth. I yawned and stretched and thought about going back to sleep again when I heard Mom's voice calling for me in the other room. I hopped out of bed, ran across the room, almost slipped and fell over my own superhero pajamas, and screamed that I did not want to wake up yet and that three-year-olds did not have to. She shouted back that I was actually four years old now and laughed hysterically. We argued back and forth until I could not stop myself from laughing aloud. I guess I really am four now, even though I wasn't actually sure what that meant. I revved up my internal engines and sprinted into the living room on the hunt for Mom so I could make her play with me. I finally talked her into playing a game or two but not for too long because she said that Nana and Poppop were going to be here soon and my brother and I needed to get ready. Suddenly my entire body turned into happiness and excitement. I couldn't believe Nana and Poppop were going to be in my house today!

I played with some of my toys in the living room before running back to my room to take off the pajamas that were probably my brother's before they were mine. I waited for Mom to be done so she could come pick out my clothes for me. I sat down on my bed and tried to remember yesterday, the day before, or anything before today but I couldn't. I just remember waking up today and knowing that I was three (or four, allegedly), that she was my Mom and that I loved playing with her, that he's my older brother and can be mean sometimes, that Nana and Poppop visiting makes me really happy, and that this is my life. I didn't know what any of this meant or why this is the life that mysteriously belonged to me, but I just *knew.* My name is Chase, I'm four, and I'm happy. Mom walked in and picked out some clothes for me and asked if I needed help putting them on or not. I smiled as big as I could and said I could do it myself like my brother does. A few hours passed by until Mom yelled from the other room that their car had just pulled up, causing my body to go into hyper drive as I ran towards the front door of our house to be the first one to greet them. Mom saw my excitement and told me that she was going to beat me to being the first, but I made sure she knew I was the winner here and that I wasn't going to have it any other way. We both laughed out loud and stepped out onto the front porch together.

Poppop got out of the car and ran over to the other side to open up Nana's door. He offered his arm and they started to walk slowly towards our front door, my euphoric heartbeat getting faster and faster. I didn't know how I knew this was Nana and Poppop, but I just knew. Just seeing them was enough to make me smile from ear to ear until I noticed her almost slipping on the sidewalk. Mom let out a little scream and told her to be careful because of the ice. A minute later and we were all in the living room laughing together. My big brother had finally walked in from his room to join us. I made sure to tell him that I got to see Nana and Poppop first before he did even though I knew he would make me regret it. About 45 minutes later, he was putting me inside the dryer, which made me laugh at first. I stopped laughing after he shut it and actually turned the machine on for a minute or so. Naturally, I ran straight to Nana and/or Mom for comfort once I managed to escape Rob and the dryer. They always knew how to make me feel better.

I ran down the hallway out of the laundry room and towards the living room, hoping to come face-to-face with Nana to hug her and tell her how scary the dryer was. However, whenever I rounded the corner everything was completely different. The scenery around me had dissolved and changed into something new. I was walking down the hallway of a school instead of my house. I felt suddenly older than the three/four year old version I had just been, but not by much. I looked around and tried to figure out where exactly I was as more and more information started to present itself. I began walking, one terrified step in front of the other towards the direction of the guidance counselor's office. Wait. Oh yeah. I'm at school and it's time for some meeting that I have to go to because Mom says I'm not like some of the other kids in my class. I don't really know what all that means, but my teacher walked me to the guidance office so that I at least knew where this special class was. I walked into one of the rooms in the office and tried to be as nice as I could to the woman my teacher left me with. Mom and Nana always tell me that manners are important, but I'm still trying to figure out how to make myself talk to people more.

"How about we start this meeting today by getting to know each other a little better," the woman said like it was a simple task instead of one that made my body shake in fear. I answered some of her questions about who I am and some things I liked to do. After a few back-and-forth rounds of these simple questions and games and other small icebreakers, the conversation started to get a little more serious. The next words came out of her mouth very slowly and carefully, almost as if each word was capable of exploding at any moment. "Would you like to tell me what you think about your parents being divorced? Is it difficult for you to have to live in two different homes sometimes?" She finished

2

the last word and paused for a while, as if waiting to see if her words had detonated anything inside my brain or not. I stared down at the floor for what felt like hours as her words settled over me with a rush of discomfort. I didn't want to be here in this room anymore but I had no idea how to say that or what this feeling in the pit of my stomach was or meant. I just knew I wanted to leave as quickly as possible and run away from whoever this woman was. But I couldn't. I sat in my chair, my mouth frozen shut in fear. I sat in silence until she took me back to my classroom.

I saw the decorations of my teacher's door as we rounded one of the hallways, excitement quickly replacing the hollow void of awkward silence inside my head. I could finally get back to my building blocks or try and read one of the books if the other kids hadn't taken them all for themselves. I knew I didn't want to talk about Mom and Dad and whatever that word was that she asked me about but I didn't know why. I had no idea what "divorce" was but it sounded scary and I never wanted to hear it again. The woman opened up the door for me and I quickly made my way over to the empty corner in the classroom. I grabbed some of the blocks and threw myself into the tranquility that came with building a little castle area on the play mat in front of me. I looked up and around at all the other kids and started to wonder whether their parents lived in two different houses away from each other too. Was I a weird kid? Was this why the teacher looks at me like that sometimes and none of the other kids? Was this why nobody likes to play with me?

Mom picked me up from school later that day after she sat in one of the rooms in the front office for a little while. Once we got home, she said that we needed to sit down and have a talk if that was okay. It wasn't a very long talk, but by the time it was over, I was left both confused yet somehow enlightened at the same time. Apparently, Mom and Dad loved each other and had me but then they stopped loving each other and found new people to love. Dad found Erin and Mom found Steven. The other kids have two parents and I kind of have four even though that doesn't really make much sense. Rob doesn't come with me to Dad and Erin's house every other weekend because that's not his dad. But we have the same Mom and the same Steven and the same Nana and Poppop. The two other brothers (Apparently they're called "stepbrothers" actually) that I have when I'm at Dad and Erin's don't belong to anyone else at my other house. I knew I had a few questions and quite a bit of confusion surrounding why my life was so different from everyone else's but I couldn't find the words in my head to try and convince my mouth to ask. I think the most confusing part was the way that Mom kept making it seem as if I had a choice on whether I wanted my life to stay this way or not. It'll all make sense eventually though, right?

I went to my room later that night and started thinking about everything Mom had told me and how confusing it all really seemed. However, at the same time it didn't seem confusing at all because that's just how my life was. All the memories that I have inside my head consist of two different houses and two different families. Two birthdays. Two Christmases. Two sets of parents. Two sets of siblings. Two totally separate lives that were never going to mesh together. Suddenly, I started thinking about how hard it was to talk to that woman in the office and how hard it seemed for Mom to talk about having to keep up with visitation and letting Dad see me so often. My mind drifted to how I would sometimes get spanked and how scary that was. I stared up at the ceiling in the dark of my bedroom and the scenery quickly began to dissolve around me again. I blinked a few times to determine if I was dreaming or caught in the grips of another nightmare but that wasn't the case. I was still in my bedroom, but not the bedroom I had at Mom's house. This was my bedroom at Dad and Erin's house. It definitely was not a dream the more I looked around in the darkness. But it wasn't today anymore, that much I knew for sure.

It was nighttime and there wasn't even a sliver of doubt in my head that I was older, but not by much. If I had to take a guess, I was late five, early six years old sitting on my bed and looking up at the glow-in-the-dark stars on my ceiling. I loved this ceiling, my mind immediately flashing back to helping Dad and Erin paint it to look like a bright blue sky with clouds during the day and a luminescent starlit galaxy at night. It may not have been a Picasso or a Sistine Chapel mural, but that didn't mean it wasn't perfect. I only held onto the happiness of that flashback for a second or two before falling back down to reality. It may have been dark, but I knew I wasn't alone in the room. The seriousness of the conversation going on right now fell over the entire room until it felt like a tangible fog. I'm telling them that I don't want to have two lives anymore. I can't tell if it's Dad in the room or Erin or perhaps both. I think it's both.

I wasn't exactly sure what had caused me to start having this conversation with them after being tucked in one night. Saying it all out loud, or at least attempting to, was the only thing that started to calm down the million thoughts in my head about my life and how different it was. That said, the moment the words were funneled and launched from my mind across the still quiet of the room my stomach contorted itself into a dense network of knots. Once the words were out, there was no taking them back which was a feeling I hadn't quite prepared myself for. The more twisted my stomach started to feel, the more words I tried to find to explain what I was feeling in a way that made more sense to Dad and Erin. The more I squinted into my own brain, the further away all the words I knew began to drift until they were completely out of sight, leaving my mind and entire catalog of vocabulary almost nonexistent. I had let the bomb drop in the room and now I was seemingly unable to elaborate or justify the decision I had just vocalized. From the perspective of my parents, my parents of this household at least, I had just randomly decided that I didn't want to see them anymore. Their 5-or-6-year-old son had just broken up with them and then stopped texting back or answering the calls.

They didn't hear that I was terrified of being spanked even one more time. They didn't understand how confusing it was to be physically disciplined for what felt like everything, especially when it never happened at the other house with my other family. They didn't get to hear that Mom made it feel like it would be easier to not have to do visitations anymore. I wasn't able to say that I hated airplanes and airports and that flying from Florida to Tennessee was terrifying. There wasn't a way for me to describe what it felt like knowing the other kids in my class all had the parents they were born with and only one house. I wanted nothing more than to clarify all of these thoughts and discuss them with Dad and Erin so that perhaps things could just be adjusted to be easier on everyone involved. I wanted them to know how hard this all seemed to be for Mom to manage. But I couldn't. The more I tried to find the right words to say, the more my stomach twisted into knots until I thought I was going to hurl right on my bed. All I could do was think about the words that *had* come out of my mouth and sit paralyzed in my bed feeling the devastation linger right in front of me.

Questions started to soar across the room from Dad and Erin but no matter how much I wanted to and no matter how much I jumped and reached out for words to grab hold of, I couldn't answer any of them. Words were coming out of my mouth as a jumbled mess that I knew wasn't making any sense. Each attempt to say something of value resulted in another knot forming in the tangled mess of my stomach. Eventually, I gave up trying altogether and retreated as far as I could in the caverns of my mind. Their questions kept coming, but I stopped listening and began to imagine a barrier between us that no words could break through. The questions then began to slow down until I could tell that I was now the only one remaining in the room. The conversation was over and it didn't feel like it could have gone any worse. Silence filled the room and left a heavy blanket of gloom and dread in its place. I stared up at the ceiling, felt the weight of what had just happened drape itself over me, and cried myself to sleep.

I opened my eyes and immediately recognized that I was in a new place once again and that some time had passed but only a week or two. My stomach was still entangled with nauseating coils of regret and confusion as I stared at the ground in front of me. I was in an office somewhere with a man that I had definitely never seen before. I knew Mom was nearby but not quite inside this same room. The man kept asking me questions about Dad, Erin, and how my life at that other family's house had been the last couple of years. Just like the woman I had met with at the Guidance Office, each question caused me to retreat further and further inside my own head until I couldn't hear them anymore. I didn't want to answer this strange man's questions. I don't understand why I'm having to sit in this office and talk to him. I wish I could just undo everything that I had said to Dad and Erin to make everything go back to normal. At this point, I somehow knew that wasn't an option. I had already let the words escape my mind and there was no backspace or undo button that could make everything go back to normal. At least Mom seemed happy that she was going to get to spend more time with me.

The conversation in the gloomy room with the strange man seemed to last forever before I could leave and go back to my house. Mom tried to ask me why I didn't tell the man anything about what had happened at my other house, but I couldn't find anything in my head to say to her either. This didn't feel right. I think they think something horrible happened to me there but I couldn't make anyone feel differently. My stomach was turning into more and more knots until I remembered what it was like when I would get spanked by Dad or by Erin. The guilt that would fill my head whenever I would wake up and realize I had wet the bed, knowing what was going to happen next. The fear that would spread like a wildfire across my body as I went to bend over Dad's knee after I had broken one of the rules that I forgot about. I didn't have to worry about spanking anymore though. A lot of this didn't feel right, not going to see Dad and Erin or my step brothers ever again. Not speaking to them at all again didn't feel normal or correct. However, not having to worry about spanking or making Mom stress about traveling to let them see me felt right. I don't know what to do or how to make this all work now. I guess I just have to accept that this is my life now and Mom is going to do what's best for me which is what she's done with all these papers and not seeing my other family anymore.

We pulled up to our house and I started to pick up some of the memories from the last year or so and figure out what point in time I was at. I was in first grade in my fourth or fifth house so far and this one was in Daytona Beach, Florida. I remember Mom and Steven getting married and being a part of their wedding, but that was a year or maybe more ago. I already finished kindergarten even if it felt like a disaster. I had two different kindergarten teachers, one that would never believe me and always say that I was in trouble and another one that screamed at us and said bad words all the time. I didn't really know what the bad words were or what they meant, but I could just tell it was words that I wasn't supposed to hear or say. The other teacher would always say that I was causing problems with the other kids because I would never be able to find any words to say whenever the other kids would get caught doing something bad. One kid asked me to cut his hair and I was the one that got in trouble because he told the teacher it was my idea and my mouth froze shut in fear when she asked me about it because I thought I was going to get a spanking. I hated spankings but that's not something I had to worry about, even if the worries were replaced with a million other ones related to not seeing my other family ever again.

Right. I only have this one family now in this pretty house in Florida that has a huge pond in the backyard. I have my stepdad Steven, Mom, and my brother Rob. I usually try to keep to myself as much as possible because Steven yells a lot and scares me, especially when he's yelling at Mom. Rob scares the absolute hell out of me because he'll fight me whether he has a reason to or not. I look at Rob and immediately get reminded of the time he put me in a dryer or hit me across the back with bamboo. Hell (if I'm allowed to say that word), just two weeks ago I was running away from him into the front yard and looked up from my hiding spot just in time to be struck in the forehead with a golf ball that he had hurled full-speed in my direction. I passed out for a few seconds and ended up having a gigantic bruise and knot on my forehead for about a week after that. Rob was 3 years older than me so he was always going to be the bigger, stronger person in our fights so I tried to avoid them as much as I could. Reading books, playing with my action figures in the sanctuary of my room, playing with our dog Shiloh, or walking over to Mr. and Mrs. Patterson's house next door quickly became my routine escape whenever Steven was yelling at Mom and/or Rob or when Rob was trying to murder me for whatever reason.

We went to the beach sometimes since our house was only about 15 minutes away, but that didn't really make me very happy. The sand irritated my skin and every time I stepped into the water, Mom screamed at me about getting eaten by a shark, or Rob came up to push me headfirst into a wave. From the moment my sandals hit the sands, I started counting down the time in my mind until I could be back in my room playing with my action figures, watching the animals on my TV screen, or running around the neighborhood. Mom always made me have Rob with me when I went outside to be safe, but that always means I have to do whatever he and his friends did which wasn't always fun (or legal). One of those times involved me following them around and trying to find frogs on the sides of houses while his friends threw rocks at each other until one of the rocks went straight through the neighbor's screen porch and into their pool. They blamed me. I'm the one that got grounded and yelled at by Mom and Steven and the neighbor. I stayed in my room instead of going outside again unless I got to go play with the Pattersons. One time they helped me with my Art project for school by creating my own aquarium when Mom said she was too busy. Mr. Patterson even let me use the hot glue gun as long as I promised to be super safe.

I'm pretty sure I was in second grade since I had a new teacher than I used to when we first moved to Florida, but she wasn't nearly as nice as Mrs. McGray was. Mrs. McGray would always let me use the bathroom when I was too shy to have used it with everyone else and never forced me to talk to the rest of the class about one of the answers to a problem. This woman wasn't nice at all and I knew that on the first day which is why I started crying when Mom started to walk away. I wanted to stay at home with her and tell her how much I knew I wasn't going to get along with this new teacher in the trailer beside one of the school buildings. However, as with any previous situation, I couldn't find the right words to say any of that stuff so I just walked to my seat and cried until I found a way to calm myself down and make the knots in my stomach disappear for a while. On the bright side, with the classroom being in a small trailer, I could always find frogs and little snakes underneath it or in the surrounding grasses.

Some of the kids in my class were nice to me, but some of them called me weird within the first week. I already called the teacher "Mom" by accident and everyone laughed at me. I hated people laughing at me so from that point forward I decided not to say anything out loud anymore unless someone came up and asked me something or talked to me first. If that didn't happen, that meant I was probably reading one of my books to try and keep my mind from going to places that I didn't like going. I missed seeing Dad but anytime I started to mention it, Mom would interrupt me and tell me that I didn't have to talk about it. She kept bringing up that man in the dark office room and how he told her that something had happened at Dad's house that I wasn't ready to talk about. Before I could think about the best way to tell her that I think I messed up, she would tell me that Dad already signed the papers to not see me ever again. He apparently signed those papers instead of fighting to see me like Mom had fought for me to do what's right. This didn't feel right but if that's what Mom says we have to do, it must be. But I couldn't stop myself from thinking about it whenever I was sitting at my desk or in my bedroom by myself.

Whenever these thoughts got louder and louder in my head and the knots in my stomach grew more tangled, I tried to find whatever I could to make them go away. I started reading books and quickly realized how much I loved letting the voice in my head read the words printed on the pages in my hands until my mind was transported to whatever world the characters were living in. When I got tired of that, which was rare, I had all my action figures in my room to play with. I would pick up a superhero one and a cartoon one and a random one that I don't remember anything about and suddenly my bedroom became a brand new universe. A universe that I had complete control over as I laid out all the names of the action figures and what their mission was on any given afternoon. My bedroom quickly became my favorite place to be because I could imagine it being a new place every time I came home from school. Today, the Captain had to take the two injured soldiers back to their home planet without getting caught by the villain that was perched on top of my dresser. Tomorrow, they would have to come back for the rest of the crew. In a few days, this storyline might already have dissolved into a new one altogether if I thought of something more interesting until it was time for dinner. Our dinners usually happened in the living room while we all watched TV which was my favorite since it usually didn't count for my hour of TV allowed per day.

I loved reading and I loved playing with my action figures and I loved playing with our dog sometimes, but sometimes I wished I had friends. The Patterson's next door are my best friends but Mom said they got pretty sick sometime last month and I haven't seen them sitting on their porch at all since then. I wished the kid that was always nice to me in class lived next door to me so I could have someone else to play with that wasn't trying to attack me all the time like my brother was. I really hated my brother sometimes, especially the times he fought with Mom and Steven over things that didn't make any sense. He always got all the attention in the house, not that it bothers me because I never know what to say anytime anyone ever talks to me. But I got frustrated when he acted like that because they give him so much attention whenever it's time for another doctor's appointment or a checkup on his ear to see if some new invention might make it possible for him to hear out of it. I don't know all the health problems that he had because Mom always said so many so fast that I couldn't keep track. They treated him so differently and so carefully and yet he was still mean to everyone.

If Mom and Steven weren't fighting with Rob, they were fighting with each other which gave me another reason to stay in my room all the time. I never really knew what started the arguments, but sometimes they got really loud and a tidal wave of panic struck my body. Luckily, I figured out how to drown out the noise by creating another galaxy inside my bedroom to send all my action figures to until they were done screaming at each other over whatever they were fighting about. I always pretended that I didn't hear them and would even deny hearing it if Mom asked me later. Sometimes she would still come into my room after and make sure to tell me that it was Steven's fault for the arguments and that he could be really mean sometimes. Steven could be really scary, especially when he's mad, so I believed her. I always gave her a hug after until she felt better. If I was lucky, she would rub my back or play with my hair afterwards until I fell asleep. I knew Steven was nice sometimes, but it was hard not to feel scared of messing something up and making him mad. Thankfully, one way to avoid getting yelled at was to stay in my room with my books, action figures, and untamed imagination for hours and hours and hours.

I walked in from playing with our dog in the backyard near the pond and heard Steven fighting with Mom again. It sounded pretty loud, so I quickly put the dog back out onto the screened porch so he wouldn't hear them and made my way to my room before they could notice me. I shut the door behind me as quickly as I could and got my action-figures out before sending my mind off into another world that existed in my head for a while. When I came crashing back down into my room, I could immediately tell something was different. Time had passed again, but I somehow knew it wasn't too long. I looked around in confusion as I began to notice my room was packed up into stacks of boxes. My bedroom door opened quickly and Mom was standing in the doorway rushing me to get the rest of my room packed up. We were moving soon. I was puzzled, but knew not to speak up or try to make sense of what was going on. Maybe if I can get my imagination to be strong enough, I can just pretend we aren't moving and everything would be back to normal with my two different families. However, that dream seemed far off as I helped put that last box into the moving truck and climbed up into the car, leaving our pastel-colored bright Florida house in the rear-view mirror.

With every red light we passed and every intersection we turned on, I got more and more clarity as to what was happening in the current time frame I had awoken in. We were moving to a state called Tennessee again, but not the same place we had lived before Florida. We were going to a place called Loudon so that we could be closer to my grandfather. I started to get excited until I realized that she wasn't talking about Poppop and Nana. This was a grandfather that I didn't remember ever meeting before. What if he was mean? What if he didn't like me? We hit another pothole, causing another memory suddenly rising to the surface of my mind. My last name was being changed. Suddenly, I recall sitting across from Mom and Steven with Rob sitting beside me, already upset about having to move. I didn't remember ever meeting Mom's real Dad so I wasn't sure why we had to move close to him. Then, to make it even more confusing, I was having my last name changed to be the same as my new grandfather's.

No more Florida. No more Mr. and Mrs. Patterson. No more giant pond in the backyard that would sometimes house alligators. No more frogs and lizards everywhere for me to play with. No more seeing the one or two people I had managed to start befriending. No more having the same last name as my real dad. All of these realities were hitting and I wanted to scream at the top of my lungs. I wanted to yell so loud that the knots tangled up inside my stomach would shrivel from the volume. To shout in a way that everyone in the living room was forced to stop their own yelling and listen. But I couldn't. I searched my head for the right words to say how I was feeling or ask the right questions but it was no use. I would just end up saying the wrong things like I had done at the other house, not realizing it would be the last night underneath those glow-in-the-dark stars on the ceiling. If I took the risk and managed to say the wrong thing, there was also the chance that it would make Steven mad and that was not something I was willing to bet my cards on. So I sat there in silence, nodded, and waited to be dismissed back to my room. Plus, Mom loved me very much so there must be a good reason for all of this happening right now. Maybe a new name will be fun! It's almost like I was getting to play a new character in a new story like I was always imagining in my head whenever I'd play with my action figures.

Chapter Two

Remember When I Lived in a Motel?

Walking into the new hallway of my new school came with an overwhelming tidal wave of paralyzing fear. Not only was I going into another new school where I didn't know anyone, but I was going to the same school as my brother. It didn't make much sense to me, but apparently this school was kindergarten through eighth grade. Each footstep on the linoleum brought my head further and further down until I was practically staring directly at my feet as I took step after step towards the Guidance Office with Mom. Rob was old enough to go directly to his homeroom class alone once he had his schedule printed off. I looked up just in time to avoid running into the closed door of the office to get my schedule figured out. I looked around at all the different kids in the same area. Some of them stood tall like giants and others seemed like they were toddlers from where I stood. Feeling the same overwhelming panic forming in the form of knots in my stomach once more, I lowered my head again while Mom led me into the office to meet with the Guidance Counselor and Principal.

I wasn't used to being introduced to the heads of the schools I had attended in the past, but I guess that's what happens when you move from a beachy city in Florida to a microscopic town in Tennessee. Not wanting to make a bad impression by saying something wrong per usual, I remained silent and clung to Mom's side as closely as I could. The tall, kind man could sense my uneasiness and forewent all the small talk. He assured Mom that I would be well cared for in the hallways of this new school and that they would do everything possible to make me feel comfortable in my new environment. Mom decided to take his word for it and surrendered me into their hands more quickly than I expected. Luckily, I didn't cry this time like I had done with my second-grade teacher in Florida. I followed the Principal along the hallway that felt like it was never going to end towards my teacher's classroom, making a stop at the library along the way. He walked me in and introduced me to the librarian in order to get my library card. She was an older woman who radiated kindness, immediately reminding me of Nana, which put me more at ease. She typed at her computer for a few moments before asking my name so that she could print out the card from her system. Without thinking, I told her and was met with an awkward stare from the Principal.

Wait. That wasn't my name anymore. I had a new name now. My heart sank into my stomach and I felt the blood rush to my head in embarrassment. I quickly apologized, fumbling over my words as I gave her the new name that I had to go by from now on. She gave me a smile, making me feel a little bit better about seemingly not knowing my own name even though I'd only had it for a few weeks now. They didn't know that though. No one would know that. How were the other kids in my class going to understand that my Mom changed my name when I barely understood it? I already knew it was going to be a difficult few weeks trying not to use my old name whenever I put my name on my papers and assignments. I already missed my old name, especially since it was the same last name of Dad. I missed Dad. I wish that undo button was a real thing. But it wasn't and I had no way of telling anyone anything to fix it. This was my new life and this was my new name, I guess.

We finally made it to my teacher's classroom where I'd be spending my time for third grade in my new school. I walked in and immediately felt everyone's eyes shift towards me and my stomach was immediately in knots again. This was my second time being "The New Kid" and I already hated it ten times worse than the first experience. The teacher gave me a comforting smile from across the room and asked me to introduce myself to the class. I tried to summon as much of a voice as I could in the moment while paying careful attention to saying my new last name instead of screwing that up again. I heard a couple of them giggle whenever they heard my last name and quickly realized it wasn't too common of a name. Great. I was already getting laughed at on my first day. The teacher must not have heard them, so I pretended not to have either as I made my way to the desk that had my name card sitting on top. I sat down in the chair, wishing I could sink further and further into it until no one could see me anymore. I definitely didn't like being the New Kid. Luckily, Mrs. Bright jumped right back into the lesson so I could let all the knots in my stomach slowly unravel at a painfully slow pace.

I started to feel more comfortable as time flashed by and I got to know some of my classmates. One of them introduced themselves by letting me know that he was my cousin which completely threw me for a loop. The only cousins I knew were from my aunts and I only saw them at Thanksgiving and Christmas whenever we'd visit Nana and Poppop. I quickly remembered Mom telling me that all of our family was born and raised in this small town so it started to make a little more sense. By lunchtime, I had gathered that practically everyone in this school was born and raised here. Everyone knew everyone already. My brother and I are the only strangers in these hallways. As if I didn't already stand out with my uncommon last name that I had to broadcast to the class, I had to be escorted to a new classroom after lunch because I was apparently placed in a different reading class for fourth graders. Great. Mom must have told them that I needed to be in a different grade level whenever possible because of how much I liked to read. So now all my new classmates think I have a weird last name *and* I think I'm a nerd. I wonder if I come home crying enough if it would be enough to move back to Florida already. Would it be enough to undo the whole Dad situation too?

The rest of the day seemed to drag by painfully slowly, even after putting myself out there by playing football with some of the other kids that my cousin had introduced me to. There were a handful of other third-grade classrooms but during recess, we all have to gather and play at the same time. Maybe this wasn't going to be so bad. Everyone actually seemed to be pretty nice to me, all things considered with me being the newest human of the entire town. I had to contain my excitement whenever I found out that we got to have silent reading time to wrap up every single day. Compared to my feelings at the beginning of today, I think I could give this place a chance even if it meant a little bit of cultural adjustment. I had traded in frogs, sunshine, and beaches with boots, trucks, and thick accents but this was life now. There's nothing I can do but go along with the new lives that kept getting presented to me by Mom.

Rob and I jumped into the back of Mom's car in front of the school and told her about our first days until we pulled up the long driveway to our big brick house on Country Lane. I hopped out of the car and into the front door, eager to run up to my room and emotionally exhale. Sure, we were in a vastly different town and state, but that doesn't mean I couldn't enjoy the perks of the new house. I had my own room once again, this one being about twice the size of the other one with a big open floor. The layout provided the perfect area to dump out all of my action figures comfortably to create whatever escape I could ever need. On top of that, there was a big window area with a windowsill that was large enough to hold me that I could hop up on whenever I wanted to dive into a book with the soothing sunlight pouring in through the glass. We had unpacked and settled in pretty quickly, with special thanks to the younger kid next door coming in to help (after first helping himself to the pizza we had ordered without much of an invitation at all). I set my backpack on the floor next to my bedroom door and stepped over to the window to look out over the new front yard in our new town. Maybe it wouldn't be too bad here. It'll be fine. New town. New name. New grandfather.

We turned up the small hill and pulled up to the first house on the right before walking inside to meet. I couldn't remember if I had ever met them before so I stayed silent like I normally do while Mom does all the talking. The house had a pretty, open living room with high ceilings. A thin, older woman greeted us as we walked in and Mom told me that she was MiMi, Poppop Luke's mother.

Poppop Luke walked up from the basement to join the gathering next. He was a tall man with a full head of dark hair. He walked up to us, carrying an aura of confidence with every step. He shook our hands, pointing out that my handshake could use some work but that he could help fix that eventually. We all sat together in the living room for a while, sipping on the best fruit tea I had ever tasted. Mom said it was one of MiMi's specialties and I could not get enough of it, even after downing two full glasses. I still wasn't able to muster up the courage to say much of anything, but they seemed pretty nice even though Mom had said MiMi was a mean person all the time. After a while we all stood up from the living room and made our way back to the car to head home. Poppop Luke asked if we would want to go fishing with him sometime and Rob answered for both of us. I had never been fishing before but my new grandfather seemed eager to be the first one to teach me so I smiled and shook my head.

I spent the ride home trying to wrap my mind around the fact that I had just met Mom's father and grandmother. Apparently he had been high school sweethearts with Nana in this same town that I was living in now. They got married, had Mom, but then apparently things went downhill from there. Mom said that he did bad things in his life and became a pretty different person whenever he would drink, whatever that meant. So they got a divorce and Nana married the Poppop that I already knew pretty well. So now I have Poppop Luke and MiMi, Nana and Poppop, and Grams and Gramps. That's what we call Steven's parents whenever we get to visit them on holidays, usually right after Nana and Poppop's house. I couldn't stop my mind from starting to wonder about my "real" Dad and Erin. I hopped out of the backseat and walked up to my bedroom to sit in the windowsill and read a book before I got too consumed by those thoughts. I wondered if everyone's family situation feels this disconnected and complicated until I drifted off into a nap.

I'm not sure how I pulled it off, but it felt like I was actually beginning to make friends here at this school, a concept I was vastly unfamiliar with up until now. Of course, I still had moments of saying weird things and getting weird looks from the other kids, but I was making progress. I had friends to sit with during Ice Cream Fridays, play with at recess most of the time, and play random games with during class breaks. I even found out one of the fourth-graders in my Reading class lived in the street behind our house. Once we found that out, Rob and I started to spend more time outside playing with him whenever we'd get done with our homework or chores. Mom eventually met his mom and we even spent some mornings carpooling to school together. I wasn't the most popular kid in school by any means, but I was starting to really like going to school and not feeling so isolated and alone like I had the last couple of years in other schools.

Naturally, there were speed bumps to watch out for with this new appreciation and understanding of friendship. One of these included accidentally tripping our neighbor whenever we were running around in the backyard, causing him to face plant into the brick wall in our driveway. Somehow, even with half of his face mauled by the bricks we still managed to remain friends. Next would come the moment of frustration whenever I lost a game of connect-the-dots with a friend in class. After throwing a small tantrum, I threw my pencil down which just so happened to enter into the leg of the girl who had just beaten me in the game. It turns out stabbing your classmate will result in a not-so-nice letter you have to give your parents as well as sitting out during the next Ice Cream Friday. But like I said, progress.

I backpedaled a little and started to keep a lower profile instead of trying to be as much of a class clown. I liked people thinking that I was funny, but I didn't want to get too greedy with my pursuit of making friends for the first time and end up losing them all in the same breath. I only spoke up if I knew for a fact that what I was saying was going to land and then did as much socializing as I could during recess with the other classes. One day, the teachers messed up the recess schedule by letting some of the seventh and eighth grade classes go outside for the afternoon instead of staying in the classroom for lessons. I looked up from the old, rusty merry-go-round to see them stampeding towards us like a herd of raging giants. Before I could even start to form an escape plan, I was being spun around on the metal circle faster than ever before. I clung to the metal pole as tightly as I could but eventually got flung off entirely. I flew into the ground just a couple of inches away. A moment later, a surge of stinging-hot pain in my leg caused me to release an agonizing wail. Somehow, I had been flung off the merry-go-round, but not far enough to avoid the wheel from spinning at maximum speed into my shin. I pulled myself away as quickly as I could, but it was too late. I glanced down to see a mixture of red and white as I looked at what appeared to be the inside of my bone as blood began pouring out.

A sickening feeling hit the pit of my stomach as I realized what was going on and the pain started to resonate throughout my body. Was I really just looking at my own bone just now? I quickly turned away, unable to keep staring at whatever it was I was staring at any longer. I don't know when I stood up, but all of a sudden I was looking down to see one foot moving in front of the other across the grass. I moved my head up to see the group of teachers I was sprinting towards while pointing at my leg, blood now reaching all the way to my socks and shoes. I had no idea what I was screaming in that moment as panic drowned out almost all of my senses and my flight response took control of the wheels. Somehow, between the blood and the flailing about, they managed to direct me to the nurse to take matters into her own experienced hands. I barely knew anything about her, so naturally I didn't say much whenever

I was escorted into her small office. She was a nurse, though, so she would probably know exactly what to do to make my leg better. She was a school nurse too, so maybe she'd know exactly what to say to make me feel better. I know that's how Nana or Mom would handle this if it hadn't happened at school on the playground.

I decided to bite the bullet and look back down at my injured shin just in time to see the school nurse putting a Band-Aid on it. More pain surged up my leg and it took everything in me not to scream. I wasn't sure what the rest of her plan was for this treatment, but this was not working. I wanted to say something, anything, but my mind immediately went blank as I searched for the right words (like it always did). I had seen my shin bone and an actual flap of the skin hanging over the gash left from the rusty merry-go-round. Yet the school nurse just threw a Band-Aid over it and told me to go back to recess with the other giants. No ointment of any kind. No sterilization. Just the small bandage and a pat on the head. The sick feeling in my stomach remained as I limped down the hallway back towards the outside. Nana wouldn't have done this. Mom would have done more. This didn't feel right but what was I supposed to say to the school nurse? She was a complete stranger to me and what if she got mad at me for speaking up like Steven would sometimes get mad at Mom or Rob. What if she was the one who was in charge of the spankings that you would get for breaking the rules at this school, something I didn't know was a real thing until we moved here.

A week or two of healing underneath the tiny bandage, which Mom immediately disinfected and treated with ointment the moment she saw, and things seemed back to normal. By the time the hanging piece of skin fell off and the wound itself healed, the only evidence that anything had happened was a smooth dent on my shin. Mom didn't seem too happy about it, but I kind of thought it made my leg look cool. A dent is ten times cooler than a scar, but that was just my opinion. Plus I would rather have experienced something that only hurt a small part of my leg than have to deal with our friend's face soaring into our brick wall. Plus, it's not like I wasn't already used to dealing with various injuries that were inflicted on me from Rob from the last few years. After proving to Mom that there wasn't any need for bandages or ointment on it anymore, I walked up to my room to start reading or playing with my action figures. Before jumping into one of those worlds, though, I walked over to the big window and looked out over our big front yard. Staring at the apple tree that we had all planted together in the front yard since apples were my favorite fruit, I couldn't help but start to fall in love with this small town and the small number of friends I was finally making, even if it meant the occasional leg injury during recess.

Part of living next-door to a family who had lived on Country Lane for decades meant we got to be a part of their regionally-famous Christmas light show whenever winter decided to make its annual appearance in Loudon. Their entire property was adorned to the max with festivity, from the mailbox to every side of the house to the backyard. It looked like a shopping mall holiday extravaganza except it was right next door to us. Our street quickly became a booming tourist spot as cars lined up every single night from all parts of the area and surrounding counties. Every now and then we would make hot chocolate on our stovetop and hand out small mugs of it to the people traveling to see all the Christmas lights down the street. Not only did Christmas mean this popular lightshow next door, but it also meant we got to go visit Nana and Poppop's house for a week. A week of pure joy and great food and aunts and cousins and helping Nana decorate the tree with her special ornaments, each one being carefully hung in the precisely-perfect spot on the branch. Waking up on Christmas morning brought all the excitement it always did as I sprinted downstairs to see what had been left in my stocking before we opened up the presents together, laughing about everything between each gift.

After the morning festivities had concluded at Nana and Poppop's, it was time to pack up and head to Grams and Gramps. Usually I was excited for more Christmas events, but Mom always made us feel like everyone there didn't really care for us that much. She would always say in little private comments that Grams and Gramps and our uncles loved Steven but didn't really love the rest of us. It never felt that way whenever we would visit Nana so I never knew how to act once we came to a stop at the end of the curved, gravel driveway at Grams and Gramps. Luckily, I could avoid the awkward moments by playing with all their dogs who crowded around the car waiting for the first door to open so they could go crazy, jump, and kiss everyone. From there it was another meal and another gift exchange while I sat in the corner of the living room in silence, not knowing if anyone there actually wanted me to be there or not like Mom had been saying. Eventually, she would ask Rob and me if we were ready to go back home and then we were giving everyone a goodbye hug. However, I'm pretty sure I heard her say that we were complaining about being here and that was the reason we were needing to leave, but I dismissed this outlandish idea that I must have misheard somehow. She wouldn't say that. No way.

I fell asleep pretty quickly on the two-hour-or-so drive back from Grams and Gramps, waking back up in Mrs. Bright's room once again and comparing stories from Christmas break with all my other friends. I started to notice just how different my stories of family visits during these holidays were from the other kids. Everyone here grew up together in school and their families were all relatively stable. There weren't these complications like my brother having a different father that wasn't around and me having another dad/family that I don't actually see anymore. I started feeling weird anytime these conversations would come around and quickly adapted to just saying "it was good!" without any specific details whenever my friends would ask how my break was. The bell sounded in the speakers in the ceiling and we all grabbed our backpacks and headed to the buses and pick-up spots to head home.

I could tell something was wrong the moment I got into the car, but I decided not to question Mom too much. There was a tense silence that filled the car that told me we were about to be given some bad news and that came the moment we pulled into our driveway and walked into the living room. I found myself sitting on the couch across from Mom and Steven which usually only happened whenever we got told it was time to pack up our bags and move again. Which was once again happening, but in quite a different way than the times before. Confusion quickly flooded my mind as I tried to figure out what black mold was and how it came to fill our entire house and how the people that they bought the house from had lied to them about the safety tests. Mom mentioned that it could be the reason that I had been getting sick so much this year and it took everything in me not to tell her that I had been faking all of those sick days because of how bored I was with the actual schoolwork and how the thought of trying to make more friends made my stomach hurt sometimes. Apparently I had asthma too which is not something that living in a house full of black mold is good for.

So just like that, we were moving out once again, but we were at least going to be staying in the same town. I got to stay in the same school with the friends I had somehow managed to make since our arrival. However, while we were still getting to stay in the same time, we had to say goodbye to this awesome house that had started to feel like home. No more sitting out in the sun room. No more planting daffodils out in the backyard once I decided they were my favorite flower. No more watching our apple tree grow while waiting for it to grow old enough to bear fruit. No more carpooling with my friend from Reading class that lived on the street behind ours. No more letting Rob talk me into ringing the neighbors' doorbells and running away before they answered. No more watching the next-door neighbor turn the street into a tourism destination during Christmas with their light shows. No more walking down the road to use someone else's trampoline even if they weren't home to tell us it was okay. All of that was quickly changing. Now, a group of guys came to examine all of our belongings in the house to analyze them, discarding and cleaning what could be salvaged from the mold infestation. After we packed up what was deemed acceptable to take with us, it was time to move into some room within a building off the highway for the foreseeable future while they determined whether or not the house was able to be saved.

I had never heard of the word *motel* nor did I have the slightest clue what it meant, but I knew right away that this was the least favorite place we'd ever lived in so far. It was a tiny room that basically consisted of four walls, two beds, and a questionable bathroom. The only redeeming quality that came with our new place was the fast food restaurant that was in front of it. I knew right away that meant we were going to get some of my favorite burgers and milkshakes more often than ever now that it was just a few steps away from our room. The room and bed I had to share with Rob might have smelled weird, but the constant access to junk food almost made it worth it along with getting to stay in the same school. Without much access to a backyard or neighborhood to play in anymore, we started going over to MiMi and Poppop Luke's house as often as we could to get out all the energy we weren't expending during recess at school.

I'm not sure what I did to convince my parents that I needed rollerblades for Christmas, but I couldn't have been happier that they made it into the list of approved items to be taken from our infected house. I decided it was the best possible time to rip them out of the box one night at Poppop Luke's place despite the fact that I wasn't given a helmet or pads or any form of basic safety gear for this new venture. I kicked my shoes off, barely able to hold still as I rushed to put on the blades at the top of Poppop Luke's driveway. My stance was very unstable at first, but after a few almost-falls I seemed to get the hang of it. I quickly advanced past the driveway test and suddenly found myself at the top of the street looking down the steep slope in front of me. I heard Steven walk up behind me as my mind tried to figure out if I was ready to try rolling down this steep of a hill. The motel we live in was near the highway so there's no telling when I'd have the chance to use these things again. Before I could talk myself out of it, I leaned slightly forward and began rolling down.

All sound left the world for a few seconds and it was just me, sliding forward in what felt like slow-motion. I looked up to see Steven standing in the street halfway down the hill in front of me with an expression of concern that was growing more and more extreme. I looked down at the roller blades attached to my feet. The sound quickly returned to my ears in a tidal wave of wheels on gravel that were picking up far too much momentum. My legs started to shake as my speed increased and I heard Steven yelling for me to hit the brakes. Panic filled my body as I tried to figure out how I'm supposed to stop these things. I was halfway down the hill at this point and I heard a scream coming nearby before realizing it was coming from my own mouth. Steven started to lean forward and put his hands out to stop me from shooting further down the hill and into the connecting street. For some reason, however, he jumped away at the last minute. The panic inside me flourished into an inferno by this point. I was either about to go into the street at the bottom of the hill and get hit by a car or go over the guardrail and down into the woods. I looked down again to attempt one more look at where the brakes might be or how they were supposed to be used. I glanced just in time to see the wheels on my right foot hit a large rock that was laying on the street minding its own business.

I felt my entire body lurch forward and the roller blades fly out from under me, leaving me to collide with the asphalt at an alarming speed. I closed my eyes, hoping it would make the pain less severe if I didn't see. I felt myself sliding across the road, pain quickly overtaking the majority of my torso and legs. Eventually, I felt myself come to a halt on the curb separating the yard of one of Poppop Luke's neighbors and the hill I had so confidently tried to conquer. I thought about standing up to assess the damage, but I was frozen in place. I could already tell by the searing pain that it was not going to be good. I heard the sound of something shaking against the street close to me until I realized it was my own body/blades that were shaking in some kind of terrifying response to what had just happened. What just happened? What do I do?

Steven ran over to me and helped me back onto my feet, carefully taking the roller blades off of my feet. I could tell he was worried, but he had no idea what to say or what to do in the situation. I didn't know what to do either and suddenly I was flashing back to the time he had accidentally slammed the car trunk on my finger a couple of years ago. Once again, I had injured myself and neither of us knew what to do or say. The pain was growing more and more intense and I started to raise my shirt and look down. My skin didn't even seem to be there anymore, causing the familiar tangle of knots to form in my stomach. It took every ounce of power I could muster to prevent myself from throwing up on the road as I took in what had just happened.

From my collarbone down to around my knees was nothing but burned skin from sliding across the asphalt. Steven, still silent and awkward, tried to help keep me steady as we slowly made our way up the hill and back into Poppop Luke's living room. Each movement sent a shockwave of pain from somewhere on my body, making the journey seem to take forever. Tears drenched my face, from both pain and fear, as I finally made it to the garage and limped in through the screen door of the garage.

I stepped through the doorway and looked around in puzzled confusion. I was suddenly standing in the Principal's Office next to Mom. I vaguely remember Mom's frenzied reaction seeing what I had done and applying countless layers of ointment. However, those appeared to be memories now that I was standing in this office while Mom talked about my wounds almost being healed enough to return. The Principal seemed somewhat skeptical, prompting Mom to lift up my shirt a little bit, the entanglement forming in my stomach from both pain and embarrassment. Something about my entire torso being one giant scab proved worthy of getting the remainder of the week off from school. We stopped by Mrs. Bright's room to grab some work to do while I was at home and then it was back to the motel. But first, I had to talk Mom into stopping for ice cream at the place in front of the motel. It worked. And it almost made up for the fact that it still hurt to sleep, move, or do anything I normally would throughout the day thanks to this rollerblading accident.

Staring out the window between the weird-looking curtains in our room did nothing but make me miss our house even more, but that didn't stop me from doing it. I missed our neighbors instead of the bizarre strangers I encounter now. I missed pretending to be sick and laying on the couch all day with Mom and watching the shows she said I wasn't supposed to be watching since they weren't for boys. I missed having my own room to read and play and anything else that would help take my mind to the other galaxies within my own head. I missed impatiently waiting for our apple tree to flourish. I missed Poppop Luke coming over, even if he sometimes argued with Mom about something with his job at the car dealership. I missed not feeling embarrassed when the other kids would ask me why I live in a motel.

I had to turn away from the window and try to take my mind off of how much everything had changed because the nausea had started to form. I walked over to the uncomfortable bed across the room and pulled out a book I had gotten from school the other day. I looked back down into my backpack and noticed the certificate I had gotten for Best Silent Reader at Awards Day. I smiled a little at the idea of my first school award before remembering the day I brought it back to the motel, excited beyond belief to show Mom and Steven. However, they didn't share in my excitement as they were in the middle of a heated argument, one of many that was happening since we had to move out of our home. I smiled at it again before sliding it inside one of the drawers inside the creepy room.

I didn't have much time to sit and simmer in the feelings that were sewn into these memories before the door to the room opened. I thought they had just walked down to go grab dinner but somehow another argument had started somewhere within this process. Mom noticed me sitting on the bed with my book open and immediately stifled the argument (she was somehow still unaware that I heard or at least picked up on every single argument no matter what). A blanket of awkward, tense silence immediately fell over the four walls that was our home now. I knew something was off about tonight immediately as they entered, as if a soundtrack was playing within the motel room to set the tone for whatever was about to happen. However, it took approximately two minutes or less for me to pick up on the type of conversation we were about to have in that motel room. I knew we were about to be told that we were about to start packing up our things to finally leave this space. However, the moment the conversation started I knew we weren't packing up to move back into the same house. Or any other house in this town.

Chapter Three

Remember When I Got Another New Name?

I stared out the window of the car in complete silence, the motel growing smaller and smaller until it had completely disappeared from view. I looked over to the seat next to mine to see Rob also staring out the window in stern, deafening silence. He had already gotten into three arguments today with Mom and Steven about the move, but we were still here in the car on the way to Knoxville. With each car we passed and every blink of my eye, another question rose to the surface of my mind. Why were we having to leave the motel right this very moment? Why weren't we moving to a different house in Loudon? Why did we have to go all the way to Knoxville to a new city and a new school? Why were we moving away from MiMi and Poppop Luke? Why couldn't I stay in the same school for once and not have to say goodbye to the first set of friends I had finally made? Why wasn't I even given time to literally tell any of them bye? I wanted to scream all of these questions the moment they shot through my head but it was no use. Rob had already argued every one of them and gotten nowhere. Once again, I just had to be the quiet kid who didn't get in trouble or argue while Rob was the opposite. I started to doze off as I stared up at the clouds, wanting nothing more than to wake up as one of the birds flying carefree between them.

When my eyes suddenly opened once again, I was sitting in my new classroom without a single clue how much time had lapsed from the day we made our move from the motel. I looked around at all the other kids in class, not knowing any of their names and none of them sitting at my table. One of the huge books from a series about witches and wizards was open in front of me. I looked up one more time, hoping the move had just been a bad dream and that I would suddenly be back at the other school with the friends I had made. Unfortunately, this appeared to be my new reality once again. I was the New Kid in a new school in Knoxville and clearly hadn't been making a great impression considering no one felt like sitting with me at this table for reading time. Eventually, it was time to walk outside to recess together as a class even though I had no idea what was going to happen when I got outside considering it didn't seem like many people liked me. I saw my school picture hanging up on the wall, uncomfortable smile and glasses being the shining factors, showing me as having the most Accelerated

Reader Points of anyone else in my grade. Great. I'm the New Kid and the Nerd (again). Suddenly sitting alone in class was making more sense.

I couldn't have been more excited to see the car pull up into the driveway of our new house, despite the sudden rush of memories that came the closer it came into view. I was ecstatic to be done with school and be home even if this was one of the least favorite houses we had ever lived in. Although, I have to admit it *was* a bit of an upgrade from the couple of months that we lived in a literal motel. I hopped out of the car and sprinted inside towards my room to read more of my wizard book until it was time to have dinner in front of the television screen again. Mom said that tonight was the night we were going to be watching a new show after we finished eating that involved people singing for a chance to become famous or something like that. It sounded pretty interesting, but it didn't really matter what was actually playing on the screen as long as Mom was letting me lay down on the couch while she scratched by back or played with my hair. It felt like that was quickly becoming the only way I could feel at peace these days.

I finished up everything on my plate and went to drop it in the sink, sulking away slowly as I felt Steven's gaze piercing through my back. I know they told me I have to start helping with dishes now that I'm getting older, but he always got irritated with me whenever I tried and did it wrong even though no one had actually shown me how to do much of anything around the house. I ran up to lay next to Mom so that he couldn't come in and yell at me before the new show started. I was pretty invested in the show within the first few minutes because it was showing all of these normal people getting the chance to sing in front of some judges to try and win a huge record deal. I immediately found myself daydreaming about what it would be like to have a chance to do something like this whenever I grew up, although I knew for a fact singing was not the gift that would land me that opportunity. I fell back down from this daydream in time to see a blonde, curly-haired woman singing like someone I had never heard before. I knew she was pretty, whatever that meant, but I could just tell that there was something about her that was special. Mom quickly noticed my fascination and how confidently I was saying that she would win the competition. She grinned, looked over at Steven and Rob, and excitedly made the announcement that I had my first celebrity crush.

I didn't really know what it meant to have a crush on a celebrity, but that didn't stop the molten embarrassment rushing into my face. I didn't know how I was supposed to respond to this kind of proclamation or what it even meant. The silence was cut short as Rob chimed in with a "so you want her to be your girlfriend?" but with laughter interrupting every other word. I felt everyone's eyes on me as I looked back at the TV for some kind of savior. Her audition finished up, she was immediately showered with compliments, and she walked out of the room with her golden ticket to Hollywood. I glanced back over, hoping they had moved onto a new subject, but it was hopeless. They were almost enjoying the fact that I was petrified beyond words. I didn't say a word before I fled to my bedroom, closing the door behind me for the rest of the night. Staring up at the ceiling in silence, I began to let my mind wander. What's a crush? Am I supposed to feel something seeing her win her Hollywood ticket? Am I supposed to have a girlfriend already like my brother? Thought after thought rebounded off the walls of my quiet bedroom all night until I eventually fell backwards into a restless slumber. Why don't I feel normal?

I woke up after a considerable amount of time had passed although I was unsure of how much time (as always). I rolled out of bed to start my usual routine as Mom poked her head in to make sure I was awake. I quickly decided to tell her I felt sick (I didn't) and followed up with a request to stay home. Something about the thought of trying to tiptoe through another day in the halls bearing the burden of my huge teeth, nerdy glasses, weird hair, and overall awkward demeanor sounded unbearable. My heart sank into my stomach when she quickly declined, stating that I couldn't be skipping school this close to the end of the year. I guess there was my answer on how much time had passed. I finished getting myself ready, begrudgingly making my way to the car as the memories of this school year started to slowly surface in my mind.

I remembered dressing up for Halloween and feeling cool for once since no one made fun of the fact that I dressed up as my favorite wizard. I remembered the teacher forgetting my birthday and telling Mom that I didn't want to have a party since I didn't know who I could even invite. I remembered playing by myself mostly during recess except on the day I dressed up. I remembered seeing one of my classmate's fall off the monkey bars and snapping his arm in half, instantly sending me back in time to the time I saw the inside of my shin bone or burned my stomach off at my last school. I remembered diving into my books or box of action figures every chance I could so that I could have fun in whatever imaginary world could be found or created. I remembered watching my first alleged crush win the competition show and feeling so happy that my prediction came true. My influx of random flashbacks was cut short as the car stopped and I was forced to hop out of the car and walk into the building to my teacher's classroom. I wished I could just force time to skip ahead on my own so I could go ahead and be walking onto the bus to head home this afternoon.

I made my way to class, paying special mind to avoid looking at my ugly school picture that was still taped to the AR Point Leader Chart on the wall. I sat down at one of the desks and followed along with whatever lesson was being taught for the day and then immediately opened up a book once the opportunity presented itself. Coming back from lunch, I noticed someone standing at Ms. Houston's desk that definitely wasn't normally there. He was tall and definitely older, but not like "parent old" at all. He had dark hair that swooped over and a set of white teeth that showed as he laughed at whatever my teacher had just told him. The rest of the class took their seats and she stood up and told us that the guy standing at her desk was her son, a student at the high school down the road. As she told us that he was a football player for the school, I took notice that his arms had muscles on them. I tried to look away from them and turn back to my book before she started teaching math but it was to no avail. I kept staring at Ms. Houston's son as she gave more and more introductory details that I had stopped being able to pay attention to. I found myself staring for some reason, even as he made his exit out of the classroom to go back to his school. I had no idea what was going on in my head but all I could think about was how I hoped he started coming back to visit her more often. I really want to be his friend. Bad.

I couldn't stop thinking about my teacher's son the entire bus ride home as I did my best to stare out the window and avoid any confrontation with the other kids on the bus. I got off at my stop and slowly made my way back to our house while I tried to figure out why I wanted to be his friend so badly and why I hadn't been able to stop thinking about him. Luckily, I had a new book in my backpack and some new action figures in my room that I could use to distract myself with. I would talk to him the next time he came into our class. I was going to say hi and tell him I want to be friends. Until then, it's time to teleport myself into some alternate dimension in my mind with the characters in my new book. I quickly lost track of how much time I was spending buried in the pages until I heard my parents coming through the door from work.

I stepped out into the living room to see what was going to be for dinner later, but I knew the moment I saw Mom and Steven that something was wrong. There was a certain weight that they were carrying about the kitchen, obvious yet invisible. I glanced over at Rob and could tell that he noticed the disturbance too. I briefly considered asking them what was wrong but quickly changed my mind to prevent potentially angering Steven. We eventually sat down in front of the television for a painfully awkward meal together until Mom announced that we were going to need to have a talk. My stomach immediately turned into knots thinking about what could possibly be following this announcement. Was Nana and Poppop okay? Was Rob going to have to go to another set of hospitals for his list of health problems again? Did I somehow do something wrong with my schoolwork? Did my teacher notice me looking at her son for too long and being weird? I tried my best to stop the various scenarios flooding into my mind until Mom and Steven finally started to reveal what was going on. The sting of their words were all too familiar, but a sting I was almost numb to at this point. Rob immediately put up a fight and launched counteroffer after counteroffer, but I quietly went to my room instead. I knew well enough by now that there's not much use in trying to change the minds of my parents.

Packing up my room once again didn't feel as painful as it had the numerous times before. I wasn't necessarily happy or even indifferent, but it wasn't the worst scenario that could have been presented to my life in its current state. I hadn't really made many (or any) friends here, the classwork was boring, and I was still carrying the weight of my Weird New Kid sign through the hallways even though I had been here for the entire academic year. I started packing up one of the last boxes of my room, tossing in the Weird New Kid sign before taping it closed for the ride to another new house to wear in another new school. I stepped out into the almost-empty living room where we had just had "the talk" only two weeks or so before. I wasn't sure how to pack up the rest of the house so I timidly sat in the corner until I could eventually feel the frustration filling the spaces where the furniture used to sit. I could tell Steven wanted me to be helping more, but I had no idea how to do so. Unable to find the right words to ask the right questions, I retreated into my room once again. I had never heard of the town we were relocating to, but I wish we were already packed up and headed there so that the tension could finally start to evaporate.

As if the universe had been specifically listening to my innermost thoughts, Mom popped her head into the doorway to ask how I felt about going to Nana and Poppop's house for the rest of the weekend. The words had barely escaped her mouth before I was already in the backseat waiting to make my escape to my favorite house in the entire world. A few minutes into the car ride to Nana's house, I was told that this move came with another significant change outside of the geographical kind. Steven had always been Steven, the man that Mom married even though he wasn't Rob's dad or my dad. However, Mom was saying now that he loves us so much that he wants us to be his sons. Naturally, questions started shooting through my mind like a meteor shower in a vast nighttime sky. I remember playing with a kid when we were younger around the same time they were getting married and I always thought that was Steven's son but then I remember he suddenly stopped coming to our house. Mom said that there was a misunderstanding and not to worry about it. Was he not his son anymore? Did Steven really care about us to adopt us like Mom was saying? He always seemed so angry and we don't usually talk that much unless Mom was sending us to him for discipline, or at least threatening to do so.

I remained silent in the backseat and stared out the trees that we were speeding past and wondered if I should actually ask any of the questions in my head. I definitely knew better than to ask any of the ones involving my biological father even if it was something that was still troubling me. The more Mom spoke from the front seat, however, the more I started to realize that this didn't seem like it was an ask but more of an announcement. My brother and I were getting adopted by Steven and he was going to be our legal father alongside Mom now. We were getting different last names once again. I was going to get rid of my legal first name and make it the nickname I had always been called along with the new last name being the same as Mom and Steven's, I mean Dad's? I stole a glance at the driver's seat, waiting for...Dad (?) to chime in with his support in the conversation but he was just staring at the road in complete silence. This didn't feel very natural or the most comfortable, but I knew at this point in the discussion that none of these things were really up for debate. This was our new reality. New names (again). New town (again). New school (again).

I ran as quickly as I could into Nana's outstretched arms after we pulled up into the driveway, my stress about all these new life changes immediately dissolving in her embrace. It seemed as if the rest of the family had already pulled back out of the driveway and gone back to Knoxville to pack up the rest of the house, something I was all too happy to be excluded from. I continued into the house and immediately felt all the worries that had been filling the depths of my mind vanish into the air to be replaced with the feelings that always came with Nana and Poppop's company. It felt that no matter what house they were living in (they moved sometimes into newer and better houses but not nearly as frequent as we did), they made special care to infuse tranquility and love into every beam and every brick before the construction was completed. The outermost walls were a barrier that kept out almost any negativity from breaking through and stressing anyone inside. However, even if some negative thought or idea managed to survive all the way inside, Nana and Poppop themselves were there to quickly extinguish it before it had the chance to wreak any havoc. Oh, and the food was always to die for, too.

I went to sleep the first night feeling refreshed and at ease, something that wasn't often the case when I put my head on my pillow each night. When my eyes opened the next morning, I could hear Mom and Steven/Dad's voices downstairs. I got out of bed, peeked out the bedroom window, and saw their car parked out in the driveway below. I thought I had only been here for a few hours but apparently time had fast-forwarded once again. It was apparently already time to pack everything back up from my long weekend stay and hop back in the car to travel back to the next phase of life, once again adorned with a new school and new name and another set of new kids to convince I was normal enough. I sat back down in bed and closed my eyes, partly hoping that I was going to open them and somehow be a grown-up that didn't have to deal with all of this. A grown-up that was living alone and done with school who didn't have to follow his parents around every 10 months to a new house in a new town for some unknown reason.

The thoughts started swarming back into my mind the moment we had pulled out of Nana's driveway and out of the protective barrier they had cast around their property. I sunk into the seat of the car and turned my head to look at everything we were passing to try and take my mind off of the discomfort that came with moving again. When this deflection method failed, I slowly began filtering through the different feelings and thoughts racing through my brain while mustering the courage to start asking some questions about this move. Of course, that came with its own set of worries surrounding what questions to try and ask. Would this question make Dad mad? Would that question make Mom tell me to be quiet? Should I just ignore the questions and wait for Rob to start complaining/asking so he could handle the brunt of whatever consequences came along? Still unsure of the best way to approach my confusion, I blended all of my options together to get a few of the answers with as little recourse and damage as possible. Each answer brought little relief to the discomfort I was feeling about having to hit the reset button once more, even if there wasn't much to reset from fourth grade in Knoxville. Nonetheless, I was pleased with myself for at least speaking up to ask a question or two for once.

We pulled up to the new house in a town called Oak Ridge that wasn't far from Knoxville but still far enough to move schools. Stev- I mean Dad landed a job as a radiation therapist in one of the cancer hospitals in town which is what sparked the sudden-but-not-surprising relocation. At first glance, the home looked like it was from an entirely different time period, but all of those thoughts disappeared when I noticed something. Beyond the edge of our backyard appeared to be a forest, a vast expanse of trees and animals almost as if directly from my imagination into the real world in front of my eyes. I didn't even need to see the inside of the house by this point, I was already preparing to run into the woods for the next couple of years or until it was time to move again. I would just run and not stop running and not come back up to go to school and have to tell a room of 30 other kids that I'm new. I would run through the trees and act out whatever story was forming in my head that afternoon until the sun went down and it was time to sneak into my bed until the next morning. I would wake up before Mom and Dad do and sneak back out and repeat the whole process day after day after day after day.

I heard Mom yell sharply for me to come inside, jolting me away from my daydream and back to reality. I turned back around and made my way back up to the front door, having almost made it to the tree line without realizing I had even been walking. The inside of the house appeared just as dated as the exterior had seemed. I was happy to see that all of the unpacking had already been done in my absence as I made my way throughout this new foreign territory that could be ours for the next five years or five months or five days. My favorite part (other than the backyard) was the stairway leading up to the second floor and how it leveled off halfway to form the front door entrance. You open the front door and are immediately met with the decision of stairs going up or stairs going down. I have no idea why this was my favorite part of the house but I had never seen anything like it and it seemed so strange in the best way.

I sat down in my new bedroom that had already been arranged and tried to calm my nerves about starting over for the millionth time in a new school full of new kids. I had about a week or so to spend walking around the woods and trying to figure out where all of the hidden treasures and pathways were located. I was worried my parents might not be okay with me going on these explorations by myself, but they didn't seem to care (or notice) too much. Dad was always busy on his computer game and Mom pretty much said yes to anything I brought up, especially when she was watching one of her shows or movies. Whenever it got too dark to meander about the trees, I was in one of my imaginary universes from the safety of my bedroom or practicing writing my new last name or calling him Dad instead of Steven. The more I write it down on paper and practice saying it, the more it would hopefully start to feel real. The more I called him Dad in front of him, the more he might start to feel like my Dad the same way that I used to feel when I would be at my other family's house before I stopped going there. This week of explorations and practices seemed to pass by with a blink or two before I was waking up in bed and getting ready to be dropped off at school for my first day.

I did my best to calm down the million nerves that were firing off throughout my body and mind as we pulled up to my first day of middle school. This was the only school system that I had ever heard of that started middle school in fifth grade instead of sixth but it's not like I could change that. Not only was I in a new school with a new name and a new dad, but I was suddenly in an entirely new phase of my educational journey. I feigned the best smile I could to Mom from the back seat before walking up towards the gym doors where she had instructed me to go. I opened the door and immediately felt like a tiny bug sitting underneath a microscope as I stepped into the large gymnasium full of students that were all collectively staring at me in confusion. My worst-case scenario of having to stand up in front of the class and tell them my name was suddenly washed away as I stood at the front of a hundred or so kids who all seemed to know everyone else in the entire gym except for me. I immediately shifted my head downward and made my way up to the first teacher that I saw and let him know I was a new student. A rush of relief came over me as he took me out of the crowded room and towards the main office to get my information printed out so that I knew where I was supposed to go.

I told them my (new) full name and had a schedule printed out shortly after that listed what quadrant of the second floor of the school I was assigned. I was given a locker number and combination which made zero sense to me. From there, I was dropped off in the middle of the giant ocean of confusion known as the very first day as a very new kid in the very new system known as junior high school. I tried to keep my head above the violent waters, but every time I turned my head there was another wave of water crashing into me. When I came back up for air after trying to understand five different teachers instead of one, here comes still having recess. When I recovered from recess, there came my entire English class laughing at me for saying my favorite singer was the one from the TV show I watched with Mom. I came up for air again, flailing my arms about in an attempt to keep myself afloat just in time to get hit with having to introduce myself as The New Kid to five different classes and five different teachers. Five classes, an awkward lunch in the confusing cafeteria, using my old last name on accident at least five times later I was walking through the front door of my house. I eagerly changed out of the clothes that were soaked through with the ocean water from my emotional first day and put on something more comfortable to go walk around the woods to calm myself down and escape everything that was going on.

Every morning waking up was another day to fall into the bland and boring routine of my new life and my new school with all the friends that I wasn't making. I floated around our sector of the building and did my best to make friends with the teachers since all the kids had already branded me as The Weird New Kid after my questionnaire card was unexpectedly read aloud for the entire class (who does that?). Once I was able to find a table to sit alone and eat the lunch that I finally figured out how to purchase (whenever Mom would remember to hand me a check for my account), it was time to meander around outside during recess by myself. Occasionally I started a challenge for myself to try to swing as high as possible without injuring myself which took a surprising amount of my recess time each day. Once I had finally survived another school day without too much damage, it was time to sit in the back of the bus and hope no one talked to me since everyone there tended to be on the meaner side. Relief would surge the moment my stop came up and I was free of the stresses and anxiety of being a new kid for the millionth time. The only thing I had to worry about from then was waiting for Rob to get home before I could go walk around the woods and making sure I told Mom I had a great day instead of letting her know how sad I was here. The last thing I needed to do was be mean to Mom and Ste...Dad and possibly get in trouble like Rob always did.

I drifted and skirted through the monotonous days where the only highlights involved learning how to use a pocket knife to whittle my own wand or sword and running wild through the tranquil woods. One day, Nana and Poppop let us know that they had decided to adopt a toy Australian Shepherd puppy which prompted Mom to almost immediately follow suit. First came the adoption of a Pekingese puppy named Chloe that Mom quickly claimed as her third child. From there, I was able to convince her to let me adopt the perfect angel from the local pound that I named Chancey. From the day that I brought her home from her spaying surgery, I knew I had just gotten my very first best friend in this lifetime. The surgery didn't go as smoothly as we had hoped so I had to sit by her side for the first couple of days while she was recovering. I set up a small bed for her on top of mine and watched her as she slept off the procedure, memorizing the various orange spots (especially the heart-shaped one) that were stamped onto her white coat. By the third day, she seemed to love me just as much as I loved her and suddenly I wasn't running through the woods alone anymore. I finally had someone that wanted to play with me. I finally had a friend.

Having the confidence boost from Chancey, I quickly tried to make friends with a couple people who walked on two legs instead of four and who weren't covered in fur. I had a class with one of them and every now and then our parents organized a day on the weekends where we would go over to each other's house for hours of mindless video game playing. His mom was really nice, although I couldn't understand her thick Russian accent sometimes. The other friend I managed to make in one of my classes happened to live down the street so we eventually started playing outside together whenever we didn't have much homework. Of course, I usually never had homework considering I always worked on it during class when all the normal kids were socializing. Whenever I wasn't having fun with these two, though, I was spending time with Chancey the moment I got home from school each day. She was such a quick learner of tricks and how to go outside without a leash. I never really knew how to take care of a dog, but I'm pretty sure she was the best one I could have ever hoped for, even if she occasionally came back from using the bathroom covered in mud and dirt.

Waking up one morning came with the realization that I felt a bit less miserable than I was at the beginning of the move. I wasn't sure what time of the school year I was in by now (time is still very hard for me to keep track of), but I didn't think I was doing too bad for myself. I have two friends that I hang out with sometimes outside of school and one four-legged best friend I got to spend all my time with at my house. On the plus side, I never had to worry about this best friend disappearing since she would have to come with me if we ever had to pack up and move again. I even convinced myself to talk more with Dad instead of keeping my distance or escaping to the woods for hours at a time. I spent an afternoon watching him play a video game on his computer that I always heard Mom complaining about since he spent so much time on it. However, it only took that one afternoon of watching him for me to get just as hooked on it. All of a sudden, he was setting up my own little computer station and bringing home my own copy of the video game so that I could start an account of my own. On top of having something in common with Dad and something to always talk about, it was as if this game had taken one of the imaginary worlds I often created in my room with my action figures and put it into a video game right in front of me in real life.

My everyday routine quickly started to change until the driving force of my life was this video game and the newfound relationship it had created with Dad. For the first time since he adopted Rob and I, it felt as if he wasn't Steven anymore and he cared more about everything. I rushed home from school each day and started to trade in my adventures through the woods with adventures in the virtual online game for hours and hours. I created my mythical characters and quickly tried to level them up and interact with other people across the world who were also playing the game. Dad would roll back in his computer chair every now and then to check on my characters' progress and to make sure I wasn't chatting it up with any potentially dangerous strangers. Of course, chatting with other people on the game was one of my favorite parts since they weren't able to see that I was The Weird New Kid at a middle school. I could be anyone that I wanted to be when I was running around as one of the characters that I created to play within the game without worrying I'd be the butt of someone's joke or the reason everyone in the classroom is laughing as your favorite female singer is unexpectedly announced to everyone.

Days were quickly turning into weeks the more time I kept devoting to the virtual world that was quickly feeling more and more like reality. I gave up most of my hopes of striking gold in the social market of this new school because it was much easier to make friends virtually with this game than it was to risk being laughed at over and over again for whatever joke I would attempt. I traded in more and more afternoons with my neighbor/classmate friend and Chancey in for afternoons spent with Dad as we both marinated in front of our computer screens living life as fictional characters in a video game. Suddenly our quiet dinners, often spent in front of the television, were filled with questions and observations about whatever new game update was going to be fixing and when the next sequel to the game was going to be released and so on. I gave up trying to talk to the other kids during downtime at school and instead worked on finishing up my homework during class and then spending recess sitting alone wondering what kind of adventures I would be getting into once I got home from school and logged on. I couldn't believe I had finally found something to spend my time on and a place where I suddenly felt so accepted for the first time.

As more time flashed by, Halloween began to approach and provided an opportunity for me to break out the same costume that so many of my Knoxville friends had loved the previous school year. This was my first chance to really make an impact on my status here at this new middle school and hopefully impress some of the other kids. I got Mom to put the scar on my forehead as I threw on my wizard robe, put on the glasses, and grabbed my wand before walking out the door. Surely this costume would be enough to grow my current social circle of two friends to at least three or four. Mom dropped me off, seeming almost as excited as I was to walk through the doors and begin the inevitable tidal wave of compliments coming my way. However, I opened the door to be struck with a tsunami of immediate regrets as I noticed that not a single other student had taken the opportunity to dress up. I turned around in continued horror as I realized Mom had already disappeared from the drop-off lane before I could demand that we go home to change. I had somehow missed the memo that middle school was the point of the academic journey where it was no longer "cool" to dress up for Halloween during the school day. My face ignited with piping-hot embarrassment as I made my way to sit down before my unescapable journey to my classes for the day.

I tried to keep my head low and disguise myself as much as possible in every class, even attempting to sit at one of the empty desks in the back rows of each room. To ensure that this would be one of the worst days of my life, however, my teachers all recognized me in the back row and excitedly had me stand up at the front of the class to show off my costume and resume my assigned seat towards the front. The remainder of my day was smirks and outright laughter directed my way no matter how much I wished in my head to disappear. There was one moment that I considered making a run for it and walking/sprinting back to my house but I knew that even if I managed to leave the building without the school catching me, I had no idea how to get home from here. Instead, I suffered through the jokes and everyone around me making fun of me all day while I did my best to drown it all out in whatever homework I could find after each lesson. The moment I heard the final bell ring, I sprinted as fast as I could to the bus so that I could sink into the first empty seat closest to the door. I threw my entire costume into the trash can the moment I got home and immediately logged into my game with tears still forming in my eyes as I tried to completely erase the last 8 hours from my memory.

Despite the horrifying Halloween experience and finding my new home on an online realm of dragons, swords, monsters, and sudden paternal bonding, there was still a miniscule glimmer of hope that I might be able to turn around my social standing at school. Whether it be from one of my phone calls with Nana that always made me feel so special or one of the walks through the woods with Chancey that always gave me a positive new outlook on life, I was determined to give this school's social ladder a new shot. One morning, I woke up to what felt like January or February with the spontaneous confidence to branch out that day and ask the girl who had the locker next to mine to the annual Semi-Formal Dance. I always heard the other boys in my classes talking about how pretty and popular she was, so I knew I probably wouldn't be the first one to have this idea but I knew I was going to be pretty early in asking someone so maybe I had a shot.

I couldn't muster the courage to force my mouth to speak the words before we shut our lockers and went into Homeroom for the announcements and pledge of allegiance. Therefore, the rest of my entire school day was spent conjuring up as many nerves and putting my mind through every possible scenario that could happen before I shut my locker and finally ask her. After what felt like an agonizing eternity later, I was shutting my locker and turning to face her. I awkwardly told/screamed at her that I had to ask her a question before I left which resulted in an uncomfortable length of silence as I stood in front of her paralyzed like a statue.

Like a bonfire that suddenly finds enough fuel to fully flourish, a surge of confidence rushed through me as I (loudly) asked her if she would go to the dance with me. My confidence was almost immediately extinguished as I watched a look of confusion turn to a look of disgust on her face. Next came laughter which quickly replaced my confidence with agonizing embarrassment. To make the entire situation worse than any of the ones I had come up with that morning, she further confirmed her denial by saying that she would rather go alone than to show up with me. She shut her locker and turned away from the locker to walk off with her best friend, both of whom were still laughing loudly enough for me to hear all the way down the hallway from where I was standing, still paralyzed from what had just happened. Knowing I only had a few more minutes to get to the bus before it left without me was the only thing that convinced my brain to force my body to close my locker and put one foot in front of the other. I stared out the window in despair the entire ride to my stop, immediately heading to the woods with Chancey with tears in my eyes as I tried to forget...everything.

I made the decision to skip the dance altogether. I skipped any form of social event of any caliber. I stopped spending time with either of the two friends I had managed to make at this school. I stopped talking to anyone at recess and instead spent the time on a swing alone or aimlessly strolling around the property. I finished my homework before the bell to dismiss class would even make a sound. There was one girl that I eventually started talking to whenever we would run laps around the track in gym class. She seemed pretty quiet at first, but very kind and funny. The other kids weren't the nicest to her either which is probably why I felt drawn to talk to her and break my vow of silence. We seemed to both know what it feels like to be the underdogs of fifth grade for no apparent reason. I also thought she was pretty, but that's beside the point. I think. The other kids eventually started asking us if we were boyfriend and girlfriend in a taunting manner and eventually I wrote her a note asking if I could start telling them yes. I said it was just an effort to shut them up, but a part of me was hoping she said yes for other reasons too. I may not have any friends here, but after she handed me a note back at the end of that school day, it looked like I had a girlfriend. I had Chancey, my online friends, the woods behind my house, and a girlfriend. That's all I needed.

Two weeks passed by along with more walks along the track and sitting with my girlfriend at lunch as opposed to the usual loner table. Two weeks of walking through the woods after school with Chancey, letting out whatever stress was clouding my mind by acting out fantasy I could come up with to project into the gloomy forestry in front of me. Two weeks of logging into my video game to sit in front of for hours and hours until Mom demanded that I log off. Two weeks of hearing more arguments between Mom and Dad or Mom and Rob or Dad and Rob or some combination of the above while I sat alone in my room wondering if they realized how loud and scary they always sound when they're like this. Two weeks of figuring out how to use the landline phone to talk with Nana whenever I needed that feeling of peace and calm that only her voice was able to bring. Two weeks until I found myself sitting in front of Mom and Dad as we were being told once again that it was time to pack up the house and move.

Chapter Four

Remember When I Joined the Marines?

I wanted to be angry and demand that we stay in this house with the cool staircase and the backyard woods full of endless escapes. I wanted to scream back at our parents immediately after they delivered the news the way that Rob was so fearlessly doing, but I just didn't care. The words that meant we were having to relocate once again were immediately overshadowed by the words of Nana having cancer being the reason for this move. I didn't know exactly what cancer was or the complexity of it, but I knew from the little I had heard on TV and from science class that it never meant anything good. My favorite person in the world was sick. She was not just casually ill, but sick enough for us to pack up our house and move two hours away to live next to her while she was being treated. Every other word being launched back and forth from Rob and my parents were immediately muffled out as I imagined losing the one person who seemed to always understand me and know exactly what to do or say to make me feel better. I could lose Nana. Suddenly, having to say goodbye to the woods, my new girlfriend, and another school full of kids that treated me so poorly didn't mean as much as it would have even seconds before.

I wasn't even going to attempt to put up a fight or try and stop this move. I knew Rob already was firing off his attacks because he clearly didn't have the same issues making friends in new places the same way that I did. The thought of living so close to Nana and Poppop's house actually brought me a lot of relief knowing that I would be able to go over there whenever instead of just on holiday breaks or special occasions. Plus, it would be easier to help Nana fight off her disease in Murfreesboro than it would be to try and fight it from all the way here. I won't have to say goodbye to Chancey. I just had to say goodbye to my girlfriend and the woods that offered me so much peace during this school year that nothing and no one else could. I started packing up everything like Mom had told me to do and sent my girlfriend an email telling her that I had to move and that we had to break up on the last day of school. That day crept up much quicker than I anticipated and I was suddenly giving her one last hug before seeing her fade off into the distance as her bus left the school parking lot. I found the Weird New Kid Jacket right before packing up the last box and threw it over my shoulder with a sigh, hardly any dust having accumulated on it whatsoever. I walked down the stairway one last time before hopping into the car, dozing off almost immediately to avoid my own thoughts on the two-hour-or-so car ride.

I woke up to Mom telling me it was ready to wake up and get dressed for my second "first day of middle school" since this school system started in sixth grade. I sat up, slowly getting used to these fast-forward phases of time, and looked around at my new room. It was definitely an upgrade from the last house, although we exchanged the exquisite wooded backyard for a quaint suburb with only one or two small trees in the front yard and a small park that was shared by the neighbors. Thankfully, I didn't have to worry about a school bus and all the social trauma that typically accompanies them because our neighborhood was a couple of blocks away from my new middle school and Rob's new high school was directly across the street. So far, it seemed like the only thing Chancey and I had to get used to was leashed walks through the neighborhood as opposed to our countless independent ventures throughout the vast wilderness of Oak Ridge. I suddenly got pulled back down to Earth from this train of thoughts by Rob yelling at me to hurry up so we could start our walk to school.

I kept the Weird New Kid vest at home since I was lucky enough to have the upper hand at how middle school operated. I knew all the kids would be scrambling around trying to figure out what it meant to rotate between four or five different classrooms so I wouldn't have to worry too much about being the outsider in front of a bunch of strangers. I walked into the front entrance of the school and quickly took notice of how modern and brand-new it looked since it had been built just the year before or something like that. I had no idea when the Oak Ridge middle school was built, but it definitely gave off 50+ year vibes. In familiar, but still devastatingly awkward, fashion I made my way to the front desk near the entrance to get my schedule and have someone walk me to where my section of classrooms were going to be. I kept my head down and weaved between all the kids freaking out about what lockers were and trying to figure out how they worked before I quickly got familiar with mine. I made my way into the classroom that would be my Homeroom, sighing as I realized I was the first kid inside. Not wasting any time trying to assess my peers or feel out my chances at making friends here (my social wounds were still fresh), I introduced myself to Mrs. Barber.

From Mrs. Barber for Homeroom and English to Mr. Sully for Science to Ms. Hill for Social Studies to Mr. Huddleston for Math, I quickly made the teachers the focus of all my social efforts. I quickly felt an attachment to Mrs. Barber and Mr. Huddleston more than the others, but there wasn't any teacher that I didn't immediately get along with. Thankfully, I didn't have to stand up in front of any of the classes and tell them all I was new and instead introduced myself along with the rest of the kids and tried to make it seem like I had lived in Murfreesboro my whole life so I didn't have to explain over and over again that my family moved every school year to a new place for whatever reasons. Not that I made any friends by any stretch, but I was doing pretty well at staying off of everyone's radar even when I was making extra efforts to befriend the teachers on the first day. Before it felt like any time had passed at all, I was already making my way back to my house with the reassurance that I at least hadn't made a fool out of myself on the first day. I let myself into the front door, exhaled all the stress, let Chancey out for a little bit, then logged into my video game to escape reality and enter my own version of reality for the millionth time.

I quickly fell in love with living just moments away from Nana and Poppop's house even though the reason behind this relocation was such a horrifying one. I knew that the illness that had fallen over Nana was terrible, but I never saw her change her demeanor at all, at least not when I was near. She had a major surgery to help prevent the breast cancer from spreading which I could tell had a deep impact on her, but I still never saw her without the smile that could light up the darkest of rooms. Instead of spending any time complaining about the surgery or her situation, she decided to ask everyone else about the details or stresses of *their* lives. Even if it was a day that she had an aggressive treatment, she'd still be sitting in her recliner, her tiny Australian Shepherd nestled in her arms, drawing out anything that was worrying or stressing me on that given day. I looked down at a letter I had just written after one of these long conversations with Nana. I read over all the words I had carefully written on the letter that was addressed to the family that I stopped seeing when I was so young. A sense of release pulsed through my body and a weight that I hadn't even noticed was there was suddenly floating off of my shoulders into nothingness. I looked around in confusion in familiar fashion whenever time slowed down and I crashed down into reality.

Somehow, Nana had managed to crack open my defensive barriers and convince me to tell her all about (my other) Dad and Erin. The letter was full of apologies for how everything was handled and how I forgave them for the spankings and everything that had scared me so much at such a young age. I didn't necessarily go into detail about how much I regret not trying to explain more before it got so out-of-hand, but the overall tone of the letter to them was positive. I gave it to Mom once she came to pick me up that day, who told me she would be sure to look up their address to mail it. I haven't the slightest idea what Nana had done to get me to open up about all of this, but it didn't seem to upset Mom and Dad which was the main reason I had kept it behind the barriers for so much time. I looked through car window on the way home, immediately flashing back to asking the girl to the dance only to be laughed at along with the dreadful Halloween costume fiasco. Thankfully, this time I had gone far outside of my comfort zone without it blowing back up in my face. Maybe things would finally start looking up for me here in this new city and this new school. Maybe I could actually branch out and make friends with some other kids instead of just the new teachers.

After being slightly forced out of my comfort zone during classwork and various projects, I found out that one of the other kids in my grade was actually my neighbor. To make matters even greater, we both seemed to be "the weird kids" in similar ways. Before I could even learn his last name, we were spending afternoons after school together and I had made my way into the invite list to sleepovers and hangouts with the entire social network of our neighborhood. Somehow, I went from the kid who wanted to be best friends with the teachers to being a part of the best friends of the neighborhood group. I had a best friend my age, I wasn't fighting with my brother as much as usual, I had Chancey, and Nana and Poppop at arm's reach. We started going to the same church as Nana, but there was something about church that was confusing/boring to me and I didn't really fit in with any of the other kids in my small group. However, I could see how happy it made Nana to see me next to her every Sunday and I knew if I put up too much of a fight about going, Mom would ground me like she does so often to Rob. Finish my schoolwork. Go to church. Avoid doing anything that Rob generally does. Make everyone happy. Easy.

Despite my efforts to avoid any form of consequence or disciplinary action, Mom started to point out how much time I was playing video games with my friends and playing the online game with Dad every afternoon/evening. Out of nowhere came the two-hour maximum limit that I was allowed to consume media each day. Naturally, I didn't think the rule would stick after the first few days until I glanced up to see her standing in the computer room doorway, arms crossed and a stern expression painted across her face. My heart pounding with sudden fear, I closed out my game in the middle of an important quest. I opened up a blank document and quickly told Mom that I was working on a school project and not playing a second more of my game than I was allowed to. I was shocked to see that she believed my last-minute efforts and I was back to staring at the blank document once she made her way back to other parts of the house. My first instinct was to reopen my video game until I realized if Mom came back in and caught me I would have to deal with being grounded for the first time in my life and suffer through weeks or months without any access to the computer or television whatsoever. Suddenly, a light bulb above my head ignited so quickly that it shattered itself into tiny pieces all across my desk.

While I couldn't technically log into the video game and escape into my favorite alternate reality, there was nothing stopping me from writing about it. In fact, I could write about a hypothetical scenario where my dreams come true and I'm actually teleported into the realms of my video game except in real-life. Before I knew what was even happening, my imagination was crashing into the keyboard like a tsunami and I was creating my own storyline with a character who was transported to an alternate, medieval dimension via mystical library book. Hour after hour introduced knights, dragons, magic spells, and any magical creature I could think of, especially villains and obstacles in the main character's way. I took a student who typically drifted along the outskirts of the social kingdom of the school and gave him the opportunity to change his story and become a hero that I always dreamt of becoming. I took a deep breath, rolled backwards in my computer chair, and stared in amazement at what appeared to be the beginning pages of a novel that I was apparently starting to write. The flicker of excitement continued to grow into flames over the next several weeks as I added more and more pages to the project until I had to break the news to my parents that my school project had been a little white lie and their 12-year-old son was actually writing a book instead. Another wave of relief arrived as my confession was met with excitement and encouragement instead of punishment.

To follow up with my good grades, tendencies to befriend teachers, and overall social standing in school systems (or lack thereof), I found myself in an orthodontist's chair to have brackets and wires permanently attached to my teeth in an attempt to make my smile prettier. Mom seemed to be worried about the other kids at school making fun of me for my braces, but it actually became an icebreaker and resulted in more socialization than normal. Kids were asking me if they hurt, how long I was going to have them, what color bands I was going to get each month, and a million other questions that actually made me feel somewhat popular for the first time ever. Not that I was worried about being made fun of for something in school (again), but I was probably just as shocked as Mom was that the braces turned out to be a successfully strategic move. I was painfully shocked, however, at what it feels like to have your teeth start to dramatically shift around in your mouth every day.

I got used to spending more and more days sitting in front of my computer to work on *The Knight of Oakville Middle* just as I got used to the pain of shifting dental bone. I took care of Chancey and continued talking to her everyday as if she was another person whenever I wasn't saying the same things to Nana and Poppop. I was even warming up to the idea of church and Christianity to try and explain the meaning behind my strange family structure and constant stress about my weirdness or my parents' constant arguments that they still think I can't hear every week. However, what I was not getting used to was the idea of being put through a disciplinary program alongside my brother. My jaw slammed into the floor as I listened to Mom tell me that my brother and I were both being signed up to join the Kid Marines in Murfreesboro. Our cousin had already gone through one year of the bootcamp-style program and our aunt couldn't rave enough about how his problematic behavior had been corrected. I had a feeling that Rob would be signed up for it, but my heart fell into the deepest depths of my stomach learning that I was somehow being signed up as well. In those few moments on the couch, I replayed everything I had ever done in front of my parents that might explain this decision. Every word I chose not to speak out loud, every action I told myself not to take because it was something Rob would probably do, every feeling I didn't talk about because I was worried it might make my parents upset to hear.

This wasn't fair. I didn't have behavioral issues. I didn't argue or backtalk. I didn't act out at school. I did my homework. I went to church. I was writing a book at the age of 12. As hard as I could try to reflect and investigate, I could not find a reason why I was being sent off to this program once a week to be yelled at by retired military men and their wives, run laps, and learn how to march in a line. I filtered all of my words of apprehension which quickly turned into words of resistance, but it was of no use. They had already signed me up and paid the fees for my enrollment and that was that. No plea or bout of tears was going to undo their decision and I had no choice but get in the car and go into the school building for my first day the week following the conversation.

I had to stand there and be yelled at by a man and his wife until I was audibly sobbing because I apparently played outside too long and missed a Wednesday night church service that week. I had to go outside and do the extreme exercises and then some more if the instructors felt I hadn't gotten the message clearly enough that they had complete control over me until I didn't even feel human. I had to try and learn how to follow drill instructions and then do more exercise as punishment for not comprehending or knowing how to ask for help. I had to do this dehumanizing two hours every single week because that's what Mom and Dad had decided was best for me for whatever unknown reason. No matter how much I pleaded with them or vented to Nana, I had no option but to obey and remain silent about being shouted at and scolded publicly like a disobedient dog. The worst part of it wasn't even the shouting, but the fact that Mom stood and watched any time it happened at check-in and didn't do a single thing to intervene.

Despite being the one who was responsible for throwing me into the program and passively motivating these angry strangers to scream and force me into submission, I eventually convinced Mom to withdraw me from the program. It took countless weeks of begging and hiding every time it was time for the weekly two-hour visit, but she finally seemed to notice what the program was doing to me. While I was ecstatic to be finally free from the weekly torment, I couldn't stop questioning why Mom would have signed me up for it in the first place. She knew more than anyone how much I hated screaming and arguments, yet that didn't stop her from registering me and telling them that I had disobeyed some church service plan that was never even communicated to me. She sat there while I was a traumatized, sobbing heap on that linoleum floor. If the program had taught me anything, it was to fear my parents even more than I had before and to think twice before telling them anything out of fear of what they may retaliate with. I would say that I was going to think twice before seriously breaking any kind of rule or disrespecting my parents, but I couldn't recall a time where I had been doing so in the first place. Needless to say, I spent more and more time isolating myself and peacefully slipping away into whatever other reality I could, whether that be in the neighborhood park with Chancey and the other kids or my video games or *The Knight.* Of course, it only took a couple of nighttime movies and her playing with my hair when I had trouble falling asleep for me to look past everything and accept that my mother was the same loving, caring woman she always was.

I came home from school one day and immediately saw her face light up when I told her I played a few games of football with some new friends during some outside time (we only get this recess time on special occasions now that we're mature, middle-school young adults). Mom had always been obsessed with football, spending her free time watching every game that she could of her favorite teams and obsessing over it. She would scream at the TV in excitement or throw things at it whenever her team would lose or the referee's would make a call that was incorrect in her opinion. Naturally, she took this casual comment and brought up a community league that she could get me signed up for. I didn't like the idea but then I couldn't help but notice how excited and happy she was to even be bringing it up for me. Plus, she was aggressively requesting me to sign up instead of forcing my registration like she had done with the bootcamp-for-small-children program. Never missing the opportunity to try and secure my spot as the favorite son, I told her that she could sign me up for the football league. Her excitement even started to spread to me at the thought of being a part of a team and meeting more kids until I first put on the uncomfortable pads and jersey, the mouth guard that increased the pain I was already feeling from braces, and was handed the playbook I was supposed to memorize.

I lasted all of three weeks and two unexpected tackles before I was hiding before practice and begging Mom to undo my registration and let me quit. I was in way over my head and the idea of getting tackled more was unbearable. I had absolutely no idea how to play the game outside of the occasional throw-and-catch at recess. The playbook might as well have been written in Latin or ancient hieroglyphs and the coaches all seemed to have the same temperaments as the retired drill instructors from that dreadful program that's still featured in my nightmares. For a normal preteen boy with a normal sense of competitiveness, this would have been motivating and inspired a desire to learn the sport or adopt a certain sense of comradery amongst teammates. However, the sport and all its obligations only brought an impending sense of anxiety and fear that I couldn't talk myself out of even if I really wanted to. Thankfully, I was able to scavenge and find the right words to convince Mom of the nauseating fear that came before every single practice and the unbearable confusion I had to feel during the first scrimmage that resulted in the tackles and aggressive shouts from every single coach. I could see the anger and disappointment in my parents' faces so I quickly supplemented with a request to take guitar lessons and maybe end up on the same show as my celebrity crush and make it big like she had. When that also fell through, I had to tell myself that they'd just have to be okay with a son whose only skill and/or potential artistic talent was starting a science-fiction novel at the age of 12.

My parents didn't have much time to be angry or disappointed with me about my trifecta of throwing in the towel on things. Instead, they sat us down one evening to let us know that our household was going to be temporarily growing by one because Poppop Luke was going to be moving in for a bit. Apparently, he had a pretty serious drinking problem (whatever that meant) and was signed up for a program near our house that was going to help him get back on his own feet. All the specifics were confusing to me, but I was excited to be in such close contact with another grandparent since we didn't see much of him since we moved away from Loudon in whatever grade that was. I quickly started to feel like our household was the heroes of the family since we had moved to Murfreesboro to help take care of Nana and now we were moving Poppop Luke in with us to help take care of him at the same time. However, my excitement was replaced with fear shortly after he had gotten all of his stuff moved in, or at least the things he had brought with him. While I had only known him for a relatively short period of time, it was as if I could hardly recognize the man that was my new housemate for the foreseeable future.

I sat down in the middle of the stairs, hidden out of sight from anyone on the first floor of the house. I heard the screams coming from downstairs as I was working away on my book in the computer room. This blind spot on the stairs seemed like the best vantage point to hear what was going on without risking being seen and aggravating anyone any further. I was used to Mom and Dad fighting enough to tune them out most of the time, but this was not a familiar noise. Mom and Poppop Luke were launching missile after missile towards each other from what sounded like opposite sides of the living room. I quickly realized that my new roommate did not particularly move in with us for fun sleepovers or to spend more quality time with us. My eyes widened as I sat on the stairway, paralyzed with fear as their screams intensified below. Why were they yelling? Why were they so angry? What was about to happen?

Were they going to hit each other? Were they going to break things? Was Poppop Luke sick like Nana is? A million scenarios raced through my mind as I heard them dive deeper and deeper into their battle below until it finally started to fizzle out. Whatever it meant to have a drinking problem or withdrawals, my grandfather *really* had it.

I wanted to ask more questions about why Poppop Luke was living with us and what kind of problems he was having, but I got too scared of potential repercussions. Instead, I eventually adjusted my abilities to tune out the outside world to include the consistent screaming matches between Mom and her father. Each battle that erupted gave me yet another reason to escape into my video games, books, neighborhood walks with Chancey, or my book. One day, after Nana had wrapped up her cancer treatments and Poppop Luke had completed his program (or at least the amount he was willing to undergo), I accidentally let slip to Mrs. Barber that I was halfway finished writing my own novel. Before I could do any damage control, I was sitting on a stool in front of the entire class with the familiar cinder block resting in my stomach as I looked down at the 50-or-so pages of *The Knight* in my hands. I looked up, trying to resist the urge to vomit and flee the school building, just in time to see the glowing smile on my teacher's face. Suddenly, her encouragement soared across the room and made its way to my vocal cords, allowing me to start reading the first few pages out loud for the entire class. I handed the microphone back to her and was surprised to hear the class clapping for the words I had printed onto paper instead of the thrown tomatoes I was expecting to receive. I just read my book. Out loud. To my whole class. And survived.

A newfound wave of confidence surged me through the remainder of the school year before spending the majority of the summer completing the full-length fiction novel. I spent hour after hour pouring all of my imagination over the keyboard and creating a world full of adventures I could only dream of. Towards the end of the summer, I rolled back in my computer chair and exhaled as I tapped the final sentence and immediately saved the file and started on a possible sequel. Part of me knew I wanted to continue this adventure into another book (maybe even a series) but mostly I just wanted an excuse to sit at my computer for an unhealthy period of time since Mom didn't monitor my time if I was working on becoming an author. One afternoon, however, she burst into the computer room in what I assumed to be anger at how much time I had been spending here. My wide eyes stared in fear until I saw that she was grinning from ear to ear before I felt the landline phone press up against my ear. A man's voice I had never heard before asked how I was doing along with a few questions. I responded in quiet, confused tones while Mom watched excitedly from across the room. My jaw dropped in disbelief as the man told me he worked for a publishing company and wanted to publish my book if I was okay with it. He started to briefly explain what that process might look like, but I had already accepted his offer and handed the phone back without a second thought.

Mom said she had already emailed the file of my book to the company and that we didn't have to worry about anything else. I don't remember when I told her that I wanted to have it published or that she could send it off to anyone, but I guess it was too late to worry about that now. Plus, she seemed so excited and happy about the publishing for me to consider bursting her bubble now. She took over the process from here, bypassing an editor and a few other phases in order to save money (apparently this company took money up front to publish books while the authors hope to make up the money in profits) and before I knew it, I had helped design the cover and it was available to purchase shortly after that. Looking down at the very first copy of my book in my hands, I couldn't believe it. Everything seemed to have happened so quickly as I gave up trying to interpret the various emotions that were swirling around becoming a newly published author and leaned into the new experience as best as I could.

The whirlwind of excitement, confusion, and accomplishment was immediately silenced and extinguished the first week or two of seventh grade during dinner. We were seated at the table, an immediate sign of something to come, instead of the usual meal in front of the television on the couch. Mom started to speak, but I immediately drowned out her words because I already knew what was about to happen. Mom would start out by telling us that we were moving while Dad would sit in silent agreement and then Rob would lash out in defiance. Arguments would happen while I tried to figure out in my head why my parents were so comfortable uprooting us every single school year and placing us in yet another new school environment. Was it because I quit football and guitar lessons? Was it because I liked staying the night at Nana and Poppop's house more than here? Was it even something that I had done or a decision made spontaneously out of boredom? I knew Poppop Jack had returned home and Nana had made it through all of her cancer treatments, but why did that mean we had to make our exit from Murfreesboro? I stood up from the table, dropped my plate into the sink, and took Chancey for a walk as I tried to process having to say another round of goodbyes to my favorite teachers and the small handful of friends I had finally managed to make here. Worst of all, I had to accept that I wasn't going to be 10 minutes away from Nana anymore.

Chapter Five

Remember When I Was on the News?

I grabbed my last bag out of the car, slamming the trunk behind me as I made my way up to the new house, the weight of the painful goodbyes to my short-term girlfriend, favorite teachers, and neighborhood friends still heavy on my shoulders. This house was new, but the neighborhood it was rooted in was all too familiar. Dad was offered his old job back at the cancer center in Oak Ridge and in the blink of an eye, we were unpacking our things into the pretty two-story house with a nice backyard that Chancey was already in love with. I hung up my clothes in my new closet of my new bedroom, deeply hoping I was going to walk into school without a single person remembering me from fifth grade considering my social status was in shambles that year. The date-to-the-dance rejection, the only-one-dressed-up Halloween situation, and my overall lack of social skills were still etched into the walls of my memories to this day. I looked around my bedroom, satisfied enough with my progress, and made my way downstairs to check in on everyone else. I was mortified to hear Mom having a conversation with a stranger in the living room, the main topic of conversation being her son who had just published a book.

I told her multiple times how uncomfortable it made me to have her telling strangers about my book. I told her that I wanted to tell people when and if I wanted them to know and that I didn't want to become a walking advertisement. She knew how angry it made me and yet she was telling the woman I had never met, the previous owner of our new house, that I was having a book published before I even finished middle school. I stormed out of the house, letting my anger steam out by playing with Chancey in the backyard until Mom forced me to come back inside after the woman had left. She gave me a lecture on why I need to be more proud of my book and try to make everyone buy a copy that I came in contact with as I sat and stared at the floor until she gave up. I didn't want to shout from the rooftops that I wrote a book. I didn't want to have to market myself to strangers on the street to sell copies. I can't help being shy when I haven't stayed in one school for more than one grade level at a time. I didn't know how to make friends, let alone make clients. Knowing I didn't want to suddenly become the problem child of the house, I told her I would try my best even if I knew that wasn't a possibility. I remembered how happy she was the day the publishing company called and couldn't bring myself to try and ruin the happiness for her by somehow undoing the book. Plus, I had already started writing the sequel so it's probably a bit too late to turn back now anyway.

The horror continued as I made my way to my first class of the day as The New Kid Who Used to Go Here So Not Technically New only to be immediately asked if I was the one who wrote a book. My heart immediately sank into the depths of my stomach and I lost the ability to speak. I envisioned staying under the radar as much as possible like I did in Murfreesboro since that approach had worked pretty well, yet I already had an entire classroom's eyes on me in the first 60 seconds. My paralyzing confusion must have been plastered on my face because the girl who asked me chimed in to break the silence by saying that I had moved into her old house and her mother had been the stranger that Mom had so eagerly told about my book. Damn it. Damn it. Damn it. My worst-case scenario that I hadn't even mentally prepared for (a first for me) was happening in real-time right in front of me.

I wanted to fake some kind of illness or emergency and flee school property as quickly as humanly possible. However, I knew that was out of the question considering it was my first day and Mom would see through whatever lie I would try to conjure up. I scrambled to find the best words to say in my head, but the only ones that could come out were a jumbled mess trying to explain that I had written a science-fiction book but that I didn't know much about how it's being published. I said something about it being 200 pages and make-believe but I knew the moment my sentences came out of my mouth that I had screwed up my pitch. All it took was one day, one minute even, for me to dig myself into a grave at this school for the second time. It was challenging enough to be The New Kid Who Has Actually Been Here Before but now I had to sit through class and wander through the halls with "*The Weird Semi-New Kid Who Wrote A Book*" branded onto my forehead along with a mouth full of braces and unkempt hair.

My anger towards my mother reignited as I realized this day would have gone much differently had she simply respected her son's wishes and kept my book private, at least for now. The remainder of the day was spent with my head as low as it could go, steam billowing out of my ears about my business being spread throughout the student body on the first day, my parents relocating me every single year, and the overall dysfunction of my life in general. I wanted to be normal. I wanted to have friends. I wanted to be proud of my book and be able to tell people about it. But I can't. I'm not. I'm not the person I wish I could be.

Keeping with my familiar course of action, I didn't approach or confront Mom about keeping my book under wraps until things could die down or I could learn how to talk about it. Questions were still launched my way, from students and staff alike, and I got better about giving vague responses or one-word answers until people eventually got the hint and moved on to other topics of discussion. The fascination with an author in the class shifted as the season changed and I began to get my feet on the ground after such an unsteady/rocky start to the school year. I put some of my mediocre investigative abilities to the test and found out some of my classmates were actually my close neighbors and made the mistake of sharing that discovery with my parents over dinner. Before I could do any damage control, Mom had reached out to some of their parents and arranged a hangout for us to help the social process along. This would have been extremely helpful if it weren't for the fact that we were all pre-teens or teenagers and having your parents assist in this process was no longer considered very cool. Nonetheless, I had no other choice but to go along with the plans and try to make the best of them, despite my track record of success with these kinds of things being virtually nonexistent.

Unable to put forth any effort in getting out of the plans, I exhaled and stepped out of our front door. The walk across the street felt miles long as I raced through every possible scenario in my head. Would it somehow be comfortable and easy with my classmates/neighbors immediately welcoming me into their circle? Would there be a bucket of pig's blood waiting for me the moment I walked in? Would I have to finally break open my shell and explain the entire plot of my book and how I managed to write it? I stopped at the doorstep that marked the end of my two-mile trek across the street, anxiety spreading like an emotional wildfire throughout my entire body. This was it. The final moment before the beginning of my social life (or lack thereof) began again within this school. The last few moments before I could never turn back on my introduction to the popular crowd. I reached up to knock on the front door only to pause for another moment. I began contemplating another plan that involved hiding somewhere in the neighborhood (maybe my old forest area) for a couple of hours and telling my parents that I had a great time with the other kids. However, I knew the consequences of being caught in that lie were far worse than dealing with the all-too-familiar awkward encounter with other humans.

His dad opened the front door before I had any more time to consider this alternative. Naturally, I was barely able to conjure up responses that made sense to the small talk questions and icebreakers. The words appeared in my head but were completely disconnected by the time they made it from my mind to my vocal cords. Realizing he was dealing with such an awkward kid, he gestured toward the stairs and said everyone was up in the room playing video games if I wanted to go join them. The stairs seemed to grow in length as I stared up from the bottom, my heart picking up its pace with each one I climbed. I stood silently in the doorway, wondering if I was covered in as much visible sweat as I felt I was or if the guys in front of me could hear my heart pounding from there. The one who lived in the house welcomed me in, gesturing to have a seat in the open spot between the other two guys while they finished up whatever round of the game they were on. I managed to calm my heart down enough to try and make small talk as it presented itself, whether it was agreeing with what girl was pretty in whatever class or sharing excitement in whatever video game was going to be released next week. There were a few moments where I saw an opportunity to throw in a joke or add some substance to the conversation at hand, but I quickly talked myself out of it. Staying under the radar was my best chance at being invited back into this social circle and hopefully making a name for myself my second time around these hallways.

Now that I had made my initial impression on my neighbor, I started taking the same route to classes with them. I saw where they all sat at lunch and decided to take a spot at the same table. I would occasionally glance out the living room window to find them jumping on one of the other neighbor's trampoline or running around acting out a video game in the real world. I was sure they wouldn't mind if I walked outside and joined them in their antics. The more I was hanging out with them, the more convinced I became that their popularity, humor, flirtation skills, and general social rankings would rub off on me. I even managed to talk Mom into buying me my first cell phone for my birthday, something that truly reflected your ranking in the social hierarchy of middle school. I quickly got all my new friends into my contact list and wasted no time sending everyone texts every day the moment school would end. My phone kept malfunctioning because I didn't get responses back very often, so I had to keep sending the message over and over again until it delivered. Between making sure my texts were sending and joining their squad anytime I saw them outside, I was sure to secure my spot at the top of the food chain.

My dreams were confirmed when my neighbor leaned over during Math to let me know they were doing a game of flashlight tag on our street later that night and I was definitely invited. I tried my best to suppress my excitement before confirming my attendance, butterflies already filling my stomach. I actually got an invite instead of waiting to see them hanging out from my window. It seemed a bit odd because the flashlight tag games usually happened on the weekends when we had a more relaxed curfew but I was in no position to question it. I finished up all of my homework for every class before the bell had time to ring so that I'd have my availability wide open once they texted me that it was time to head over. The bus ride home took ages before I was finally home and eagerly awaiting their texts. I went through every outfit combination in my closet (I still hadn't convinced Mom to buy me some clothes that the other kids seemed to always wear) trying to find the best thing to wear for my first genuine social hangout that I'd been organically invited to. After what felt like another eternity, I got the go-ahead to make my way across the street for the game of flashlight tag with my new circle of close friends.

I floated out the front door, skipping steps off the porch as I quickly made my way across the street. I got to the driveway and noticed a strange hush fall over everyone gathered in front of the garage. My feet returned to the ground and my pace slowed as I tried to fight off the feeling that I had just walked up on them talking about me. I took a few more steps forward, hoping the insecurities forming in my mind would fall off with each impact on the concrete. Another second of silence that lasted hours stopped me in my tracks as more doubt began to rush over me. The others took a few glances at one another and suddenly ran into the garage. Before I could open my mouth to ask a question, they had returned and were opening fire on me from the front of the driveway. I froze in disbelief until I felt the sting of the plastic bullets colliding into my skin. Between my nonexistent pain tolerance and the sudden realization of the situation at hand, tears began to form immediately as I turned to run back home. I felt more and more bullets hit my back, arms, and calves as they chased after me, their laughter piercing my ear drums as their bullets pierced my skin. I tripped as I made it to my driveway before scrambling up as quickly as I could inside the front door. I ran past the living room and whatever meal Mom had prepared for everyone and up the stairs toward my bedroom.

I threw myself onto my bed, burying my teary face into the pillows in disbelief at how wrong I had been about everything. I could still hear their laughter and comments about how I should "write another book about this" as they enacted their pellet gun ambush. They did not want to be friends with me. I sat up to examine myself in the mirror, each bruise and welt a reminder of how many times I threw myself into their social circle under the illusion that I was welcome. I knew I couldn't tell my parents what had happened because it would just make the situation that much worse. As much as it hurt, both literally and emotionally, I was going to have to look past this and pretend it was fine. Stay under the radar and see how my social standing survives being shot and publicly bawling my eyes out as a result. I laid back down as Chancey jumped up onto the bed beside me to try and figure out why I was crying. Just for fun, I told her what had just happened even though I knew she had no way of understanding a word of it. Nonetheless, she curled up close to me in an attempt to console me, an attempt I would kill to have been a successful one.

Walking through the doorways into school the next morning with as brave of a face as I could muster was not the easiest, especially the closer I got to my assigned classrooms. Even as I kept my head down, I could feel their eyes on me, each gaze stinging like the plastic pellets that they had shot me with the night before. Awkward silence filled the room like a dense fog as I took my seat and avoided their eyes. One of them eventually spoke up and said that the ambush had just been a joke, adding in an awkward laugh at the end of the sentence that lingered throughout the room for a few moments. I looked up, gave my best attempt at a smile, and assured him that I knew it was a joke and tried to return the laugh. Seeming validated, everyone shifted their eyes back to their own side conversations before the teacher began her lecture and the rest of the day resumed like normal. As much as I had wanted to scream and launch myself up from my chair, I knew my best chance at recovery was to pretend to find the humor in getting The New Kid's hopes up for friendship only to literally shoot them down from the clouds. My new plan of action would be to continue to stay under the radar, avoid inserting myself into plans from now on, and hope that I'm able to eventually make at least one or two meaningful friendships.

With the popularity of cell phones and text messaging still in full effect, another culture shift overcame the hallways as something called social media started to arise. Instant messaging sites, online profiles, and other various platforms began to insert themselves into the everyday lives of everyone at my school and everyone at Rob's high school. In what felt like a week, we all collectively went from depending on landline phones and word of mouth to make plans together to being able to reach each other and connect instantly in a million different ways. My computer that used to strictly be for video games and writing *The Knight* and its sequel was now a way for me to attempt making friends when I wasn't at school. Thankfully, Rob had already created profiles on everything without permission and gotten those shouting matches out of the way by the time I was ready to beg permission to create profiles and usernames of my own. It took a little bit of convincing that I wasn't going to be viciously murdered by posting a song I was listening to or a survey I had taken when I was bored, but she eventually gave in after I reminded her I wasn't the problem child of the household. Additionally, I agreed to go door-to-door in the neighborhood selling copies of my book in return. She knew I would hate this, but it was a worthy sacrifice if it meant a potential increase in my social standings with everyone at school.

With every day that passed, I spent less and less time playing the video game with Dad or finishing up my book's sequel (that no one, including my parents, knew I was writing). Social media quickly took up the majority of my free time and desires, providing me an opportunity for research and action at the same time. I suddenly had a glimpse into who was friends with who, what music was popular among all the Cool Kids, what types of posts seemed to be the most liked among the various social circles I had added to my online friend groups, and a million other insights that quickly stoked my hopes at making a social recovery that I could never have imagined before this new phenomenon. Where I would usually stammer and stutter trying to piece together the right words during a social interaction, I was now able to take a few deep breaths and read the words I was going to say before I hit send. Not only was I able to improve my contributions to any given conversation now that it was online, but I could passively look at everyone else's conversations and begin studying the other kids and how they spoke amongst each other without anyone seeing. Social media had suddenly given me a two-way mirror to allow social research in secrecy so that I didn't seem weird and creepy the way I would have if I had sat at a lunch table with a pen and paper to take notes on middle school dialogue. Before I knew it, I had even secured two best friends that I could finally add to the "top friends" section of my online profile, something that I had to keep hidden on my page until now.

Seventh grade picked up its pace as I continued to stay under the radar of social interaction unless I was specifically invited to join. The publishing process reached its final stages, aided by the fact that Mom completely bypassed so many phases, and we got the first batch of copies delivered to us along with the website information for anyone who wanted to order online. From there came the terrifying reality that I was going to have to try and sell copies of my book to strangers around the neighborhood. I sat up alone in my room, quietly plotting a way to get out of having to take on this task. However, I came to realize that putting my efforts into going door-to-door meant I wouldn't have to try as hard to talk about it to anyone at school. Mom had been mentioning how she wanted to sell as many copies as possible for whatever reason, but she didn't say that those sales had to come from my classmates. Before I knew it, I was knocking on every door I could find and all but begging whoever answered to help me follow my dream as a young author by supporting my first book. Much to my despair, though, Mom let it slip to another parent and word began to spread around the school. The first morning that I saw the familiar novel being passed around in one of my classrooms brought an immediate nausea that followed me the remainder of the day.

As much as I attempted to stay under the radar for my own potential popularity's sake, Mom was determined to make me a bestselling author at the age of 13. With her enthusiastic marketing skills, I got a couple of calls from some of the newspapers around here and in Knoxville asking to write a piece about my book. I awkwardly answered their questions over the phone as Mom excitedly stood beside me and listened. I hung up and put the phone back down onto the counter only to pick it back up for another newspaper call. I put it down again only to pick it up once again to be told that the local news station wanted to set up an interview to be televised later that week. Mom took the phone from me before I could hang up to confirm the interview and even suggested that they do the interview in the library at school in the middle of the day. I felt that familiar feeling in my stomach as any chance of making a social comeback at this school went up in flames with one single phone call.

Unable to see the terror that was consuming my every thought, Mom could not be more excited to drop me off at school the day of the interview. She gave me a hug before driving off, unsure if she was going to be able to make it or not to the big event. I walked through the doors, my head low and my mind racing through the possibilities of getting myself out of this. Coming to no conclusion that wouldn't result in my public execution via my parents, I sat through my classes until I heard the intercom sound above me. The voice came through, asking my current teacher to dismiss me so that I could go to the library for an interview. I sprinted out of the room as quickly as I could, my classmates' giggles and jabs still ringing in my ears as I made my way to the library. I stood outside the doors for a few moments as I attempted to figure out what in the world I was going to say in front of a camera about the book I didn't actually want anyone to know about. I had enough difficulty talking to kids in my class, how was I supposed to talk to a complete stranger knowing that it was going to be broadcasted to several counties and cities? I took a deep breath, told myself that Nana and Mom were both ecstatic about me being on the news, and stepped through the double-doors towards my imminent doom.

I walked over to where the cameras had already been set up, immediately feeling like the person who was late to his own party. A woman who radiated charm and warmth greeted me and went right into the details of the interview. I tried to give her my full attention but I couldn't help but look around the library to see a few kids gathered around chattering amongst each other. I continued scanning the room, passing over one of my favorite librarians as she beamed an encouraging smile that was overflowing with pride. My eyes completed their scroll of the room and fell back on the journalist in front of me. I could tell she was waiting for my response to the explanation that I had barely heard so I gave her the best attempt at a vague reply and a smile. Clearly able to detect my overheated fondue of confusion and nerves, she gave another quick summary of how the interview was going to go, a few questions and a read-through of a few paragraphs to wrap it all up. I gave an attempt to seem eager and excited as she began her questions, but all I could think about in my mind was the sounds of the cameras and the fact that my parents weren't there. With each question, I felt smaller and smaller until I was a tiny ant underneath a microscope by the time I finished the last sentence of the reading of whatever random page I anxiously picked in a hurried panic. The camera crew packed everything up and I was on my way back to class, hanging my head in shame at how much my nerves had probably radiated off of my every word.

I had to suffer through several viewings with my family as we all saw the story air later that night on the news, Mom rewinding it over and over again. I wanted to mention that they could have watched it in real time had they come to the school but I figured that would cause more issues than benefits. Instead, I sank further and further into the couch as I was forced to relive the disaster over and over again. However, I quickly realized that by tanking my first major opportunity to market *The Knight*, I simultaneously wrecked the odds that I'd sell many more copies or be asked to do an interview for it ever again. A certain peace suddenly rushed over me as I imagined the buzz starting to die off from the book. No more jokes from the other kids at school. No more being put on the spot by Mom in front of strangers. No more getting shot with plastic bullets only to be told to "write another book" about the experience. A smile I had forgotten how to make stretched across my face as I stared up at my bedroom ceiling with hopeful, almost-teary eyes and imagined a world post-novel where I made another best friend or two. Maybe even a girlfriend, who knows?

I woke up the next morning with the same passion for my newfound plan to bury any and all news about my book. Shut down any conversation about newspapers or news stations. Change the subject when it was brought up. Ignore anyone that asked about it at school. Instead of developing a book I had spent so much time working on, I started convincing myself that it never happened. With each passing week, there were fewer and fewer people asking me things about it. Fewer people pointed out all the grammatical or formatting errors because we had bypassed getting an editor. Fewer people asked me why I wrote a book only to start laughing at me before they could even finish their sentence. Once the buzz had completely dissipated for the most part, I picked myself up from the bottom of the social hierarchy of middle school. I could tell that Mom was disappointed that I wasn't a global bestselling author making millions, but I couldn't have been happier to go to school without carrying the burden of marketing myself to an audience who already didn't have the best opinion of me to begin with. I knew I had made the right choice when I found myself writing a love note to one of the girls in my grade and asking her to be my girlfriend (once my new best friend had given me a significant pep talk of course).

My heart skipped several beats whenever I saw her walking towards me later that day, a folded piece of paper in her hand. She handed me the paper before scurrying down the hallway with her friends. I slowly unfolded it, almost passing out from my own nerves a couple of times in the process. The tiny *yes* that I saw delicately written on the page in cursive suddenly wiped away everything bad that had happened that year from my mind. All of a sudden, I wasn't the Weird New Kid Who Wrote A Book. I was the Normal Kid Dating A Pretty Girl. I stared at the piece of paper for a few more moments as if it was going to somehow change into a rejection letter or disappear altogether before making my way home on a cloud. However, I knew that her parents hadn't gotten her a cell phone yet so I would have to wait to share my excitement at her acceptance until the next day at school. In familiar fashion, I couldn't wait to tell Chancey the good news that I had worked up the nerve to ask out a girl as we laid in bed later that night. I decided to wait to tell my parents or Rob until some more time had passed just in case she changed her mind by the end of the week.

For whatever reason, she didn't change her mind and revoke the decision to be in a relationship with one of the most unpopular kids of the school. By the next week, we were walking the hallways between classes and sitting together at lunch every single day. We were talking on the phone with each other at night via landline phone while she was trying to talk her way into a cell phone. With every day that passed and every set of eyes that saw me walking around the halls with my new girlfriend, another unfortunate event seemed to have vanished altogether from existence. Slamming my locker to see her suddenly standing behind it made the jokes on my first day back about my book disappear. Finally taking her hand in mine on the way to the bus after school obliterated the millions of texts I used to send to the other guys in my grade after getting my first cell phone. For a poetic, full-circle moment, we were invited to play a huge game of flashlight tag together as a package invite which made the horrifying ambush experience suddenly a memory that was far away in the distance. It turns out asking a girl out was all I had to do in order to establish myself within the social order of middle school after all. That was, however, until it came time for the paparazzi to start investigating.

I didn't know what to think when I looked down at the text from one of her friends asking if I was going to kiss her Friday night during the flashlight tag game. The concept of a first kiss was among many conversations in friendship groups and had come up numerous times in some of my hangout sessions with some of the guys in the neighborhood before the bullet ambush. However, I had always been able to avoid the concept considering girls didn't really like me and I was the Weird New Kid the whole time. Suddenly, an immense and nauseating pressure began to build up in my stomach as I realized the expectation was there for me to make the move for the first time this weekend. How do I kiss someone? What if she hadn't asked her friend to ask me about it and didn't actually want me to make the move? What if this is another trick and my girlfriend pulls out a gun to ambush me? Do I even want to- I cut my thoughts off and tried to take a deep breath to calm my nerves. I responded "probably" or something vague and nonchalant and began to make plans in my mind of how I was supposed to go about making this monumental childhood moment come to life in the days to come. However, try as I might, I couldn't calculate a scenario in my head that would smoothly result in me making the first move and sealing the deal for the sake of the relationship and my own social ranking amongst the other guys in my classes, a friendship group I was only halfway certain was even valid to begin with.

Suddenly, I found myself hiding in a playground set in a random backyard of the neighborhood face-to-face with my girlfriend as we awaited the designated seeker to make their attempts. My heart was racing as an awkward silence that was almost tangible filled the wooden castle. We both knew what the other was thinking without a single word being spoken and I was fully convinced my heart was beating so loudly that it was vibrating the wooden planks of the structure. My brain kept telling my body to just inch closer to her and just make the move, but all it could do was sit paralyzed in fear and stare directly ahead without saying a word. The awkward silence continued until the rays of light shone through the gaps of the wooden planks and released my body from its own paralysis. I let out an uncomfortable laugh and muttered that I guess we had been caught before quickly leaving the wooden castle and joining the rest of the group. A look of disappointment was painted across her face for the remainder of the evening.

The next week or so came with situations exactly the same as the first, the look of disappointment becoming somewhat of a permanent fixture on both of our faces with each first kiss that didn't happen. Each time, I'd sit and stare at the ceiling, barely able to fall asleep for most of the night in shame and guilt. Each time, I'd tell myself that I was going to seize the opportunity the very next moment I saw her and just do it even though I knew each time was going to be the same. Why did it always go fine in my mind but never in person? Why could I text her friends about making the move but not actually make it? Why did the thought of kissing my girlfriend prove to be such a paralyzing concept? Why did everyone else seem to be so invested in whether or not "it" had happened? Why did everyone else want me to kiss her more than I di- I stopped my thoughts again as the bell rang to free me from the prison of society for the day. I kept my head down, partly in shame and partly to avoid my friends and girlfriend as I made my way to the bus and headed home. Eventually, the male and female best friend that I had somehow managed to make/keep tried to chime in and give me support/encouragement but by that point I had no desire to talk about it whatsoever.

I stared in the mirror at the outfit of blatantly-obvious hand-me-downs from Rob that I knew didn't fit me well. I had no idea what a Bat Mitzvah was other than it was a Jewish tradition and one that my girlfriend's best friend was celebrating. By this point, we were barely talking and our hangouts were basically nonexistent thanks to my ineptitude in the kissing department. However, I knew I still had to show up tonight despite the awkwardness of not attending the religious ceremony and only showing up for the party (Mom said that we shouldn't be forced to attend other religious activities that aren't our own). I looked out of the backseat window the entire drive to the fancy lakeside restaurant in town. A feeling of dread had set in the moment the car pulled out of the driveway, a feeling that was completely affirmed as I walked into the venue to see my girlfriend who made eye contact with me but didn't come over to meet me in the doorway. I quickly scanned the rest of the crowd, doing my best to appear unaffected and not showcase the internal misery I was already feeling. Thankfully, my best friend had noticed my entrance and walked up to greet me and give me the rundown of anything I had missed from the ceremony and the party so far. He seemed somewhat nervous which quickly confirmed what I knew what about to happen, something that apparently the whole party knew.

I didn't have much time to sit and ponder everything before my girlfriend had finally made her way over to me to ask if I would come talk to her. I saw her lips moving, but the words were already drowned out as everything seemed to move in slow-motion while my fear became reality. My eyes moved across the room as she began the break-up speech in front of what felt like everyone else in the whole school. My heart sank and I wanted nothing more than to sprint out of the restaurant, rip off these stupid clothes, and sulk in the tranquil silence of my bedroom for the rest of eternity. Knowing that wasn't a possibility, I did my best to smile through her words that were hitting me like a pillowcase full of bricks to the stomach. We had a reassuring departing embrace that brought no reassurance to my mind and that was that. I quickly made my way to the closest bathroom stall to let out the tears I had been holding in from the moment I walked into the party. From there, all I had to do was mingle around the other groups of kids from school while trying my best to not seem phased by my first heartbreak that had been ten million times more public than I could have ever anticipated. My parents couldn't have arrived sooner by the time the party was over and it was time to leave, replaying every missed opportunity I had had to kiss my girlfriend and save the relationship the entire drive home.

I wasn't sure what was going to happen next now that I no longer had a popular girlfriend to walk around the hallways with. Visions of all my newfound friends abandoning me or plotting more ways to shoot me with plastic ammunition flashed through my mind as I sat in bed dreading the next week at school. Chancey hopped up onto the bed with me as if she knew every thought that was currently troubling my conscience. She cuddled up close to me and laid her head across my chest as if to reassure me that everything was going to be fine. Whether that was some kind of profound wisdom she possessed or an optimistic gesture, it helped to put my mind at ease in a way I could have never accomplished on my own. The network of friends I had managed to gather may get smaller now that I wasn't so popular but that's okay. I lost one of my first girlfriends because I couldn't bring myself to kiss her but that's okay. I only had two best friends and one of them was busy with her boyfriend nowadays but that's okay. My brother was never going to let me rest once he found out I got dumped and still never kissed her but that's okay. At the end of the day, the fact that we would probably move for whatever reason in the next few months since the school year was ending made these things seem fairly manageable.

With my first best friend filling most of her free time with dates and make out sessions with her boyfriend who wasn't too scared to make the move, I started to spend more time with the other close friend I had been able to keep around the last couple of months. We had opposite classroom schedules and teachers so we spent the majority of our time outside of school at his house or mine. We quickly came to realize his mother was much more laid back than mine so most of the time we tried our best to hang out around his place, walking all around town or climbing random trees in his neighborhood until the height came to be too intimidating. His sense of humor and overall demeanor was just as weird as mine, although he had a much better way of hiding it and making it adaptable to the general public. His parents were divorced which made it that much easier to vent about the various dynamics and strange issues of my family the more we got to know each other. Before I knew it, we were staying the night at each other's house almost every weekend and hanging out as much as we could throughout the week after school, sharing whatever weird jokes came to our mind or going to the regionally-famous ice cream place down the road the moment we got our allowance.

I had planned on going over to his place again one afternoon after school but those plans were intercepted by Mom and Dad who sat Rob and I down in the living room. I braced myself for another move that would have me finishing out the last few months of seventh grade somewhere across the world. The words that came out of my parents' mouth, however, were far more serious and much more upsetting. Another grandmother, this time Grams instead of Nana, was diagnosed with cancer that appeared to be at a pretty serious stage of development. I immediately saw how each word seemed to sting Dad as it was spoken, as if each one made his mother's illness that much more of a reality. I expected to be told to go upstairs and start packing up our bags, but Mom told us that Grams was actually going to be moving in with us here and getting treatment through the cancer treatment facility that Dad works at. It felt as if our parents were expecting some form of hesitation or backlash from us, but we were actually excited to have another person living in the house despite the unfortunate circumstances. I knew Grams loved Chancey about as much as I did and it would probably help Dad be in a better mood to have his Mom around so often. In fact, the more days passed after her arrival, the only person who seemed to be tense about the situation was Mom herself.

I started to sense the tension levels rise whenever Mom and Grams got to being in such close contact as the days and weeks passed. There had always seemed to be a certain disliking between the two of them for as long as I could remember so I was worried this would be a repeat of the time that Poppop Luke had lived with us. However, there were only moments of awkward silence or tense jabs back and forth which didn't really compare to warzone that the house had transformed into at random times back then. Typically, I would go outside with Chancey, go over to my best friend's house, or hide away in my room and read/work on my book's sequel whenever it got too awkward in the house. Whenever Grams would be at treatments or out of the house for some reason, Mom would mention something she had done or said to me and/or Rob for whatever reason. At times it felt as if she assumed we felt the same tension or negative feelings toward Grams and Gramps despite the fact that we got along just fine with them. Nonetheless, I would listen to the complaints without offering much feedback or response like normal until I could make my escape from the conversation and go off into my own little world until it was time to go to bed.

In a stay that felt like it was unfortunately only a weekend long, Grams had completed all of her necessary treatments and was packing her things back up to head back to her house. I knew Mom felt a tad bit too much satisfaction to see her go, but I was going to miss having someone else to talk to everyday and I knew Chancey was going to miss having someone to play and cuddle with while I was at school or over at my best friend's. Nonetheless, we had our parting hug and I watched her reverse down the driveway and drive off into the distance along with what was left of the seventh grade academic year. A rollercoaster and emotional train wreck of a year was finally coming to a close as I laid in bed one night and reflected on my survival. I knew I wasn't one of the popular kids by any means, but I wasn't at the bottom of the totem pole which was at least a start. I had made a few breakthroughs by surviving an ambush, doing damage control about my career as a published author (or lack thereof), convinced a girl to date me for a month or two, secured one or two solid friendships, and created social media profiles to keep myself on my toes with social research to hopefully make some more breakthroughs next year.

I was, oddly enough, excited to confidently march into my final year of middle school which means it was about the time for my parents to sit us down in the living room to let us know that we were packing up and moving again. Which they did.

Chapter Six

Remember When I Broke My Teeth?

Once again, I found myself staring up at the ceiling in disbelief after taping up the last box of things before the move tomorrow. Tears were already filling my eyes as I imagined how horrible tomorrow would play out. Putting off as much sleep as humanly possible, I laid in bed with Chancey and held her as close as I could. She could tell I was upset about something and did her usual cuddle tactics to try and cheer me up. Morning came in the cruelest of ways to remind me that my worst nightmare was becoming a reality today. The boxes around my bedroom stood as another brutal reminder that my life was quickly coming apart at the seams. I took a few deep breaths, gave Chancey as meaningful of a hug as I could muster, and made my way downstairs. Not wasting any time, Mom told me I needed to get dressed before we made our way to breakfast at the family's favorite restaurant, as if that somehow made everything sunshine and rainbows. As with any situation I was dreading, time passed at warp speed until I was suddenly standing in the parking lot holding Chancey as the other car pulled up the spot next to ours.

Watching Mom take the leash out of my hands and place it into the hands of these strangers made the brick that was already in my stomach all day grow twice its size. I gave her another hug and a few treats before I was forced to watch her climb up into their car and drive away into the distance. Mom turned almost immediately and began walking to the front entrance of the restaurant as if we had just gotten rid of a trash bag of old clothes and not my best friend in the entire world. Not having much of a choice in the matter (or any of this at all), I followed her into the restaurant and sat in silence. Silence was the only way that I could try and process the fact that my parents had just made me give away my favorite friend in the world. Sure, we were getting to stay in the same school since we were moving just a few miles down the road but why did that mean I had to give away Chancey? Mom was getting to take her dog that we had gotten at the same time so why did mine have to go? Why did she have this new house lined up before even having the courtesy to discuss the idea of giving her away? I tried to answer these questions in my mind but kept drawing blanks and I knew I couldn't ask them directly because that would just cause arguments, something that was already present enough in the house as it is without my input. To make matters worse, Mom seemed to be confused why I was silent and emotional at breakfast and insisted I be thankful to be taken to my favorite restaurant as if a stack of blueberry pancakes was enough to mend the fact that my best friend had just ridden off in a stranger's car to go live on some kind of farm in the middle of nowhere.

I did my best to feign tolerance as we finished up our food before heading to the new place to begin unpacking. Had this been a normal morning, I would have been excited to see how nice the new house was. It was uniquely rectangular in shape and an eye-catching blue all over with a spacious front porch and a long balcony stretching across one entire side of the second floor. My parents seemed to be picking up on how the Chancey situation was impacting me and moved Rob into the smaller bedroom and gave me the second largest one on the top floor. I still had to share the upstairs bathroom with my brother, but the spacious layout that gave me access to the balcony and enough room to have my computer set up in my bedroom made that sacrifice a manageable one. A hallway led out of my bedroom and opened up to the computer room that Dad had already set up before opening up to the stairs and the open living room and kitchen on the floor below. Even through the gloomy haze of emotion I was viewing everything in today, I couldn't ignore the fact that this was one of the nicest houses we had ever lived in. However, the moment I stopped to take that in, the reality of what I had to give up in order for us to meet the one-pet rule that our landlord apparently enforced interrupted every thought.

Summer break passed in a flurry of sleepovers at my best friend's place where I quickly began to feel like his mom's second son, a beach trip that we took as a family in Florida, and as much social media research as I could accomplish on a daily basis. I had convinced my parents to get me the newest mp3 player that came in the form of a phone-like device with a touchscreen and wireless internet connectivity. Suddenly, I was able to connect to the internet and log into my social media sites from anywhere in the house instead of being confined to the computer desk in my room. Between browsing all of the online profiles to see the music people were listening to and the jokes that seemed to be funny, I was getting slightly more confident about my final year of middle school that was quickly approaching. By now, I knew I had permanently locked in a best friend but I couldn't help hoping this could be the year where I really broke the barriers and branched out a little bit more before it was time for the hellscape of high school. In familiar fashion, I spent the night before the first day staring up at the ceiling anxiously awaiting my fate and feeling more alone than ever without Chancey cuddled up beside me.

Getting to walk through the same school doors for a new year was a strange feeling that I was not used to but quickly fell in love with. Seeing only a few new faces as opposed to *being* the new face of society was incredible. I had hyped up my behind-the-scenes social research online this summer and quit texting guys so often now that I realized that wasn't a popular thing for a teenage guy to do. For one of the first times, I felt like a (relatively) normal person making my way through the groups that had already gathered in the halls catching up on everything that had happened over the summer with their friends and families. A few people asked me how my summer had been and I had to quickly catch myself before saying anything about losing Chancey or finishing *The Knight*'s sequel. If I had learned anything from my life so far, it was that no one wanted to be given sad news and that the kids in this school did not need to hear anything about my literary works that I had written. Instead, I mentioned my new mp3 device and the beach trip we had taken with a big smile before making my way to my first classroom when the bell rang.

The rest of the day resumed as any other normal first day would have, each teacher giving the supply/reading list for the course and an idea of what to expect. After almost getting onto the wrong bus that would have taken me to the old house, I finally made it home in one piece with the relief that nothing major had transpired the whole day. Of course, that came to a close whenever Mom greeted me later that afternoon to deliver the news that I was somehow going to be interviewed again. The feeling of dread must have immediately shown on my face because Mom quickly followed up to inform me that the interview was at my old middle school in Murfreesboro and that it wouldn't be shown anywhere close to here. She went into some details about the interview being shown on the morning announcements across the entire school, but all I was hearing was that I was getting to see Nana *and* all my favorite former teachers while missing a day of school here. The next thing I knew, I was waking up in Nana's house and making my way downstairs for the breakfast I could already smell from my room here. As expected, the waffles came with a few words of encouragement to have fun at the middle school today and not let my nerves get the best of me.

Compared to the last time I was walking into a library for an interview, my nerves were hardly even an ounce of a problem. Something about the fact that this was happening in a school I wasn't attending and that I was about to make a round through my old classrooms that now housed a bunch of kids I've never met made the interview a breeze. I went through the fact that I started the book while I was a student here, covered a few of the plot points, dropped the website that anyone could order it from, and made my way down the familiar hallways. I made it to Mrs. Barber's class just in time to receive one of the best hugs and catch up before I got to watch myself on the television in her room after the various other school-related updates. My previous English teacher could hardly contain her excitement after the interview came to a close and a few seconds later she was taking her current class down memory lane when I had first started writing *The Knight* and reading portions of it in her class. From there, I made my way to my former Science and Social Studies classrooms before wrapping up at Mr. Huddleston in time to get his stamp of approval and words of encouragement for whatever my future held in writing.

The words of encouragement and support from my former teachers cemented themselves into my mind the entire ride home to Oak Ridge. They were so genuine and drenched with good intentions without any idea of what the first book had done to my social career at a new school. Mom, Nana, and my previous teachers all saw so much potential in *The Knight* without seeing how horrible it made my first few months here. A book that had caused so many jokes, snide remarks, and even that formative ambush from what I thought were my best friends. I had loved writing the novel that was full of so many fantasies and realms that I would have killed to make a reality, but I was closing that chapter of my life quickly. It had taken several months of effort to close this chapter and prevent it from being opened again by anyone else in the hallways of my new school. Once we got back home, I quietly went upstairs and stared at the computer on my desk upstairs for what felt like hours. Scrolling through the 200-or-so pages of the sequel I had written, I couldn't help but imagine what Mom would do if she knew I had started and finished it. Another round of publishing and interviews would ensure any chances I had of maintaining this newfound, neutral social ranking were buried. I took a deep breath, deleted the entire file that no one else knew existed, and decided to put an end to my writing altogether.

I quickly settled into the routine of being a semi-normal eighth grader now that I had wiped my slate clean of the previous year. Classwork came pretty easily from my new teachers and I got into the habit of somehow finishing my homework before the class bell rang each hour. Not having to worry much about assignments or studying proved to give me that much more time to scroll social media and continue my research methods for making myself as likable and relatable as humanly possible. Right on cue for my attempt at a lifestyle shift, my orthodontist decided it was time to remove the metal brackets and wires that had been implanted onto my teeth for the last two years. Having almost forgotten what it felt like without metal appliances, it took several days to get used to having a normal set of teeth all day. For the first time in two school years, I could open my mouth to smile for picture day at school instead of giving my best attempt at a soft smile or mysterious grin that would always come out horribly no matter what. It was going to take a few more weeks of practicing in the mirror to figure out what my signature smile was going to be but I was excited nonetheless to be free from the pain and maintenance of braces.

As the bell rang to signal the end of Advanced Algebra one afternoon, I gathered my stuff and prepared to follow one of my acquaintances (still working on the "friends" thing) to the next class. Before

I could get to the doorway, however, a girl I had only seen from afar stopped me to say that she loved my new smile. Not knowing how to react, I stumbled over whatever words I could convince my mouth to say before running off as quickly as possible in order to avoid a full-blown conversation. Although I had noticed her in my class a few times over the last couple of weeks, the only things I knew about her was that she was a grade below me and that she was incredibly pretty. Naturally, I spent the remainder of the day beating myself up over the fact that I had likely blown whatever chances I had to get to know her more with my lackluster response to her compliment. Later that night, however, I decided to reach out to one of our mutual friends to get her number or online username. Having no way other than email to contact her (strict parents), I hoped for the best and sent her the best attempt at a flirtatious email. Of course, this meant refreshing my inbox every five to ten minutes for the next few hours awaiting her response. Seeing the notification for a new message from a new sender sent my heart into hysterics as I realized I hadn't blown my chances after all.

Between emails and eventual texting back and forth (I was able to get her number with parent approval), I got the hunch that we both had a crush on each other. The next step that came was to bother my one best friend constantly until he was tired of hearing me talk about her and convinced me to take the leap of faith and just ask her out. Realizing that confidence wasn't my strong suit by any means, I wrote out a note to slip her way after our class one day. The pros of not asking in person when I had the obvious opportunity meant spending the rest of the day waiting for her written response like we were in the Stone Ages. To the entire galaxy's amazement, I got her reply and the girlfriend proposal had been accepted. I found solid ground with my social status, got my braces off to reveal an almost-perfect smile, *and* convinced another pretty girl to go out with me. Eighth grade was pretty damn awesome.

I quickly found out that her mother was an employee of the school so she had already researched and found out everything there was to find out about me. Nonetheless, she asked her daughter to invite me over for dinner to find out a little bit more about me after the first week or two of walking around the hallways together. Surprisingly, I found myself carrying casual conversation like a pro between my girlfriend, her parents, and her little brother. We all were getting along as well as I could have hoped and I began to think they genuinely liked me. Dinner wrapped up and I offered to help clean up the dishes, a move her mother seemed to be impressed by, but was told not to worry about it. The rest of the night was spent sitting on the couch with her and arguing over which movie we should watch. Convincing myself it wasn't too soon, I reached my hand a little distance across the couch cushion to hold her hand. I felt her hand go into mine without any resistance and couldn't help feeling butterflies at how much I had grown over the last year or so. After what felt like forever, I was able to ask girls out and carry conversation almost as well as a normal person while keeping my grades in check too. All too soon, Mom called to let me know she was outside waiting to shuttle me home after my date.

Holding hands, flirtatious text messages, and putting my arm around her at the movie theater in town quickly became the status quo. Changing my social media profile pictures to a selfie of the two of us was the cherry on top of the beginning of a great year. However, the paparazzi roaming the hallways of middle school had other expectations in mind as the pressure suddenly appeared that I should have already made the move by now. Random questions started to arrive from strangers, her friends, and my friends alike and ranged from "why haven't you?" to "are you going to this weekend?" and everything in between. The pressure built up more and more with each invasive question until it had formed a solid brick of anxiety and nerves in my stomach. I started formulating the best plan to seal the deal and finally get this milestone out of the way as I made my way to her house to have another dinner and movie night on her couch. Within five minutes of the movie, we were already cuddled together on the couch which presented the most perfect opportunity for me. This was finally it. My heartbeat began to accelerate to an insane pace once again. I was about to finally kiss a girl for the first time.

Driving home in Mom's car, I couldn't have held my head lower in shame. I couldn't believe that I had let another opportune moment slip through my fingers. She was one hundred percent expecting to be kissed that night as much as I was one hundred percent ready to cross the milestone off my bucket list to relieve the immense public pressure. Once again, I screwed everything up by letting the most confusing fear paralyze my entire body until I was frozen in place for the entirety of the movie until I got the call from Mom from her car outside. Why could I not just bring myself to simply lean over a few inches and just do it? Why couldn't I just do one peck at least? Even on the cheek? She had said yes to my proposal to date each other so it's not like I was just walking up to a stranger asking them to make out. Didn't we like each other enough to kiss? Why did it feel like I was only wanting to do this because everyone else -

The car came up to a halt in our driveway which was enough to pull my mind back down to reality. I swiftly exited the car and ran up to my room without a single word to anyone else in the house. I closed the door to my bedroom and buried myself under the sheets and pillows until I was completely in my own world and at peace. I wanted nothing more than to take another walk through the woods somewhere with Chancey by my side, nothing but the wilderness and my own imagination to keep me company without the stresses of the real world constantly scratching at our ankles. Time and time again, I convinced myself that I was starting to become normal like the other kids at school and yet I was physically unable to kiss my girlfriend like a normal person? I tried to ascend above my own thoughts and worries while hiding in my bedroom but the only thing I could see was the expression on my girlfriend's face as I left. It was the same expression of subtle disappointment that was painted on the last girlfriend's face after each failed attempt at a kiss. A nauseating mixture of guilt and self-loathing swirled around my stomach until I was able to slip off into a painfully inadequate sleep.

Almost exactly like the last time, there were countless opportunities to make the move but each and every time came with the same paralysis and inability to kiss my girlfriend. The painful look of disappointment grew deeper on her face with each date until I knew it was about to be over once again. Another week passed before I got the inevitable break-up text that sent me into a downward spiral of self-loathing once again. Another week of miserable sleep as I stared up at the ceiling wondering what was wrong with me that I couldn't reach this milestone in a normal teenager's life. Another week of keeping my head down in class hoping I didn't make eye contact with her. Another week of her thinking I must not have liked her at all when in reality I just seemed broken when it came to this simple human interaction. I liked having a girlfriend, didn't I? Did I not enjoy having someone to walk around the hallways with? I wanted to have my first kiss with her, right? I forced myself to try and put these thoughts and self-doubts to rest and keep moving forward if it was at all possible.

There was only so much time that I could pretend to keep the thoughts at bay before they began to overcome the semi-stable mental blockades. Shifting my energy away from scrolling through everyone's social media to further my social skills in secret, I began to look up any articles I could find about why someone would be seemingly unable to accomplish what should be a simple first kiss. I skimmed over the articles quickly, unable to find any golden answer to my problems outside of being too nervous/scared. I jumped from articles over to videos that were meant to teach people how to be a better kisser, hoping that somehow seeing an instructional video would make it easier the next time I convinced a girl to go out with me. After watching 20-or-so videos, I shifted over to whatever videos I could find on the platform to make me laugh and unwind a little bit. This journey down the rabbit hole of "videos you may also like" landed me watching a compilation of animals in the wild doing anything from accidentally doing backflips to kissing each other. One of these videos caused a video titled "bears kissing" to show up in the related videos section with the thumbnail preview causing my heart to erupt into panic mode.

I threw my device down and frantically looked in all directions in my bedroom to make sure no one had seen the suggested video that popped up on my screen. Once I confirmed I was alone (as always),

I cautiously picked it back up and stared at the preview on the screen for a few moments. Panic was still coursing through my entire body but for whatever reason I was entranced by the thumbnail and couldn't bring myself to close out of the app. Without thinking, I pressed play. The video that was suddenly being streamed in front of me was not an ordinary couple kissing each other. In fact, I'm pretty sure this kind of kissing was something that my parents had made jokes about on TV shows before and something that had been brought up in church a handful of times. Guilt immediately rushed over me as I realized the type of video I was watching along with another wave of guilt as I fully realized it involved two men. I quickly closed out, cleared the history on my device, and threw it back down on the bed. I stared up at the ceiling and tried to force my heart to stop racing and the strange sensations to subside. What had I just looked up on the internet? Why did it not gross me out? Why was I still thinking about what I had just seen? Why did I pick up the device and pull it up again?

The next morning, my stomach immediately twisted itself into a million knots as I reflected on the rabbit hole of videos I looked at the night before. I triple checked that my history had been cleared once again even though no one knew the passcode to enter into the device anyway. However, I still felt as if *I WATCHED PORN LAST NIGHT* was branded onto my forehead for my parents and brother to see while I got breakfast. Classes that day became various phases of panic and self-sabotage as I tried to figure out how I had gotten myself into the situation yesterday. While I had started out by accidentally clicking the video of two guys kissing and accidentally watching more than half the video, I shifted over to the normal kinds of videos like that. That balanced everything out and made me more normal, right? My brain was performing an intricate set of mental gymnastics going back and forth until I thought I was going to have to run out of the classroom to puke. Even if I had canceled out the gay intro to the rabbit hole of video searches, I had still done something evil. It was bad to watch inappropriate videos like that, especially that particular genre, and look at what I had done. Another wave of panic crashed into me as I imagined my parents finding out and having to explain what I had done to Nana. My mind flashed back to the times that Rob had been caught looking up videos like that on the family computer and how angry our parents had gotten as a result. I couldn't let myself suddenly become the next problem child of the household.

Making a solemn promise to myself that I'd simply stop looking up those kinds of videos, I began to pray every night that the evil curiosity that had attached itself to me would be extinguished. The next night I found myself in the bathroom going down the same rabbit hole of the dark corners of the internet. Once again, I felt sick to my stomach afterwards. Prayer came again later that night only to repeat the process over and over and over again. Out of nowhere, I started sneaking off to privately browse the videos that I knew I wasn't supposed to be watching as if it were some kind of drug that I had gotten my first highs from. When I wasn't looking up explicit material, I was looking up any information online as to how to stop myself from looking it up again. When I made certain no one was around me to see, I even looked up if sometimes looking up videos that didn't have girls in them meant something. With each new search my stomach would twist into itself further and further until I couldn't bear it any longer. Why was I suddenly having this problem with online videos? Why could I not just stop myself from doing this? Why, no matter what type of video it happened to be, did I keep focusing on-

A few irritated knocks on the bathroom door nearly sent me into cardiac arrest as Rob shouted that I had been in the bathroom way too long. I ran my hair under the running water and grabbed a towel to at least give the illusion that I had been showering before exiting. I fell onto my bed and did my best to turn my mind off of the newfound hobby I seemed to have tripped and fallen into. I grabbed the device again, this time to look up some bible verses that could be applied to this sort of situation and began to read through them for a while. If there had been any messages that were repeated for my entire life so far, it was that prayer and religion could fix any issue. I began reading more and more verses until I felt too tired to continue. With tears of guilt and frustration welling up in my eyes, I prayed as deeply as I could to wake up healed. I wanted nothing more than to wake up and feel normal. To wake up and feel like a normal teenage boy. A boy who wasn't looking up videos on the internet that were raising even his own eyebrows in confusion. A boy who would walk up to his former girlfriend after class tomorrow, apologize for screwing up, and finally kiss her.

When my independent efforts seemed to have little to no effect, I started asking my brother to tag along when he'd go with his friends to church. He seemed confused at first but thankfully agreed to it. Eventually, I met one of his youth leaders that seemed incredibly popular and started hanging out with them anytime he'd come by the house to see Rob. I was impressed at how easy it was for him to talk and hang out with pretty much anyone and was ecstatic to find out he was pretty much a youth leader for any grade instead of just high schoolers. It took all of about two hangout sessions before I found myself confessing that I had stumbled upon a sinful habit of looking up explicit videos on the internet now that I had such private and quick access to the internet. I left out the part about the videos sometimes being of the only-male variety because I knew it wasn't an important detail. I knew once I could kick the habit of watching the videos in general, I wouldn't have to worry about the small, insignificant details like that.

I felt a portion of the weight that had been following me around for the last few weeks evaporate into the air as my new youth leader told me that he completely understood what I was going through. He mentioned having his own past, and sometimes current, issue with online pornography and how difficult and isolating the problem can be. He provided a few more verses and some other perspectives on biblical stories that could be tailored to help someone battle this kind of situation before dropping me back off at the house with my newfound confidence and refreshed outlook on life. We exchanged numbers after this confessional and decided we would do our best to hold one another accountable for this specific issue and any other issues in life that may present themselves to us. Of course, that also meant the harsh reality of admitting to each other when we would succumb to our own hormonal pressures and browse the darker corners of the world wide web. I was still having difficulty accepting that I had gotten myself into such a twisted, complex habit but it felt nice not having to deal with it alone at least.

I kept a sheet of paper in one of my dresser drawers that had a tally system, one for every day that I hadn't logged onto *that* part of the internet. At the end of each day, I grabbed a marker and added another triumphant tally next to the one from the day before. However, whenever I would crumble to the pressure I would have to go through the torture of scribbling through however many tallies I had accumulated up to that point. One afternoon in particular, I had to suffer the emotional toll of scribbling through the longest "clean" streak of 17 days which prompted me to rip the paper into several pieces in anger. I looked up to see my brother standing in my bedroom doorway, a puzzled expression on his face. Not knowing how long he had been standing there or what all he had seen or heard (did I say anything out loud?), I spiraled into a panic. He must have noticed my reaction because he just continued to stare in silence and watch me suffer for an eternity before asking what was wrong. I stumbled over a few words and said something to the effect that I had lost some kind of online gaming streak with one of my friends at school before gathering the pieces of my sexual sins tracker to throw them into the trash can and make my way downstairs as if nothing bizarre had just happened at all. Suddenly, I could feel the brand on my forehead announcing that I had just watched two men going to town on the internet return for all to see. Thankfully, I said a few extra prayers that night that would eventually kick in and heal me from all of this so I could move on with life.

When I finally settled into a pretty steady routine of hanging out with the youth leader and growing my tally streak to longer and longer stretches, my parents decided to sit me down to have a talk. My mind immediately shot towards having to pack up my room and prepare to move to a new school in a new city halfway through the school year. I gathered a mental list of all the reasons why this was not going to happen and even went far enough to say I'd move in with my best friend if all else failed. Instead of the worst case scenario coming out of their mouths, however, they told me they were no longer comfortable with me spending so much time with the youth leader outside of actual church activities considering how much older he was. My mind immediately shifted to defense mode, something that was very unfamiliar for my parents to see, and I demanded that they change their minds. The thought of losing the progress I had been making on my religious healing thanks to an unexpected friendship drove me to hysterics. I made the mistake of saying that I was going to hang out with him anyways since he was a church friend which only caused them to threaten me with a suspended phone line and zero internet access for an undetermined period of time. Accepting my defeat, I sent him a text message relaying what my parents had decided on my behalf before retreating in shame and silence up to my bedroom.

Though it was expected, my friend honored my parents' wishes that I had relayed in the text and stopped all communication with me other than casual small talk whenever we'd see each other at church. Naturally, we drifted apart to the point where we stopped even the most minor communications and I was suddenly isolated once again in my journey to spiritual revival. The marker tally system quickly became a thing of my past until I decided altogether that I didn't have to face the fact that I had any form of issue if I simply pretended it wasn't happening. Every stealthy retreat to the bathroom and video genre of the day did not exist the moment I cleared my browser history and returned to normal life. I would reap whatever amount of enjoyment I was deriving from my secret session, even if it added to the confusion, and simply erase the entire experience from my memory afterward. Eventually, this habit would become a random phase of childhood to never look back on once it moved along to infect someone else instead of me. Until then, my prayers every night would be enough to keep me in line and moving forward. God was eventually going to reach down and decide I had suffered enough and heal me back to normal.

Walking downstairs after yet another video scroll that simply never happened, Mom interrupted the emotional spiral I was experiencing internally to say the dreaded words. Once again, I was finding myself sitting down on the couch across from her to await whatever it was that warranted this particular family meeting. I wasn't very phased with this "we need to talk" meeting considering Dad and Rob weren't a part of it so it couldn't be that tragic of a conversation. Right on cue, however, my mind wandered into the hypothetical scenario of my mother having somehow figured out my internet history on a device that she definitely didn't know the passcode to. Had I somehow leaked my own history by using the wireless internet? Had I left it unlocked on my dresser somehow? Did she contact the company who manufactures the devices to somehow convince them to remotely unlock it? Were the videos she saw me look up at least the normal kind of videos or had I just been caught watching-

Mom cut off my train of self-deprecating, panicked thoughts to let me know that my biological father had reached out to her. After several years of having no contact with me since the days of my early childhood, he wanted to meet me again. He was in the military and was going to be going overseas and he didn't want to leave any stone unturned before making this journey considering how unpredictable the job is. Realizing the weight of the decision that was being put in front of me, I sat alone with all the thoughts and feelings swirling around in my head that had quickly replaced the brief feeling of relief that my secret(s) had not been discovered by my parents after all. My mind immediately jumped back to all the confusion that I had felt all those years ago and all the regret I had about being unable to communicate what I wanted to communicate before it had been too late. It had been so long since I had thought about how much I regretted how everything had played out and wondered how often they still thought about me, if at all. What would they even say if I agreed to this meeting? What would I say?

I was still sitting alone with my thoughts and hypothetical scenarios that I was creating, silently reflecting as much as possible before responding to my mother's question. She took my silence as an opportunity to remind me just how difficult of a decision this would be on her and the rest of the family. Without any hesitation or pauses, she explained that my biological father had signed away his parental rights and that it was illegal for him to see me now and that my brother and I had been adopted by a new man who loved us and provided for us and that I shouldn't be scared to decline this invitation to meet again. My optimistic thoughts that had been swirling around inside were quickly contaminated with how complicated this offer would make everything. I would apparently have to process paperwork for this to happen, explain to Dad why he wasn't good enough to be my only Dad, and put my mother through even more stress about it all. Not wanting to make my family more complicated or disappoint anyone else with my own decisions, I told her not to worry about this and that I would hold off on meeting my father and the rest of that side of the family that I would still think about late into the nights that I couldn't get myself to fall asleep.

The inability to fall asleep occurred more and more often in the following days and weeks after turning down the offer. What if I made the wrong decision once again? What if he went overseas and didn't make it back? What if something bad happened to him and he thought that I didn't care about him? As much as I tried to ignore these thoughts and downplay all the potential downfalls of the decision I had to make, I couldn't help but think the worst. Eventually, I had to tell myself that the pros somehow outweighed the cons in this scenario. I told myself I could have added stress to Mom and Dad's life if I had made a different decision. What if agreeing to see him again somehow drove my parents apart? What if Nana and Poppop had been disappointed in me for allowing them back into my life when it had felt so scary getting spanked and disciplined all those years ago? What if Rob found out that I had been able to see my biological father again when he had tried so many times to see his to no avail. The scenarios I created in my head all seemed to have devastating effects on the people I cared about so maybe I made the proper decision after all. Eventually, I began filing these regretful thoughts away to the furthest corners of my mind where I also stored the thoughts about my secret internet habits.

As if the universe was ready to send me a much-needed gift, I got the opportunity to spend a weekend at Nana's house which provided a much-needed escape from reality. Without any wireless internet access, I didn't even have to worry about caving under the pressure of my own secrets. All I had to concern myself with was helping Nana with her cooking, watching movies and eating ice cream every night, and walking around the backyard with Poppop as he explained all the updates and renovations they had done to the deck and landscaping. After I got the full backyard tour, I decided to act out one of the scenes from the sequel to my first book out on the boulders once Poppop had gone back inside. My grandparents' backyard quickly transformed into a magical forest and then a violent ocean with the boulder being my ship and then a battlefield where I was finally conquering the kingdom's traitorous knight and his evil dragon. Escaping into this imaginary realm quickly made all of my life's worries disappear as the only thing that mattered was the next move I was going to make and the next adventure I was going to create and project into the landscape in front of me. I quickly dodged the dragon's attack and ran around to get a different vantage point for my next attack. However, my foot unexpectedly lodged into a network of tree roots that had been hidden by the fresh layer of mulch, causing me to launch forward face-first into one of the boulders.

I rebounded off of the boulder into a crumpled heap on the ground as I tried to process what just happened. Looking down where my foot had finally freed itself from the roots and back towards the boulder that was now branded with a fresh, unknown scratch on its surface, I began to realize. Hesitantly, I moved my tongue around the inside of my mouth to inspect the crime scene. I paused when the reality hit me like a speeding train when the tip of my tongue filled the space that a portion of my teeth once filled, shooting an agonizing, blinding pain throughout my body. Before I could process anything further, I was speeding through the backyard, up onto the back deck, and into the house. Once inside, I ran towards Nana with my arms flailing about in fear and regurgitating whatever words I could force my mouth to make. I had no idea who or what had instructed my feet to start running inside or who had picked the words to try and explain the situation to Nana, but I knew more than anything that she would know what to do because she always did. Without any hesitation, she wrapped her arms around me as I sobbed uncontrollably into her shoulder. Eventually, she managed to calm me down enough to explain just what had happened out in the backyard.

She took me to the nearest bathroom so I could see the number the boulder had done to my face. Thankfully, I had fallen tooth-first into the stone so all the damage was to my teeth and not my actual face. Nonetheless, as you can imagine, there was quite some damage to two of my teeth. Despite having just gotten my braces removed to reveal a perfectly-aligned set of teeth, I was suddenly missing a semi-circle of bone inside my mouth. I had somehow avoided any facial damage and any damage to the rest of my teeth or the permanent retainer that was still resting, fully intact, on the back of my lower teeth. I gave an attempt at a smile in the mirror and immediately started sobbing again as I realized I had just gotten this new smile and had somehow already ruined it. How was I supposed to explain to my parents who had paid for my braces that I had broken my teeth playing an imaginary game by myself in the backyard? I knew they argued about the money the braces cost when they didn't think I could hear them and now I put their money to waste by shattering two of my teeth. I felt Nana's arms around me once again which only made me sob that much more. I wish I could just stay here and not have to return home to break the news to my parents at all.

Nana was able to sweet talk her dentist into seeing me on short notice to fill the gaps in my teeth with a semi-permanent material until my regular dentist could come up with something better. While I was getting the work done, she also decided to break the news to my parents for me whenever she somehow sensed how stressed I was about telling them myself. From there, all I had to do was convince myself that I was the only one who could *really* tell that half of two of my teeth were artificial. The moment we got back to her house, I ran to the nearest bathroom to stare at my smile for no less than 15 minutes since I had only seen it under dentist office lighting. I immediately spotted the imperfections in my newly-repaired smile, a devastating blow to my newly-acquired self-esteem.

I sat in silence for the entire car ride home once Mom and Dad picked me up from Nana and Poppop's house. Although the words weren't spoken aloud, I sensed that they were upset about the fact that they had funded my new smile only for me to literally shatter it playing some kind of imaginary game outside. While I knew they were angry, they thankfully kept it to themselves the entire drive home until it was time to return back to my normal routine of classes, social media research, and secretive internet scrolling to be followed by immediate prayer. I made certain that I covered my face anytime I laughed around the other kids at school and that I gave a soft smile in any photos that were taken just in case the lighting made the fake parts of my teeth more obvious. Of course, this was a pretty simple task to accomplish when you only have a small handful of close friends that would even ask you to be in their selfies to begin with.

As time crept along through the semester, I began to notice a group of two or three girls in my grade that I got along with pretty well. They all appeared to reflect the same degree of careless, "weird" personalities and were quite happy to be seen associating with me in the hallways which was something I wasn't accustomed to in the beginning of a friendship. Deep down, I was also thrilled and eager to make a couple of new connections so that I could give my best friend a bit of a break from constantly hanging out every single chance I could. Leaning into how much I was getting along with them, I started spending more and more free time with them between classes and at lunchtime. I added them all on the various social media platforms until it became pretty clear that I had somehow stumbled across a new set of friends to add to my very small collection. After arriving home from school one afternoon, I spent a pretty decent amount of time staring up at the ceiling wondering whether or not we were to the degree of friendship to be able to hang out outside of regular school hours. I finally decided that I was just going to go for it and ask my parents if I could plan some kind of hangout here or a movie theater vibe or something. I made my way towards the living room to ask Mom if this was something I could make happen.

As I walked down the hallway towards the stairs, I realized there was an argument brewing between Rob and my parents. This wasn't anything new, so I quickly descended the stairs and found an empty spot on the couch so that I could ask them about my newfound plans with my newfound friends right after they wrapped up the argument. However, I quickly noticed the intensity of the conversation brewing more and more until Rob and Dad were hurling words laced with fiery anger across the room back and forth at each other with little to no remorse. I sunk further and further into the couch as I watched each attack, each word more angry and damaging than the one before for both sides. I knew this argument was more serious than the average one but I had no idea of any way that I could intervene to calm the tensions that had clearly grown out of control. I glanced over at Mom who seemed to be in the same position that I was, both equally unsure of what to do at this point.

Dad launched one more verbal attack as Rob was storming up the staircase. I was certain that it wouldn't land since my brother was accelerating up the steps so quickly, but I dreamed too soon. His words collided into Rob as he approached the very last step before the hallway that would have led him to his bedroom to cool down. Only pausing for half a second, my whole body tensed as I watched Rob turn from the top of the stairs with a newfound expression of frustration distorting his entire face and body. He began stomping back down the stairs, obviously eager to return an attack of the same caliber back towards Dad. He was hurling insult after insult with every step until he made it to the bottom of the stairs and they both stared at each other in silent, growing anger. In what could have been five minutes or five seconds, my brother and dad collided into each other in a pile of swinging fists and indecipherable insults. I covered my eyes for a brief moment out of sheer panic and opened them to see Dad shifting enough of his weight to overpower my brother and take him into a much-too-tight chokehold. The room fell completely silent until Mom let out a shrill, powerful scream once Rob's face started to turn purple from the intensity of the chokehold. I froze in place, unable to comprehend exactly what I was watching unfold a few feet in front of me.

Mom continued her screaming and then suddenly threw something in my direction, the collision from the object breaking my trance and snapping me back to reality. I looked down to see our landline phone laying in front of me and turned back to face Mom who had thrown it at me. She yelled for me to dial 911 as I picked the phone back up from the ground. Without thinking, I did as she instructed and put the phone up to my ear. All of the crime shows and movies that I always watched with Mom suddenly rushed to the front of my mind as I answered the operator's questions on the other end of the line and explained that there was an incident of domestic violence between my dad and brother in our home. I set the phone on the coffee table after she assured me someone would be on the way to our place as Mom managed to separate the two of them before any serious damage had been done. I stepped outside for some fresh air from the house that was now clouded with tension and anger. I noticed two different police cars enter our quiet little neighborhood a few moments later.

I met the officers at the front porch and gave a quick summary of everything that had happened before they stepped past me and into the living room. I took a few deep breaths before stepping back through the doorway. However, by this time I was just walking into the living room as they were walking back out with my brother in handcuffs. My jaw dropped at the sight that was playing out in front of me, my brother being escorted to a cop car with Mom wailing behind them to treat her son special and Dad standing with a stern expression from the far corner of the room with his arms tightly folded. I stood for a moment in shock before closing the door and looking over at Dad, the two of us being the only ones left in the house by this point. Without saying a word, he gave a slight nod which I took to mean that it was time to go up to my room while he figured out the rest of the situation before Mom came back. Not wasting another moment, I quickly ascended the staircase and fell directly into the pillows on my bed, shutting the door behind me. What was meant to be a moment of me simply existing without a single thought or movement was shattered with the torrential downpour of emotions and thoughts at the fact that I had just been forced to call the police on my own family and that my brother had apparently just been arrested because of it.

Looking around at the various, and somewhat conflicting, patterns on the floor, I couldn't help but count the seconds that ticked by without a single word being spoken. Not daring to risk making direct eye contact with the therapist, I continued this head-down approach for the entire hour. The woman didn't really ask any direct questions to me and instead spent most of her effort trying to force Rob and Dad to open a channel of communication so that they could discuss what had happened in as healthy and safe of an environment as possible. However, she quickly came to realize that was about as impossible a task as any. Therefore, the excruciating session became a way for Mom to cry about what she had to witness, Dad and Rob to sit with arms folded in silence, and me to stare at the ground wondering why I was required to be here in the first place. The car ride home was somehow even more silent, with awkward tension filling the inside of the car like an ominous fog. We started eating dinner at the dining room table for the next week while everyone continued their silence until eventually we shifted back to whatever sense of normalcy had been in place before the violent incident. Dinners moved back to the couch in front of a television, awkward small talk began again, and the eggshells that had been scattered around the floor of the house the last few weeks started to shift into hollow attempts at compliments and conversations to try and seem like a family who hadn't just had the police visit their home a few weeks ago.

Instead of asking my new friends to come over for a movie where they could be subject to police questioning at any random time, I joined their plans at the theater in town one night. One of their parents was nice enough to pick me up and drop me off afterwards. I walked up the front porch steps and into the living room, excited to tell my parents that I had a new group of good friends and how I had accidentally fallen down the movie theater steps in front of everyone (with the lights on and a full crowd and everything). Mom and Dad were sitting on the couch seemingly awaiting my arrival, their stern expressions immediately extinguishing every ounce of excitement I had been carrying. She motioned for me to sit down at the opposite end of the living room across from them. A familiar brick of anxiety and panic formed in my stomach as I prepared to explain that something had hacked my music/internet device and that it wasn't me that looked up any of those videos on the internet, especially *those* ones. The silence that followed sitting down caused the brick to multiply about a hundred times before one of them finally spoke to ask me if I had been at the movies with that group of girls I go to school with.

The panic inside my stomach that had almost ejected every piece of candy and popcorn onto the floor was quickly replaced with confusion as I answered her question. The conversation then shifted to my parents telling me I wasn't allowed to hang out with them at the movies or in public anymore if I wasn't trying to date one of them. My confusion grew even more and I immediately put up my defenses and asked why I was suddenly not allowed to have friends outside of school when it was something I had longed for so long. The question lingered in the air for an uncomfortable amount of time before it was met with Mom explaining that it simply didn't look good for me to be hanging out with a group of girls at school or at the movies if I didn't like one of them. A sickening network of knots formed in my stomach as I finally picked up on what my mother was insinuating. I had finally found some new friends who wanted to spend time with me and my parents are forbidding me doing it again because they think it makes me appear gay. I studied the expression on her face as her words struck me, an expression of concern and slight disgust that added a hundred more knots to my stomach. Without thinking, I muttered, "so this looks bad on who? Me or you?"

Panic rushed over me again as I realized I had said the words out loud and not just in my head. Not knowing what to do considering I had never mouthed off to my parents, I quickly stood up and stormed off to my bedroom. My steps were quick to give off the vibe that I was upset, which was true, but also because I wanted to get away as quickly as possible out of pure fear. Once I was in the safety of my room, I tried to process the fact that my own mother was worried that her son seems gay to other people. She was worried enough to keep me from having a social life with a new group of friends and worried enough to say it to my face with a horrifyingly uncomfortable facial expression. If my own mother was thinking this, what were the other people at school thinking? Is this what people were talking about whenever I wasn't around? Chase can't get his first kiss and now he has female friends so maybe he's gay? Tears were already flowing out of my eyes as all of these hypothetical scenarios made their way to the forefront of my mind. Once again, I started praying with the intense passion and ferocity that Nana always told me about. I pleaded with every ounce of emotional power I could muster for the being above receiving the message to come down and fix me so all of these problems would disappear. I kept launching prayer after prayer until I finally slipped off into a night of constant tossing and turning.

Thankfully, my parents didn't bring up my retaliation the next morning as I got my breakfast ready before school. As it usually went in our household, the morning was filled with aimless small talk or silence as if the previous night hadn't happened whatsoever. I rushed through the status quo and put my headphones in the entire car ride to school as Mom dropped me off. Walking through the front doors, I was completely convinced that every set of eyes was on me and every set of lips was whispering that I might not like girls. I was already certain of the visible brand on my forehead, but I began to feel a sturdy metal cuff form around my ankle that I'm sure everyone else could see too. It started as one singular, dark metal ring but by the end of the day it had become twice as heavy with a few intertwining links attached to it. No matter how much I tried to inconspicuously reach down to investigate, I couldn't feel the rings with my fingertips or determine if anyone else could see them. However, each footstep in the hallways felt a little heavier with each worry that I was the topic of every single conversation I walked past. By the end of the week, my entire mind was consumed with dread and panic that everyone in the whole school was somehow watching my internet browsing from behind my shoulder in what used to be the privacy of my bathroom.

My prayers at night were filled with more and more desperation and passion as I realized just how little power I had over the habits I had fallen into. Lying in bed at night contemplating the existence of the tattoo on my forehead and the hefty ankle cuff quickly became a normal routine before throwing myself into an ocean of prayers that were being ignored. I knew my choices were the wrong ones and I had been dousing my life in secrets and sin but I couldn't seem to stay away from the feelings I had been discovering. The worst part of these newfound habits, as much as I would hope otherwise, was the isolation. I was constantly tormented with the possibility that I wasn't the only one who knew they existed. The worry followed me everywhere and nowhere, piercing my thoughts when I was with my friend and completely drowning me when I was alone. Whenever anything goes wrong in life, like face planting into a rock or having to move schools, I always ran to Nana or Mom for immediate relief. However, I couldn't tell a single person about the videos I had been looking up or the ways they made me feel. I knew that this was just a phase and that I'd get back to normal whenever god stopped ghosting me, but no one else would see it that way. If my own mother seemed suspicious about going to the movies with a group of friends, what would everyone think if this secret somehow got out?

Attempting to escape my own mind's hypothetical traps, I went over to my best friend's place only to immediately notice he wasn't himself. Wondering if this was how everyone else had been seeing me the last few months, I tiptoed around the observation to see if he would reveal what was going on in a natural way. When that didn't work, I stopped whatever small talk he was attempting to use as a veil and demanded he tell me what was going on, adding in a laugh to make the exchange seem less icy. My best friend froze in mid-sentence and immediately started to break down in front of me. Caught completely off guard, I tried to do what I thought Nana would do in this situation and put my hand on his shoulder and told him everything would be okay and that he didn't have to talk about it if he didn't want to. I was halfway expecting him to be upset about a girl not liking him back or rejecting his offer to go out (something I was dealing with quite a bit these days) but reality was much worse. His mother, the woman who had basically accepted me as part of her home the last year or so, had been diagnosed with an awful form of cancer. I did my best to ignore the gut wrenching entanglement in my stomach and try to find the bright side of this horrible delivery of news.

My mind immediately went to Dad and the fact that he worked in a cancer treatment facility and would know exactly what to do in this situation. Not knowing the specifics of his everyday work or hardly anything about cancer, I told him I'd see if we could do anything that might help. Even if he couldn't somehow treat her illness for free or make it all completely disappear somehow, I was going to find a way to fix this. By now, I had seen two of my grandmothers make it to the other side of the battle with this disease so there was definitely hope. However, whenever Dad came home from work the afternoon that he said he would try to reach out to my best friend's mom, I knew by the look on his face that the news wasn't great. Apparently, they had communicated to some extent and he wasn't able to convince her to come in for a treatment plan or second opinion on her diagnosis. Instead, she was planning on fighting the illness in a completely natural way by sticking to a strict diet and taking an abundance of natural vitamins and supplements.

My ignorance of how cancer works or what treatment was like was overshadowed by her confidence in her plan and the optimism it inspired. Her son seemed content with her plan after the initial shock of finding out about the horrifying diagnosis so I did my best to reflect that optimism despite my Dad's loyalty to medicine and technology. This sudden burst of optimism also carried me down the stairs one afternoon to finally ask Lilley if she could reach out to Chancey's new family for an update. I had been wanting to ask her for this favor for a few weeks now that the sudden abandonment and all those swirling emotions had settled. However, I didn't know if there was a right or wrong time to ask something like this since we hadn't had many significant interactions since I had snapped at her about forbidding me to hang out with a group of new friends because of their gender and my lack of romantic pursuit(s). Something felt right about reaching out for an update and the thought of seeing a picture of her sparked a sense of calm and euphoria at the same time. A photo of her with a big smile on her face after spending the day running around the boundary less farm that she got to call home now.

The euphoric anticipation followed me for a day or two while we waited to get a response to my mother's email to the new family. Walking in from school, I followed up again only to notice a certain hesitation before my mother's response. My backpack hit the ground with a solid thud as I lost all control of my motor functions. I looked down to see my legs walking themselves into the guest bathroom in slow-motion. My body collapsed into a heap before my brain could even turn on the light switch after the words struck me in the deepest pits of my stomach from across the room. From somewhere came a restrained sob in the dark until I realized the sound was coming from me. Finally feeling like I had control of my body back, I reached up through the darkness until I felt the toilet paper to wipe my nose and stinging eyes. Not knowing how long I had been in the rarely-used guest restroom, I opened the door quietly to peer out into the hallway. Noticing the change in the brightness of the light coming in from the windows, I tiptoed quickly to the staircase and up to my room while Mom's back was turned in the kitchen. Not wanting anyone in the house to see me in this state, I retreated to the furthest corner on the upstairs to try and reason with the fact that Chancey was gone.

Every memory suddenly flashed through my mind and projected itself onto the chilled tile of the balcony upstairs. The temperature of the air and the tile was making my legs numb but I didn't care and it didn't matter. Mom's words kept playing in my head between every snapshot of running through the woods together and cuddling on my bed. My best friend was gone and I wasn't even given the courtesy of knowing until months later. While I had been enjoying family time at Nana and Poppop's house for Christmas a couple of months ago, my best friend was having the last seizure she ever had to worry about. The confused, terrified look on her face as I had to hand the leash over to a family of strangers and turn to walk away was the next to project itself onto the tile until I found myself sobbing uncontrollably once again. She didn't make it six months in her new home before her illness took over. Whether they had forgotten to give her the medication she needed or this was just too much for her body to handle, she was gone and she went without knowing how much she meant to me. She passed wondering why I gave her to a family that didn't know or understand her and how she had saved a young middle school boy's life who had never felt more alone until she came into the picture.

My eyes looked around at the balcony of this new house and felt sick to my stomach even being here. I couldn't believe this was how our story was ending. My parents forced me to give away my best friend because we had to move down the street. Forced me to give her away only for her illness that once woke me up in the middle of the night in a panicked frenzy to take her away less than six months later. I could, and should, have fought them for once about the move and clung to a few more months with her. The ending could have been the exact same, but at least she would have gone with my arms wrapped around her instead of a stranger's hand, if they had even given her that small comfort in the first place. My best friend deserved better than to have this fate. She deserved more love than this world had dealt her. I heard the door open a few feet away, snapping me back into reality as I noticed Dad standing in the doorway while simultaneously realizing how long I had been sitting out here now that the moonlight was casting small bits of light across the long balcony floor.

He stepped through the quiet stillness and hovered a few feet away from where I was sitting. Eventually, after several minutes of uncomfortable silence, he asked if I was alright. The idea of translating every emotion brewing in my mind into words came and went in the same breath. I knew opening up, especially to Dad, was not going to bring my four-legged friend back. Nothing was going to bring her back to this earth or this home again. At this point, remaining silent was the best thing I could do considering the anger I could feel blazing inside at the circumstances that led to her leaving this world without me even knowing. How was I supposed to explain to the man I rarely exchanged words with that I was furious about being forced to move for the millionth time and that it was because of their decision to move that I was sitting here devastated in front of him. My retaliating remark regarding having a few female friends hadn't changed anything, so why risk a full-blown assault on my parents now? Without even lifting my head, I mumbled that I was fine and quickly heard the door close once again.

Chapter Seven

Remember When I Failed My Permit Test?

Standing in front of the seven colossal buildings that made up my new school for the next four years made me feel like the most microscopic, insignificant speck on the social radar in the best way. After another summer break of hanging out with my still-only best friend and his mom, talking about plans to conquer this next adventure, and endless hours of even more social media research the moment was finally here. On top of scrolling through everyone's music playlists on their online profiles, I started listening to hours of internet and car radio to get a semi-stable grasp on the most popular music. I could carry a conversation with someone while simultaneously gauging whether or not my next joke or statement should be released from my mind or not. My eyes couldn't stop scanning this massive campus and how each building looked like its own tower of education that I got to call mine now. I couldn't help but allow myself to have an ear-to-ear grin as I hopped out of the car to go inside. With the other middle school and ours funneling together with all the other strangers throughout these buildings, I was finally able to have a pretty clean slate as I walked into the front doors for the first time.

Being a high school freshman in a school campus of this magnitude meant I was practically a new kid again but in a good way. Everyone who wasn't born and raised in this town was a new kid now. Hardly anyone here knew I had written a book (or a sequel and a partial third installment that all no longer existed). Hardly anyone here knew I had asked out at least a dozen girls, dated two, and still hadn't had my first kiss. Hardly anyone here knew I barely kept my head above water in the middle school hierarchy the last two years. The ones who *did* know these things about me had already forgotten about them, didn't care, or didn't have a single class anywhere near mine. To make this fresh start that much more exciting, Rob had somehow graduated and moved off to go to college in Murfreesboro down the road from Nana and Poppop's house. For the first time in my life, I was a confident new kid at a new school who could enjoy living like an only child without having to share the upstairs or the bathroom with a single person other than myself. Plus, with my brother moving out, I only had to worry about overhearing Mom and Dad arguing with each other instead of with him all the time.

Hearing the new-to-me bell chiming brought me down from my gilded clouds of the new life I was about to embark on. I grabbed my backpack from the other side of the booth, a tactic I had taught myself to make it seem like I wasn't sitting alone and that the person across from me had gone to the bathroom or something. Looking around at the gigantic cafeteria and the cascading levels of booths and chairs, I realized I had no idea how to get to my locker from here. Or my first class. Or the other five or six classes after that. Panic immediately set in as I made my way up the ascending plateaus of seating areas until I reached the main entrance of the school next to the main office. I glanced down at my printed schedule for this year but the course names and room numbers may as well have been in a different language. Of course, the swarms of people around me all looked completely settled and seemed to know exactly where their footsteps were leading them. Not wanting to risk looking like an idiot, I snuck into the main office to discreetly ask for directions from someone behind the desk.

Luckily, my locker and first classroom were just up the staircase to the left. I took a deep breath, tried to make my shoulders broad and chest high, and walked into my very first day. I found an empty seat towards the back next to the only two people I recognized. They were talking about skipping the assigned summer reading for the incoming freshmen and I quickly agreed with a chuckle despite the fact that I had read both of the novels twice. The conversation shifted into their fun summer plans and vacations before the final bell sounded and the announcements began to disperse through the intercom system. I glanced back down at my schedule and the names of all the courses Mom had picked for me with the help of a guidance counselor. My grades were fairly decent, but I wasn't fully convinced I would be able to keep up with all the Honors classes she chose on my behalf. However, they would apparently set me up to be in the highest class structures for Junior and Senior year which would surely guarantee me a spot in any college I wanted to apply for. Not that I had given any thought to college, but going for free sounded like the best route to attempt so I put my apprehensions about courses aside while shifting my focus on finding my footing in this massive new school.

The first day of high school found me caught in a violent tide that barely allowed me to push my head above water for more than a few seconds at a time. I would be in one classroom attempting to learn that teacher's name along with the names of 30 strangers before I was suddenly sprinting from building one to building six to try and make it in time for the next bell to do it all over again. I kept looking for familiar faces in the hallways and classrooms but only a small handful of acquaintances seemed to share any classes with me. Thankfully, I was able to find a couple of friends to have lunch with after I did my best to navigate the confusing cafeteria system that was going to take some getting used to. However, we were apparently allowed to apply to have lunch off-campus anywhere in town once we made it to Junior and Senior year. By the end of the gruesomely exciting first day, I barely had enough time and energy to chase after the bus after it almost left without me. I plopped into the first empty seat I could find, unable to even attempt to begin my investigation on the social system within high school buses. Not remembering the exact location of my stop, I had to walk about a mile to get back to the house and immediately collapse onto my bed.

By the second and third week into this exhausting-but-also-exhilarating new routine, I got at least one solid foot on the ground as opposed to the first day where I felt caught in the clenches of a riptide in the middle of the ocean with no land or life in sight. Knowing no one I was passing knew who I was enough to be making fun of me gave me that much more time to sprint from one class to another. The opportunity of being a stranger in the majority of my classes allowed me to become the kid who seemed normal enough and said something funny every now and then. The tension I always felt with my English teacher and his crude remarks were immediately overshadowed with how much I quickly fell in love with my Spanish teacher afterwards. Having my own beautiful, brand-new computer in front of me to work on independent projects in Graphic Design quickly became my meditative escape every day. Lunch was always followed with a walk down a creepy, dungeon-like hallway with my best friend on the way to our next classes as we tried to condense a full day's conversation about girls and how much cooler it felt to be in high school. I noticed he had stopped giving many updates on his mom's health and decided to respect that by not prying as much as I usually do. The rest of the classes that took up my day were pretty neutral blurbs, especially Math and Civics.

After several long weeks of building up my social status day by day and walking a mile home because I was too intimidated by the bus driver to ask him to stop closer to my house, my home life began. Walking through the front doorway was always followed by a snack and a seat at the dining room table to immediately finish up any homework that I hadn't managed to finish before the classroom bell sounded. Knocking that out of the way first gave me the rest of the evening to browse through social media profiles to see anything new and add anyone that I had any semblance of a conversation with that day. When I started to feel invasive or annoying with my occasional posts or requests, I'd switch from one device to the next by turning on the television in the living room to watch a few hours of cooking shows to give myself new ideas and inspiration in the kitchen. Nana always joked I was eventually going to take her crown for Best Cook in the Family and that she should have never let me help her grate cabbage when I was little whenever her hands would be in too much pain from her arthritis. I knew she was joking and that I'd never bypass her status in any kitchen but it was reassuring to know I had her approval and know that I was at least the best cook in my own household.

After several weeks flew by, I found myself sitting in Spanish class trying not to crack up with laughter at my friend sitting behind me, one of the ones I had gone to the movies with before my first retaliation against Lilley. A noise came from the other girl who sat in front of me which caused me to turn back around with a bit of concern. I had not made a very good impression when I tried to become her friend in the first few weeks because I asked if I could have one of the snacks in her backpack. To try highlighting the specific snack I was referring to, I reached down to hold it up to her across the room working with someone else in the class on an assignment. The color had completely fled from her face as she noticed what I was holding up for the entire class to see. It turns out the "snack" I had seen in her backpack was actually a tampon that happened to have a bright, colorful wrapping to it. Agony rushed over me as I thought I had done something else to make her hate me but instead she greeted me with a smile. She delicately placed a Halloween-themed envelope on the desk attached to my chair before turning back around to face the front of the classroom.

I quickly unwrapped the envelope to see that I was somehow being invited to a Halloween party by the girl who I assumed hated me. With how much more quickly time flew as a high schooler, I hadn't even realized that Halloween was this weekend. Furthermore, to add onto that surprise, that also meant my birthday was right around the corner also. My mind instantly reverted back to the day I showed up to school in a Halloween costume in fifth grade only to realize I was the only one in the whole school who dressed up. Thankfully, after putting out some feelers, I realized this wasn't going to be a Halloween party where people dressed up so I could avoid the pressure of finding a socially-acceptable costume or the dread of showing up in the only costume. After what felt like no time at all, I got dropped off at her house and took a deep breath on the sidewalk outside. I took a few moments to reflect on the fact that I had managed to build up my social status here to move from a kid who got ambushed by plastic bullets to the kid who got invited to a party. With each footstep towards the front door, a memory of my social journey would flash across my mind until I was stepping through the doorway into my first social event of high school.

The night passed by in a flurry of shoving desserts in our mouths, talking about which teachers were the best and worst, taking as many selfies on our digital cameras as possible, and laughing about everything and nothing. I floated out the front door on a cloud once Mom called to say she was waiting outside. While I knew I wasn't a socialite or one of the popular kids of school, I had achieved some form of status after all the years of hard work and social research I had put into it. I was finally at a place where I could carry normal conversation with people enough to have a number of places I could sit at lunch and talk to people before a class started instead of reading a book or working on homework that we hadn't even been assigned yet. We pulled into our garage and I hopped out to run upstairs and hop online to see if anyone had uploaded any of the pictures we took tonight since I didn't have a digital camera of my own yet. Walking through the bathroom before entering my room, however, I stopped in my tracks once I noticed something out of the corner of my eye in the mirror. My forehead, while not as bold and noticeable as before, had started to reveal the *Check my Internet History* tattoo once again. Looking down, I saw the ankle cuff had also formed once again though not as prominent as before. Did anyone else see this at the party tonight? Had it been there this whole time since the first day of high school? Shit.

Just in time to get my mind distracted by this sudden remembrance of my own secrets, I found myself nervously sitting in the cold chairs of the lobby next to Dad. He seemed somewhat annoyed to have had to take me to take my Permit test at the Driver's Center, but Mom had been too busy and I wanted to reach this milestone as soon as possible. Before I could sink into any more feelings of guilt, I heard the woman up at the front desk area finally call my number. I shot out of the chair like a rocket and followed her instructions and was taken to the computer that I'd be taking the test on. I studied the online handbook for several nights earlier in the week but now that the questions were flashing in front of me on the screen it was as if my entire brain had been wiped clean and reset. The final question was submitted and I sat for several moments, frozen in complete horror, as I was shown to have failed my Permit test and that I'd have to come back after a week to give it a second attempt.

The entire ride home was spent in silence as I felt Dad's annoyance and frustration build when he realized I hadn't even passed the exam. Another week that felt like months passed and I found myself back at the Driver's Center, bound and determined to dominate the test this time with Mom's encouragement behind me. This time the test felt like it was over in a matter of seconds and I was ecstatic to see the green flashing screen as opposed to the ominous red one. Eager to begin my journey behind the wheel, I convinced my parents to take me driving for the first time under their supervision the moment we got back home. Despite my confidence going into the test, I was mortified to be controlling a vehicle for the first time as I moved through the streets of our old neighborhood at a speed of about five miles per hour. Mixing up the acceleration and brake pedals a few times, I could sense the impatience and annoyance filling up the car until I finally pulled to the side of the road and said I was finished. We resolved to try once a week for about an hour or so until I could build my confidence up in a more baby-steps kind of approach.

I decided to skip the bus one afternoon after the final bell rang and instead spent the next 20 minutes socializing with a handful of other kids. Eventually, everyone else was picked up by their parents so I decided to go wandering throughout the hallways with my best friend once we realized we hadn't had a chance to actually explore the place since we were busy sprinting from one class to the next in order to avoid being tardy. We were suddenly mesmerized with how lucky we were to be a part of such a beautiful high school. Compared to the one building we had attended for middle school, this seven-building campus was absolute royalty. The next three-and-a-half years were going to be filled with so many social opportunities that we were both going to tackle together until we somehow made it to the very tops of the social hierarchy. We started laying out an imaginary, tentative roadmap for social domination as we rounded an unfamiliar hallway when I felt my phone buzzing in my pocket. I saw Mom's name flash across the screen and pressed the ignore button as I assumed she was upset about me skipping the bus or something else. When she immediately called back, I took a deep breath and answered.

Standing alone in the quiet stillness of my bedroom, I looked around at all the boxes I had packed up with the same frown etched into my face since I answered the phone call. A frown that formed when Mom frantically screamed through the phone that MiMi had passed unexpectedly. A frown that carried through the funeral that seemed to happen a mere hour after the news had been delivered to my ears. A frown that persisted through the conversation that we were going to be moving once again, this time next door to Poppop Luke, so that we could help him now that his mother/best friend/roommate was no longer with us. A frown that walked through the beautiful hallways as I counted down the final days at this high school with all the friends I had finally made. A frown that was soaked by the tears that formed on the way home from my last day after having to say goodbye to all of them. The frown that now stood in my bedroom looking over the favorite house that I was also going to have to say goodbye to.

A number of emotions kept rushing over me in waves that collided with each other as they rushed in from all directions. Anger seared as I thought about my parents ripping me out of yet another school when the academic year wasn't even finished only to be met with sadness as I realized I had lost another great-grandmother. I watched Nana lose her mother several years ago, who we all called Nanny Sally, and how devastated everyone was by the loss. However, I had not fully grasped the concept of death in the ways that I did now as I sat on the bed pondering all the questions I had never gotten around to asking either one of them. Anger and sadness barely had time to battle each other before the tidal wave of fear consumed both of them as I reflected on the diagnosis that Poppop Luke had gotten just a few weeks after he lost his mother. As if the sudden death and moving plans weren't sufficiently tragic enough, cancer had infected yet another member of my family and we were apparently the only ones willing to uproot everything to help take care of it. A wave of dread quickly formed to combine with fear as I realized I was having the rug I had spent the last three years carefully creating completely pulled out from under me. My grandfather was sick. We were moving. I was about to be the New Kid once again and everything I had worked so tirelessly now meant nothing. I collapsed onto the bed and did my best to keep my head above the waters and tears that were quickly building up all around me.

Watching my favorite house, favorite friends, and favorite city grow smaller and smaller in our rearview left a nauseating, hollow feeling in my stomach. Every mile we drove closer towards Loudon brought another harsh reality to the forefront of my mind. I was about to become a part of a high school that was one small building instead of seven massive ones. The student body of Loudon was about to be a small sliver of the bustling population within my previous high school. Each bump or pothole Mom directly ran over immediately reminded me of the death of MiMi and the cancer that was quickly occupying my grandfather's throat and neck muscles. Whenever that panic slowly subsided, I was left to ponder over the fact that I was about to be forced to walk through another set of school doors into a building where I *might* know two people that I was friends with in third grade if I was lucky enough for them to still be here and recognizable. I noticed the same sloping street that I had fallen down on rollerblades all those years ago come into my line of sight to signal we were arriving. The only silver lining crept into my head to let me know that, at the very least, no one here knew I had written a book and I had already deleted all the files from my computer that could suggest otherwise. I hopped out of the car only to catch a quick glimpse of my reflection in the car window, my forehead emblazoned with my internet secrets tattoo to quickly extinguish whatever glimmer of hope I might have felt about this new, forced adventure.

I tried to stifle the worries of any chance of other people seeing this tattoo and constrictive anklet as I unpacked the boxes piled up in front of me. Our new house was literally next door to Poppop Luke's place, though you'd never guess it based on the difference in values. We had traded in the luxurious, modern house in Oak Ridge for a downsized, ancient structure that looked like it could very well belong in a low-budget horror film. My room was about half the size of the old one and stuck between my parents room and the living room. I made the mistake of walking down the stairs before I began unpacking only to find a creepy, unfinished basement crawling with unidentifiable insects and puddles of standing water. Immediately slamming the door shut behind me and sprinting back upstairs, I vowed to never return to whatever that room was intended to be unless absolutely necessary. As if this move wasn't stressful enough, I noticed Rob's car parked outside and immediately got nauseous as I remembered that Mom told me he was withdrawing himself from college already and moving back home for a while. I walked silently past his room nestled between Mom and Dad's and mine and shut the door. I threw myself onto my bed that hadn't even been assembled yet and tried to stop the whirlwind of realizations and emotions swirling around inside my mind and stomach. Goodbye Oak Ridge, any sense of privacy at home, living like an only child, and everything else that used to bring joy to my life this year.

After a night of restless tossing and turning and staring at the ceiling, I found myself walking up to the front doors of a new school for the millionth time. Slowly putting one foot in front of the other, I realized just how much of a culture shock I was about to experience. On my quick journey to the guidance office alone, I noticed an abundance of camouflage clothing and a variety of different boots that I had never seen in such a high volume before. My campus of multiple buildings was now one with two long stretches of hallway and a cafeteria making up the entire floor below. Two excited cheerleaders did their best to paint each classroom in the best light as they gave me a quick tour of the new school. They eagerly searched for an excited expression on my face when they pointed out the mechanic shop and farm on the grounds and seemed disappointed when I didn't adjust the look of shock and fear from the moment I walked through the doors that morning. Whether I was ready for it or not, they dropped me off by the gymnasium doors to walk into my first class for the day. Looking at the schedule they had handed me, I realized that this school operated on an entirely different schedule system and I'd be taking four different classes every semester as opposed to seven-or-so consistent classes for the entire school year.

I pushed through the metal doors after fighting with my own apprehension to join a gathering of other students across the gymnasium. I did my best to ignore everyone's eyes immediately shifting to look at me the same way I was trying to ignore the fact that everything about my life changed dramatically overnight. However, each footstep seemed to make my heart increase its pace and a new knot form in my stomach as I ventured toward what appeared to be the teacher for this class. Not knowing what words I was supposed to use in this scenario, I simply held out the piece of paper the guidance office had given me and waited for him to respond. After a half-second skim of the paper, he gave a silent nod and gestured toward the gathering of other students.

I kept my head low in hopes that I wouldn't be asked to announce my name to the entire room and go through some form of awkward ice breaker that would inevitably ruin my social rank on day one.

Thankfully, this man didn't seem interested in getting to know any of us as he quickly ran through the class details and told us to go get changed in the locker rooms. Of course, I had no idea that I'd need to bring a separate set of clothes on my first day so I got to sit awkwardly in the stands awaiting the rest of the kids. Today was apparently going to be spent in the weight room near the football field. The reality began to set in as we walked across the parking lot that I had absolutely no idea how to exercise in general, let alone lift weights for specific muscle groups. I immediately found the nearest corner to blend into as everyone else started going towards the various equipment. With how familiar this small building was, I quickly realized I was in a gym class with a bunch of football players that the teacher already loved. With each plate of weight that all the kids added onto a bar or machine, the smaller and smaller I felt standing as both a figurative and literal outsider in the various corners of the room. I gave my best attempt at feigning activity but I knew I was standing out like a sore thumb to the rest of the class and the teacher. I quickly figured out where the bathrooms were and fled to escape the awkward energy that was filling the weight room.

I wandered through the doorway and past a locker room and showers that I assumed to belong to the football team until I came across a couple of urinals and stalls. For a brief moment, I stood alone in the bathroom and my head felt like it had finally stopped spinning for the first time that day. For whatever reason, standing alone at the urinal put my mind at ease and for that moment I wasn't worried about the kind of impression I was making on everyone so far or the fact that I had no idea how to exercise like a normal person or the fact that I was in another new school for the hundredth damn time. I stepped away from the urinal only to have the brief moment of peace and clarity plummet from the ceiling and shatter into a million shards of panic across the locker room floor. Out of nowhere, there were several guys that walked in from the weight room, took off their clothes, and turned on the shower faucets that were hanging from the ceiling a few feet in front of me. Before I even had time to begin processing the scene playing out in front of me, one of them was walking directly up to me, completely naked, with an outstretched hand to introduce himself. Cue the panicked entanglement of knots and bricks immediately forming in my stomach.

I could only assume that I was witnessing some form of football and/or gym ritual with how casually they had all undressed and started showering, especially the one who walked up to make small talk with me by the urinals. A million different thoughts raced across my mind as I tried to figure out how the hell I was supposed to respond to this unexpected situation I had found myself in. Do I mimic their comfortability level and act completely casual about the fact that everyone in front of me was naked?

No. They were likely teammates and/or people who had all grown up together in the same town since birth and I definitely wasn't on that same level. Do I take *my* clothes off to show them I'm just as-no, absolutely not. Have I already looked too long? I've never been in front of naked people until this very moment so the etiquette was a mystery. I quickly shifted my eyes up towards the ceiling before everyone could start to see the tattoo on my forehead that would somehow reveal I had watched a video or two on the internet that involved locker rooms like this. The panic overcame my entire body and I sprinted out of the locker room without a word while doing my best to keep my eyes straight ahead.

Thankfully, I heard the same group of guys laughing as we all made our way back to the gymnasium at the end of the class. While I wasn't ecstatic about being laughed at, I couldn't help but feel relieved that I hadn't been weird or started a rumor on my first day that I stared at a bunch of guys showering in gym class. Wait. Was *I* the weird one for thinking it was weird to get naked and shower in front of each other? Was this just a small town bro code kind of thing to do? Was I supposed to just be completely comfortable being naked in front of them? Was this some kind of test that they gave to all the new kids on their first days? If so, had I passed? Was I supposed to stick around longer and answer all the small-talk questions from the guy who had walked up to shake my hand? What would have happened if I hadn't fled the entire situation without saying a word? Why did I have to tell myself to stare up at the ceiling? Why did I feel the need to glance downward while everything was happening? Why did I have to literally force myself to look away and exit the situation? Why was a part of my mind still imagining-

A much-louder, much-more-obnoxious bell sounded from the speakers above that harshly let everyone know that the class period was over just in time to stop my train of thought in its tracks. I grabbed my backpack despite the fact that it was completely empty and made my way to the next class to repeat this same process, although hopefully with less nudity. And then the next class. And then the next class. And then the next class. Suddenly, I was starting to settle into a new routine at a new school in a new town within a new society. While it was quite a shift, I started getting used to having four long classes every day as opposed to seven small ones. All of my classes were located within the two long stretches of hallways so I didn't have to worry about sprinting across a campus through several buildings to try and make it on time. My attempts to make a decent impression the first couple of weeks were met with confusion as I tried to shift my mind from a school of thousands to a single building with maybe a few hundred students. All the social research I did the last few years was specifically tailored to the kids at Oak Ridge and Loudon was quickly starting to feel like a new planet entirely. After the first few failed attempts at jokes and small talk, I resorted to keeping my head down and actually paying attention in my classes even though I had already learned every piece of material being covered in every class so far.

By the third or fourth week in my new school, I was called into the guidance office after sending a text to Mom in my final class for the day. I was mortified to walk into the office to see her sitting in a chair across from one of the guidance counselors for the school. I wanted to turn and sprint as far away from the building as possible but the front desk volunteer had already noticed me enter the doorway and motioned me to go have a seat. Anger immediately started to brew inside the more I realized that my mother had taken my "please come pick me up from school I'm so bored" text message to be something serious enough to have a guidance counselor meeting about. The counselor, someone I had yet to meet, thanked my mother for coming in and began by asking what had prompted me to send "such an emotional signal" to my mother while I was in class. Wanting to immediately extinguish the fire that was starting to form, I tried to disengage whatever warning alarms had gone off in either of their heads from hearing that I was miserably bored in all of my classes because I had already learned everything that was being lectured on.

Unsatisfied with my methods of trying to brush off the significance of the text messages and overall demeanor towards my new school and new classes, Mom pressed for more answers. She started using the same tone of voice that I noticed her use whenever she was describing my brother's problematic behavior to people who were completely unaware of our household dynamic. I intercepted the conversation and spontaneously unloaded all of my thoughts before the situation could be labeled as my fault. Before I could stop myself, I was completely spilling my guts in front of a stranger and my mother just to take back control of the narrative that I was to be blamed for my feelings. I missed Oak Ridge. I missed the friends I snapped my back in half to make for years. I missed the classes that were actually interesting and challenging. I missed not having to force myself to keep my hand down so that the other kids in the class wouldn't make fun of me for knowing the answer to the problem. I missed Joe and his mom and the warm sense of welcome I would always feel in their house. I went into detail about how it felt to have the rug completely ripped out from under my feet all the time. Moving from a colossal, massively successful high school campus to a small town in the middle of nowhere with only two familiar faces, one being my cousin and one being the girl I accidentally stabbed in third grade. I missed the nice house and the nice bedroom I used to have. I missed living alone while my brother was away at college. I missed when my great grandmother was alive and my grandfather didn't have cancer. I felt alone. I felt bored. I felt terrified. I missed my old life that had been taken away.

94

Silence fell over the office as I exhaled and fell back into the stiff back of the chair to await their response. However, my attempts to somehow change my circumstances failed as they both took turns explaining to me, in the same tone they'd use to speak to a small child, how I was just going to have to deal with it because that's just how life works. If I wanted to go back to my old high school, they'd have to pay out-of-county tuition and I'd have to wake up early enough to ride with Dad on his way to work. The house we're living in apparently costs a great deal less than the one in Oak Ridge and allowed us to take care of Poppop Luke while he was undergoing treatments. I was stuck here. It doesn't matter that I'm miserable. The counselor pulled up my course schedule and suggested switching out one of my classes for a more advanced version of the course which I was surprisingly on board with. However, I would have to suffer through the other aspects of my predicament until I naturally caught up to the academic material and began making progress in my social life once I could finally figure out how to make friends here. Mom told me I could ride back home with her instead of returning to class as if that was going to somehow make up for everything that I had just unloaded. Nevertheless, I grabbed my backpack and followed her out to the car.

Realizing I had no escape plan that could work somehow created the motivation to try and make the most of it. Starting my social research from scratch once again, I started to figure out how a small-town high school operates. I finally made a friend only for them to vanish the moment I started to feel somewhat comfortable around them or made a weird joke or tried to hang out with them at lunch. When my constant attempts to befriend the popular kids in person weren't landing, I started shifting my focus back to social media to see what kind of progress I could make online. I began adding the small handful of people I had any kind of interaction with and message them seconds after they accepted. While there were a few people that didn't seem to mind, I found out pretty quickly that Loudon followed the same social code that found it strange for a guy to follow/message another guy on social media or text them after school unless there was a precise reason for it. Laying down in bed each night, I found myself staring up at the ceiling in agony over the fact that I was somehow reliving the horror of middle school all over again and all my social research was rendered useless. Every morning it seemed that the tattoo on my forehead was bolder and bolder even though no one else could see it. I glanced down every now and then only to see the anklet starting to form more chain links, a new one after every internet scroll in my bathroom. An icy splash of water across my face and extra scrubbing on my ankle in the shower quickly became part of my regular routine as I tried to ensure they stayed hidden.

Enduring the painful agony of forcing myself onto a new student body and hoping they accept me lasted for the entirety of the first month or two of the semester before I started to somewhat feel like an actual student. The new math class proved to be slightly more interesting, but for the most part all of my classroom lectures and assignments were things that I was taught in middle school. Therefore, the only thing I had to worry about in my free time was learning how to adapt to a small-town culture that proved to be painfully different from what I was so used to. After constantly reminding myself not to ask every pretty girl out and not text every popular guy to try and become his best friend overnight, I started to feel less and less miserable roaming through the hallways of Loudon. One of the girls I had befriended for the day even invited me to one the school dance that weekend.

I felt surprisingly content looking at my reflection in the bathroom mirror while wearing whatever I was forced to wear out of my brother's closet. I wasn't a socialite by any means at this new school, but I was surviving. It was only the first couple of months and I had at least been informed about a school dance even if I didn't have an actual date to accompany me. That being said, I still made sure to keep a low profile when it came to the actual dancing and focused more on sneaking myself into as many pictures as possible. If all the pictures happened to be uploaded to everyone's social media profiles, maybe more people at this school would realize I existed and try to be my friend if they saw me in other people's photos having fun.

After managing to befriend a group of guys for a week or two without them completely abandoning me for texting about hangouts too often, they asked if I was going to go to Thursday Club with them. As if I didn't feel like enough of an outsider as it was, I had to admit that I had no idea what they were talking about. They chuckled before explaining that it was a religious-ish club that recruited high schoolers all across the country to meet one night a week for fun, games, a brief religious message, and a fast food run afterwards. Naturally, I accepted their implied invitation and was excited to see several other popular kids at this week's meeting that was held in the lower level of a doctor's office down the road from my house. I quickly realized this was a golden opportunity to try and catch up on my reputation, or lack thereof, amongst the social players of this school. On top of Thursday Club being a prime social opportunity, I also got a dose of religion that I could use as fuel for my nightly prayers to fix my internet habits and permanently remove the forehead tattoo and ankle cuff that were still plaguing my mind anytime I passed a mirror. I knew I was the only one who could see them but I couldn't help but wonder if it was just a matter of time before everyone else became aware of them too. I stopped my mind from wandering too far into that hypothetical situation and started paying as much attention as possible to the skits, bible talks, and social interactions among the popular kids.

The weeks soared by as I sat through the same four classes every day, attended every Thursday Club meeting, browsed through social media and the occasional dark corner of the internet in secret, and even asked a girl out who actually accepted the proposal. However, I quickly repeated history and lost the girlfriend because of my cursed inability to initiate the fateful first kiss. As if I was living through a nightmare, I found myself back in the same situation of losing a girlfriend because I couldn't kiss her and hallways of people knowing about it enough to start drawing their own conclusions. Suddenly, the ink in my forehead turned a shade darker and the small chain links connected to my ankle had formed a small concrete orb that I started to feel with every footstep through the halls packed full of skeptical teenagers. Instead of repeating my previous strategy from middle school, I gave my best attempts to laugh along with any comments about not having my first kiss yet or being dumped and focused my energy on building up my small network of friends here. My entire life quickly became social networking, social media, Thursday Club, trying to learn anything I could about sports since that was what everyone here seemed to regularly talk about or do, and church whenever our household would go together as a family or the random occasion that a friend would invite me to go with theirs.

As more and more time passed, I realized my best course of action was to simply become a sponge or chameleon to whatever environment I was finding myself in. If I was at church, I was fully absorbed in whatever words were being preached in the service. If I had a friend stay the night and he threw out the idea to sneak out at midnight to go wander the town, I immediately agreed. If a group of my friends suggested riding out to a little bridge on the outskirts of town to jump into the mysterious waters, I jumped despite my own internal questioning on the quality of the water below. If country music was being blared outside the drive-in restaurant after Thursday Club, I learned the lyrics and all the different artists that were popular. I also started to notice that age didn't seem to be a divisive factor among social groups the way it had been at my other schools. Everyone here pretty much grew up with each other so it wasn't abnormal for Seniors to be friends with Freshmen or siblings to have the same sets of friends. This made hanging out much easier when everyone seemed to have at least one friend or sibling-of-a-friend with a driver's license and a car to transport everyone around to church, the sketchy bridge, one of the four fast food restaurants in town, or someone's house to pass the time. By making one solid friend, you pretty much opened the door to their entire network of friends until eventually you knew everyone in the school by name.

When it wasn't a Thursday night and I couldn't convince anyone to hang out with me, I was stuck inside the house. While I typically kept to myself in my room scrolling through social media or random articles or sexually explicit material, it was difficult to drown out the other noise now that we were living in such a smaller place. I heard every argument across the spectrum whether it was between Mom and Dad or both of them against Rob. There was even the occasional rumble between Mom and Poppop Luke. The topics of all these different battles ranged anywhere from Rob not having a job and hanging out at the skate park with kids who were probably my age to Dad being pissed that we moved so far away from his job and even the occasional screaming match that didn't seem to focus on any topic at all. I was accustomed to arguments within the household and was usually able to drown them out but the ones involving Mom and Poppop Luke were completely unpredictable. Much like I had to witness during fourth grade, his body was going through hell except instead of withdrawals, he was going through withdrawals *and* cancer treatments. However, every few weeks or so, Mom would sneak over to his house and go through his things until she'd eventually discover a pack of cigars or a half-empty bottle of vodka which was just enough of a spark to ignite her fuse. Her fuse immediately went out and she'd storm downstairs to start chastising her father, igniting his already-short fuse as well until the entire house was a warzone.

Whenever these arguments became too loud to drown out or too chaotic to avoid, I would slip out the nearest door of whichever house I was in. As if it were playing a cruel trick, the universe decided it was going to give me back the forest in the backyard that I had loved so much in fifth grade. Out past the backyard and down the street a little laid a huge stretch of woods between the road and a large river. I quickly felt right at home as I made my escapes from home to wander through all the trees and steep inclines for hours. I almost forgot how much I had missed aimlessly walking through a forest with nothing but my thoughts and imagination to keep me company. Naturally, it took a few of these escapes to work through the waves of sadness that came with my melodramatic return to the woods. However, once the adjustment phase was over I started making these ventures a weekly ritual even if there wasn't some kind of catastrophic battle going on at one of the houses. I may not have had Chancey by my side or any of the friends I eventually made back in Oak Ridge, but at least I had a place to escape once again whenever I needed a brief sense of peace.

One afternoon after school, the guy who had walked up to me naked in gym class on my first day came over to hang out. Mom sold my video game console in a yard sale without telling me the week prior so we quickly ran out of things to do to keep our minds entertained. Rob, as he typically does, walked into my room to invite himself into whatever our plans were despite the huge age gap. The thought of the three of us confined and cramped inside my room made my heart start to race. Without thinking, I threw out the suggestion of going on a walk through the woods I found down the street near the river. The three of us made our way through the backyard, down the winding asphalt for about a mile, and walked into the first accessible opening in the trees. Rob took the reins of the conversation and quickly asked my newfound friend if I was one of the popular kids or if I had finally managed to get my first kiss. My stomach turned into knots and a fiery anger started to grow inside me as I immediately regretted the fact that I had allowed anyone else into my secret realm of the woods. I faked a few laughs to try and extinguish the anger before I gave myself the chance to lash out at my brother in front of a potential new best friend. Another knot formed as the thought of my friend and his mother flashed across my mind and I made a mental note to send him a text or something to check in since we had fallen out of regular contact with the whole spontaneous relocation and new school thing.

Rob moved past the topic and changed course a bit to lecture us on how we needed to make the most of the next few years. He wasn't actually lecturing us, but instead encouraging us to go after every crush, attend every sporting event possible, and just make the absolute most of any fun opportunity we could. He was moving onto the subject of preparing as early as possible for college applications when a clearing opened up in front of us to stop him in mid-sentence. Taking a few steps forward through the thick entanglement of branches revealed a decent-sized bluff that overlooked the riverbank below. A few more incredibly-careful steps forward revealed that this cliff overlooking the beautiful banks below was at least fifty feet from the ground below. In familiar fashion, my brother didn't think twice about walking right up to the edge of the bluff and even started to lean over the edge to get a closer look. As if that adrenaline surge wasn't enough, he reached one hand out to grab hold of a small tree that was growing out of the side of the cliff's edge and looked back to see if we'd dare him to reach out his other hand.

I knew my brother more than enough to buy into his attempts to make me dare him to do something dangerous. All it would take was one "you won't do it" for him to reach out his other free hand or something much more dangerous. I immediately demanded he back away from the edge of the bluff, threatening to call Mom and Nana (who had arrived a couple hours ago to visit for the week) if he didn't. However, before I could follow through with my threats, my friend gave in and taunted Rob. With a quick smirk, having received the only encouragement he needed to seek a thrill, my brother reached out his other hand to grab hold of the nimble branch in front of him. Time slowed down to a glacial pace as my heart fell into my stomach watching my brother freely hanging over the edge of a cliff with only the support of a miniscule tree keeping him afloat. I watched in horror as the branch slowly bowed under the weight of my brother until it couldn't handle it any further, a bone-chilling snap eventually erupting from the base of the branch. My body quickly became paralyzed from sheer terror as my brother fell further and further away from the tree that had been holding him moments ago. In what was either a single second or an entire year, my brother disappeared from view until I heard a thud somewhere below that caused my own legs to collapse underneath me.

I remained in a crumpled heap on the forest floor for an unknown period of time, eyes still wide and body still frozen from terror. There was no way in hell my brother survived a fall of that great of a distance. I just witnessed my brother's death in front of me. The thud of his body hitting the river bank area fifty or so feet below was ringing in my ears until my friend's screams finally broke through and I registered that he was violently shaking me back to reality. Feeling began to rush back to my limbs and I pushed myself back onto my own two feet and cautiously took a couple of steps forward. Not willing to take any chances at this point, I quickly got on all fours in order to peek over the ledge. An enormous tidal wave of relief washed over me as I saw my brother down below, somehow on both feet and moving around. I shouted down below to tell him to lay down and stop moving in case he damaged something further without realizing it but only received an indiscernible sentence shouted back up at me. I looked around at both sides of the bluff but quickly realized there was no way to safely make it down to where he had fallen without sliding down and hoping for the best. Unsure of what else to do, I told my friend to stay here and make sure my brother stayed as still as possible while I called Mom and sprinted home.

I burst through the front door to see everyone scrambling around the house in hysterics about what I had just told them over the phone. Nana was locked in the bathroom and literally couldn't stop getting sick from worry and concern over my brother. I eventually got through the doors to my bathroom since I knew where the doorknob keys were but my grandmother remained motionless in the corner of the bathroom floor unable to move or speak. I gave her a quick hug and moved about to another part of the house where Mom was dialing 9-1-1 and anyone in her phone's contact list that would answer to see what she was supposed to do for an emergency in this town. She noticed I had entered the house and immediately threw me into the car to take her to the exact spot where Rob had fallen. The ambulance pulled up a few moments after we had parked on the side of the road and I did my best to direct everyone down to the embankment where my brother appeared to still be conscious and walking around. The paramedics quickly determined there wasn't a single way they could safely and efficiently bring a stretcher down through the woods and back up to the ambulance and made a few calls back to their station. With some assistance from a combination of emergency services workers, they traveled by boat to get to the part of the riverbank my brother was at and took him back to the dock to be transported to the hospital.

After a couple of weeks in a hospital bed under heavy observations and various tests, my brother returned home. By some stroke of miraculous luck, he only suffered a concussion and a broken thumb from the fifty-foot drop to the solid ground below. After only one or two people saw me standing by an ambulance on River Road, I walked back into school having to address rumors on what near-death experience I had survived. I always heard that news travels fast in a small town, but I had no idea just how fast word got around and how inaccurate the gossip could be. I did my best to set the record straight, but a small part of me was happy to be receiving any kind of attention for once even if it was at the expense of my brother's reckless endangerment of his own well-being. Even after denying the rumors that I was the one who suffered through a traumatic fall, my social standing in the ranks of Loudon finally seemed to land on its two feet for the first time since suddenly moving here. Whether it felt accurate or not, the semester was already wrapping itself up and preparing to set the kids wandering the two hallways free for the summer. However, while having a big backyard and access to the woods again and being able to make exceptional grades with minimal effort were nice, I still couldn't help but wish I was ending the school year back in Oak Ridge.

With my grief and longing for my previous town and school, I finally worked up the nerve to send a message to check in on everything with my former best friend. We had both been overwhelmed with just how quickly time seemed to fly and how much was happening at all times in high school that we pretty much fell out of contact with each other. After a few messages back and forth with normal small talk, I hesitated a few moments before asking how his mother was doing. A few minutes that felt like hours passed before I heard the ding from an inbox notification that catapulted my glass heart directly into a concrete wall. I sunk down into my desk chair, my soul descending even further into the most unknown depths as I read the words on my screen over and over again. Without warning, the feeling of guilt rushed over me as my mind attempted to mull over the fact that I had allowed myself to fall out of contact with my closest best friend in Oak Ridge and had missed one of the most monumental tragedies of his life. The woman who had practically been my second mother for two years lost her battle with cancer months ago and I was only hearing about it today.

I'm unsure how much time passed by as I sat in front of my computer screen, reading his message over and over again trying to convince myself this wasn't real. Convince myself that I hadn't fallen out of the loop. Convince myself that I hadn't missed the news of her passing and missed the funeral. Convince myself that I hadn't abandoned my closest friend when he was one of the only ones there for me through my worst moments of middle school. I had no idea what I was supposed to say back to his message. No idea what I could possibly say to make up for my own selfishness. No idea what to do to even come close to making him feel better or make myself feel better. I sat up a little in the chair and put together the best sentences I could form with the destroyed fragments of my mind. I offered my most sincere condolences and apologies for being nowhere to be found during all of this. Thankfully, he accepted my words despite their inability to change anything. I re-added his phone number from the last time I had lost it during a device replacement months ago. We both promised to never fall out of contact for so much time again, although I couldn't help but notice a sinking feeling that our friendship would never recover from this, at least not to the extent of greatness it had been at one time or another. I stood up from the computer desk in the corner of my room, did my best to pick up all the pieces of my soul that had shattered below, and walked out of the room in tense, lonely silence.

A few weeks lingered on as I pushed my guilt and sadness over the most wonderful woman's death further and further to the back of my mind. I knew I couldn't change anything or go backwards in time so I knew I had to just try to move forward as best as I could. I briefly brought up what had happened to Mom and Dad who casually expressed how sad of a situation it was before quickly moving on to some meaningless conversation topic without realizing how affected I was by the tragedy. A number of days later, Mom approached my doorway and paused. Her silent approach was one I had recognized all too well from my past and I immediately knew I wasn't about to enjoy what we were about to discuss. In familiar fashion, my mind immediately began forming hundreds of hypothetical situations to attempt to prepare me for anything that might come out of her mouth in the next few moments. Every single "Nana had another episode and fell again" or "Poppop Luke's cancer is getting worse" or "We know what you've been looking up online" that flashed across my mind created another tangled knot in my stomach until I was certain I was about to throw up before Lilley even spoke the first word. She took a few steps forward and rested at the bottom corner of my bed for another painfully-silent moment. "Your biological father is back from overseas..." she said quietly.

My mother remained at the edge of my bed as she went on to explain that Ryan had returned from his overseas tour he had been sent on because of the war. He was seemingly back in America for good and was extending another invitation to meet me once again after all these years. Suddenly, all concerns over my own grief and the guilt I was feeling about my own internet habits was overcome with the option being presented in front of me. My mother continued to inform me that this was ultimately my decision but started to go into the ways that it might affect our family the same way she had done a year or so ago back in middle school before my father had been shipped off for war. Finding a newfound confidence buried deep within the depths of my body, I cut my mother off before she could go into these potential consequences once again. Instead of firing off a hurtful remark, I simply told her I wanted to consider this invitation on my own and come to a decision without anyone else's ideas of what may or may not result from the choice on the table.

There were a few seconds where she appeared taken aback by my response, but agreed to it nonetheless by stepping out of the room. I laid back down and stared up at the ceiling as I started mulling over the various thoughts and emotions that were developing inside of me. My eyes closed and my mind immediately turned into a projection screen with memories streaming onto a blank stretch of canvas. Early memories running around Ryan's house and laughing at the top of my lungs switched to visiting Nana's mother in a nursing home with her which quickly switched to Nana's mother's funeral. From there the screen switched to show a young version of myself helping MiMi make her famous fruit tea in the kitchen of Poppop Luke's house only to immediately switch to her funeral that we had attended just a few months ago. The screen went blank for a few seconds only to flash back on out of nowhere with a still image of my best friend's mother that I never got to say goodbye to. I quickly opened my eyes to shut off the mental projections and sat up in bed almost having to gasp for air at all the visuals my mind had just conjured so quickly. My mind immediately flooded with dread as I imagined somehow losing my biological father without getting a chance to ask him any and every question or say goodbye. Without pausing to think of how anyone else in the family might react to a decision I wanted to make, I walked into the living room where Mom had retreated to and told her to let my father know that I accepted his invitation.

Mom slowly pulled into the parking spot outside of the restaurant and paused for several uncomfortable seconds. She didn't seem very ecstatic that I had agreed to meet him again, but I hadn't backed down from my choice nonetheless. That being said, my heart was still racing uncontrollably as it pumped nervous energy throughout the rest of my body. I slowly pushed myself into the booth to sit next to Mom as we waited for Ryan and Erin to arrive. I stared down at the silverware folded tightly inside a napkin and tried to avoid making eye contact with my disapproving mother. Though I hadn't specifically asked how Dad was taking the news of my decision, I imagine he wasn't thrilled either. However, thinking back to how easily they had dismissed my best friend's mother dying, I'm not sure there was any hope of finding the right words to convey everything I was feeling about this particular situation. I knew Dad had legally adopted us all those years ago, but parts of me couldn't help but wonder if he actually viewed me the way he would view a biological son. How was I supposed to simply explain to my parents that I probably messed up everything all those years ago when I told them I didn't want to visit my father anymore and that I was just trying to make up for whatever lost time I could? If they could create so many battlefields and warzones out of thin air over all of these years, what would they do with something actually substantial like that?

Ryan walked through the front doors of the restaurant and made his way over to our booth. He looked practically the same as I remembered him looking when I was a little kid. A smile quickly lit up across his face as he saw me and I quickly rose out of the booth to greet him with a hug. All the nervous energy and worries about what he might act like or whether or not he resented me faded as we picked up right where we'd left off the last time. We went back and forth asking random questions, updating each other on what life was like now, discussing the million-and-a-half schools I had attended, very briefly covered my book, and joked as if we were just two long lost friends reuniting at a local bar. We put each other's phone number into our phones after we finished up the last few bites of food before sliding up out of the booth. He hesitated a moment before asking if I would be okay with meeting Erin again. While I admired the fact that he came alone, I quickly assured him that would be completely fine. He gave me one final goodbye hug before agreeing to text each other from time to time and planning the next meet-up. I hopped back into the car and could tell Lilley was a bit uneasy at how well the meeting had played out but decided to ignore it the entire way home as I took control of the radio station playing through the car speakers.

Chapter Eight

Remember My Bonfires?

I stood outside the tall double-doors of the main hall of school with a much more solidified confidence than I had when I walked through them on the first day last semester. Summers in tiny towns zoomed by much faster than I was used to, flying through Thursday Club meetings, trips out to the questionable waters under that small bridge, and even a month or so of infatuation with the girl I accidentally stabbed with a pencil back in third grade. While I had convinced myself we were meant to be the fated high school sweethearts who lived happily-ever-after, the spark fizzled out before it had much time to develop into even a small candlelight. All that was left after she assured me we weren't going to run off away into the sunset together was a small stream of smoke and the realization that my forehead tattoo was a few shades darker and the tiny chain links on my ankle cuff had started to form a larger orb of concrete at the end just in time for the first day of a new school year. I took a few deep breaths and stared at myself in the mirror for a few moments that morning, telling myself no one else could possibly see the ink under my skin or hear the concrete dragging behind my every step. I took another look at my new school building, did one final double-take to ensure my shirt didn't suddenly have *I sometimes watch dudes online* printed on the front, and walked through the doorway once again.

As it turned out, the first day of a new year goes much more smoothly when you already know the name of every student and teacher in the building and don't have to worry about sprinting until your lungs collapse to make it to each class on time. I wandered around the hallways, stopping at each different clique of students gathered around discussing how their summers went. That familiar buzz and feeling of excitement that only a new school year could bring was running rampant throughout the entire building and even seemed to excite the faculty/staff members. I bounced around from group to group and tried to pick up my almost-decent social status back where it had left off until the first bell sounded in the speakers above. Right on cue, everyone in the hallway scattered and it was every man for himself as everyone rushed to their first class to get the best seats and make sure they secured a spot next to their best friend. With a semester of experience and research at this new school under my belt, I liked my chances of making a name for myself among the ranks this year. I had a pretty decent grasp on what kids here found humorous and what music was popular and how dating seemed to work and anything else I would need to understand for social survival. All I pretty much had to do was know when to make the right jokes or keep my mouth shut and avoid accidentally telling anyone my secrets or that I pretty much had two Dads now after this summer.

With the way my class credits transferred over from Oak Ridge to Loudon's schedule system, I got stuck in a History class that was typically reserved for only freshmen. While I was dreading having to endure this tragedy, I quickly realized the teacher of the course was one of the funniest humans I had ever met and quickly started trying to absorb and mirror his antics as much as possible. Additionally, the only other student who transferred from another school last semester had the same issue as me so I at least wasn't the *only* sophomore in the class. This also gave me that much more of a head start into learning the names and personalities of the incoming class and that much more of a chance to make more friends. As if this wasn't enough good luck on its own, I snagged a spot in a Culinary Arts course. I already knew the class that allowed me to pretend to be one of the famous chefs I always watched on TV would be my favorite, but I wasn't quite expecting just how therapeutic it would be to spend an hour and a half learning anything and everything there was to know about the culinary world. For an entire hour and a half every single day, I was able to put aside the stresses of building up a decent social reputation to survive a new town, my parents constantly fighting, starting a new relationship with my stepmother and biological father after ten years of zero contact, and the whole questionable internet search history thing.

I fell headfirst into an exciting new semester's routine of Thursday Club meetings, playfully talking down to freshmen, culinary escapism, ignoring the feelings I was experiencing on my internet scrolls, attending a few different churches that my friends went to, staying the night and sneaking out to ravage the town after dark, and settling into the life and culture of the tiny town of Loudon. Out of nowhere, I realized how quickly time had been passing and noticed I was a mere month or so away from a monumental birthday: 16. Not one for surprises, Poppop Luke told me that I was going to be handed down the new car his brother and he had purchased for their mother in 1997. With how little MiMi had used the vehicle and how persistent my grandfather was with caring for cars, it still felt like a brand new car and only came with about 35,000 miles on it. For whatever reason, Mom came up to me one morning and dropped the keys into my hand before slowly walking away. Confused, I followed her and asked when she was going to take me to school. She smiled and looked at my hand and signaled it was fine for me to take myself. Being a month away from 16, I knew it was illegal for me to be driving a car without a parent in the car but I wasn't going to decline Lilley's generosity. I nearly sprinted over my own feet and hopped in the driver's seat of my new car that was parked next door. I parked at a Mormon church across the street from the high school in case they randomly checked parking tags and walked into the front door like a king, my keys hanging around my neck on a lanyard like a glorious trophy.

I wasted no time letting everyone in the hallways and classrooms know that my parents already let me start driving to school by myself. With the newfound excitement, confidence, and recognition this brought I decided I was going to give my best attempt at throwing a Super 16th birthday party for myself. Sitting in class that week, I wandered through a million different ideas and tried to brainstorm what I could pull off that didn't cost a lot of money or potentially set me up to be embarrassed if no one showed like every party growing up. A gymnastic center with tons of trampoline flooring and foam pits immediately came to mind after we had gone there for an all-nighter Thursday Club event. Mom booked the event and made close to 50 invitations in envelopes since that was the most guests we'd be allowed in the building. However, the company called her back and asked for a credit card to put on the invoice for the booking. After hanging up on them, she casually walked over and let me know that every guest would be expected to pay a portion of the bill if they decided to attend the party. While I had been invited to only one or two parties my entire life, I had never been asked to pay to attend. Thinking on my feet, I quickly told her to just cancel the reservation and started to consider throwing the entire idea of celebrating my own birthday in the trash. How was I supposed to have a huge bash in a small town without traveling to the closest city which came with a giant price tag attached to it?

Quite literally out of nowhere, I glanced over next door at Poppop Luke's backyard as the spark of an idea came to my mind. I quickly stood up from our back porch and walked over to the small circle of bricks that were placed there in hopes of a permanent fire pit fixture at some point. Not wasting a single moment, I ran up to the sliding back door and opened it up to quickly ask my grandfather's permission to finish up the pit and have some friends over for a birthday fire. My social research so far this year had at least shown me that bonfires and hayrides and everything in between weren't just popular in movies and television shows. Before I knew it, I was creating an online event and sending out invites to anyone and everyone I could think of. I rolled back from my computer desk after sending at least a hundred social media invitations to long lost friends in Oak Ridge and anyone I had ever had a single conversation with in Loudon. A literal and figurative exhale of relief escaped my lips as I realized I had actually pulled off the self-appointed task of a birthday party. Excitement began to flood into every part of my body until it immediately rushed out to be replaced with a feeling of dread. What if no one showed up? What if everyone showed up but as a joke? What if this became a repeat of the plastic bullets ambush?

Over the next week, however, I got the vibe that quite a few people were actually planning on coming to the party. The online RSVP's were rolling in with each passing day and people were starting to pass me in the hallways and said they were excited for the bonfire next weekend. I talked my watched-my-brother-fall-off-a-cliff friend's older brother into driving us to find firewood and bringing it back to my grandfather's backyard since he was the only person I knew well enough who drove a truck. Between semi-legally obtaining an abundance of chopped firewood, hooking up my radio system to the balcony in my grandfather's backyard, and spending about $25 on random snacks and sodas, I felt fully prepared for whatever the birthday party may or may not entail. Mom had even promised me to get one of the fanciest cakes I had ever seen since it was a milestone birthday. After what felt like an eternity of waiting and double-checking with everyone in the entire state on their attendance, it was finally time to get ready for the big night.

I put on the nicest pair of casual clothes I probably owned, plugged the stereo system into the outlet on the balcony, and took a deep breath to try and calm my nerves and anxious excitement. I blinked twice and suddenly the sun had set and there were 50-60 teenagers scattered all around my grandfather's backyard that was now adorned with a blazing fire at the center of the brick circle I had built. I turned the speakers up a little more before making my way back downstairs to mingle with all the small groups and cliques that had formed. Everyone was either gathered by the fire or laughing in small groups or watching the athletes of the school playing whatever game they had made up on the spot to play in the spacious yard. A permanent smile was plastered onto my face as I tried to absorb the fact that my 16th birthday party was such a huge success. I moved to this small town less than a year ago, went through another awkward phase, but still managed to pull myself back up enough to host a huge party in my own honor. Not only were there a huge number of people here thanks to the social media invitations and word-of-mouth confirmations, but everyone seemed to be actually enjoying themselves too. I took a step back and glanced over the entire scene laid out in front of me and couldn't help feeling intoxicated by the rush of pulling this off.

Out of the corner of my eye, I noticed sparks coming from the sliding glass doorway as Lilley carefully walked out to greet me with my cake. A grin formed once again, this time from ear to ear, as I took in the moment. The greatest cake I had ever received by far, my new friends showing up and filling up the backyard for me, a roaring fire that I had helped build, and everything in between brought a tidal wave of happiness over my entire body. Everyone sang the painful song, I took a deep breath, and blew out all the candles in front of me, simply wishing that this feeling stayed as long as possible and that I didn't somehow lose all the progress I had made here. Some of my closer friends chuckled uncontrollably as I struggled to extinguish all the candles as my parents performed the ceremonial gifting of the car keys as if I hadn't been driving myself to school every morning for the last month. The party seemed to shift into slow-motion as I looked around at all the people and smiles frozen in place. A smile grew on my face once again as I tried to think of ways to bottle up the happiness radiating inside me. Time kicked back into its normal pace and I was suddenly hugging all of my friends goodbye as they started to make their way home or to whatever plans they had made for the remainder of the night. A couple of my friends were staying the night with me over at Poppop Luke's and we quickly worked together to pick up all the cups and paper plates that were scattered around the yard before heading inside for the rest of the euphoric, unforgettable night.

I had about three or four days after passing my driver's exam to soak in the glory of being able to (legally) drive around town whenever I wanted before my parents sat me down to let me know the costs that come with owning and driving a car. They quickly let me know they were willing to pay for my car insurance, but not gas or maintenance costs associated with the vehicle or any free time activity expenses whatsoever. I put on my best second-born charm to try and convince them to give me some form of chore list for a huge allowance, but it proved to be of little use. I even threw my good grades and good behavior into the mix to try and avoid the "we made your brother get a job at 16 too" argument but they stuck to their guns even though I knew we were spending far less money to live here than we were in Oak Ridge. After a few hours of the silent treatment and pouting in my room, I hopped in the car and drove around to the handful of businesses in town to ask if they had any job applications I could have. I had barely pulled back into the driveway after turning in the first round of papers before I had a phone call from a fast food chain asking if I could come in for an interview. Not having any "nice" clothes of my own, I once again selected the lesser of all evils I was able to find in Rob's closet and anxiously made my way to the restaurant.

Not knowing a single thing about job interviews, I nervously sat outside the McDonalds for a few moments trying to calm my nerves. I quickly played over the articulate, complex words of advice of "just be yourself" that I received from my parents when I told them how nervous I was. I quickly realized my random breathing exercises were doing very little for my nerves, if not making them worse. I thought about just turning the key inside the ignition and fleeing the interview altogether, but ultimately hopped out of the car and made my way inside instead. In an almost inaudible tone, I told the first employee I saw that I was here for a job interview only to notice this employee had no idea what I was saying and pointed towards the back of the restaurant before returning to her work. Giving it another go, I gave my best attempt at relaying the message to one of the cashiers that didn't have anyone waiting at their register. I was instructed to have a seat at one of the empty chairs in the dining room and wait for a manager to come speak to me, a task that only doubled my already-high levels of anxiety. After what felt like three hours of agonizing anticipation, a woman with short hair and a variety of facial piercings made her way over to me. I immediately shot up out of the chair I was sitting in to shake her hand, briefly considered performing a curtsy for some reason, and sat back down for my line of interrogation.

She started with two or three simple questions regarding my name, age, school performance, and recreational hobbies. I tried to answer confidently but my voice kept shaking uncontrollably as I threw in that I made straight A's and even attended church, something that was true enough to where I didn't feel that bad. She asked a few more completely unrelated questions that didn't seem related to the job whatsoever before cutting the interview short. I started to hang my head in embarrassment and shame as I realized I must have blown it. However, she quickly followed up saying that she had more important things that needed her attention in the back and that I seemed "normal enough" for the job if I wanted to accept the minimum-wage salary offer. Not wanting her to change her mind in the time it would take me to consult with my parents or ponder any of the other applications I had placed, I graciously accepted. Grinning from ear to ear, I made my way home without even the slightest idea of what specific job title I had accepted or when my first day would be or anything at all other than I was now officially employed for the very first time.

It only took one or two instances of freezing up in front of a customer while I was training as a cashier for someone to move me over to the fry station. I thought I had conquered my fear of being able to somewhat hold my own when talking to strangers but something about the uniform and all the confusing buttons on the screen in front of me crossed all the wires in my brain that handle my social skills and confidence. After a few weeks, I managed to connect the wires back in the proper ports and experienced fewer and fewer awkward freezing spells when a customer would ask a question. I still hovered over the French fry station sometimes, mostly to help during busy periods but also to taste test all the products more times than necessary. Before too long, I had memorized the buttons and how to operate the screen during an order and started to feel more and more comfortable living the life of the part-time American worker. Between the interactions with strangers and the more-often-than-not occasion of friends coming through the doors, I treated this new adventure as an extension of my social research on my quest to socially dominate this small town. As if this wasn't exciting enough, the random experiences of working in the fast food industry also gave me that much more to post about on social media, especially the occasions I could easily make jokes about to help convince people I had some semblance of a personality.

After about the second or third $150 paycheck, I began walking around the hallways of school like I was Jordan Belfort himself. My gas tank was full every week, I bought any shirt or shorts the moment I decided I wanted them, I offered to pay for prospective friends' food after Thursday Club, and even bought a new cell phone that ate two full paychecks at once. Needless to say, there was hardly any money that existed in my checking account at any given point, let alone even the thought of a savings account. Since I wasn't a legal adult yet, I had to have at least one parent on my bank account with me. Therefore, Lilley immediately saw how quickly I was able to burn through a paycheck every two weeks and decided to sit me down to have a talk one afternoon on my day off. I figured she was going to tell me that she was going to start putting a daily spending limit or some other restrictive action to properly teach me about managing money, but what she suggested was something quite the opposite of what I predicted. "It's about time we start looking into and really thinking all those years without child support." she said calmly, as if she was mentioning the weather or a funny commercial she had seen on TV.

Perhaps it was the fact that I had just had to speak with police for someone trying to steal money out of my cash register or the man who decided to scream at me for the ice cream being broken (it wasn't) (it never is), but my mind didn't immediately dismiss what Mom was saying. She went into how proud she was for being the "bigger person" by choosing to start a new relationship with my father and stepmother, but quickly shifted the conversation to how difficult it had been all those years ago when I was so young. Paperwork, legal fees, therapy, and everything was being laid out in front of me to explain everything my mother had to go through. To conclude her explanation, she mentioned that all forms of child support payments were halted when all the paperwork was finalized and processed. My mind immediately went to the fact that Dad had married Mom around this time and thereby agreed to help raise my brother and I. She could tell my mind was a bit puzzled because she responded to my silence by insinuating that she would not have gone through all of that work if I was going to change my mind later down the road, especially after allowing Dad to legally adopt me. I sat in silence across from her with a puzzled expression as I mulled over her words.

She could clearly sense my apprehension about discussing anything related to money and decided to go into more detail. Lilley apparently already reached out to my father and established a plan where he would wire some additional money about once a month into the same bank account I had been using to house my paychecks from work. With how quickly the conversation was moving, I quickly felt overwhelmed with uncertainty and confusion. Apparently, Ryan only felt comfortable supplying any form of additional income if the money went directly to me instead of through my mother so he agreed once he knew it was my own bank account. However, Lilley assured me that she would be having a closer grip on the bank account and observing it more in an attempt to teach me how to better manage my finances. A sense of relief came over me as I realized I might have a little bit more spending money on top of the money I was earning from my part-time job. Mom wrapped up the discussion by encouraging me to keep this discussion about Ryan's payments and her bank account monitoring strictly between us instead of involving anyone else in the household. I didn't think much of this disclaimer as it was pretty standard behavior at this point for our house.

Not knowing what exactly I was meant to do with the extra income that started to arrive in my account after the first month or two, I spent it. A new pair of shoes that caught my eye here, a nice pair of shorts there, and suddenly my account was back to double (or sometimes single) digits once again. I logged into my account online one afternoon to check my balance like I was starting to do more and more often. My heart dropped into my stomach as I noticed a negative symbol next to the number that usually represented how much money was present. Fighting back the urge to vomit all over my computer desk, I quickly pulled up the recent transactions to see a number of dollar amounts being swiped out of my account at places I had no recollection of going to. My first instinct was to sprint across my room to check my wallet only to find my debit card safely tucked in its designated pocket. The relief that came with knowing I hadn't had my card stolen only lasted a few seconds until the realization hit me of what was actually going on. A small flame sparked inside my stomach where the nausea had been a few moments ago, quickly expanding until a fiery rage had completely consumed my insides.

I stormed into the living room and grabbed Lilley's purse to begin searching for her wallet without pausing to confront her with words. By the time she jerked her head from the couch and started shouting, I had already pulled out the debit card she had secretly asked the bank to create that was linked to my bank account. She stopped her words mid-sentence and stared back at me, eyes darting back and forth between me and the card I was holding up. My eyes started to form tears, not from sadness but from seething anger, as the reality was confirmed in front of me. My mother, the woman who was my main source of comfort and support whenever Nana was too far away, had taken control over my bank account in order to have access to the money my father was sending for me. My mother drove my bank account into overdraft mode. We launched harsh words back and forth at each other in an effort to defend each other's anger. She insisted that I had misunderstood everything and that it wasn't her excessive swiping that drove my bank account down but my own inadequate management. Screaming at my mother was very unfamiliar territory, but I couldn't stop myself at this point with the amount of anger welling up inside. I immediately thought back to the last time I had been even remotely close to this anger and I suddenly saw myself back in eighth grade when she had told me I couldn't hang out with my new group of friends because it "made me look gay."

The shouting match eventually drew the attention of Dad and he quickly made his way into the living room to investigate what the hell was going on. By this point, I had yelled enough to lose my voice and my points still seemed lost on my mother. Dad quickly stepped in between the two of us and demanded I tell him what was happening. I knew I couldn't summarize the situation without revealing my mother's plot to get my father to pay for the "years of no child support" which would just result in even more shouting matches between the two of them. I spent the next two seconds pondering whether or not it would be worth the prolonged arguments that would inevitably lead nowhere and cause nothing but more chaos. I turned away without saying a word and stormed off to my bedroom with as loud of a door slam as possible. I flung myself onto my bed, feeling halfway defeated and apathetic and halfway proud of myself for actually standing up for myself against Lilley. While she definitely didn't accept responsibility for draining my funds, she seemed to at least acknowledge that it wasn't going to happen any longer. I knew this likely meant a stop to the supplemental income, but I also wouldn't have to worry about having to watch my bank account like a hawk to make sure it didn't go back into the negatives once again. I let out a long, exhausted breath before rolling over in bed and trying to suppress the flickering embers of anger that were still radiating from my pores.

There were no more follow-up screaming matches in the coming days but I knew the issues were as resolved as they could be when she didn't ask the whereabouts of the debit card I hadn't returned to her purse. After a few text messages back and forth with Ryan to summarize what had happened, we decided it was best to stop the wire transfers each month into my account. Instead, he assured me that anytime I ever needed anything that I couldn't afford or if I ever ran into a rough patch that he'd help out in any way that he was able to. While I knew I'd have trouble ever working up the nerve to ask my father for financial assistance if I needed it, it was still enough reassurance to put this entire ordeal behind me as much as possible and continue moving forward. If anything, this gave me all the motivation to start spending more time outside of the house whether that meant spending more time with friends or picking up extra shifts at work when they were available. I slowly started to understand Rob's constant arguments throughout his childhood more and more each day.

With more and more time being spent outside of the house with my growing network of friends, I quickly started to see just how different my household was. By the time I had stayed the night with two or three other friends a few times, I saw how wildly different their entire family dynamics seemed to be. Their parents took time to ask me a variety of questions about my life and my classes and seemed to take a genuine interest in who I was and how I came to be one of their son's friends. Not only did they seem to have a desire to get to know me, but they also had a complete understanding of their son's entire life and the lives of their sibling(s) and other friends. The more families I met, the more common this familiarity seemed to be with everyone else but me. The parents knew what projects, essays, or exams were coming up. They knew the names of all their teachers. They knew what teams we were playing in football or basketball that week. They knew the names of their other close friends and what their parents did for work and exactly what part of town they lived in. At this point, I wasn't completely certain my parents could name two classes I was taking this semester, let alone what assignments or tests were approaching. The most important detail I began to notice, however, was the fact that none of these other households seemed to be a warzone with landmines scattered all across the floor waiting to erupt into a fiery screaming match at any moment.

Part of my mind told me I was overreacting and thinking too much into this extended social research into family systems. While this was an easy way of explaining my observations and tossing them aside, other parts of my mind started to whisper that perhaps my childhood hadn't actually been that great and that my mother might not be the beaming beacon of love and support that she had always painted herself to be in our young, susceptible minds. These different voices argued back and forth with each other in my head until I could hardly hear anything in the outside world. Eventually, I pushed the thoughts as far as I could into the depths of my head and decided to stop thinking about family altogether. In its place, I started picking up more shifts at work, hanging out with any friend I could outside of school, focusing more and more on social media as it continued becoming more and more of a prominent presence in our daily lives, and making myself miserable in the darker corners of the internet through secret visits to the bathroom only to cry myself to sleep or prayer right after. Between trying to convince god to fix me and worrying about whether or not my parents were decent parents at all, my head started to get more and more clouded with stress in ways it never had before.

Thankfully, I had a number of different outlets I could use whenever things got too cloudy and noisy in my head. Now that I was old enough to drive, I could simply hop in my car and take a drive to try and relax. When that didn't work, I had a job that let me pick up shifts whenever I wanted to for the most part which guaranteed a mental distraction with how quickly my brain was used there. When those options didn't seem to be very effective, I started throwing more bonfire parties and using my network of friends and social media to ensure there was a pretty decent crowd each time I threw one. The neighbors never seemed very pleased to have cars lining the streets, but for whatever reason my parents and grandfather seemed too happy that I was finally building up a social life to care too much about the occasional police officer being called to make sure no one was drinking alcohol or doing anything too reckless. After the last one wrapped up and classes got dismissed until the New Year, I tried to be thrilled at the social reputation I had built myself from the ground up and the life I had seemed to create here in this small town. However, each time I began to soak in the euphoria, I instantly reminded myself of my dark little secret getting bolder on my forehead and heavier around my ankle along with the fact that I was starting to doubt everything about my childhood and the way I was raised.

What I wasn't expecting was the reality of "winter break" not being something that applies to your job even if it was just a part-time one. At first I was repulsed at the idea of not getting to sleep in every single day of the break and even considered faking some kind of family emergency or terminal illness to get those few weeks off of working a drive-thru line or front lobby cashier. However, I quickly remembered what my mind and body tended to do whenever it was left alone for too long and my mood about having to work completely shifted. I told one of the managers that I could come in more often until the new semester started as long as I got a few days off around the actual holidays so that I could spend some time with family. I wasn't willing to risk not soaking in the love and comfort that Nana and Poppop's house brought or playing with the million-and-a-half dogs that lived at Grams and Gramps. My manager seemed willing enough to agree to the deal and suddenly I was bouncing from drive-thru shifts to fryer shifts to front cashier shifts and even the occasional lobby maintenance shift which basically just meant I had to clean up the bathrooms and any messes that kids (and adults) made on the tables and floors. These extra shifts made time fly by and all of a sudden it was as if I was already zooming through the holidays with Nana and Poppop, Grams and Gramps, and all the aunts, uncles, and cousins that came with both of those gatherings.

I wasn't sure if it was the fact that this holiday break came with much less free time or if I was just growing up faster than I expected, but time wouldn't stop flying by. Not only was time flying, but this break from school didn't feel nearly as special when I was having to clock in for shifts at work and also try to fill all my free time with hangout sessions to avoid spending much time at home and risking any arguments. However, I didn't have to be burdened with the task for too long with time moving as quickly as it was. In what felt like a blink, I was waking up and throwing on the first articles of clothing I saw for another first day of school. I pulled into the closest spot I could find in the parking lot that wasn't reserved for the football players via their unspoken rule that was understood and somehow accepted by every staff member, teacher, and student. It turns out there isn't as much of a buzz or excitement coursing through the hallways when everyone returns from such a short break, but it was still refreshing to be surrounded by people my age once again. I made my way from group to group as they shared everything they had gotten for Christmas as exchanged schedules to try and figure out what classes they had in common. A smile stayed printed on my face, roaming all over the spectrum of smile types like ear-to-ear grin and the soft smile of quiet contentment, until I tripped and face planted onto the linoleum tiles of the hallway. I quickly picked myself up off the ground and looked around for what or who could have caused me to trip. The painfully-familiar entanglement of knots in my stomach immediately formed as I glanced down to see a fully-developed shackle and iron orb attached to my ankle.

I immediately rushed to the nearest restroom, hoping no one was able to hear the sound of the metal ball dragging behind me as I ran. Thankfully, the first bell had already rang so there was no one else in the bathroom I entered. With no one around to see, I ran directly up to the first mirror and looked at my reflection in front of me, completely horrified to see the tattoo on my forehead had returned with a few layers of fresh ink. My jaw dropped slightly as I stared at the words *Check his Internet History* that were emblazoned on my forehead twice the size as before. I leaned in closer only to see there were other words in thin, faint writing that seemed to say *check his texts* and *look at his inbox*. My heart began racing as I tried to process how quickly these secrets were starting to become a part of me uncontrollably. Leaning forward with my hands gripping the sink in front of me, I thought I was going to collapse onto the small, square tiles of the questionable bathroom floor. I quickly found my footing again, not wanting to risk whatever illness could be lurking on the floors, and tried to calm my thoughts. I knew there was no way anyone else could see the tattoos or the ball-and-chain that was growing heavier and heavier, but it seemed like only a matter of time before they would start to. Another bell sounded above to quickly interrupt my mind from the onset of a panic attack. I was now late to my first class of this first day of the semester. Shit.

I quickly cupped my hands together and tried to gather as much water from the sink as possible to splash across my face, washing enough of the ink on my forehead down the drain. After I managed to rinse it all and dry my face with the sandpaper towels, I wrapped the chain around my ankle until the iron orb was suspended off the ground and resting against my ankle. From there, I sprinted out of the bathroom and made my way to my first class in an attempt to remedy the horrible first impression I likely already made on the teacher that morning. Thinking on my feet, I quickly grabbed the printed schedule out of my backpack and crumpled it up a little in my hands until I was standing outside the room I was supposed to be in. I took a few seconds to catch my breath and make my face look as confused as possible. Feeling satisfied enough, I opened the door slowly and gave my best "I got lost and then couldn't find my schedule" performance as possible. Oscar-worthy.

The teacher didn't seem too frustrated as I made my way to one of the only available seats near the front of the room. After a few minutes of going over the ways the class was going to operate and everything we were to expect from the semester, my mind immediately drifted back to the bathroom. I wanted to be surprised at how the tattoos and shackle had grown, but I knew exactly what had caused it whether I wanted to believe it or not. After the awkward intrusion of my first class, I gave my best efforts at paying attention to everything that was being discussed. This plan worked, of course, for approximately three minutes before I was zoned out and falling down the rabbit hole of my own self-reflections and thoughts. I replayed every single text message and online message I had sent to guys over the holiday break. I retraced every friend request I sent to guys who had come across my social media feeds whether I actually knew who they were or not. Every attempt to hang out with my friends here so far suddenly played out in front of me. Why could I not stop myself from being weird like this? Why was I not this annoying with all the female friends that I had made? Why hadn't I been able to find a girlfriend in so long? While I had built up a pretty impressive social standing during my short time here, I was simultaneously retracting back into being annoying and...questionable. Damn it.

Thankfully, the bell chimed above after what felt like only seconds away from the previous one to stop my mental spiral from getting too treacherous. I gave my best attempt at meandering through the hallways and classrooms throughout the day without seeming too bothered at how the morning had started. When I was least expecting it, I walked into Honors English class and immediately knew the teacher for the class was going to be one of my favorites. Her dry sense of humor instantly resonated with me and, despite her class seeming pretty difficult, I knew this semester was going to be one for the books. Not only did I meet a formative, life-altering English teacher but I also got the chance to add another Culinary Arts course to my agenda to ensure I had another hour-and-a-half of therapy every day. Thursday Club leaders were already flooding into the hallways at lunch on the first day to let everyone know that meetings would be starting up again in the next few weeks. A few of my close friends even invited me to start attending their church more regularly since they were doing a sign language performance sometime in the next two months. What had started as a truly chaotic morning quickly shifted gears and everything seemed to be falling back into a normal place before I found myself hopping into my car to head home after another first day.

Despite filling my every free moment with friends, church, Thursday Club, or work, I found myself always coming back to my ankle chain and forehead ink the moment I was alone in my room for even a brief moment. I was attending church services and participating in the sign language performance practices on top of the Thursday Club meetings which I had never missed once. However, even with all of this on my schedule alongside work and school, I would still find myself sneaking off to the privacy of my bathroom every single time the temptation made its way into my mind. Even with my friendship networks growing and developing more and more every week, I still acted weird when it came to online interactions and excessive texting whenever it came to my circle of guy friends even when I was completely aware of it. The more control over my social reputation and my religious efforts, the less control I seemed to have of this innocent little middle-school curiosity that was violently taking over my high school life with every passing day. Somehow, in my head, if I was able to resist scrolling through the videos online, I had to immediately balance that out by sending an annoying amount of strange text messages or social media chats to the friends I had made over the last year. On the off chance I received replies from my friends or strangers online, I at least had the chance to become closer friends by oversharing whatever was troubling me at that given moment.

Deep in the dimly lit corners of my mind, I knew this newfound way of strengthening friendships or creating new ones was not a logical or reasonable one. I knew it was even borderline manipulation. However, the moment I had the fleeting emotion or slight inconvenience it was as if something took over my body and forced my fingers to send out the messages. To make matters even more difficult, the entity that took over my body never reached out to the handful of close female friends but instead focused its outreach on a collection of popular guys around school that I had hardly exchanged ten words with or a complete stranger whose profile came across a *People You Might Know* section of my feed. It was as if the only solution to my worries and stresses was to become best friends with any and every one of these hand-selected popular guys and the only way to do so was to bombard them with a barrage of texts, calls, online messages, and face-to-face interactions. Of course, every single time this happened my mind would spiral. Were they going to react negatively to these messages? Were they going to ignore me? If they replied kindly, were they actually wanting to be friends or did they just pity me? Above all of these hypothetical situations, of course, was the scenario in which they looked at these messages and got suspicious and shared that same, specific suspicion with everyone in the school. All of a sudden, despite having built up an impressive social standing at this school, it felt as if I was walking through the same middle school hallways full of people whispering about me and wondering if I liked girls and/or loudly pondering why I was such a weirdo.

Thursday Club's debut meeting for the semester came just in time to cut through my emotional crisis and give me another dose of hope for self-healing my dark secret(s). I parked my car outside the same doctor's office they still used to host meetings and excitedly made my way inside. The Leaders got right to business by silencing all the side conversations from the audience and welcomed us all back for another exciting season. They eagerly announced that there were also going to be three new Leaders joining our county's club in an effort to expand communication throughout our high school to hopefully recruit more kids. A hush fell over the students as the three new Leaders made their entrance into the basement where we were all huddled together. The new additions looked like they could have just stepped off the set for a magazine cover photoshoot. The men were sporting tall, muscular builds and the woman was donning freshly-blonde hair and trendy clothes. With the three of them all looking like supermodels, every single set of eyes were set on them and practically every jaw in the room was on the floor. They seemed to notice how awestruck we were, causing all of us to snap out of it and act normal but not before my eyes lingered a few moments too long on the wrong Leader.

The opening session continued like any normal meeting in the past before we were all heading to the drive-in restaurant down the road to hang out and maintain the traditions of Thursday Club. Much to everyone's liking, the new Leaders joined in on the traditional fun and made their way from clique to clique to introduce themselves further and get to know us. For whatever reason, a bundle of nerves formed when one of the new guys made their way over to me and started asking some basic questions to break the ice. I froze for a brief moment, petrified at the idea that he was immediately able to see my forehead tattoo and ball-and-chain attached to my ankle. The knots in my stomach twisted and turned into a complex entanglement until it felt like I was going to pass out or throw up, or perhaps both. By some miracle, I was able to force my mouth to form a string of replies to his questions that were hopefully normal enough. A sense of relief rushed over my mind and immediately untangled my stomach as the new Leader asked to exchange numbers and possibly plan a hangout sometime soon. He handed me my phone back after putting his number in and I quickly decided to head home before I had a chance to ruin this potential new friendship or risk anyone seeing the secret that felt like it was branded on my body at this point.

I walked through the front door and down the hall towards my bedroom, completely unnoticed by anyone else in the house like usual. I sat down on my bed and couldn't help but look around the room. What used to be my sanctuary and escape when I was so much younger was now just a bedroom that felt more like a prison the moment I laid down each night. I tried my best to ignore how excited I was that one of the new Thursday Club Leaders seemed to want to be my friend, but I couldn't escape the swirling euphoria that came with feeling noticed by someone who was clearly popular and desired amongst the rest of the kids that were there tonight. It's normal to want to be friends with cool, popular people. It's totally normal to feel this excited about having his number and being able to shoot out this text about how nice it was to meet and how excited I was for this season of Thursday Club. Pressing the send button, however, brought nothing but turmoil and nausea into the pits of my stomach. I already wished I could unsend the message and play it cool and normal for once but it was already too late. Why did I get this intense urge to be friends with certain people and then try and manifest it into reality by any means? Eventually, I was able to calm my thoughts down enough to start to doze off but not before I started to notice a dismal haze forming up in the corner of the ceiling. It didn't have any distinguishable characteristics that I could notice through my drowsy vision, but its presence definitely felt ominous as if it was sneering at my emotional spiral from my attempt to befriend one of the male Leaders instead of the new female one.

Morning came all too quickly as I jolted awake in my bed and immediately looked around for the dismal fog that I had seen the night before. Satisfied that it must have been a nightmare, I hopped out of bed and made my way to school. The new Leader had replied to my text which threw a wrench into the plans I devised right before I fell asleep which entailed me actually leaving people alone instead of pestering them into being my best friend. If anything, I had a pretty decent network of close female friends that I could text whenever I felt sad instead of online strangers or popular guys at school who definitely weren't reaching out to be best pals with me whatsoever. Naturally, I sent an immediate reply back and completely ruined my plans before I gave myself a chance to even begin them. In search of some kind of reassurance, I told myself in the rear-view mirror reflection of my car on the way to school that I was going to tweak the kinds of messages I was sending instead of abstaining from all communications. I would be normal and talk about hot girls or whatever game was coming up that week/weekend instead of talking about how my family life makes me sad or how alone I feel sometimes. If I could just shift the tones of these messages and texts to people at school and online, maybe I could actually continue building my social reputation even further as opposed to compromising it once again. Of course, this would inevitably be easier said than done as I realized my tattoo seemed to have grown a few shades darker and the iron orb on my ankle a few pounds heavier.

I remained in my car in the parking lot for several minutes once I pulled up to the school, suddenly terrified of walking in. What if the Leader had shared with some of the other kids that I had weirdly texted him out of nowhere? What if one of the football players I had texted told the whole school that I was a depressed weirdo who texted guys too often? What if some of my female friends start flirting with one of the guys I'm trying to be best friends with and he brings me up and how emotional and unstable I seem? How was I supposed to explain why I text guys I barely know or message people online who live halfway across the country instead of opening up to one of the girls I spend so much of my free time with? I took a few deep breaths and tried to calm the torrential hailstorm of hypothetical situations forming in my mind. Another look in the mirror proved that the tattoo wasn't showing anymore and I made my way into the main hallway, making sure to smile to everyone I passed along the way. I stopped at a few groups on my way to my first class and managed to convince myself that I had nothing to worry about. All my friends were still talking to me like nothing was out of the ordinary and I even got a head nod and a shoulder pat from one of the football players I had regrettably texted a few nights ago to unload my emotional problems on. Everything was fine. I think.

A few more weeks passed before I realized just how awkward of a web I had spun with my virtual/real-life behaviors. One bad afternoon or an exhausting shift at work would send me into a spiral that I decided to fend off by shooting off a text to one of the football players or my new friend within the Thursday Club Leaders. From there, I would send more and more messages even if they hadn't responded to the first one until I was practically sobbing in my bedroom pondering the idea of breaking my phone into several pieces. For a few brief moments, that felt like the only possible solution to keep me from texting guys in the most annoying way possible when I was already worried enough about my reputation as it is. I would battle with the idea until I realized how unreasonable it was right as sleep finally crept my way. From there, I woke up to freaked out replies asking if I was okay because they had been asleep or busy when I reached out. Not wanting to risk any further damage, I would laugh it off and say everything was fine as if that was somehow going to erase the damage I had already done and stepped two steps backwards and that much closer to becoming the school's Weird Kid once more.

No matter how many times I tried to play it cool whenever I saw people at school or at Thursday Club that I had sent an embarrassing number of messages to, it slowly began to eat away at my soul. Night after night, the same pattern would repeat itself. Watch a video I definitely shouldn't be watching as a totally normal, totally heterosexual guy. Cry myself to sleep after. Get home from work and think about what I watched online the night before. Send a text to one of the popular athletes. Send another when they didn't reply. Send one to the Thursday Club Leader even though you said you'd start leaving him alone. Cry myself to sleep waiting for someone to reply to distract myself from my own thoughts. Wake up the next morning with my stomach in knots of embarrassment. Hop in the shower to try and wash off the agony that was quickly becoming my every single day. Try to make it through my week without hearing anyone talking about my weird communication habits or questioning why I was texting other guys and being weird. Rinse and repeat. Over and over and over. After a month or two into this emotional roller coaster of a semester I was being forced to ride for whatever reason(s), the ominous fog began to appear more clearly in the upper corner of my room. However, instead of a potential hallucination happening in the mere moments before drifting off to sleep, it was hovering there the moment I got home and threw myself on to the bed after a Thursday Club meeting.

I immediately jolted up off the bed and somehow landed on both of my feet and stood there for a few moments, absolutely frozen from head to toe in fear. After blinking a few times to ensure what I was seeing in front of me was real, I tried to take a step closer to examine it further. There didn't seem to be any distinguishable features, though the closer I stepped towards the condensed haze on the opposite side of the room, the more evil it began to feel. I paused after the third step as my forehead started to sear with pain along with my ankle where I had started noticing the shackle and chain. I threw myself onto the bed once more, this time covering my head with as many pillows as possible and hoping the entity was just another twisted form of my imagination that had hacked into the vision system of my brain. After what I felt to be enough time had passed, I cautiously peered through one of the pillows only to see the dark cloud hovering up in the corner of the room. It hadn't moved closer to me or moved at all whatsoever so I slowly sat up on the bed to try and figure out what the hell was going on. However, the longer I sat perched on my bed staring at the abysmal haze the more I started to notice thoughts popping into my head.

Part of me knew I should slide off of the bed and sprint out of my room as quickly as possible and likely never return, but the other parts of me remained sitting there in complete stunned perplexity. I wasn't sure how I knew this but these thoughts that guided my fingers to type out all the texts and online messages or click the "add friend" button to complete strangers had been coming from this cloud in my room. I leaned forward slightly and could almost feel the "send your Leader a text about the meeting tonight" forging in the center and shooting across to my head. I looked down to see my hands already typing out the message even though I knew I would hate myself for it the moment I hit send. I threw my phone down as anger began to grow inside me as I realized whatever this thing was had been responsible for backtracking towards being the Weird Kid when I got my first cell phone. A cindery glow began to form from the center of the cloud that quickly distracted my mind. I slid a bit closer across the sheets on my bed only to feel a piercing pain shoot across my brain as a thin beam of light came from the fiery orange center directly towards me. All of a sudden, the enormous guilt and shame from my secretive internet scrolling, my constant texts and messages to dudes, and everything in between crashed into me like a tsunami all at once.

Immediately regretting not running out of my bedroom the moment I noticed this cloud, I was forced to sit on my bed and experience this wave of sadness that was connecting me to the cloud. I wanted nothing more than to flee, but I was paralyzed by this point. It was almost as if the beam of light from the smoldering center of the fog was a channel directly into my mind as more and more shame and sadness began to funnel in. After a few minutes, my entire brain seemed to be full of negative thoughts. Visions of video clips I had shamefully watched online were suddenly projected onto all four walls of my bedroom. Embarrassing text messages that I sent some of the popular athletes at school and attractive strangers on the internet were now flashing across my television and computer screens. On top of my embarrassing habits being magnified onto my walls, every time my eyes would blink I would find myself in one of the several scenarios where I was expected to give a girlfriend a first kiss but found myself too paralyzed. I felt the uncomfortable warmth of tears running down my face with the sudden onslaught of memories and emotions being funneled by this bizarre entity that had made itself at home in my bedroom. Within moments I was sobbing uncontrollably and felt myself plummeting towards the lowest rock bottom I had ever felt until the cloud suddenly burst into a million small lights with a pop. The texts, explicit videos, messages to strangers, the ringing in my ear, and flashbacks all halted immediately. However, the tidal wave of relief immediately diverted away from me as I looked down to see my house key positioned in my hand and a fresh slash on my ankle.

Chapter Nine

Remember When I Made that Prayer Page?

Holy shit. What the hell had I just done? I stared at my ankle for what felt like hours trying to wrap my mind around the fact that I had just attacked myself. A million-and-a-half thoughts were shooting across my mind and rebounding over and over again against the walls of my skull while my stomach twisted into itself. Half of these thoughts were the memories of every single joke I had heard throughout middle school and high school about kids who were depressed and/or harmed themselves and every single mention of self-harm in classroom lectures that always resulted in someone laughing. I was now one of those kids that people try to make fun of. I'm one of those depressed kids who hurts them self whenever they got sad. One thought, however, that was more pronounced than any of the other racing emotions and words was the fact that this had worked. While the slash on my ankle was already burning, it had completely gotten rid of the cloud in my room and all the havoc it had been wreaking on my brain. No abysmal cloud apparently means no risk of anyone in my family walking in to see the evidence of my secrets projected onto my bedroom walls. No cloud means no ringing in my ear or the sense of dread and hatred funneling into my brain. One quick slice and the agony was over.

The next morning, I hopped out of bed at the first chime of my alarm to eat breakfast and hop in the shower before anyone else got up. I slipped on a pair of jeans despite the warming temperatures so that no one saw my ankle until it had enough time to heal and look normal enough. As if the tattoo and shackle-and-chain weren't enough secretive burdens to carry, I now had to worry about anyone at school or at home seeing that I had attacked myself. The thought of Nana finding out crossed my mind and was almost enough to bring my breakfast immediately back up as my knees almost buckled beneath me. I took a few moments in the bathroom to take some deep breaths and collect myself before darting out of the house as quickly as possible into my car. Without a moment's hesitation I turned the radio to the Christian station and prayed while driving, only halfway paying attention to the road in front of me. My conscience pleaded with the omnipotent being above to heal my ankle, forgive me for doing it to myself, and mend the broken parts of my mind and body that were allowing me to get into such complex sinful habits. I parked my car in the first open spot I saw and made my way into the school trying to appear as normal as possible.

A week or two passed by in a flash before I walked into my room after a painfully-long shift at work to see the cloud positioned once again in my room, this time slightly larger than before. Instead of taking its time or waiting for me to examine it like before, the fiery core immediately shot towards me and I was spiraling once again. The entire process repeated itself in an eerily step-by-step fashion until there was an accompanying cut on my ankle next to the first one. In more disbelief than the week before, I stared at what I had just done in agonizing disbelief before collapsing into sobs and burying my face in my pillows. A few minutes passed before I found myself staring at my phone, quietly contemplating whether or not I wanted to text my Thursday Club Leader or one of the jocks at school that I was trying to force to be my best friend. My mind projected a scenario in front of me that showed me walking through the hallways as every set of eyes focused on me and every clique whispering about me as I passed. The jock(s) read my texts about what I had done and immediately shunned me and spread the word around the whole school/town/state/country/world. Shaking my head until that haunting imagery disappeared, the next scenario that played out in front of me showed me and the small handful of guys in my life I felt compelled to befriend hanging out together. They read my texts and immediately hopped in the car to come check on me and we became the best friends I could have ever asked for.

I blinked and suddenly the virtual scenarios my mind was projecting in front of me vanished into thin air faster than the villainous cloud had. I reached across the bed and picked up my phone, pausing to stare at the keys lying next to it for a few seconds that felt like hours. A few deep breaths later, I was sending a text to the Leader saying I really needed to talk about something serious. A brief sense of confidence came out of nowhere and I went ahead and sent a follow-up text that gave a quick summary, carefully tiptoeing around the cloud part and the online video secrets that brought it into existence. Without thinking, I went ahead and did the same with one of the popular jocks at school that I had been maintaining a general friendship with over the last few weeks for whatever reason. Before I knew it, the secrets that I had engraved into my ankle were no longer my own secrets and I had brought two or three others into this ominous circle. Thankfully, the two or three reactions I received in response didn't make me think they were going to disown me or tell the world what I had just revealed. I laid my head down on my pillow an hour or so later. My head was racing unbearably as I tried to figure out how I was supposed to walk through the halls at school or go to Thursday Club knowing that anyone knew what my ankles looked like under my jeans and could do whatever they wanted with that information now. Sleep did not arrive for quite some time as I unsuccessfully tried to shake the feeling of wanting their responses to be...more. They seemed concerned, but a small voice coming from the corner of my ceiling whispered *I know why you wanted more from them* before I drifted off into a restless sleep.

What started as a confessional text exchange quickly turned into sending texts and online messages to the Leader and the two or three popular kids/athletes every single time I had a bad day or thought the cloud was about to show up. Even when I wouldn't get a response, it was like the dark cloud was following me around and controlling my fingers like a puppet on a string to send more and more texts in addition to the ones that hadn't been replied to. The Leader and the popular jock quickly turned into three which grew into five which grew into a number of online strangers. I was praying and pleading every hour of the day for some kind of intervention before everything started to get out of hand, but it was no use. By whatever means necessary, I *had* to be best friends with them. By now, I had constructed a spider web of people who knew about my sinister self-destructive habit that were hopefully going to keep it to themselves. Not only did I have to worry about what my parents might do if word got around to them, I also had to worry about my social reputation that I had carefully constructed here completely collapsing overnight. What would happen if two of the popular kids somehow became close friends and told each other what I had confided in them? Would they not have anything to do with me if they knew other people knew and it wasn't just them? I had somehow created a spider web that would take one person speaking to the other to completely unravel the entire thing and take everything down with it.

By morning, the cloud would be gone but the texts and private messages would still be lingering in my soul as I slid on jeans once again despite the outside temperature that was rising faster than my anxiety levels with the passing weeks. Another morning trying to make sure my parents didn't stroll past my room and see my wounded ankle. Another week hoping that my brother (when he wasn't staying with Nana and Poppop for extended periods of time) didn't run into someone at the local skate park who somehow knew about my habit enough to share it with him. Another stroll through the hallway and passing someone who I had shared my secret with and pretending like they were nothing more than an acquaintance so I didn't seem obsessed or potentially blow my cover to anyone else. Another week of Thursday Club and avoiding any kind of eye contact with the Leader who had completely stopped replying to any texts I sent and was only coming to every other Club meeting by this point. I tried to focus on whatever lesson they were trying to teach but my mind was wandering off in the distance pondering if I was somehow to blame for his string of absences. To conclude this emotionally-taxing weekly routine, another Sunday morning in church (provided I was able to get off work) and small group to silently beg and plead during prayer times that I would magically stop wanting to look up those videos online, add those strangers on the internet, and send those texts to the popular guys and maybe send a text to one of my close female friends for a change the next time I felt low.

The abhorrent haze continued to show up in my bedroom while continuing to take up more and more space as it grew in size and strength. The stronger the cloud grew, the more strained the friendships I was so heavily focused on seemed to be. After a few more weeks of annoying texts and unrequested confessions whenever I wielded my key, the replies stopped altogether. The new Leader stopped attending Thursday Club, seemingly taking the other two new Leaders in his wake until our high school's Club was barely holding on by a few threads. Any form of social interaction halted between me and the three or four popular athletes I had been sharing my problems with since the cloud had appeared as they all seemed to understandably move on from trying to fix me. However, despite the spider web of social connections I had started to weave this semester, it didn't appear that any of the people I had trapped into being best friends with me had revealed my dangerous little secret to anyone else. That being said, the cloud was still becoming more and more of an issue whether I was sharing its actions with anyone or not.

Not surprisingly, each time I fell victim to my own hands, the cloud grew even more until it felt like it was detaching from my bedroom wall and following me everywhere. The forehead tattoo stung constantly while the ball-and-chain wrapped around my normal ankle grew denser and heavier. With the fear of people seeing my forehead and the burden of dragging around the weight of my secrets that were starting to pile up, I could hardly take the added stress of feeling like the cloud was hovering above or behind my every step. Assuming it would somehow be unable to follow me into church, I asked the girl I had accidentally stabbed in third grade only to fall in love with last summer if I could come to the next available church service of any kind. However, I still felt its presence almost breathing on the back of my neck like an ominous, dense dew even after I stepped through the large front doors of the church building. Unable to focus on anything being taught that night, I knew I could still give Thursday Club a shot to see if there was any possible place I could go without feeling weighed down by my own ominous shadow. I pulled into the familiar gravel parking lot of the doctor's office and made my way inside. While it seemed all good so far, I immediately noticed just how few of the other regulars were here. With my entrance, there were actually only four of us instead of the usual 20-30. I made eye contact with one of the only remaining Leaders that I was pretty decent friends with and I could tell this was not about to be a very fun Club meeting.

Between the emotional rollercoaster I had been on this semester and the overwhelming dread that had manifested itself into some psychophysical form, the last thing I was expecting to hear was that our Thursday Club was over. The night's meeting could not have been more abnormal as this Leader went on to explain that they couldn't sustain the necessary logistics to keep our Club running, especially with the resignation of the three new Leaders that lasted all of two months here. They let us know that we could meet on a more one-on-one level every now and then to discuss life and our journey with Christianity and/or we could attend the Lenoir City Thursday Club if we wanted to. I knew this kind of announcement was inevitable with the loss of almost every single Leader, but something about the timing of this announcement felt like the final rug of my life being pulled from underneath my feet. As everyone started making their way out the door and towards their cars, I could feel the tears starting to well up in my eyes and a sense of urgency mixed with adrenaline pulsing through my veins. Without pausing to analyze, I called out the name of the now-former Leader to ask him if he had a second before heading back to his house. He seemed a little caught off guard but quickly accepted the request once he saw the importance painted on my face.

With everyone else completely out of earshot, I took a deep breath and started to explain what was going on in my head. Completely out of my element, I let loose that I had tried to bond with one of the new Leaders since he seemed so popular and it was easier to talk to someone closer to my age. He nodded his head in understanding as I pivoted away from wanting to be close to him and towards the fact that I completely opened up to that Leader about the feelings of depression, hopelessness, and constant stress. Something deep within my mind told me not to tiptoe around the subject, so I took another set of deep breaths until I let slip the habit I had formed with my keys and ankle that I had also confessed to that former Leader only to have him ignore my messages and then vanish from Thursday Club altogether. My stomach began to twist into knots and my brain immediately dammed up the channel between my brain and my mouth before I let slip the internet secrets that had contributed to the forehead tattoo and ankle chain that was, much to my dismay, becoming more and more tangible by the day. There were a few moments of icy silence while the other Leader processed everything I had just unloaded on him. Much to my surprise, he didn't stand up and immediately flee the building and instead wrapped his arms around me in a caring embrace. A few moments later, he was explaining to me that it was important that I share this news with my parents instead of keeping it bottled up or trying to determine which of my friends at school/church/Thursday Club was best to tell next.

Knowing I couldn't keep the secret for much longer anyway, especially with how powerful the dark haze was growing with each burned bridge in my social network, I agreed. In the days following this spontaneous confession, I did everything possible to try and back out of telling my mother all the way up to the point where the Thursday Club Leader was sitting in my bedroom helping me call her in to talk. He urged me to just be myself and assured me that everything was going to be just fine since mothers will always love their son no matter what. His words of encouragement lingered in my mind as I turned my head to face my mother who was now standing inquisitively in my doorway. I opened my mouth to speak but not a single sound escaped my lips. My eyes started to well up and I immediately threw the blanket over my head. Suddenly, the entire hour that he spent hyping me up to reveal this dark secret had completely vanished. No matter how ready I felt only mere moments ago, I couldn't bring myself to say a single word whatsoever let alone something as grim as admitting that I had been harming myself with keys. All I could bring myself to do was hide out of sight underneath this blanket and wait for someone else to break the silence for me.

After what felt like decades, my newfound friend began explaining to my now-very-confused mother that something serious had happened. My eyes wandered over in the direction of where he was sitting on the other side of the blanket covering my head as he explained that he had only recently been told but that there have been a number of people I had been talking with who had been trying their best. He delicately told her that I had hit a very rough spot with everything that was going on at school with having to find myself at another new school and the chaos that came with having such difficult dynamics with my family. Sticking to the main points I had discussed wanting to share with her before I found myself unable to speak, he explained that there was no reason to freak out and that everything was pretty much under control now. He assured her that this discussion was simply meant to explain what had happened and how I had been feeling but that I had gotten through the worst of it and was on the way to recovery. After laying the groundwork, I heard him pause and wait for me to jump in and when I didn't pull the blanket from over my face, told my mother that I had gone through a brief period of cutting my own ankle.

Not wanting my brain to create hypothetical images of what my mother's face might look like, I immediately removed the blanket I had draped over myself once the final words had been released into the air. I expected my mother to break down in some kind of way, to run over to the bed and take me into her arms. I expected her to be shocked but thankful I had told her and that I had gotten through the worst part of it, even if it had been without her. I wanted her to congratulate me for coming clean and hug me for an hour while telling me everything was going to be okay. However, when my eyes made the arduous journey over to make contact with hers, the face that was staring back at me was nothing of the sorts. Instead, I was met with an icy stare and a mouth that dropped open in horror and a type of almost disgust that I had never seen on her face before. The voice that erupted from her lips was fueled with anger and laced with venom as she spoke to me as if I had broken one of the household rules. "You did *WHAT?!*" she exclaimed and took a step towards me in the bedroom. "What the hell do you mean you've been *cutting* yourself?" she continued, each word dripping with disappointment, anger, and disdain.

My mother took another step forward into my bedroom, the somber light from my ceiling shining down on a woman I could barely recognize. In the handful of seconds that had passed, the woman standing in front of me wasn't the person who tucked me in at night or played with my hair when I had trouble falling asleep for so many years. She wasn't the person who took me with her to the movies to see all of her favorite rom-coms or the one who let me stay home from school to watch soap operas with her all day. She wasn't the person I ran to the moment something went awry when Nana wasn't close by. Instead of the parent who let me drive to school before I had my actual license, a dictator now stood in front of me towering over my bed. Her words were menacing as she scolded me for what I had just confessed as if I had stolen candy from the gas station by our house in elementary school or plagiarized an essay. The woman who was supposed to listen to my worries and administer the perfect words to calm me down was nowhere to be seen. In her place was an angry, disgruntled woman who made sure I knew that I was in big trouble for what I had done to myself at my lowest of lows. Eventually, as she realized we were not the only two people in the room, she made her exit after telling me we would discuss this further in the coming days. I looked over at the Leader, a hopeless expression forming on my face as he nodded in agreement.

I gave him a parting hug in the driveway and told him that I'd keep him posted with any updates before I found myself sitting in my pediatrician's office the next day after one of the most restless nights of my life. Following in the same footsteps as Lilley from the night before, my doctor scolded me for the decisions that had led up to this unfortunate meeting. Once again, I attempted to explain that I had confessed this in the aftermath stages and it wasn't an issue I was overwhelmed with any longer but neither of them would hear a word. My eyes eventually glazed over as I stared at the wall in front of me. With someone reinforcing her stance on everything, thoughts of medicines, therapies, and even facility treatment began to fill the spaces of the uncomfortably chilled office. I wanted to speak up but I knew it would be an aimless venture as they further convinced themselves that I was a danger to myself and that I needed drastic, immediate medical attention. By sitting in stubborn silence instead of acknowledging the ideas that were bouncing off the tacky walls in the room, I managed to escape the medical office with a simple therapist referral instead of something more dramatic. I already knew how the therapy session was likely going to go, but I knew I had to agree to *something* to right this horrible wrong that I had apparently inflicted our household's immensely respectable name.

The hour-long visit to the stranger's office crept by as painfully slow as I imagined it would. The therapist seemed nice enough and deeply intelligent, but after seeing how my own mother reacted to hearing the news of my self-harming habit, I was not very inclined to open up to a complete stranger. I skated through the session by saying as few words as possible while staring at the various patterns of the carpet flooring until I was released from her captivity. The words and answers I did decide to give must have convinced her that I was in a stable enough frame of mind because she didn't suggest a follow-up appointment or sending me off to a psychological facility despite how much Lilley had likely already planned to do. The car ride home was plagued with awkward, tense silence until we finally pulled up to the house. I walked through the front door and went directly to my room without a sound, closing the door behind me. To pour salt on the wound, Lilley came by shortly to open my door and let me know that I wouldn't be allowed to close my bedroom door for a while and that she'd be checking in regularly until "I got back to normal" with a concerned tone in her voice that made my blood boil.

The (only) silver lining of my parents' reaction to my confession was that it gave me the proper motivation to keep the dark cloud at bay for the foreseeable future. While their concerned questions and check-ins only lasted for a week or two after the required therapy session, I knew that if they happened to notice a fresh cut on my ankle again, I would be immediately shipped off to a prison or some psychological institution. Instead of giving that possibility any fuel, I threw my focus into staying as busy as possible in whatever capacity possible. I began trying to mend the friendships I had damaged during my rock bottom. As soon as any extra shifts became available at work I would pick them up. When work wasn't an option, I threw myself into small groups at church or any church-related activities whatsoever. When those options fell through, I was doing my absolute best to spend any free time with friends or driving around town with the windows down or something. Worst case scenario, I spent more time learning as much as I could about the various social media platforms that were becoming more and more intertwined with society. It wasn't an easy transition by any means, but after a few weeks of work I began feeling more and more like my normal self again as I took back the reigns of my life.

Right on cue, my brother broke the news to our parents that he was in a pretty serious relationship with a new girlfriend. While this wouldn't typically be groundbreaking news, the part where the woman he was dating was still in high school and pregnant with someone else's child was the exact distraction I needed to finally shift their focus away from me for a while. As with any significant event in the household's past, concern for my sinful self-sabotage had been replaced with the next significant event that came along. Lingering stares at my ankle were suddenly replaced with lingering stares at the growing belly of Rob's new significant other. Worries about whether or not I was going to suddenly relapse into a dark depression vanished into new concern over whether or not his girlfriend's home was stable enough to support a newborn. Moments later and the idea of her moving in with us for the remainder of the pregnancy were being discussed. As with most discussions, Lilley explained that this is what felt right and so this is exactly what was going to be happening. A week or two later would find Rob's lover bringing all of her bags into the house whether there was room for another person (technically two) or not. Not only did this mean I was getting a new roommate in an already-crowded house, but I would also be sharing the school hallways with my brother's new girlfriend who was carrying a child who wasn't his but was going to apparently be living with us for the foreseeable future.

Naturally, I threw myself even further into whatever social opportunities that allowed me to escape the confines of the house now that I was no longer being kept under Mom and Dad's magnifying glass at all times. When I wasn't at school or at work, I was texting any and every friend in my phone to see if they wanted to drive around or play video games at their house. If I wasn't hanging out at the fast food restaurant (on the clock or off at this point) or at a friend's place, I was going to small group sessions or sign language practice for an upcoming performance for the main Sunday morning service in a month or so. I was slowly feeling more and more at home with this church and the close group of girls from school that encouraged me to come back each week. After they convinced me to start practicing with them to do a sign language performance to a religious song without me somehow having a panic attack at each practice, I knew I had made a good decision. However, even with the distractions I was putting myself through, from friends to church to social media to those private moments in my bathroom that still plagued my entire existence, having someone who was practically a stranger move into the house took an emotional toll on everyone inside.

As it turns out, I only had to worry about sharing the hallways at school for a brief period of time. She went into labor about a month or so after moving in which apparently gets you out of school for a while after a lengthy hospital stay. Everything happened very quickly and all at once until suddenly I was being woken up one morning by Lilley who immediately placed a newborn child into my arms. I had no idea how I was supposed to hold an infant, but somehow in that moment everything felt alright for a change. In that moment, with this little girl nestled in my lanky arms, I wasn't recovering from being at rock bottom a month or two ago. I wasn't a weird kid who still sent friend requests online to men I've never met before. I wasn't a teenager sitting in church during the day and hiding from his own internet browser history by night. For those few minutes, the dark cloud and tattoo/shackle simply ceased to exist. The only thing that existed or mattered right now was right there in front of me being calmly rocked back and forth. However, the moments that this feeling lasted could have fit in the tiny palms of her innocent hands before time seemed to catch itself back up. With what seemed like a single blink, chaos immediately began to flow into the house once again.

After the angelic first meeting of this newborn child, Lilley immediately started to question whether or not Rob's girlfriend was the best fit as a parent. With Rob not being the biological father, she also raised the question of whether or not it was his place to be supporting the two of them especially with him still living at home with us. Arguments became a normal occurrence once again, shouting matches filling the quiet of the house at all times. Sometimes they were between my parents. Other times they were between Lilley and Rob's girlfriend. Rob made appearances in as many as he could fit himself into until even Poppop Luke came over every once in a while to chime in. After what felt like ages, Lilley decided to gather us all together to have another family discussion. Sticking with her normal methods, this discussion involved what she felt was needed to be done in order to remedy this tense situation we had all found ourselves in. Naturally, I didn't have much input into this discussion since I fled the house or kept myself barricaded in my room anytime one of these battles broke out. I wasn't sure what was really going on or why everyone was on edge with each other, but long story short my mother suggested Rob's girlfriend move back in with her family in Oak Ridge. However, before wrapping up this discussion, she made sure to emphasize that the baby should stay behind with us.

With everything moving so quickly and suddenly, I wasn't exactly sure how many conversations were had or how thoroughly they were discussed before Rob's girlfriend moved out of our house. With the countless screaming matches between my mother and her, it was pretty clear that she wouldn't be returning for quite some time. Rob decided to end things with her shortly afterwards when he realized just how complicated everything was getting and how much their compatibility was clouded with doubt. However, the most shocking and spontaneous event amongst all of these was the fact that I was apparently a big brother now. We had another family meeting and instead of telling us that we were going to be packing up and moving to yet another city/school, Lilley told us we were officially adopting the little infant. I wasn't sure how they managed to convince Rob's ex-girlfriend to legally agree to this adoption or how it was going to be funded but that didn't seem to be a worry that was brought into the discussion. Overnight, I became the middle child of the household. Even with all the chaos and how sudden everything felt, though, something about adding this precious gem into our family just felt right.

Getting my final grades and walking back out of the front doors of the school once again as sophomore year came to a close, I couldn't help but feel an overwhelming sense of pride in myself. Each footstep on the linoleum tile in the hallways and the firm sidewalk outside toward my car brought another memory and/or challenge that I had overcome in the last year or so. One step and I was back in that restaurant after agreeing to meet with Ryan and Erin for the first time since I was six and spending the next year reviving a relationship with them. A few more steps and a few "have a great summer"s and I was discovering that Lilley had drained my bank account behind my back. Another step or two came the overwhelming dread of realizing I had tried to force so many different popular guys at school (and across the country online) to be my best friend. From there, I quickly revisited the free-fall I had taken to rock bottom as my social habits and attempts to hide the forehead tattoo and ball-and-chain on my ankle resulted in actual attacks on my own ankle. One final step as I approached the side of my car parked on the side of the school brought forth the realization that I had somehow picked myself up from these pits of the rock bottom. Sure, I had confessed (almost) everything to my parents and dealt with the repercussions of that, but the wounds healed up without any major scarring for the most part and my social reputation was still mostly intact. With the semester and the gut-wrenching rollercoaster of a year growing smaller and smaller in my rearview mirror, I made my way home to play with my new baby sister.

With classes out of the way, my schedule quickly became shifts at McDonalds, playing with the newest branch of my dysfunctional family tree, any and every possible church event/service, and crying myself to sleep when religion didn't erase my dark secrets. The weeks flew by now that time apparently moves faster with age. Shifts at the front lobby and drive-thru window blended into tickle attacks to make my baby sister giggle which then transitioned into church pew after church pew and then into more bridge jumps down into the suspicious waters by the outskirts of town. Before I knew it, it was time to help the church out with their Vacation Bible School, a weeklong event they put on every summer as a way of entertaining and educating the youths of the community.

However, by the end of the week during the preacher's final sermon I was struck with a feeling of desperation. He was going on about how we need to listen to the calls from above and follow through with them if we felt compelled to chase after salvation. If we didn't want to spend eternity burning in hell, we needed to save ourselves. Out of nowhere, my mind was flooded with feelings of desperation that forced my legs to rise out of my pew and move one foot in front of the other on the way to the front of the church. Once there, I threw myself down on the altar and tearfully pleaded silently for whoever was listening to heal me. Surely this all-powerful entity would hear me now and finally get rid of the thoughts and urges I was feeling anytime I passed one of the jocks at school or saw a stranger's profile picture online or anytime I was left to my own devices for too long.

A few moments later I felt someone's arm embrace me from behind and then another arm guiding me to a room behind the altar. Away from the crowded service room, I sat down with the youth leader and my close friend (yep, the girl I accidentally stabbed). The youth leader took control of the conversation and asked me if I was willing to put in the work that came along with being saved and if it was something I was going to be taking seriously. He pressed further and asked what it was that compelled me to make my way to the front of the church. Paying special attention to my words so that I didn't reveal too much, I started to reveal some of the key points of the last few months. However, he cut me off pretty quickly and said, "Oh, the cuts on your ankle that you put there? I already noticed those a while back." which was enough to leave me stunned and speechless. While he made sure to follow-up the statement with something about my past not defining the person I was at this very moment, I couldn't help but wonder why he hadn't approached me at any point if he had noticed I was feeling low enough to put myself in harm's way. I decided to brush off the comment and lean into the conversation in front of me and all the options that were being discussed. A blink of the eye or two later and I was calling Nana to excitedly share that I was "saved" and baptized in a pool in front of the whole church.

Unfortunately, the holy water that I was submerged in to signify my salvation was either a dull batch or one that was designed to have a delayed reaction. I was on cloud nine that morning but within a few days, the dark cloud reappeared to follow me around all day until it got me alone that night to get me onto the internet and sneak away to the bathroom for the millionth time. While my youth leader didn't know about this particular habit of mine, I kept repeating our conversation over and over again in my head where he mentioned how much of a commitment this new life would be and how much effort it would take. I just needed to try and stay focused, ignore the cloud, and if I fell short in the meantime, attend more church events. Thankfully, an opportunity was right around the corner for me to not only surround myself with more religion but have a nice escape before I had to start mentally preparing for another semester. Despite our school's Thursday Club having fallen apart, the Leader who had helped me make the confession to my mother told me I could easily go with the Thursday Club Summer Camp that was in a few weeks. I agreed to do a bunch of random yard work and other various chores that took care of some of the fees and then a community fundraiser helped cover even more of it. After that was all factored in, I somehow managed to convince Lilley and Dad to cover the small remainder of the cost.

Upon boarding the bus and having my phone taken for the duration of the entire week, I quickly discovered I was the only male student from my school attending this trip. There were a handful of girls that I was friends with but clearly I wasn't allowed to room with them once we got there. Therefore, I was placed in a cabin with the Lenoir City guys that I had met maybe once or twice when some of us started transitioning to their Thursday Club after ours crumbled. I figured we wouldn't be spending that much time in the cabin but that theory was quickly debunked when I walked into the cabin to see several of the guys running around without a stitch of clothing on. Apparently they had all been on the same football team since elementary school so showers were a pretty public thing and a practical stranger from their rival high school wasn't going to change that. I immediately diverted my eyes to the floor before anyone could accuse me of staring at the wrong parts. The last thing I needed was another school full of people possibly seeing the secrets branded on my forehead.

Bags were unpacked into these cabins in whatever state we were in before everyone met up for the first meal. There were several different Thursday Clubs from all over the place so everyone began mingling and exchanging numbers and social media usernames within the first few hours. The week flew as I did my best to mingle with the other guys in my cabin while simultaneously doing my best not to look at any of them naked, something that proved to be very difficult considering they walked around naked 75 percent of the time. There were hikes and zip lines and various lake activities throughout the day to keep everyone occupied and entertained. The nights typically consisted of some form of concert and/or religious sermon before we all returned to our cabins to resume the discussions with our Leaders until it was time for lights out. By the end of the week, I finally opened up to the cabin full of strangers and gave a little insight into some of my struggles with my family chaos but decided at the last minute to leave out the ankle issue and the whole "sometimes I look up videos of guys on the internet and by sometimes I mean often and since middle school" since they didn't seem to be the type of guys who would handle that conversation very well (especially after I saw them naked all week even if it was against my will). While it was a pretty fun week with some good heart-to-heart conversations, I couldn't wait to get my cell phone back and head home to start getting ready for Junior year.

There was something quite different about walking through the tall front doors of the school this time around. The sensation was subtle, but the first footsteps on the cold linoleum tiles as Juniors felt recognizably more confident and powerful. There was no denying this was still the same yee-haw town in the middle of nowhere, but it felt as if we had earned our place at the top ranks for the first time. We were already friends with the now-sophomore class, but there was a certain look of intimidation that the incoming freshmen that only strengthened the confidence we were feeling. There was even a handful of faculty/staff members that we were on a first-name basis with (whenever nobody important was around of course). The energy buzzing throughout the hallways carried us through the first few weeks of another new semester with another round of classes with another round of social climbing. Social media was completely synonymous with everyday life and required scrolling at least every other hour as tweets were sent and selfies were posted to let our online networks know that another academic year had indeed kicked off. It felt refreshing to be surrounded by other kids once again, especially now that I wasn't worried about which ones I had confessed my depression to the night before against their will.

It took less than a month, however, before I walked past a group of football players with my friends and heard the word "faggot" spoken just loud enough so that I'd hear. My heart fell into the pits of my stomach as they erupted into laughter. The knots in my stomach were infused with fiery rage and embarrassment, but I pretended to ignore the group of idiots and quickly resumed walking with my friends. Sure, this wasn't the first time something like this had happened since I moved here, but it wasn't something I was expecting to still hear now that we were all Juniors and rising to the end of our high school journey. Sometimes it was blatantly calling me that word. Sometimes it was rumors circulating through the halls that I was only best friends with all the pretty girls because I'm secretly gay. Other times it was the feeling you get when you walk past a group of people and you just *know* you were the person they were just gossiping about. There were even the occasional posts online plainly asking if I was gay or actually into girls but had no game at all. Church had been doing a decent job at suppressing those rumors, but I still felt the need every few months to make some kind of online post venting about how absurd all the speculation is just because I don't "treat women the same way the football players do" or something to that effect. However, even with all these efforts in motion, the dark cloud from my bedroom was seeming to take up more and more residence inside my mind. The tiny little thought cloud was constantly floating there, telling me that maybe people really were starting to see my forehead and ankle chain after all.

A few weeks into the semester, my boss told me that too many people had quit and they were going to need me to start picking up more shifts. She started explaining that she had no choice and that I was one of the stronger team members, but all I was hearing was that I wouldn't really be able to attend all the church services and I might not even get to go to Thursday Club once it began again up at Lenoir City. Not knowing how to say no to any kind of authority figure other than my parents, who were feeling more and more like strangers by the week, I nodded and immediately barricaded myself in my room after my shift. I knew my friends and the leaders would understand having to make my boss happy, but a part of me was terrified of being overwhelmed by the dark cloud once again. What if my church attendance was the only thing keeping it from reappearing? What if the moment I miss a service, the whole world suddenly sees the tattoo on my forehead revealing my internet search habits. I know it wasn't realistic, but my mind couldn't stop replaying the scene where my search history was put on display for everyone to see the night of the first key incident. There were ebbs and flows on how often I fell into temptation and looked up those kinds of predominantly-male flicks but what if falling out of my religious routine completely sent me flying off the rails? I couldn't help but imagine what Lilley would do if she caught me at another low point...

Suddenly an idea flickered into view inside my head that might just resolve my entire issue while simultaneously improving my social ranking even further. I shot out of bed and flung myself into the office chair in front of my computer and pulled up one of my social media pages as fast as I could, as if the idea was suddenly going to vanish out of my brain if I didn't accomplish it this very instant. A few million clicks and keyboard smashes later, I rolled back in the chair with an enormous sense of relief and a halfway-exhausted sigh. In about twenty minutes, I had created an online group that I aptly named Prayer Requests. From there, despite being the group's creator, I made any participating member able to post to the feed. A quick bio would quickly indicate to any confused member that the group's intended purpose was sharing prayer requests of any kind and receiving feedback that other members had read their requests and were offering up their support. Pleased with the overall layout, functions, and bio, I added everyone on my online friends list to the page before logging off and heading to bed. Since I wasn't able to physically attend church in person, I was going to create my own version of church through social media to keep all my demons at bay while helping others too.

The next day at school, I paraded through the hallways like I was a King who had just taken back the throne from an evil dictator. A handful of people came up to tell me how good an idea Prayer Requests was and how they were excited to see it take off. All I had done was create an online space for anyone to give their religious testimony, vent about life, request support, and anything in between but it had started to feel as if I had created some kind of new community that people were excited to be a part of. Of course, one or two of the less-friendly jocks of the school approached me to ask how to remove themselves from the page altogether. However, I brushed off their hostility and kindly showed them the wonder that was technology and how to remove yourself from an online forum and/or adjust your notification settings and continued about my victory tour through the halls. All of a sudden, the guilt I was feeling about having to miss all of the church services started to vanish as I discovered a way to stay connected to the religion that was going to inevitably heal my brain even if I wasn't physically present in a pew. I attended Thursday Club in Lenoir City, tried to attend actual services if I could get the day off work, managed Prayer Requests and my own personal social medias, and still pleaded every night. The abysmal haze, tattooed secrets, and hefty concrete ball attached to my leg would be taken care of in no time!

A few weeks passed before I could even realize what was happening, Prayer Requests had grown outside the confines of East Tennessee and branched out into surrounding cities and states. My friends were inviting their friends to join and then those friends invited their church members to join and so on. Even a few teachers and staff members at school stopped me in the hallways to share their support for the group and reveal they had heard it circulating around their church and social groups. I began checking the page multiple times throughout the day to watch the number of members and posts continually rising until it felt like I had somehow created something really substantial. About a week later, I was told I was even going to be featured in the new school newspaper as their first Student of the Month feature. After the most awkward photoshoot in the main hallway by the vending machine (?) and a few questions about how it felt to have created Prayer Requests and tweet jokes and host bonfire parties, I got to share with my parents and Nana the article as they inflated my already-exploding ego.

After chatting for a little bit, I realized the girl who helped put the article together actually lived a short walk down the street from my house. Naturally, I invited myself to hang out there one afternoon and immediately fell in love with her entire household. From the brutally honest parents to the chaotic toddler that terrorized everything and everyone in his path, I was in love. It only took a few afternoons to realize this was another family where the parents actually knew things about the kids and were emotionally invested in their lives, classes, friends, and dreams. Therefore, like always, I spent as much time as possible in their living room instead of my own and before long, I even labeled their place with the nickname "The Safehouse" for the jokingly-hostile, actually-loving environment. The Safehouse quickly added itself to my escapism routines until I found myself only being at my own house to sleep and play with my baby sister. There was a brief moment where it felt surreal to be filling my days with Thursday Club, school, a job, The Safehouse, and anything and everything that wasn't my house when only a few short years ago my bedroom and my action figures and imagination was my only source of happiness. However, I quickly battled the surreality by reminding myself I had built my social confidence from nothing and it wasn't my fault that I was starting to realize that the dysfunction and chaos of my household wasn't the status quo for everyone else.

While I still missed our original Thursday Club, particularly the club we had before the new Leaders came in and ghosted after we (I) opened up to them, Lenoir City's Thursday Club was actually kind of an upgrade. They had twice the number of students every week, a bunch of popular guys and beautiful girls, *and* their drive-in restaurant where everyone went afterwards wasn't caught selling meth out of the back. It also gave me the opportunity to start meeting new people and continue building onto my social empire, even if they *were* students at our rival school. After a few weeks of regular attendance, I had even convinced one of the prettiest girls to be my girlfriend while we were at the drive-in restaurant waiting for our milkshakes. I could hardly contain my excitement and was practically giggling the whole way home before running inside to update my relationship status on social media so that everyone could know I had a pretty girlfriend. Surely between Prayer Requests and a beautiful girlfriend, those rumors would stop lingering around the hallways that Chase was weird and/or might like boys. Of course, I could almost feel the weight of the abysmal dark cloud pressing down on my shoulders as it hovered above me as I clicked the *Save Changes* button on my profile. I quickly prayed for it to finally be extinguished so I could carry on with my life, finish high school, and marry my newfound girlfriend. Please let this all be gone by the time high school is over. The cloud. The tattoos. The ball and chain. All of it. I needed to be normal.

My girlfriend and I spent the first week texting back and forth nonstop into the early hours of the morning. We couldn't get enough of all the nonsense high school romantics talk about with each other and quickly realized how much we had in common and how much we liked each other. We talked during classes. We talked while I was taking orders at the drive-thru window even though my managers would always get pissed when they caught me. We held hands at the next Thursday Club meeting at her high school. We threw whipped cream from our milkshakes onto each other's noses. I even got a few congratulatory comments from some of the jocks at school that I would normally expect to call me a slur. Everything was falling into place and that I had somehow gotten through the worst times and was so close to approaching a new golden shore of life.

Whether I was ready for it or not, our new relationship hit a devastating rough patch the very first weekend in the sense that she stopped replying to my texts. I kept checking my phone Friday night during my shift, but her name hadn't popped up on my screen once since I clocked in. About 30 minutes before I left to head home, I checked my phone again but nothing had changed. Naturally, I sent about four texts back-to-back by this point but it was clear that she had no intention of texting me back whatsoever. My mind spiraled hysterically as I sat in my room after work trying to contemplate why she was ignoring me. Had someone told her I had tried to force a former Thursday Club Leader and some of the jocks at my school to be my best friends? Maybe someone found out I had attacked my own ankle for a few months and told her that she was dating a freak. Of course, the scenario my mind was conjuring up and flooding my entire brain with was much worse. I couldn't stop panicking at the idea that someone somewhere had somehow discovered my internet search history and let her know that her boyfriend might not like her in the way she thought I did. Before I could even attempt to extinguish this hypothetical situation, my eyes were welling up with tears before I drifted off into an endless night of restless sleep.

When I still hadn't heard back from my girlfriend Saturday evening, I went over to the Safehouse after work to discuss my options. They knew something was wrong the moment I walked through the doors, immediately ducking to narrowly avoid a flying toy truck that the toddler had thrown at me. After a quick summary explaining that we had been in love a few days ago but she stopped responding to my texts for over 24 hours now, everyone in the house assured me that I deserved better. A few moments passed as I mulled over their suggestions and pep talks. I hesitated a few moments before ultimately deciding they were probably right and I wasn't overreacting to the situation whatsoever. I took a deep breath, typed out the breakup text, and hit send. While I was devastated that such a perfect relationship had come crashing down after its first week, I couldn't help but feel a sense of relief that I had been the one to officially pull the plug. I was unsure of why she wasn't texting me back, but me sending the breakup text instead of vice versa definitely gave me the upper hand if the reasons were anything like what my brain had conjured up to explain everything.

The next afternoon, I finally saw her name come across my phone screen which caused my heart to unexpectedly fall into my stomach. After unlocking my phone right away to read that she had been at a church retreat and they took her phone for the duration of the weekend trip, I felt like a complete moron. I was going to ask why she hadn't just let me know this beforehand, but by the time I had convinced my fingers to start typing she had sent another text saying it was spontaneous and she didn't even have time to let her parents know. We sent a few messages back and forth for a little bit, but it was very obvious that the damage had already been done with my break-up text I sent before finding out what was going on. Even with the cloud being held at bay, it had still somehow made its way into my head and caused me to sabotage yet another relationship. Updating my social media relationship status once again felt like squeezing a lemon over a paper cut with the "we can definitely still be friends" text being the salt that was added on top.

Celebrating my 17th birthday with another bonfire gathering in my grandfather's backyard didn't feel quite as special as the milestone 16th party. However, I couldn't have been more excited to see how much more the attendance had grown from the previous year with the friendships I had developed and the new ones I had gained from Lenoir City. Of course, it would have been nice to have celebrated it with a girlfriend but at least I had somewhat gotten in the good graces of some of the football players that would have never attended now that they saw me date a pretty girl (even if it was for only a week or two). For the fifth or sixth year in a row, however, I blew out the candles with the voice in my head wishing desperately to wake up the next morning with a completely healed brain. A brain that wasn't so impulsively eager to become best friends with the good-looking popular guys at school no matter what for no apparent reason. A set of eyes that didn't have to be told every single second to look straight ahead or at the ceiling every time I walked into a locker room after gym class. A set of hands that didn't type that certain website or those certain keywords into the search bar whenever they were alone in the sinful, dark corners of the internet. And lastly, a set of parents that didn't seem so chaotic, dysfunctional, and the polar opposite of any family I spent time with outside of the house.

Unfortunately, I woke up every morning for the next few weeks only to see the *I sometimes watch videos of men online* tattoo as bold as ever on my forehead looking back at me in the mirror. Splashing water on my face each morning helped it disappear for a little bit, but it returned the following morning every time no matter how much I prayed the night before. The steel chain and iron orb attached to my ankle started to increase in weight until I was convinced everyone around me could hear it dragging behind me on the linoleum tile or notice me struggling to walk like a normal person with the resistance it was putting against my leg. With classes being pretty easy this semester, my brain quickly became swarmed with suspicion that everyone around me was close to discovering my secrets and that it was only a matter of time before someone figured it out. From there, they would inevitably share it across the entire school and state and the small social kingdom I had built from scratch would catch flame and become a pile of ashes within 24 hours. The worst part about these thoughts is how unpredictable they were and how quickly they flooded in, one after the other. Walking down the hallways and laughing at something one of my friends had said would all of a sudden be eradicated with *your laugh is suspicious* and *you're walking with too many girls right now* and other hopeless feelings that would immediately turn my stomach into knots with no warning.

One afternoon after school, my stomach churned for another reason when Lilley said that we all needed to have yet another family discussion. With Rob jumping back and forth from living here and living with Nana in Middle Tennessee, this discussion only featured my parents and me. I hesitantly sat down on the fireplace across from where they were both sitting and braced myself for whatever was coming. Within the first couple of words out of my mother's mouth, I detected a tone I knew all too well after these 17 years under her roof. A fire much more aggressive than the ones I threw parties with began to form in my chest as I pictured myself having to pack up my bedroom into a million boxes for the millionth time. The arsenal in my mind was stocking itself full of words to hurl towards my parents to let them know I was absolutely not going to be uprooting myself and moving to another new school when I was almost to the finish line as it is. However, the artillery was paused and forced to stand down almost as quickly as it had equipped itself. Lilley must have detected the immense anger and tension building inside me because she very quickly assured me that we weren't going to be moving to a new school system at all. In fact, we were moving right next door into Poppop Luke's house to live with him.

Anger quickly transitioned into confusion as my parents explained we were just doing a simple move from this house to the house next door to help my grandfather care for himself and the home since it was just him over there now. The cancer treatments last year had been effective from what we could tell, but there was a sneaking suspicion in our household that he was still secretly smoking and drinking and hiding it from his doctors. Of course, it made it harder to hide such behavior from your doctors when part of your treatment staff is living in the same house which is probably what inspired this move. On top of keeping a closer eye on Poppop Luke, we would also apparently be saving money by not having to pay rent in exchange for helping to keep the house clean and operational. While it was inconvenient to start packing up the house once again, it wasn't too much of a burden to bear considering it wasn't going to result in me being The New Kid once again. That didn't mean I didn't pack up and tape the boxes with resentment painted all over my face anyway.

We carried over all the boxes and furniture into their new rooms and I immediately noticed something seemed off. I walked through the front door and noticed the main floor bedroom had seemingly been cleared of MiMi's belongings that very morning. A vast majority of the things that were previously there were now down in the basement. On top of the feeling of hastiness that lingered throughout the home, Poppop Luke wasn't there. Like the lightbulb string I had to pull down in the basement area, I quickly remembered that he was gone on a fishing trip that he took every year with his brother and friends. I couldn't help but wonder why we were in such a hurry to move and why he wasn't...Oh god. Were we...surely not. My mother's made some wildly reckless decisions before but even *that* was crossing the line for her. I brushed my suspicions aside and moved the boxes into my new room in the recently-finished basement bedroom. I specifically demanded that I get this room since it was the furthest away from the chaos upstairs and gave me a quick and easy escape route through the back door anytime I wanted to leave without being interrogated. I went into hyper drive to unpack as much as possible before falling asleep on the freshly-assembled bed in the corner of my new bedroom.

Screaming and shouting woke me up in a frenzied panic as I tried to figure out what the hell was happening upstairs. It took all of sixty seconds of listening in on the altercation for my suspicions to be confirmed. I wasn't sure if Dad was involved in anything at all, but Lilley definitely moved us into Poppop Luke's house without running it by him. We moved into someone else's house while they were on vacation without actually getting a firm confirmation that we were allowed to do so. Oh my god we were parasites. I wasn't sure if I should go upstairs to try and calm the storm down or just steer clear of the chaos like usual. Realizing the storm would likely calm itself down all on its own, I decided to keep my distance. I walked off the stairway towards my room to throw on some clothes. The Safehouse was going to live up to its name for the millionth time as I slid out the back door to let things fizzle out on their own. By this point, I bypassed even knocking on their front door and walked inside and started venting my frustrations to anyone who was awake and willing to listen, even if it was just the chaotic toddler.

Somewhere between getting older and spending more and more time outside the house with other families, I realized that the only person who was genuinely the same person my whole life was Nana and Poppop. Within the last few years, my mother was practically unrecognizable from the comforting, warm spirit I saw her as growing up. Rob was somehow easier to get along with compared to the evil demon I had to defend myself from during my entire childhood. Dad went from silent dictator to best friend to silent statue and everywhere in between over the years. Other Dad was back in my life and couldn't be more of an emotional (and sometimes financial) support system even after being separated from each other for so long. Everything and everyone was seeming to change so much and I couldn't (or wouldn't) process it all. Except for Nana. Through this emotional venting session, I realized she was always the same glowing beacon of light throughout any situation no matter who or what was involved. At least I still had her and Poppop. I still had Grams and Gramps too, although Lilley had made it pretty clear to us over the years that they didn't care for us too much. But could that verdict really be trusted now that I was starting to get old enough to think for myself? Was anything I was made to believe growing up actually true at this point?

My phone buzzed in my pocket to interrupt my train of thought that I was spewing directly out into the Safehouse living room. Shit. It was Mom. I hesitated a moment before accepting the call, deeply fearing the consequence if I hit the ignore button. She still sounded a bit upset but the fury wasn't laced in between her words that way it had been about an hour or so ago. She politely asked if I could come back home and help her with some more of the unpacking. Feeling somehow guilty from her tone, as if I was the one who had decided to move into someone's house without explicit permission, I agreed. The Safehouse gave me a reluctant nod of approval and said that their door was open if I ever needed. When I marched up that same hill I had slid down stomach-first all those years ago and into the front door, it was like I could physically see the landmines and eggshells scattered out across the floor. Poppop Luke and my parents weren't speaking a word to each other, but I could feel the tension and sense the fuses waiting for a spark to erupt back into more arguments and screaming matches.

I called Nana while I continued unpacking some of the boxes downstairs once I made sure I was out of earshot. After a quick summary of the moving and the screaming match that resulted from it, all she could really tell me was that my mother and her father had a lot of issues with pretty deep roots that were impossible for anyone to really understand. Mom had always mentioned a pretty rough childhood, but I assumed everything had been processed and resolved by now. Everything just seemed so confusing with how hostile the house was quickly becoming. I realized I was very accustomed to a hostile environment from the constant fighting growing up, but this felt different. It didn't feel quite as surface-level as the arguments that would erupt between Rob and Dad or Dad and Mom or some other combination. Nana assured me that everything was going to be fine before we hung up the phone, her words lingering in my mind like a calming high. If this move was going to ensure one thing, it was that it was time for me to spend even *more* of my time outside the bricks and drywall that was now caging all these deep-rooted issues and tension. All I had to do was avoid any crossfire from their constant battles for another year and a half and then I could fly from the nest altogether.

With another semester wrapping up faster than I could keep up with, thoughts of the future made this school break that much more impossible to relax. I had always been a fan of our guidance counselor, but I'm not sure if she was that much of a fan of me by this point. The entire Junior class was collectively signed up to take the fated standardized test that would dictate what colleges we could pursue, but I was already stopping by her office once or twice a week in panicked frenzies. What score did I need to make in order to go to college for the lowest possible price tag? What did I need to do to properly apply to a college? Could I only apply to a few or should I apply to every single school in the country? How do I know what my major is going to be? What is a major? How do I study for a standardized test? What if I wake up with strep that morning? What if I bomb this test even though I've aced every test at this school? Despite my suspicions, however, she always welcomed me into her office with open arms and put even my most dramatic hypothetical scenarios to rest. Of course, I still found myself stressing about somehow sabotaging my own academic future in between hanging the tree ornaments I was helping Nana with before moving on to help her with the food prep.

Winter Break might as well have been three minutes long with how quickly we all found ourselves filing back into the hallways at school. With social media invading more and more of our lives, there was less of an electric buzz that came with this return. With everyone seeing every event and every unwrapped present moments after they happen online, there was less excitement to share all the details with each other in person. Thankfully, there was still the excitement of a new set of classes that comes with every January that came with its own guessing game of figuring out which friends were in which class before the time came to actually enter that class and fight for the best seat. Although the initial surge of excitement about Prayer Requests had dwindled to a lull, there were still a few people who would go out of their way to say how much they enjoyed the page. I always smiled in return and thanked them for the support since maintaining the page was still a daily task, but I couldn't help but feel a certain gloom hovering over me as I realized how much the page had helped others without helping to cure *me* whatsoever.

I still had to worry about the tattoo on my forehead that was starting to branch out and spread all across my face and arms. *I watch videos of guys online sometimes* began to appear all over until I felt it was undoubtedly visible to everyone else. I still had to worry about the gigantic iron orb attached to my ankle that was dragging behind every single footstep. Not only were there eggshells and landmines covering every square inch of the house, but now they were scattered all across the linoleum tile of the school hallways too. However, instead of a broken shell or triggered mine erupting into a screaming match at home for some (or no) reason, it was much worse here. The consequence of setting one of these off was another look of speculation that I may be hiding who I really am. Despite the absurdity of someone who ran Prayer Requests, attended every Thursday Club, and went to church anytime he didn't have to work being accused of being gay, the suspicion seemed to linger all over the school until it was all over the town and throughout the entire state. Sometimes it was just a brief speculative glance. Other times it was a whisper to their friend that I swore I could hear. The more extreme cases involved yet another group of jocks or randoms directly calling me a faggot and erupting into laughter at their own joke like they were the opener for a Dave Chappelle show.

The main difference (and absolute worst part) of these landmines and eggshells throughout the school was that they were somehow even more invisible than the ones at home. The ones at home were fairly predictable to the point where I knew the exact words or tones that would create a fiery response depending on the person or combination of people I was observing. All Lilley had to do was ask my grandfather what he had been up to that day with a slight accusational tone and his fuse would be ignited in no time. All Dad had to do was mention something about her spending habits and she would erupt into defensive screams until everyone fled from whatever part of the house the scene started in. But at school, these were completely unpredictable. Walking through the hallways without realizing I was in a group of all girls. Walking to a class without paying attention to how my walk itself might appear to a group of jocks coming the opposite way. Being completely silent anytime anyone ever brought up their first kiss or hooking up with someone. There were only so many times I could explain that I was abstinent and that I just haven't found the right girl to have my first kiss with. There were only so many ways I could laugh it off and avoid everyone's doubt. Anything and everything was fair game to anyone and everyone I encountered anywhere.

Thankfully, I was able to address these rumors at large from time to time with carefully-curated posts across all of my social media accounts. One day I'd highlight the fact that I took my Christianity so seriously that I wasn't willing to compromise it with hookups. Another awkward conversation in a social setting would prompt me to throw out the "I take my promise to God and Nana too seriously to throw it away on a one night stand or a pointless makeout session" or whatever else I could conjure up at the last minute. A few weeks flew by before I went out of my way to remind my virtual networks that I was respecting women by being such a devoted Christian and that it was pretty horrible for people to use that to try and make a gay joke or accuse me of not liking girls. In private, of course, I pleaded at night for these public service announcements to actually kick in so that I could stop worrying about the dark cloud and the invisible tattoos and medieval house arrest bracelet and secretive internet habits. Once those kicked in, I could finally and firmly put all of these absurd rumors to rest and everyone would finally leave me alone. In the meantime, I would just continue venting to my best friends and online strangers about how straight I was and how annoying it was that I was always having to clarify that over and over again.

When I wasn't able to escape reality through social media interactions, I fortunately was able to escape into the culinary world for an hour or two every day this semester. I had lost track of how many classes I'd already taken or what level of Culinary Arts I'd achieved and it didn't really matter to me. All I cared about was completely forgetting anything and everything outside of that kitchen the moment I stepped inside and punched in my entry time (the teacher thought it was a good method to get us used to the real world). We were learning about the various complexities of biscuits one morning when it dawned on me that this could be my potential future. Nothing felt more therapeutic than being in the kitchen baking a cheesecake for Nana's birthday or preparing dinner for the family every now and then. I was the happiest when my mind was intertwined in a recipe instead of the real world. Suddenly, I was envisioning my future as a famous chef or a TV personality on the Food Network like the many I had fallen in love with over the years. What was stopping me from giving that route a try, especially since I didn't have an abundance of other options knocking at my door?

Visions of a famous, successful career within the culinary industry began to manifest themselves at every free moment. The mental images immediately flashed across my mind when it wasn't working on the *Me Book* project our English teacher assigned us where we were challenged to write about ourselves 20 years in the future in whatever kind of profession and society we wanted. Anytime my brain wasn't focusing on math tests or the random movie our (insert heavy air quotes) history teacher was playing for us that rarely had anything to do with history, it was imagining myself in a televised cooking competition taking home the crown. I only had three actual classes this semester with the fourth and final period of the day intended to be spent at my job in order to write two essays for my "co-op" class that stressed the importance of transitioning into the working world as soon as possible. Whenever I actually used that free period to start my shifts earlier, my mind immediately imagined what it would be like to climb my way out of this fast food restaurant, put myself through culinary school, and shoot for the stars and beyond.

All it took was one conversation with Lilley to bring all these dreams crashing down as I mentally prepared to take the dreaded college entrance exam the following morning. I casually brought up that I wasn't that worried about what score I'd get considering I was wanting to go to culinary school anyway. I didn't realize this was one of those invisible eggshells but apparently it was an ostrich-sized egg. Lilley erupted into immediate disapproval and demanded that I change my attitude and adjust my goals in life because there simply was no feasible way for me to actually excel through culinary school and land a job that paid me well enough to provide for my wife. Feeling absolutely defeated by my mother's lack of support, I threw the test-prep textbooks she spent hundreds of dollars on in the deepest dresser drawer I had to be forgotten forever. If I couldn't pursue the career I was actually passionate about, I would simply let the universe decide which college I could get into, if any, by completely winging the test. Slamming the drawer shut, I threw myself onto my bed to let my mind simmer in the anger that she had just conjured. Don't ever hang out with too many girls because you'll seem gay. Don't ever confess to any kind of depression or self-harm or you'll likely be thrown into a facility. Don't ever pursue your passions because you probably won't make it and bankrupt yourself. Got it.

We all filed into the main hallway the day of the big test and waited to be sorted into our designated classrooms. While I was still riding the "I didn't study and I don't care" mentality, I could visibly see the nerves on every other face in the Junior class. Some people were even crouched and leaning against the wall with a stack of index cards in a last-minute attempt to study right before this allegedly-important state exam that was going to shape our entire academic future. Continuing with my apathetic vibe, I spent the last few moments chatting with any and every clique of other students I could up until mere seconds before the deadline to be seated in my assigned classroom. A million bubbles between scheduled snack/water breaks later, I handed in my final answer sheet to be graded by the state officials. From there, all of our fates would be signed, sealed, and delivered back to the school in a month or two. I barely listened to the closing statements and directions before I was racing out to my car to meet up with whatever friend(s) wanted to waste the rest of the free day together. Part of me almost started to wonder if I had just thrown away my entire future with how little I prepared for that exam, but I quickly tossed those worries aside.

Time continued to rush by in a flurry of shifts at work and school days that seemed to last approximately 30 minutes in total. Panic started to set in whenever everyone started mentioning that they'd been asked to prom by the exact person they were hoping for. When the hell did it become time to start worrying about prom? I started running over all the questions in my head to start preparing for one of the most important nights of any high schooler's life. Who was I going to ask? What was the best way to ask her? Could I think of a way to ask her in an amazing way so that it goes viral on the internet? How do I get a suit? Do I have to drive us in my car or do I get a fancy car for the night? What group of friends were we going to go to dinner with beforehand? Was there going to be any big plans for after the actual dance? Should I try to throw a prom bonfire? Was I going to lose my virginity somehow? How was I going to afford all of this?

For whatever reason, the prom panic amplified one afternoon until it felt like I was drowning in a monsoon from the imaginary pressure. I was working at the front cashier stand at work when I noticed the Safehouse household stop by to say hi (a very normal, Safehouse thing to do). Without sparing a second to process the thought as it appeared, I yelled for one of the girls who lived in the house and asked if she wanted to go to the prom with me. Her look of surprise confirmed my fears as I realized how tacky it was to ask a girl to prom while in your McDonalds uniform literally in the middle of your shift. She hesitated a few moments before saying yes but by that time I was already mortified at my stupidity and lack of thought process. It took all of a week before she rescinded her acceptance. She said it was because she didn't want to go to prom if her Safehouse sister didn't also get asked, but I was certain it was actually because I had screwed up the promposal so horribly. Sitting up in bed one night trying to avoid the dark cloud's temptations, I started to focus on the fact that I was probably going to go to prom by myself, if I even went at all.

Every single one my close female friends seemed to be asked to prom every five seconds over the next week or two until I felt like I was literally the only person in the school who didn't have a companion. I was getting ready to mentally accept that I was going to be flying solo for the event until I bumped into one of the random friends I made in an Art class the previous semester. I had always thought she was pretty and fun but she didn't have any social media or even a cell phone so our friendship kind of fell off whenever the class finished up. After chatting for a few minutes in the hallway, however, she let me know that she finally joined modern society and had a phone now. One thing led to another and we were texting back and forth nonstop. Even at work I couldn't help but check my phone every thirty seconds to type back whatever reply. I hated how long it took for us to connect outside of class, but I was thankful nonetheless. After a week or so of constant back-and-forth chatting, I knew I had found the girl I wanted to ask to prom. Now I just had to figure out the best way to go about asking her to make sure she said yes (and hopefully not back out a week after).

Sitting in therapy, I mean Culinary Arts, the next day discussing the various intricacies of cake baking and decorating, the golden idea hit me. Why wouldn't I just ask her through a cake?! Perfection. I immediately got started with the planning and created the recipe so that I could also use the promposal for my culinary project for the quarter. With my teacher's enthusiastic approval, I jumped into the kitchen right away and had the beloved creation in the oven in no time. I scheduled time to come in early the next morning and during my free period that was meant to allow me to get to work early. In no time, I was putting the final touches on the project and piping out icing to spell out "Prom?" on my creation. I decided to add a few last-minute floral decorations made out of frozen icing before submitting it all for final approval. I took the teacher's beaming smile as a sign of approval before making my way to the library before the final bell rang to dismiss everyone to go home for the day. I texted one of our mutual friends to make sure everything was ready and my potential prom date was still in the library for the surprise. Butterflies were fluttering throughout my entire body as I practically sprinted through the double-doors of the library holding a giant bakery box, almost dropping it three times.

The element of surprise was completely on my side as I slid the box toward her at the desk she was working on with a number of others, my friend who helped me plan the whole event included. Looking completely shocked and confused, she opened the box and her jaw completely fell to the floor. At first I thought she was going to decline for some reason (my brain is a fun place) but then some emotion returned to her face as she jumped up to give me a giant hug to officially accept the invitation. The final bell rang to interrupt the celebration and she had to hurry to catch the bus but we were already back to texting before she even made it to her seat on the way home. I floated back home on cloud 9 to get ready for yet another shift at the drive-thru window and/or fry station wearing my rose-colored glasses the entire time. I couldn't have been more excited for prom despite the fact that a week or so ago I was contemplating not attending the event whatsoever. After another day or so of excitedly getting to know each other, I realized it was time to give dating another shot. Instead of just asking her to prom, I might as well ask her to be my girlfriend too.

The last thing I wanted to do was fall short of my promposal with such an important question. Therefore, I asked another friend for her input in putting together the best dating invitation possible. With spring approaching so quickly, I found myself filling up an Easter basket with colorful eggs that each contained a small note stating something I admired about her. I left the basket in her assigned seat for her very first class of the day with the largest egg holding the official request in the center of the basket. I felt pretty confident she was going to say yes, but that didn't stop my nerves going crazy for the next two hours as I waited for some kind of response whether that be verbal or in the form of a letter. Finally, the bell rang after what felt like an eternity and I made my way to where her classroom had been. She was standing outside the room waiting for me, a letter folded up in her hand. She quickly handed me the note before scurrying off to her next class, making me immediately think I was about to unfold a rejection letter. My heart sank as I delicately unfolded her response only for excitement to rush right back through my veins as I saw the *yes* printed neatly in delicate handwriting inside. I had a prom date *and* a girlfriend. God was finally answering my pleas. Everything was getting back on track.

It took a week of walking through the hallways together, hands intertwined every now and then, for me to realize the knots forming in my stomach once again. As much as I hated to admit it, the cloud was looming over my head every single moment of the day. Intermingled between every hand hold, hug, and text message exchange, it whispered in my ears that it was calling my bluff. Was I actually wanting to be in a relationship or was I just obsessed with everyone around me seeing that I had a girlfriend? Did I actually have romantic feelings for her or did I simply want all the rumors to stop circulating around the town? No, that's absurd. I liked her. I liked girls. I liked the conversations we have. I loved walking around in front of people with her. Wait. No, that's not the right thing to think. Right? These thoughts kept rebounding at rapid speed around the walls of my mind until I felt like I was going to pass out or throw up (or both) in my last class of the day. What had I gotten myself into? The bell rang and I exited the classroom only to see my girlfriend meeting up with me a few steps into the hallway. I was headed towards one of the back exits to head to my car, but I could tell that she was lingering around in anticipation for something. Suddenly, the knots in my stomach amplified and twisted even further as I realized she probably wanted me to kiss her goodbye before I left.

Not knowing how to react, and not wanting to accidentally throw up on her or all over the floor, I quickly hugged her and practically sprinted out the doorway on all fours towards my car. I avoided even looking at my phone for the rest of the entire day as I contemplated all the different feelings and thoughts rushing through my brain. Before I knew it, I was writing out an extensive letter to her that explained that we were probably more suited to be good friends. Of course, I paid special attention to make sure none of my actual thoughts made it onto the paper. Something about God wanting her to be in my life as a friend instead of a potential wife seemed to make more sense than "this evil cloud keeps following me around and making me watch videos of dudes online and trying to make me look down in the locker rooms and keeps threatening to tell you and the rest of the school if I don't break up with you" in my mind. After reading back over the letter three more times, I folded it up and slid it into an envelope I found in Lilley's computer desk. I awkwardly handed it to her the next morning and spent the entire day trying to fight the urge to throw up at the twisted situation I created for myself. Thankfully, she didn't seem too upset and still agreed to go to Prom with me next weekend. It's totally normal to date someone, break up, and then still go to prom with them, right? It's still possible to have the most memorable night of our entire lives even with a little tense/awkward history behind us, yeah?

There were only a couple of days before the big night and I was pacing around my bedroom after work trying to make sure I had checked off everything on my list to make sure it was all perfect. I asked my parents if there was any way they could help me out with all the costs associated with everything but they both said that was what my part-time job was for. Thankfully, my manager agreed to let me work a crazy amount of shifts the last week or two (on top of assignments/exams) to try and make up for draining my account down to $10. Between buying our tickets, renting my tux, and setting aside enough money for the pre-prom dinner we were going to, my account was fried. Poppop Luke came through to save the day by letting me borrow his fancy SUV for the special occasion so I at least didn't have to worry about trying to rent some kind of nice vehicle. We were going to go with another group to a nice property on the outskirts of town, even further away from that sketchy bridge we always jumped off of. As far as I could tell, I had just about everything covered. There was even a reservation made at the gymnastics studio for a huge group of us to go jump and flip around like maniacs afterwards. It was shaping up to be one of the best nights ever and yet I still couldn't stop myself from bouncing around my bedroom from total anxiety. Eventually I felt myself drifting off and collapsed onto my bed.

Suddenly I found myself walking into the front doors of the main venue where they were holding the dance with my date. Loud music was blasting everywhere and she immediately sprinted away from me towards the dancefloor, a decision that didn't seem like her whatsoever. Something felt incredibly off about the dance but I didn't spend too much time trying to decipher it. My mind kept trying to remember picking her up, posing for photos, eating dinner, or any of the various events prior to our entrance but everything was blank. I shook off my confusion and made my way over to one of the tables to set my wallet and other burdens down before grabbing a quick snack. The entire venue was swarming with people that felt like complete strangers but also felt like my friends at the same time. My date was nowhere to be found so I made my way to the dance floor by myself instead. Something still felt incredibly surreal about tonight's long-awaited formal event, but I was doing my best to just make the most of it while awkwardly dancing alone to the song belting out of the speakers. Out of nowhere, the dance floor was swarmed with a gaggle of the school's jocks, athletes, and various other genres of eligible bachelors.

I wasn't too preoccupied or stressed about their spontaneous appearance until they all began making their way towards the area where I was dancing. Without a second thought or missing a single beat, they were crowded around me until I was submerged into their group. My heart started to pick up a few paces as I looked around for all of their dates, and mine, but there was not a single girl to be found on the entire dance floor. They all began to move in closer and closer until we were all practically dancing against each other. Panic began to course through my entire body as I looked around to see if anyone else was noticing that we were all grinding with each other. However, nobody seemed to be paying any attention whatsoever. A few more glances around the room later, I let my stress go and completely leaned into the vibe and started reciprocating their effort back. The twenty-or-so of us didn't seem to have a care in the world as our bodies danced into one another, only somewhat matching the beat of whatever song was playing. Slowly, I began to feel a set of hands on my waist that started guiding the direction my body was swaying. The song changed as another set of hands found their way to my arms and more and more until I couldn't tell which hands belonged to which person. And I didn't care.

My mind was completely letting go of all its worry as I leaned more and more into whatever the hell was happening on the dance floor with this group of jocks. Then, out of nowhere, I heard an enormous click and the heat of a gigantic spotlight hit my face. I heard the sound of all twenty sets of shoes scurry off like a stampeding herd while I stood frozen in place. The spotlight was still shining on my face and it appeared the venue was suddenly packed to the brim with faces staring at me with their jaws hanging wide open. I heard an array of gasps from the crowd as I glanced to my left to see the only other person that apparently didn't run off with the rest of them. It was the school's only gay kid and I quickly realized his hands were still holding my waist from whatever that group dance session was. Not only did I notice the entire school, faculty/staff included, staring at me erotically dancing with the only gay guy, but my date was also standing there with her arms crossed in disappointment and tears already welling up in her eyes. I started to say something to her and explain that this was all a misunderstanding but she ran off towards the doors before I could convince my mouth to say anything. I turned back around to face where she had just been standing only to see my parents, Nana and Poppop, Ryan and Erin, Rob, and Poppop Luke also staring at me with various looks of shock and disappointment painted on their faces. Shit.

I shot up in my bed in absolute hysterics, sweat dripping off of my forehead and my lungs barely able to expand fast enough to breathe. My eyes shot in every direction trying to understand how I was seeing my bedroom when I had just been standing on a dance floor under direct spotlight after being caught dancing in a huge crowd of men. Wait. It wasn't real? It was just a dream? I mean, it was just a nightmare? I let out a long sigh of exhaustion and let my head collapse back on the pillow as I tried to calm myself down. It was just a nightmare and it's the morning of Prom. Prom hasn't happened yet and all of that wasn't real. Everything was fine. I laid there for several minutes before finally getting out of bed, too terrified of what my mind would conjure up in dreamland if I were to doze back off again. I cautiously made my way to the bathroom to turn on the shower to try and take care of the fact that I was drenched with panicked sweat. While the water was warming up, I stared at my reflection in the mirror, forehead tattoo as bold and irritated as ever staring back at me. Why in the hell did my brain create some mythical Porn-Meets-Dance-Dance-Revolution scene in my dream? I mean nightmare. More importantly though, I began to ask myself why the hell I enjoyed it so much until the spotlight caught us? In a moment of panic, I found myself shattering my mobile mp3/internet device that I had owned since middle school. With the shattered fragments of metal, glass, and plastic now in the trash, maybe I could eliminate the dark cloud altogether once and for all. Sure, my cell phone had internet access, but it also had the capabilities for contracting viruses and that's one conversation with my parents and the cell phone company I would be avoiding at all costs.

The shower washed away all the little tattoos for the time being as I spent the day getting ready for the big night. With the eerie, unsettling dream still lingering in my thoughts, I was determined to make this first Prom Night one of the best nights of my life. A few texts back and forth with my ex-girlfriend/current date and a quick chat with Poppop Luke confirmed everything was good to go. I gave myself one last look in the largest mirror I could find in the house to make sure I had put on my suit properly and that I looked as good as I possibly could. My green vest shone brightly with my jacket hanging loosely over my painfully-thin frame in the mirror selfie I snapped before heading out the door. My grandfather tossed the keys to his SUV to me in the driveway before telling me not to get into *too* many wrecks tonight with a smile. I got Mom to take one last picture of me standing in front of his fancy, masculine SUV with my tuxedo jacket heterosexually slung over one shoulder before heading to her house. I tried to shake off any last lingering thoughts about my nightmare, but a small part of me couldn't help but fear that it might be some form of premonition of what was to come later this evening.

The drive to her house in the middle of nowhere gave me the perfect opportunity to further agonize over the dream for 20 minutes. I pulled into the long driveway and knocked on the front door, halfway expecting her brother or grandparents to greet me holding a gun after the way I had broken up with her after a week or so. Thankfully, they welcomed me into the house as warmly as I could have hoped for while we all waited for her to wrap up the final touches to her hair and makeup. My throat was bone-dry from the combination of meeting-the-ex's-family and had-a-gay-dream-last-night nerves so I drained a glass of water almost immediately. I heard a door open and turned around to see her making her way into the living room where we were all sitting in anticipation. Her blonde hair was pinned up in a beautiful arrangement above the long green gown that rested perfectly on her delicate shoulders. Her nails were painted a soft grey with little sunflowers carefully painted on in a way that only she could somehow pull off with a prom dress. We snapped a few pictures together on her back porch before hopping in the car (after making sure I opened the car door for her, of course) and making our way to the enormous property for professional photos.

We had no idea what to expect in terms of the property we were going to other than an address so we spent most of the ride speculating what it could possibly look like. She casually mentioned that this was actually her first school dance and how excited she was which couldn't have possibly made me feel any worse about the mess I had created between us. She looked absolutely stunning and couldn't have been more down-to-earth and I had completely dragged her into a relationship only to end it right away because of my own paranoia. The nightmare once again flashed across my mind and served as a painful, bitter reminder of what was actually lingering beneath my decisions. Why was it so hard to figure all of this out? Why had God still not fixed my brain so that I could just be normal? Why did I have to sit here wondering if I had made a mistake breaking up with her as we're literally on the way to prom together? Why did I have to create this paralyzing premonition in my head of accidentally getting caught scandalously dancing with a group of guys on the dance floor? The crunch of the gravel underneath the huge tires of my grandfather's car jerked me out of my emotional spiral and back to reality as we turned onto the driveway of the property.

Both of our jaws basically fell into our laps as we came up on what might as well have been called a mansion and parked next to some of the other cars close to the front door. Everyone else seemed to be gathered together and acting completely normal about the size and stature of this massive estate so we quickly did our best to collect ourselves and match the mood. A couple of my best friends were already there with their dates and taking pictures together at various locations across the lawn. It appeared like we were the last ones to show up to the scene so we quickly jumped in with the group photos and tried to get in as many shots as possible despite the fact that I couldn't recall paying a single one of the three photographers here. Was I supposed to pay one or all of them? I'm sure they'll let one of us know at the end who we need to pay, if anyone. After another round of quirky, random photo poses we all seemed pretty content with the portfolios we had all created. As much as I didn't want to leave such a glamorous place, we hopped back in the car and headed to grab a nice dinner before making our way to the venue for the big event.

Pulling up to the venue after emptying our plates of every ounce of food brought a peculiar nausea to the pit of my stomach. I wasn't sure if I had simply eaten way too much or if I was still hung up on my dream, but a small part of me considered fleeing the scene the moment I shifted the car into park. After a few calming breaths and the fact that my date had already hopped out of the car from sheer excitement, I took the keys out of the ignition and concealed my worries in the middle console before hopping out to join her. A tsunami of relief washed over me as we walked through the doors and I saw that the interior layout of the venue was completely different from the one my brain created. We eagerly checked in at the front table and filled out our votes for the Prom Superlatives to be announced at the end of the night before heading over to one of the empty tables. Being such a small high school in the middle of nowhere, I assumed the budget for a prom was pretty low. However, the venue was decorated fairly well for the "magic carpet ride" theme for that year. We all looked at each other and realized we had all been hit with the same surge of excitement. The moment had finally arrived. We were here.

No one was thinking about our college entrance standardized exam or what papers were due next or where we were considering going to college or anything. For once, we left our cares at the door and weren't thinking about anything. The only thing on everyone's mind was making the most out of these next three hours while we had them. Smiles flashed all across the room as we all danced (if you could call it that) to whatever song was blaring out of the speakers. Compliments were bouncing off the walls as everyone compared dresses, corsages, tuxedo styles, nails, and everything in-between. Even the guys who were typically rude to me in the hallways and the Most Likely To Use a Homophobic Slur bunch seemed unusually kind tonight. I flocked from social bubble to social bubble trying to take as many pictures and join into as many conversations as possible while everyone was riding the happy train. My date and I danced together for a bit until some of my friends pulled me into their dancing circles and then another one pulled me into theirs as I eventually became an accessory to any and every clique there in some way or another. In this moment, time seemed to slow down a smidge as I reflected on how long it took me to finally get to this point. I had various different groups of friends that I could comfortably pop in and chat with when there was such a long stretch of my life when I felt lucky to have even one. I was at my Junior Prom and surrounded by friends and having the time of my life. Nothing could possibly make this night any better.

A sudden paralyzing screech from a microphone that pierced all of our souls at once, followed by a few taps to further gain our attention, brought all of our dancing to a halt. For a brief moment, I thought we were about to get a lecture about how a few of us had snuck into the wedding reception at a different, closed off part of the venue or that someone had been caught spiking the drinks. Our fears quickly dissolved as they began to announce that the votes for the Prom Superlatives for this year's event were all tallied and to listen up for the winners. The group of friends we had taken photos and got dinner with walked back to our table to take a breather while we watched the traditional ceremony begin. I fell into my chair, completely exhausted after dancing and selfie-taking for so long. One of the chaperones tapped the microphone once again as she pulled out the sealed lockbox containing the list of winners. One by one, we heard names being called out through the loudspeaker as students made their way to the front of the venue to be awarded their sash. After a variety of categories like Best-Dressed, Most Elegant, and Most Adorable Couple, it was time to get to the top two: Prom Prince/Princess and Prom King/Queen. There was a dramatic drum roll made by everyone stomping their feet as Princess was called: unsurprisingly one of my best friends. The drum roll returned once again as they announced Prom Prince.

My jaw fell straight onto the plastic-lined table in front of me as I waited for reassurance that I had heard the principal correctly through the microphone. I felt one of my friend's hands pat my shoulder and give me a slight push onto my feet. I floated up to the front on a cloud of shock mixed with euphoria to take my position next to my friend. One of the other chaperones carefully draped a sash over our shoulders and handed us fancy scepters. My eyes scanned over the crowd of smiling faces and clapping hands as time began to slow down once again. A smile finally formed on my face as I started to realize I actually *wasn't* hallucinating. I just won Prom Prince of my Junior Class. My mind was on cloud nine and there wasn't a single thought in my head other than the pure joy of this exact, slow-motion moment. This was the same feeling I felt once I saw how many people came to my first bonfire party on my 16th birthday. Actually, that's not true at all. This feeling was 10 times better than that. I was officially one of the Popular Kids. I pushed through being a book nerd, getting ambushed with plastic bullets, getting called a fag every other week, and even a completely dysfunctional family to land right in this happy, perfect moment.

The King and Queen were announced shortly after as time returned to its normal pace. We all had to hover around by the front of the dance floor to have our pictures taken for the yearbook before I got to float back to my chair. There was a split moment when I noticed the black cloud appear in the distance and try to inch its way closer in a likely attempt to remind me of the dream from last night, but one more glance at my prized scepter eliminated it completely. The DJ made the announcement that there were only a couple of songs left before the Prom was officially over so our table quickly jumped up to make the most of it. After a few more rounds of hectic dancing, screaming the words to one of our favorite anthems, and even a slow dance with my date, the principal came back onto the microphone to thank us for coming tonight and to make it home safe. We all made a last-minute trip to the snack/beverage tables before slowly making our way through the parking lot to our cars. We leaned against our cars, lingering and reflecting on what was such an incredible night. Laughing about all the crazy dancers and the way some of us literally snuck into a wedding made us almost forget that we had all paid for those after party plans at the gymnastics studio. Luckily it was only a few minutes down the road from the venue.

The entire drive was spent reminiscing on just how fantastic Prom had turned out to be and how excited she had been to finally attend one before graduating in a few weeks. I asked her about her plans for college as we approached the gymnastics gym. It turns out she was only going to be going to college about 25 minutes down the road in a small town called Athens that I had never heard of. Apparently they are famously known as The Friendly City as well as the site for one of the most popular dairy companies in the country. When I brought up how worried I was about money and test scores, she lit up and let me know if I did well enough on that exam we took that there's a pretty good shot of getting a full tuition scholarship to her college. I started to get excited until I realized the likelihood of getting a great score back was slim to none after I intentionally didn't prepare in an act of maternal rebellion. Not wanting anything to ruin the euphoria of tonight, I quickly tossed these stresses back into the middle console and headed toward the front door of the venue. However, we quickly realized things seemed a bit off when we saw a crowd of other kids gathered at the front door instead of inside the establishment.

As eager as we all were to get inside and expend the last few ounces of energy we had on the bouncy floors and trampolines, it didn't look like that was actually going to happen. Everyone gathered outside the doors as we walked up sported an angry, disappointed face. The girl who had organized the event from the Senior Class was standing at the front of this crowd, her facial expression more of an embarrassed, defeated one. Once she realized the crowd had just about everyone who had signed up with her, she let us all know that she had somehow missed the mark in finalizing the reservation with the building's office. Therefore, the doors were locked, the lights were off, and there wasn't a single employee on site to remedy the situation. On the bright side, however, she was able to redistribute everyone's money back to them on the spot. After a quick phone call, I got the idea to have a few people over to the Safehouse afterwards instead. A part of me was actually a bit relieved that the gymnastics place didn't work out because the Safehouse felt like a more authentic way to wrap up the perfect night. Something about sitting in the living room of these friends that actually felt like family by this point was the cherry on top as we laughed about anything and everything while reflecting on every single detail from the last five or six hours. I drove my date/ex back home to her grandparents before it got too late, giving her a long hug and thanking her for an amazing night before floating back to my bedroom on the last remaining wisps of my Prom cloud.

Hearing the guidance counselor's voice project over the school's speaker system calling the Junior class to report to the auditorium the next week was enough to completely eradicate the buzz from winning Prom Prince. Oh god. The only possible explanation for this sudden summoning was our scores coming back from that official exam that was to determine our eligibility to the majority of colleges. The majority of us seemed excited and eager to get to the auditorium as quickly as possible while my feelings couldn't have been more opposite. It was almost as if the gigantic weight attached to my ankle that I was so accustomed to from over the years had doubled. There was this dense orb of my deepest, darkest secret on one ankle and now a huge cinderblock of dread attached to the other. I kept replaying that morning over and over again in my head with each footstep. I was so upset at Lilley for completely diminishing my celebrity chef ambitions that I was willing to completely sabotage my own collegiate career out of spite. It felt like an eternity had passed, but I finally approached the doorway. I took a few deep breaths before pushing through the door that suddenly felt like it weighed 2,000 pounds.

My guidance counselor handed me my envelope with a smile, jokingly mentioning that its contents might make a difference on how many times a week I made a trip to her office. I tried to return her statement with a laugh but an awkward grunting noise came out instead. I ducked my head down and made my way back to the main hallway to carefully open up the letter to see my score. My heart skipped several beats as I triple-checked to find my name at the top of the document and that I hadn't been given the wrong envelope somehow. Sure enough, there was my name neatly displayed next to my official score of 29 in a bold font. A perfect score on this exam was 36 with the average being around 20. By some stroke of miracle, I had landed a 29 without studying or preparing whatsoever. Surely something had been miscalculated somewhere between the school and the facility responsible for grading. Even if that was the case, however, I wasn't going to be the one to bring any kind of attention to it.

Nana was the first person I called once I came back down to Earth, quickly sharing the good news about the exam score and filling her in on the whole Prom Prince accomplishment. She screamed her congratulations over the phone and assured me that I shouldn't have any issues getting into any college I applied to now. I hung up the phone with her words of encouragement beginning to form tears in my eyes as I felt one of the weights on my legs disappear. I knew it wasn't a perfect score, but this was above the average enough that I felt pretty confident in receiving a pretty decent scholarship once I figured out which schools I wanted to pursue. I pondered the idea of taking the test again and actually preparing and studying the next time around to see if I could get closer to the perfect 36, but I quickly tossed that idea aside. 29 was phenomenal in my mind and taking the test again meant going through a bunch of paperwork and paying out of pocket for all the fees. I knew Mom wouldn't be paying for a second test after paying for all of those textbooks that I never opened and I definitely wasn't going to pay for them so that was that. I put the scoresheet back into its envelope and stuffed it into my backpack before returning to class. A few of my friends were comparing their scores but I did my best not to bring too much attention to mine in case there actually *had* been some form of miscalculation. I just wore an accomplished smile, kept my letter snugly concealed in my backpack, and floated through the remainder of the semester on a cloud.

Chapter Ten

Remember When We Graduated?

In the spirit of a spontaneous summer vacation, I decided during one of my shifts to kindly give them a thirty-minutes notice for my resignation. Something about the Prom Prince win, the unexpectedly high exam score, and the rush of ending another school year told me I didn't need to be bogged down with a part-time job. Instead, I deserved a summer break with as much socializing as possible, especially considering how many of my friends had just graduated and were about to go off to college or boot camp. I wasn't sure how I was going to necessarily fund this sudden (f)unemployment but I could cross that bridge when I needed to. Plus, with my good grades and exceptional college exam score, my parents were due for some kind of allowance program. Of course, this train of thought might just be my bitterness that still existed from the time Mom drove my bank account into the negatives and stole the money Other Dad and Erin had been wiring me. That bitterness also caused me to briefly consider reaching out to them after I quit to seek out some assistance but I quickly and shamefully discarded that idea almost as soon as I conjured it.

This decision caught up with me rather quickly, accelerated by the catalyst of my parents not agreeing to pay me any kind of allowance for my academic success whatsoever. Despite my efforts in pointing out how different my expectations/rewards were compared with my brother's when he was my age, they weren't budging. Something about me being mature enough to realize my academic journey wasn't the same as his and my baby sister costing a lot of money kept them from saying yes to any idea I suggested. Eventually, I stopped budging and swallowed my pride and submitted applications all over the place. I had about $80 to my name which meant I had about two full tanks of gas and three or four hangouts involving food left before I hit zero. Just as I started rationing out which friends I was going to have lunches with and how effectively I could space out my drives, my phone started buzzing in my pocket. The number on the screen was one that I didn't have memorized, but the area code was local so I decided to answer it anyway. An older woman's voice greeted me on the other line, a voice that was somehow intimidating and inviting at the same time. She wasted no time in small talk and quickly informed me they were hiring at Sonic if I was serious about the application I had submitted.

I graciously accepted the offer and found myself driving to the drive-in restaurant the following day for an interview. Although I didn't have much experience in the actual kitchens of fast-food restaurants, I must have charmed the managers with my customer service skills and the fact that I hung out at this very restaurant after every Lenoir City Thursday Club since our school's fell apart. They offered me the position by the end of the interview and even asked me if I knew of anyone else who was looking for a summer job. In what felt like the blink of an eye, one of my friends who had just graduated and I were learning how to work in a fast food kitchen. From the grill that seemed to be a mile long to the fryers that could hold 10 different baskets of 10 different items at once, the whole area felt like a sauna. It was a painful process for our bodies (and skin) to adjust to, but eventually it felt as if we could race through a busy afternoon or dinner rush with our eyes blindfolded. Of course, getting a paycheck every week instead of twice a month made this tough adjustment that much easier to process. Plus, having access to as many burgers, corn dogs, grilled cheeses, and cheese sticks was the cherry on top.

In the meantime, my friends decided to upgrade the ways in which we spent our free time away from anything work/college related while simultaneously accepting that it was okay to hang out with Lenoir City even if they were our sworn rivals. The questionable bridge above questionable water was quickly replaced with the collection of cliffs above pretty blue water, each one ranging from 30 to 55 feet drops. When I wasn't hiking the mile and a half to these life-threatening cliff jumps or sweating my life away in a scorching kitchen, I was at the Safehouse or at home. The more time I spent playing around the house with my little sister, the more tolerable the house seemed to be despite the constant screaming. Thankfully, I still had social media and Prayer Requests to manage down in my room anytime the arguments got to be too loud or uncomfortable upstairs. Prayer Requests had a couple thousand members by this point but it didn't require too much maintenance other than making sure no one's account got hacked and started flooding the page with ads for "free sunglasses" or something. As for social media, I was starting to really get the hang of the concept of establishing an actual online presence if I could just figure out how to make more potentially-viral posts like some people were. Once I figured that out, it was only a matter of time before I blew up and become rich and famous like they did so I can launch myself as far away from this tiny town the moment I graduate.

The older my baby sister got, the more times I started to come home from work to see one of any number of my friends in my living room with her. Apparently, my mother started a habit of going through my social media to find some of my friends from school and took it upon herself to message them for a babysitting job so that she could focus on her at-home job. At first I was a little uneasy with the idea, but if it gave my friends an opportunity for income while also getting them over to the house more often than they already were then I guess I could get over my annoyance. About halfway through the summer, Lilley even let me know that she was going to invite one of the close friends who had been babysitting pretty often to the beach trip we were planning on taking right before school started back. The idea, or at least the idea that was explained to me by Lilley, was that she could tag along with us in exchange for watching the baby while we were there. With a babysitter tagging along, my parents could do more of their own thing throughout the week and my friend got to come to the beach with me. It was a win-win situation all around.

As if the situation couldn't get even more exciting, Lilley called me into the master bedroom of the house to have a chat. She was watching some kind of romance and/or serial killer movie with my baby sister next to her playing with some kind of electronic device. I wasn't too sure about her already getting addicted to technology at such a young age, but this was pretty much the norm by now. My mother went on to explain that if I wanted to, I could invite two more of my friends to tag along on the beach trip. The current babysitter had apparently already asked our other close friend to come which left me to find a guy to come along to balance out the genders of the group. Therefore, I quickly shot a text to my friend that I had been working with this summer to see if he was available. With him having just graduated and planning on attending the community college down the road, he was all in. I wasn't sure what sparked my parents into letting me have multiple friends come with us to the beach, but I wasn't about to question it. Especially since it meant I would have to drive separately, avoid the crying baby for the 7 hour drive, *and* have our own vehicle once we all got down there for the whole week. We tried our best to pick up a few extra shifts to get some extra spending money until all of a sudden we were waking up early to throw our bags in the cars and head out.

My car only held the guy friend and a large portion of the luggage that wouldn't fit in Mom's car with the two girls, Dad, the baby, and migraines. With my friend and I taking turns driving my car, the seven hours or so passed by in a flash until we were all face-to-face with the ocean at last. Something about the salty breeze, the sounds of gulls overhead, and the fact that I was with some of my best friends standing on the cool sands mimicked the same euphoria from when I had the Prom Prince sash draped over me. We soaked in as much of the moment together as much as we could before my parents called for us to come back up and help unpack the car. We walked into the suite and quickly unpacked our things and settled into one of the four bunks on the opposite side of the large bed where Mom and Dad were going to be sleeping. The four of us gathered our minds together to try and map out everything we could do for the next five days to make it as unforgettable as possible. Even if one of the girls had to carry my little sister on her hip anywhere we went, we weren't about to waste this golden opportunity of a week.

We bounced from the ocean to the pool for the first couple of days before deciding to take a short drive to see what kind of entertainment options were around the area. We quickly found an outdoor shopping mall down the road that the girls forced me to park inside so they could take a look at some of the shops. From there, we grabbed a quick lunch before driving back to take a long walk along the sandy beach and plan out what we were going to do that night. After a half a mile of walking and joining in a random beach volleyball game with some strangers, we decided to go to the pier later that night. I did my best to avoid staring at some of the guys that were playing, but I couldn't help but feel happy when they suggested to the girls that we join them at the pier later to ride one of the rides or something. Naturally, I poked fun at their excitement and did everything I possibly could to ignore the cloud in my head that was whispering "maybe they'll invite you on one of the rides too" over and over again.

It took the girls an excruciating hour and a half to finish getting ready after we had dinner with my parents. The other friend and I sat out on the bunks trying to be patient as our annoyance grew more and more. After what felt like an eternity, they finally came out of the bathroom and we made our way downstairs. Mom and Dad decided to join us at the last minute but assured us they would keep their distance and do their own thing while we did ours for a while. Surprisingly, she seemed to keep her word and went off in a different direction after I agreed to ride the nauseating spinning teacup ride with her. The girls eventually found the guys they had played on the sand with and naturally started flirting as much as possible while we surveyed our surroundings for any potential girls we could flirt with. When neither of us found anyone in our vicinity to pursue, we did everything in our power to embarrass them in front of their crushes. We asked them, just loudly enough for everyone to hear, if they were still having trouble with that rash and started calling them by the most embarrassing nicknames we could make up on short notice. They seemed furious at first, but eventually they realized it was best that we stick to our group of four anyway. A few more rides later and everyone, myself especially, seemed exhausted from the day's festivities.

I volunteered to drive us all back to the hotel once I realized my parents had already left an hour ago. Halfway back, I pulled into a gas station to go ahead and fill my car up in anticipation for the drive back home. With my friends all but passed out already, I hopped out as quietly as possible and started pumping the gas. However, every second, the pump automatically stopped itself. Confused, I took the pump out and placed it back on the holder to start the process all over again. I tried inserting it into my tank again, this time manually holding the pump only for it to force-stop me from pumping any gas whatsoever. Frustrated, I walked inside to ask the cashier if the pump was out of order. The man behind the counter looked at me with an awkward, sympathetic expression before explaining to me that my card had been declined. Knowing that I had deposited two paychecks into my account before we left, I knew that there must have been some kind of error so I tried the process once more at another gas station across the street only to have the same outcome. I quickly pulled out my phone to check my bank account balance only to find that there was approximately $4.29 in available funds. Right underneath that, a transfer of almost three hundred dollars had been processed earlier today. Right into my mother's bank account.

Rage fired through every single vein in my body all at once until the corners of my vision were a blurry crimson. The anger took complete control and before I could even realize what was happening, I was screaming through the phone at my mother for what I had just discovered. Ignoring the demands to have my paychecks returned to my bank account, Lilley deflected by saying how expensive this trip had turned out to be since I just *had* to have my friends come along. It took everything in not to throw my phone into the ocean hearing her defenses, especially considering the huge vacation idea came from her mind instead of mine. When I attacked those defenses, she shifted to claims that I had owed her from this and that over the last 17 years to which I furiously brought up the fact that I hadn't asked her to give birth to me. Something about being potentially stranded in Florida with no access to my own money to even get gas into my car in order to get home had caused me to toss away all concern for the way I was retaliating. This was the final straw and it's not like I had anything to lose at this point.

The phone call ended after she finally agreed to return a small portion of the money into my account so that I could fill up my tank and possibly get a meal or two (a radical compromise and concept in her mind apparently). After filling my friends in on the situation on the drive back to the hotel, I confirmed that what she had done was completely out of line and not something their parents would ever consider doing. I took a few deep breaths in the car, trying to calm my anger and nerves so I could hopefully enjoy the small remainder of this trip as much as possible. However, each inhale and exhale brought forth a realization about how dysfunctional my family really was. It wasn't normal for a mother to secretly drain their child's bank account, inevitably stranding them 7 hours away from home. It wasn't normal for a mother to go through her son's social media friends trying to find a babysitter without ever paying them (something my friends had started conveying to me). Another round of breathing only brought forth even more memories from the past that did nothing but amplify my internal frustrations. It wasn't

166

normal to live in a motel for a semester. It wasn't normal to forbid you hanging out with your first set of friends because they were girls. It wasn't normal to move every single grade level. It wasn't normal to have fights nonstop every other day for as long as you can remember your entire life. It wasn't normal to stop seeing your father. It wasn't normal to try and have your child punished when they share that they struggled with self-harm. Nothing was normal and I was fucking tired of it.

After punching the steering wheel a few times, I decided it was time to get out and go back into the room to join my friends. We tried our best to enjoy whatever we could the next day or so while I completely avoided all contact with my parents unless it was absolutely necessary. I knew Lilley (and myself) well enough to know that any significant conversation at this point would do nothing but start a war. The four of us quietly hung out beside the pool or along the shore until we found ourselves packing up our bags and throwing them in the cars once again. I was getting ready to play rock, paper, scissors with my friend to determine who was going to take the first driving shift when I noticed something unusual at Mom's car. She was discreetly (or at least her version of discreetly) handing out small slips of paper to each of my friends before hopping into the driver's seat. Confusion and instinctive anger began to surge once again as I walked up to them to learn more. A few moments later, I was looking at four sticky-notes with a variety of numbers scribbled on them, each of our names at the top of one of them. We had just received a Lilley invoice. A literal bill written on an office sticky-note for what we each allegedly owed her for this beach trip.

I tried to sleep off my rage in the car, but it was no use. The resurgence of anger was too seething to ignore and I had never been able to sleep in a moving vehicle anyway. I instructed my friends not to say a word in response to the notes and then immediately throw them away once we got back. If Lilley complained to their parents or tried to force them to pay it, I told them to ignore that too. If anything, their parents could always claim they had paid those dues through unpaid babysitting shifts. After that, I was more than willing to be the shield standing between my mother and them if she planned on seeking anything further from them. My mind was still trying to wrap itself around the concept of inviting a group of teens on a beach trip for free and then ambushing them on the last day with unofficial, unexpected tabs out of nowhere. Once we got home, I hugged my friends goodbye, reassured them not to worry about the notes, and went straight downstairs to my bedroom for the remainder of summer break. By this point, I had no intention of salvaging the situation. All I could think about was blasting through Senior Year as quickly as possible and moving out the first chance I could.

The bone-chilling beeps from my phone's alarm shot me out of the bed about two or three hours before I would have liked. I rolled over, silenced the squealing, and noticed I already had a text. "First Day of Senior Year. Drama Free. Let's do dis!" flashed across my screen from one of my best friends, clearly already awake and eager to bust through the main hallway for our last First Day. One more year of high school. One more year in this tiny town in the middle of nowhere. One more year of managing the name and reputation I somehow built for myself over the years. One more year of Thursday Club. One more year of hoping no one could see the tattoos all over my body or the cumbersome weight sealed to my ankle. One more year of having to live under the same roof with a woman who I barely recognized from the one I had grown up with. One more year of wishing Nana and Poppop lived closer. One more year of getting to live at home with my little sister who was so adorable it hurt. One more year of memories to make. One that I was going to be late for if I didn't get out of bed soon.

There were a number of different decisions to make and paperwork to fill out over the summer that I naturally didn't do. Therefore, I had about an hour after we all walked into school to figure out the final touches to my schedule. With my standardized test score, I was able to snag a scholarship that could be used to cover some dual-credit classes that would take place at the community college in Lenoir City a couple of days a week. Since these were college courses, they held a different weight in terms of my grade point average on top of the fact that they counted as college credits. While these were huge opportunities, I signed up for the English and Statistics courses mainly so I didn't have to physically be in the high school until the second period for the majority of the week. There was another Biology dual-enrollment course that was actually being taught at the high school but I declined signing up for it since it would probably interfere with my social life more than I'd like. Plus, I had quit the summer job at the drive-in restaurant and I didn't foresee Lilley or Dad offering to buy the textbook I would probably need for it.

Once we got more information about the class schedule for the community college and how that was going to play a part in our Senior Year, I made plans to carpool with one of my best friends who I was crowned Prom Royalty with. We made the plan to meet at the school parking lot in the morning and then take turns driving to the community college depending on which class we were headed to that day. The remainder of my day, thankfully enough, contained an Art class and a Volunteer Period. Typically, the volunteer course was spent shadowing and assisting one specific teacher but I quickly decided that I was going to do everything in my power to use it as a free period. I would either linger around and help the office workers that I had developed a nice relationship with or float around to a number of my favorite teachers' classrooms and socialize with them and their students both. Realizing how much of an easy ride this semester would likely turn out to be, I considered asking a favor from the guidance office and enrolling me into the dual-enrollment Biology course even though I had missed the deadline. Then I quickly decided against that and instead deemed myself worthy of a stress-free semester.

Our college courses started about two weeks after the high school semester started which gave me another reason to love being a hybrid student. English was going to meet three mornings a week with Statistics meeting the other two mornings. This meant we got to sleep in later than everyone else, show up to school anytime we wanted before 2nd period, show up with whatever coffee/breakfast in hand (an awe-inspiring accessory in these hallways), and the opportunity to bring up that we were already in college classes during any and every conversation with the underclassmen as possible. Sure, I still had to deal with a chaotic home life full of perpetual fighting and shady babysitting arrangements and the whole dark cloud thing, but if I could just get through this final year I would finally be free of that. There was no way in hell I was going to let that abysmal haze follow me to college. The Prayer Requests page, my time in Thursday Club, and the constant pleas every night were going to finally kick in before then. From there, I'd finally find the girl of my dreams over the summer or during freshman year and then the rest will be history. Once I figured out where I'll be spending said freshman year, of course.

As I expected, time started flying by even faster than it had before as our senior year launched itself forward on the tracks whether we were buckled in yet or not. Carpool sessions in the morning quickly became live concert performances between the two of us and whatever new albums had just released. Fridays became devoted to football games even if that meant attending the ones at Lenoir City when our teams were at away games. Thursday Club was still a weekly routine as I injected my presence into their social networks while still balancing my friends on my home turf. With my bank account running on fumes, I decided to answer one of my Lenoir City friend's calls to work at one of the popular retail stores at the mall in Knoxville. Through some act of religious miracle, they hired me after my interview despite the fact of having zero experience and wearing very out-of-fashion hand-me-downs that didn't fit. However, I lasted two total shifts before I realized driving 30 minutes to work only to fold the same stack of clothes for 12 hours was not my calling.

Just in time for my bank account struggles which blended into my dark cloud struggles which blended into my "three essays in English and three exams in Statistics pretty much determine my entire grade this semester" struggles which blended into my family struggles, a new youth group in town was formed. One of my friend's mothers decided to take on the task of forming the group and meeting once a week at the church specifically to try and alleviate the pressure and stress she knew we were all facing as Seniors. Everyone who attended seemed to really take the time seriously and kept the life talks very meaningful for the most part. There were a few meetings that I was struck with the spontaneous urge to come clean about the cloud that had been following me around since like middle school, but I knew deep down that would change everything and there was no way to take that confession back. Therefore, I spent my time talking about how difficult it was not having a job and having a mother that I was quickly starting to realize is much different from the person I thought I knew. These were typically met with "well, that's just being a teenager" and "well she's always going to be your mother and she loves you" responses which just further increased my irritation but it was still nice to have a venting session once a week anyway.

Before I knew it, it was already time to start thinking about how I was going to celebrate my next milestone birthday: the big 1-8. Deep down, I knew the only logical plan was to host a bonfire once again but I wanted to make sure that this one was as over-the-top as possible with more attendance than ever. Poppop Luke, always being the supporter of my dreams that he was, immediately granted my request to have a huge party again so the only thing I had to worry about was getting the word out and finding the best music to play. A couple of weeks before, however, I found out one of the baseball players made spontaneous plans to have his own birthday bonfire on the same night as mine. Tragedy. Absolute tragedy. At first, I was furious considering his actual birthday was the weekend after my party so it seemed like he was just trying to sabotage mine. Once the anger subsided, I realized it wasn't worth the stress even if there was a way to do something about it. I still sent out a hundred or so invites out to everyone across social media and then sent a few follow-up texts to the friends at the surrounding high schools to let them know they could bring anyone they wanted from their schools. The last thing I wanted to do was have my random friends come and feel super uncomfortable around the very-unique breed of Loudon students.

Letting go of the stress, AKA pretending it (and all my other issues) didn't exist, of whether or not my friends were going to come to my bonfire gave me enough room to start worrying more about my little sister. An epiphany came to me one night as I isolated myself in my basement bedroom after a fight had broken out between whoever about whatever. The epiphany, which sent chills up my spine, brought the realization to the front of my mind that my baby sister was quickly starting to have the same childhood experiences that Rob and I had. On top of her origin story being out-of-the-ordinary, she had already lived in two different houses. She was already surrounded by spontaneous arguments and shouting that she had no way of understanding or avoiding. As much as I'd like to, however, I knew there wasn't anything I could do to make the eggshells or landmines scattered around the house disappear for her sake. I couldn't snap my fingers and make Mom/Lilley and Dad/Steven (?) get along and fall head over heels for each other. The snap couldn't mend whatever damaged bridges existed between Lilley and Poppop Luke. The only thing I could do was try my best to make my baby sister laugh, smile, and distract her from the fighting whenever I was home.

As it turns out, it wasn't the easiest task to protect your infant/toddler sibling from a house that's constantly on the brink of destruction when you're also juggling Senior Year. From Thursday Club, statistics study sessions, essay writing, youth group, and, most importantly, planning my 18th birthday party, it was impossible to be at home all the time. Rob said that he would try his best to be on big brother watch, but I knew he was hardly ever around between his random job and his new girlfriend whenever he wasn't hopping back and forth between our house and Nana/Poppop's. Poppop Luke had already fallen in love with her and, whenever he wasn't involved in arguments with Lilley, started playing with her throughout the house all day. He quickly donned the new nickname "Paps" that we promised to help her learn once she started getting into the swing of speech. When all else failed, at least I could bank on a friend or two to watch her whenever they were babysitting to make sure she wasn't around whenever things got tense. Of course, this also meant having to hear from those friends that my mother never paid them for doing so, but that was a battle I was willing to endure if it meant another set of eyes on my sister when I wasn't around.

Right before I thought I was going to crumble from the suspense and stress, it was finally the night of yet another milestone birthday party. I blinked in the midst of trying to establish a rescue plan for my tiny sister and somehow appeared in the backyard looking out at the number of people that had showed up despite that other guy trying to throw one on the same night. There was anywhere from 50-75 people all gathered throughout the yard. Some of the guys were throwing football towards each other, an audience of girls watching them. Others gathered around the bonfire pit making s'mores and laughing at each other's random jokes. There were even some that were just walking up with gift bags and cards in hand for the occasion. Emotion was rushing over me as I realized just how much I had succeeded with my plans in such a short span of time, even with the speed bumps along the way. There were so many people who came to my birthday party, ranging from various schools in the area even. Another wave of emotion struck me as I realized this would be my last birthday bonfire since this time next year I'd be a freshman in college. Thankfully, a birthday cake with bright candles and an eruption of singing

171

pulled me away from these thoughts to bring me back down to earth to soak in the remainder of the occasion.

This night quickly got filed in with the other moments of pure euphoria from my time here at Loudon. Nothing could have made my final high school birthday party any more magical than seeing all the friends I had made show up just to celebrate and have a good time with each other. For another evening, we were all able to forget about waiting to hear back from college applications, filling out the confusing financial aid applications, and the various assignments and exams that were going to be determining our finalized GPAs. We were all just a bunch of kids once again in a tiny town in the middle of nowhere just trying to have fun and make each other happy. I didn't even get mad at the small number of guys that had tried to sneak alcohol to make it *that* kind of a birthday party. Instead, in a shocking turn of events, I pretended not to notice and let them all chug it in what they thought was privacy by the side of the house and made sure they didn't act too foolishly throughout the night. I wasn't a regular Christian, I was a cool Christian.

After the party ended, a few of my close guy friends stayed the night once everyone else made their way home. We got the wild idea to sneak some of Poppop Luke's vodka and put it in some of the sodas leftover from the bonfire. However, I quickly poured mine down the drain due to both the gruesome taste and the overwhelming guilt. I couldn't run Prayer Requests, go to Thursday Club, and attend the new weekly youth group just to secretly get drunk with my friends even if it was my birthday. We spent the rest of the night laughing through the old memories we had from the last couple of years and trying to figure out what was going to come next after graduation until we all drifted off to sleep. Once I woke up, I decided to lean into the legal adulthood narrative and head to the gas station to buy my first lottery ticket. Once the buzz wore off and the reality of wasting money on a game of chance set in, I realized I was going to have to find another job. I couldn't keep begging Mom and Dad for spending money only for them to say yes once every 15 times. While it was nice not having any obligations after school, my car needed gas and my social life needed funding.

Paying special attention to how my experience working in retail went, I shifted my focus back towards the restaurant industry. However, since I was freshly 18 years old and knew everything there was to know about the world, I shifted my gaze away from the fast-food job market. With two of my best friends following closely in my footsteps, we landed in front of a manager snagging server jobs at the Cracker Barrel in Lenoir City. Something about taking on the adventure with two of my best friends made the transition into an actual restaurant much less terrifying. We were trading in minimum-wage paychecks for a dependence on the gratitude of restaurant guests. We had a $2 per hour salary but that was basically used to cover income taxes or something so our only source of income was about to be the tips we earned from each table to be given out at the end of every shift. Therefore, we wasted zero time in throwing on our brown aprons over our pastel-colored button-up shirts and memorizing every square inch of the menu. In between our memorization sessions, we were taught the strict customer service standards the restaurant proudly instilled into every single location across the country.

While I imagined starting a new job that was so different from my jobs in the past would be incredibly stressful, it actually provided the perfect escape that my mind needed. It was almost as if this new employment with a fast-paced restaurant environment was the updated version of the woods in my backyard I would always escape into with Chancey back in middle school. My routine quickly became school, using the Volunteer period to knock out any homework, work, socialize in person and/or online, sleep, and repeat and I couldn't have been more pleased with that. While learning how to greet tables, write down every aspect of their order, get their food out on time, and general maintenance was difficult to juggle with writing essays, learning the unholy concept known as statistics, a social life, and being a big brother, the structure provided me some kind of peace somehow. Plus, with all my time being devoted to all of these various responsibilities I hardly had any time or energy to worry about falling into the evil cloud's temptations on my phone's internet late at night.

Once we finally finished our training, we were set free to have our own tables, sections, and shifts. We started to actually see the money at the end of each shift which struck a fire beneath our feet to truly memorize the ins-and-outs of the restaurant that much quicker. We began quizzing each other during the day at school, halfway for fun but halfway to test our actual knowledge before we had to don the famous brown apron later that day. That being said, memorizing the menu and keeping drinks full was only half the battle. The three of us quickly realized that earning a decent tip from a table was both an art form and a miraculous display of good luck. As the weeks passed by, I learned how to read a table during the first introductions to get a feel for the type of service they were wanting during their meal. Sometimes, making conversation was a vital variable while other tables wanted complete silence. Other tables were a complete mystery and you had absolutely no way of gauging whether or not you were doing a good job until you checked the system after they left to see whether or not they tipped you. The more time we spent trying to figure out what it meant being a server in a fast-paced restaurant environment, the more we realized there was no true way of figuring it out. It was a lot of social research, physical labor, and pure confusion all wrapped into one (or sometimes three) shifts during breakfast, lunch, and dinner time.

I came home after a lunch shift one Saturday afternoon to find the two girls that had gone to the beach with us sitting in the living room. A smile spread across my face as I saw them playing with my little sister, an assortment of toys spread across the carpet. I ran downstairs to change out of my work clothes and came back upstairs to an absolute warzone unfolding right where I had been standing only moments ago. Lilley and her father were shouting at each other at the top of their lungs, my best friends caught in between them. Not giving myself time to consider my options, I jumped in between the battle to escort them all back downstairs into my bedroom to try and figure out what was going on. I shut the door leading into the stairway downstairs, my mother's shouting between sobs still piercing through the door. Once we were in the safety of my room, I immediately pressed the two of them for answers as my sister sobbed. They seemed to be just as confused as I was but each crashing sound or shout from upstairs seemed to somehow jog another memory or detail until I was able to string together enough of them to determine what had happened.

Since we had moved into my grandfather's house (without permission), we had all somewhat taken on the responsibility of keeping the house in order. In exchange for helping out around the house, Poppop Luke would often write out a check addressed to the grocery store in town so that Lilley could just handle all the shopping/cooking and hand them the check for the amount at the checkout line. This system had been in place for several months now without any form of issue and there were meals prepared almost every evening and the house clean for the most part. However, that system apparently failed today. Based on all the details I was able to extract and piece together from my close friends and the various screaming from upstairs, it had failed quite miserably.

In familiar fashion, Poppop Luke had gone upstairs that morning and laid a check out on the counter to be later used by Lilley at the grocery store. However, it slipped his mind to partially fill out the check to be addressed to the grocery store. She quickly noticed the fact that he had essentially left out a blank check and took it upon herself to seek a reward as compensation for one thing or another. Not only did she seize the opportunity to fill out her father's blank check to an amount that met her standards, but she sent my two best friends down to the local bank to deposit it into her bank account for her. With the check being enclosed inside an envelope, they agreed to run the errand not having any reason to think the request was out of the ordinary at all. However, once the bank teller opened the envelope and saw the amount written, suspicion arose. Seeing that neither the owner of the check nor the owner of the account requesting the deposit was present, she immediately walked away from the drive-thru window. From there, she called Poppop Luke considering he knew practically everyone in town and had banked there since it opened. Naturally, he confirmed that the check was fraudulent and that he would never send two high school students to deposit a check he had written, especially for that amount. I had walked in approximately sixty seconds before he decided to storm upstairs and confront Lilley for the money she had attempted to drain out of his account behind his back.

We heard my grandfather eventually retreat the battlefield and return back downstairs, the slamming door shaking the whole house. The three of us quietly walked past him back upstairs without making conversation or even eye contact. Once there, I tried to assess the damage of the emotional wreckage upstairs. I had never seen my grandfather that furious but I also hadn't seen Lilley this distraught in quite some time, if ever. My mind immediately imploded into a million different thoughts and feelings as I tried to figure out what I was supposed to do in this situation. While I hadn't gotten along with my mother very well over the last year or two, I still didn't enjoy seeing her hysterically sobbing in the aftermath of this fight. However, my grandfather also didn't deserve to have a check be stolen from him in an attempt to steal that much money out of his account by his own daughter. Suddenly, a tiny spark of anger emerged that tipped the scales in my mind. If he decides to go through with the threats we overhead to get law enforcement involved, my best friends would be involved in the legal repercussions. Since she had passed the fraudulent check for an absurd amount off to them, they would likely have to be involved in whatever trial or other various legal proceedings that emerged. A few more sobs, however, would bring my mind swinging back towards painful indecision until I couldn't take it anymore.

Knowing that there was absolutely nothing I could do to make everyone happy in this situation, I resolved to console everyone while remaining a distant, neutral observer. I hugged Lilley, I checked in on Poppop Luke (he was the furthest thing from a hugger), I hugged my best friends goodbye, and I hugged my sister as tightly as I could. She seemed unaffected by the absolute hellscape of this afternoon, but my concern couldn't help but accelerate as I pictured the rest of her childhood like this. I heard the front door near the garage open. Dad appeared in the doorway, practically dripping with sweat from a long bike ride he usually took every weekend. He looked at me holding my sister so tightly with a look of confusion before another outburst of sobs resounded from their bedroom. He briefly let out an exhausted sigh before asking what he had missed. Unsure of the best way to really describe everything, I gave him a summary of the afternoon before passing my sister off to him and heading back downstairs.

Once downstairs, I called work to ask if anyone wanted the night off so I could eagerly take their shift and take my mind off of my own family for the rest of the weekend.

As I expected, The Great Battle of 2012 had a ripple effect over the next few weeks as everyone tried to ignore the elephant in every room. Awkward, tense silence filled the entire house to the point that it was almost unbearable. Any time I wasn't at school, at work, or with friends I was burrowed away in my bedroom downstairs away from everyone else in the house. I knew the dinosaur-sized eggshells and nuclear landmines were going to linger for quite some time after the fight, but I wasn't expecting Mom to start mentioning the idea of moving out because of the tension. Quickly intercepting these ideas as soon as they were mentioned, I assured her that I would not be joining these plans if they involved moving cities once again. This was my Senior year and I was firmly putting my foot down for once. If she actually went through with moving away from Loudon, I was prepared to do everything in my power to keep myself here. After all, I knew my grandfather would never kick me out of the house so I could always bank on that safety net if need be.

It only took the promise of more social freedom and more distance between my mother and my online friend list to find myself unpacking the last set of boxes in my new room upstairs. She had somehow found a new townhouse to rent just down the road *and* convinced me to join her on this new adventure in the span of about six days. By this point, as long as I wasn't having to relocate to a new school, moving hardly phased me. I collected my bedroom and unpacked it all in the same day within two trips before reluctantly helping my parents unload their things as well. The fact that this house was much smaller with the only two bedrooms being one foot away from each other was an inconvenience but I was hardly home enough to begin with so it wasn't too bad. Moving again might as well have just been another essay I had to write for a class or another exam I had to breeze through before getting to leave and hang out with my friends. Plus, I only had to worry about hearing my parents arguing as opposed to everyone in the house. And if I've learned anything in these 18 years of life, it was how to ignore the sound of my parents yelling at each other.

Acceptance letters started arriving in the mailbox as the time to wrap up another semester came closer and closer. While I was excited to know for sure that I was able to get into the four or five schools I had applied to, I was more concerned with the scholarship opportunities that my beloved guidance counselor said should be arriving in future letters over the next several months. She had helped me officially submit my application for federal financial aid and was there for all the other questions since my parents didn't seem too concerned with my questions and concerns anytime I tried to vent to them. This was the first time I was seeing official documentation for the income of my parents which confused me the more I looked over them. I know I had technically taken a finance class at some point in school but all these legal income documents might have well been in a foreign language. Furthermore, their income seemed to be somewhat decent, at least compared to the money I was making, which didn't make a lot of sense considering the financial trouble we seemed to always be in. Moving every year, constant arguments about money, having to say no to so many opportunities growing up, etc. kept replaying over and over in my mind as I stared at the numbers that were allegedly going into their bank account every year.

I quickly tried to brush away this confusion, deciding it was a bit too late to worry about it all anyway now that I was mentally preparing for life after graduation. Instead, I pushed it all to the back of my mind and just hoped the federal government realized my parents weren't going to be providing me with any form of assistance for college and took it upon themselves to assist instead. If that didn't work out, along with scholarships from the school itself, I guess I would just work every single breakfast, lunch, and dinner shift for the rest of eternity so that I could pay for the only thing that would guarantee me a nice job four years from now. Just in time to remind me just how close we were getting to those moments, our final grades were starting to get returned back to us. The final for statistics was another exam with the final for English being yet another essay. The Art final and Volunteer Period final were just as simple/nonexistent as I expected them to be when I signed up for the course. Thankfully, I didn't have to worry too much about the last fall semester's grades and instead got to see the dual-enrollment courses work their magic on my overall grade point average. After that, the only thing left to do was shout out "See you in January!" one last time to all my friends before walking out of those giant double doors in the front hall towards my car.

My favorite part of the rush of yet another winter break is the further release it gave me from my tumultuous household. There were more opportunities to pick up shifts every day meaning that much more money now that I was really starting to get the hang of serving and psychoanalyzing every table within a few seconds. Not only did the new job provide an escape from reality, but another guaranteed trip to Nana and Poppop's house was just what my mind needed to finally feel peace once again. The moment I entered the doorway of her home, all of my stresses ceased to even exist. There were never any arguments or screaming matches. Another trip into their spell around their property line that eradicated any chances of confrontation or tension whatsoever. On the rare occasion that there *were* tense moments, they both knew exactly how to divert that energy away from the house and immediately knew exactly what to say to dissolve the situation. This holiday was no different as we made our way into their sanctuary for a few much-needed days away from reality. As it turns out, trips over to Grams and Gramps's house were also a nice escape from reality whenever you tuned out the passive-aggressive warnings from Lilley that were inevitably going to be made the mornings of our arrival.

On the dreaded drive back home, I couldn't help but wonder which school I was going to end up going with after scholarship offers were mailed out. Should I go with the university down the road from Nana's house? She already made it very clear that I could live with them if I didn't want to immediately dive into dorm life. Should I go with the college down the road from Loudon? Poppop Luke, his brother, and Nana's brother had all graduated from there so there was a bit of sentimental value to consider there, along with a more favorable chance of landing a larger scholarship due to my familial connection. Would I end up going to the big university in Knoxville to be a tiny fish in a gigantic ocean of other students? No matter which option I went with, I could rest assured that I would absolutely not be staying at home. As long as I was out of the house for once, and potentially surrounded by Nana's shroud of encouragement and support, I would be content. The possibilities of my future continued to race across my mind like three different movies trying to project onto the same screen until I eventually dozed off in the backseat of the car on the way home.

The familiar, yet still psychologically jarring, screech of my alarm jolted me out of my bed to remind me that it was time for my final first day of high school. Ever. One last hoorah. One last glance in the mirror seeing my dark secrets staring back at me before getting into my car. One final trip through the double-doors. One more semester before it was time to say goodbye to these two hallways we called home for eight hours a day the last four years. A goodbye to the teachers that now felt like family. A farewell to the subtle stares and whispers along with the more direct homophobic slurs hurled at my face. A final shot at boosting up my social presence, both in the area and online, before it was time to start all over again from scratch wherever I happened to land in August. This was the main thing that kept my mind from going into full-blown emotional breakdown mode. The reality that I was finally going to be free of the few tormentors, the dark cloud, and my own dysfunctional family was enough to keep myself motivated and sane through the nostalgia. After we all soaked in as much of the excitement throughout the hallway as possible, it was time to start mentally preparing for our list of courses for this final stretch.

As it turned out, the dual-credit English class had another course that corresponded with the one from the previous semester that we all signed up for once again. Four more essays, getting to sleep in, and getting to know our teacher that much more was too good to pass up. On top of that, it meant we pretty much knocked out an entire freshman year English requirement while we were still in high school so it was a win-win situation. There was, ironically enough, an economics course that I had to take but thankfully it was taught by one of my favorite teachers. Thankfully, I only had to take it for half the semester because the second half of the semester was Civic Government which I had already completed during the one semester I spent at the high school in Oak Ridge. Another opportunity to take a Volunteer Period almost summoned another euphoric cloud to fly me through the final semester until I remembered I had to take Senior Project this semester if I had any plans to actually graduate.

Senior Project was a course that instilled fear into us ever since freshman year and was imperative to earning the official diploma we would allegedly need to be functional adults within society. We had to select a career path that we were passionate about or at least somewhat interested in. From there, the entire semester was spent shadowing someone within the community in that field of work, writing an essay or two related to the subject, creating a portfolio that documented our experience and reflected our thoughts, and a number of other miscellaneous assignments. Finally, once this entire portfolio was completed and constructed into a binder, we would present the project to a mystery panel of judges. The presentation itself had to be a certain number of slides containing a certain amount of relevant information and the speech portion had to be immaculate and lengthy enough to satisfy the judges. If you managed to pull all of this off on top of your other classes and any extracurricular obligations, you were deemed worthy of attending graduation. If not, you either tried again during the summer school program or didn't officially graduate. No pressure, right?

With everyone else seeming to know exactly what career they were going to focus their project on, I wrote down the first job that came to mind so I didn't appear as unprepared as I felt. Guidance Counselor. I looked at the words that my hands had just written down on the sheet all on their own. The more I thought about it, though, the more it started to make sense. My guidance counselor here had been my guiding light for the last two years so the thought of being that for another stressed student one day sounded incredibly fulfilling. If only I could spend the shadowing portion of the project in our own guidance office. Since that would never fly, I cranked the wheels in my mind to work at hyperspeed. Suddenly, the perfect idea popped into my head. A surge of accomplishment and even a tinge of excitement rushed over me. Wait. Why was I getting excited about a school project? I regained my composure, storing the idea in a safe spot in the caverns of my mind until I needed to access it again. The intercom in the ceiling above beeped, interrupting the teacher's dull explanation of all the preliminary work we were going to need to do before we could officially begin the shadowing process.

Speak of the angel, an office worker said there was a student in class who needed to report immediately to the guidance counselor's office. My name was then announced through the speaker.

Confusion swept over me as I slowly made my way towards her office, each footstep shooting a hypothetical explanation across my mind. Each potential scenario was somehow more farfetched than the last so it was thankfully a short amount of footsteps until I found myself in her doorway. To enhance the confusion, three of my close friends were also sitting in the office, clearly awaiting my arrival. I knew the guidance counselor and my friends well enough to know that something was definitely off about whatever it was we were about to discuss. Awkward eye contact was made between all of my friends and I which was all I needed to activate the best friend telepathy and know that none of us knew what was about to happen next. The guidance counselor motioned for me to come inside and close the door and I cautiously obliged.

Words finally came out of her mouth now that we were all present and had a tad bit more privacy. Every one of our jaw's practically fell onto her desk as she explained that she had an ethical obligation to meet with all of us together based on the communication she had received from two of our parents. She didn't have to spell it out for us to know it was my mother and probably the mother of one of the beach trip/fraudulent check best friends. When her introduction was met with confused looks and silence, she went on to explain that one of our parents had confiscated a cell phone and gone through every text message and email exchange which prompted this meeting. Apparently, one of the countless emails that was inspected mentioned wanting to just "run away from everyone and everything" to another friend. Seeing this prompted the one parent to call another parent (who I knew to be Lilley already) in hysterics. From there, they apparently arrived to the conclusion that our little social bubble of four or five was planning on committing a suicide pact before graduation. Two of our parents thought that we were all secretly planning to simultaneously kill one another based on a stress email.

Surely this wasn't real. This couldn't actually be happening. This wasn't a real conversation that we were all collectively having to have. The dam shattered in my brain to give way to the tidal waves of emotions all over me. Fury. Embarrassment. Confusion. The entire spectrum of human emotion seemed to be colliding against one another inside my mind and body until I literally wanted to disappear as much as my mother apparently thought we wanted to. We each took turns slicing through the silence settling over the room to assure her that these concerns were wildly unnecessary and that we were all completely sane, or at least we were prior to this chat. Her facial expression as she took in our words told me that she believed us and that she didn't quite take the phone call seriously but at the same time she wasn't able to simply disregard it. She had listened to me vent often enough to understand that the relationship I had with Lilley, and her perspective altogether, was pretty convoluted at best. Thankfully, she assured all of us that the phone call and discussion wasn't going to leave this office so we didn't have to worry about this being one of the last impressions we made on the administration and student body. She released us with an earnest smile and we returned to our classes.

We all quickly checked with each other to confirm once again that everything that just occurred had actually occurred and wasn't just a group hallucination. I made my way back to my classroom alone, trying to wrap my mind around my mother and how everything seemed to have gone so off course. The same woman I had watched movies and soap operas with, cuddled with after nightmares, and ran to whenever anything went wrong was now suddenly an evil villain out to ruin my life at any chance. Somewhere along the way, she turned into this woman who refused to let me hang out with one of my first groups of friends because of "how it looked", freaked out and tried to punish me when I tried to have a heart-to-heart about the whole key-ankle situation, and now went behind my back to my guidance counselor to accuse me of some suicide pact with my best friends. I quickly remembered that Nana had just purchased her first smartphone so at least I could send her texts now whenever I felt this overwhelmed. I finally made it back to my classroom doors after what felt like an eternity of walking through quicksand. I took a deep breath, tried to put all of this at the back of my mind (a space that was getting to be very crowded nowadays), and walked back in.

Time felt like it started launching forward in a blur of waiting tables at work, watching my sister grow up way too quickly, knocking out papers for English, avoiding the house, watching movies and driving around with friends, more social media obsession, and Senior Project. After making the decision to shadow the youth leader from the church I used to regularly attend, I expected a feeling of reassurance and resolution from my lack of attendance over the last year. However, she maintained a strict sense of professionalism every time I arrived while still passively conveying her disappointment that I had to choose my job instead of attending every church service. I swallowed my pride and continued to focus on the Senior Project aspect of the partnership and assure myself I had done the right thing with Thursday Club, the Prayer Request page, and the youth group meetings that had eventually dissolved by the end of last semester. God would eventually notice all of that, along with my constant pleas every night, and take care of everything after graduation anyway so I didn't get too caught up on not having the enthusiastic friendship with my former youth leader that I secretly hoped for.

Prom season showed up once again despite the fact that it felt like we were still in January and figuring out what the semester's classes would look like. I had pretty much knocked out all of the shadowing and various assignments for Senior Project and English so I had all the time in the world to stress about who I was going to prompose to. I hadn't had any luck in the girlfriend department in quite some time, so there wasn't an obvious crush to ask, court, break up with, and still go to Prom all in the same month. After some careful consideration, I decided to ask the girl who had shifted from girl-I-accidentally-stabbed-in-third-grade to girl-I-fell-in-love-with to girl-I'm-best-friends-with. I casually asked if she wanted to get dinner at the restaurant I worked at one evening. Since food was the main way of hanging out in small towns she happily accepted, not realizing I had already worked closely with one of my other best friends who got the job with me. Halfway through the meal, she came out with the flowers and the chocolates on her serving tray that spelled out "PROM?" and carefully placed it all on the table. The surrounding tables responded with a crescendo of *oooh*'s and *aaah*'s as my best friend's mouth dropped open in surprise. A Millenial Casanova, am I right?

After a few moments of suspense, her face transitioned into a smile before she jumped out of her chair to hug me. She wasn't one for theatrics or big displays of affection so I was worried I had gone a bit too over-the-top but she quickly diffused my worries with a short and sweet "yes" after she sat back down. I quickly snapped a photo to preserve the memory (and to post my success to social media) before we went back to our meal. The excitement quickly flourished as we started discussing the various details of Prom and graduation and life in general. What dress and tuxedo color combination were we going to land on? What schools were we still trying to decide between? Were we all going to keep in touch during college? After college? Do we want to get dessert? Do we live in a society?

A few weeks after my successful Promposal, one of my friends I had met through Lenoir City's Thursday Club sent me a text. It took me a few reads before I realized that she had actually asked if I had any existing plans on going to Lenoir City's Prom and if I would go with her if not. It took approximately half a second for me to respond with a huge acceptance speech once I checked to see if they fell on the same weekend or not. Then again, I probably still would have said yes if they were and somehow found a way to hop back and forth between the two. Even if it meant picking up more double shifts on the weekend, I would make enough money to support two different Proms. I couldn't think of a more fitting way to wrap up Senior year and my entire high school experience than going to two dances and basking in my own social development. Little Chase whose only friends were the characters he read in books all throughout elementary and middle school wouldn't even know how to process this information. Life felt pretty great.

Right on cue to follow up a highlight, my parents decided that it was time to shake things up and return to Poppop Luke's house. Lilley said something about being over the last argument and needing to keep a closer eye on her father to make sure he didn't relapse. However, between Poppop Luke not being quite ready for her return and not being able to break the lease on this new place, Dad ended up moving back in instead. I quickly saw through the smoke and mirrors and realized this was actually my parents being separated. I noticed they were arguing more, so I decided to be optimistic that a break from each other might do some good. However, my mother quickly dropped more news to shift the living situation right back into the tense, uncomfortable phase. Rob got engaged to the girlfriend he had been seeing for a while and, for some reason, was going to be moving in with us. Not knowing how this was going to work considering this was a two-bedroom townhouse, I stared in confusion. However, she quickly informed me of her solution to make all of this work smoothly: make the living room her bedroom.

What felt like overnight, Dad moved into Poppop Luke's house, Rob and his fiance moved into the upstairs bedroom, and Lilley moved all of her bedroom furniture to the living room right next to the front door. Watching all of this moving and rearranging not only gave me a headache but sealed the deal on me keeping all of my friends as far away from this townhouse at all costs. As a matter of fact, I may as well just keep myself out of the house even more so than normal at this point. However, in what felt like another five seconds, Lilley told me she was moving back in with my grandfather and Dad and that I could invite one of my best friends to live in the townhouse with me while she was still supporting the lease. She knew my best friend who I worked with was exhausted from living at home with her numerous siblings and figured this place could be a nice break for her. Not thinking for even half a second, I was already helping her unpack all of her things in the bedroom upstairs that we were rearranging to hold the both of us. We had absolutely no idea how we had convinced both of our parents to let us live in a townhouse together with my brother while we were still high school students but the last thing we were about to do was ask questions and help anyone come to their senses about this monumental opportunity.

With the universe sticking to the theme of monumental opportunities, I received a letter in the mail from the college 30 minutes down the road that so many of my family members had attended. Having already received my acceptance letter a few months ago, I knew this had to be something related to scholarships because I had already gotten another similar letter from another school. I took a few deep breaths to try and calm my nerves before anxiously tearing open the letter. After the brief introduction, my heart almost exploded after reading the "Congratulations! We are pleased to inform you that you have been selected to receive..." which went on to explain that my full tuition was going to be covered. I wasn't sure if it was my GPA, the standardized exam score, my family's history with the college, or some combination of all the above but I was stunned. After reading back over it three times to ensure I wasn't mistaken, I started jumping around the house uncontrollably. I was just offered a full tuition scholarship. None of the other schools had offered me something this substantial. There's no way I could turn this offer down. Wait. Did I even know what tuition meant? Oh well. That wasn't important.

I met with the guidance counselor the next morning to have her read over the letter and confirm my interpretations. We chatted over some of the specifics of accepting a college offer and what to expect after that before she helped me mail off my official acceptance back to them. The immense weight of college was finally lifted off my shoulder the moment I put the letter into the mailbox, leaving only the weight of the dark cloud to worry about. Of course, that was going to disappear once I started packing up my things and actually moving out in August. Part of me figured that the scholarship offer and my official acceptance was something my parents would deem worthy of celebrating. However, it seemed with the whirlwind of everything going on with my best friend and the townhouse, my brother trying to figure out how to pay for a wedding, my little sister getting older by the minute, and my parents potentially splitting up seemed to take all the focus away from me. Therefore, I decided to celebrate minimally with my close friends while trying to still work extra shifts to be able to afford the upcoming dual-Prom adventures.

My best friend and I quickly started to fall in love with the roommate concept now that we were carpooling to school and work, catching each other up on anything and everything happening in real time, and getting to live in a house unsupervised. Therefore, it was only right that we invited a couple of our friends to hang out at our new place one Friday night after we decorated the place with all the lavish decor we could find at the dollar stores nearby. Living out a typical teen movie plotline, one of my friends convinced my brother to buy a 12-pack of beer from the gas station about five minutes into the hangout session. Naturally, I felt somewhat uneasy about testing our limits so soon after moving in but the fear of being seen as "that kid" overcame that uneasiness. Therefore, I kept my mouth shut and just rolled with it. Something about the smell of beer made me want to vomit so I decided to stick with my soda while a couple of my friends took care of the 12-pack. I had tried some of Poppop Luke's vodka that one time to impress some of my friends when they stayed over, but that wasn't agreeable with my pallet either. Plus, how was I supposed to beg in my prayers to be healed and cleansed of the dark cloud if I was consuming alcohol behind the omnipotent being's back?

Unlike the popular shows and films about situations like this, the hangout was just a simple one with a couple of friends and didn't turn into some raging block party that inevitably ended with a police chase. Thankful that we hadn't been busted and nothing/no one had been damaged, we started considering making this a regular thing as we settled more into living without parents. Even Rob and I were starting to get along better than ever without parental presences around. However, this peace was quickly disrupted before we had the chance to plan another minimally-alcoholic hang. We were woken up early one Saturday morning by one of our best friend's mothers as she entered and started screaming at her daughter on the couch in the living room. From there, the entire day was spent being screamed at by my parents and my roommate's parents back and forth. Our friend had her phone confiscated again and her mother went through all of her messages the same way she had done before we had to all explain that we weren't planning a ritualistic suicide pact. From there, she relayed the information to my mother and the parents of my now-roommate.

The morning screaming quickly transitioned into afternoon screaming which just evolved into evening screaming. If I wasn't getting yelled at by one set of parents, it was another set or my own. The friend who stayed the night on the couch was quickly taken from our house by her mother but that just gave way for my parents and my roommate's parents to interrogate and intimidate us. What were we thinking? How did we not expect them to find out? Were we alcoholics now? Did we get pregnant the night of the huge party? Were we prepared to be grounded until graduation and then some? Everyone's words and voices blurred into one another as I stared straight ahead trying not to explode. That was, until, I heard my roommate's stepdad randomly say that I needed to be doing a lot more work if I was worried about people at school thinking I'm a homo. My head jerked over to make eye contact with them, trying to determine if I had actually heard those words correctly. I looked over at Lilley, wondering when she was going to step in to defend me. Instead, she stared over at them and then back at me without a single shred of concern on her face whatsoever. The memory of the conversation we had back in eighth grade about my group of female friends was suddenly blazing in the forefront of my mind once again. Deciding I had heard quite enough the last eight hours or so, I stormed off to my bedroom in silence.

Unpacking the last box back into the basement bedroom at my grandfather's house felt incredibly bittersweet. Sure, the bedroom was practically a private oasis, but it wasn't quite as peaceful as living away from my family altogether. Apparently, all concern over breaking the lease early and whatever consequences may come from it was thrown out the window whenever Lilley found out about our evil, sinful rager. My best friend was forced to return back to her house with all of her siblings. She had apologized for what her parents said and for going along with the idea for the 12-pack of beer, but I told her it was fine and our paradise was bound to come to an end eventually. Two best friends living together without any parents whatsoever was only too good to be true for much longer. I took a few deep breaths and crashed onto the bed. There was only going to be a few more months of living at home to suffer through. Then I'd start my brand new life at a brand new school, one that *I* actually made the choice to relocate to for the first time in my life.

The realization that there was so little time left in this semester brought forth the plague of senioritis in full effect. I quickly lost all motivation for anything related to school with each passing day. My grades were pretty much final by this point so there wasn't really a reason to stress about the last two months at all. Or attendance. Or impressions. Even my desire to make as many friends as humanly possible within the building began to diminish once I realized I wasn't going to be seeing them for quite some time after May, if at all. The point came to where all of the Seniors were starting to be asked what their Senior Quote was going to be, a famous portion of the annual yearbook. Without batting an eye, I filled mine in the moment the sign-up sheet was passed onto my desk during a Senior Project progress update meeting. The ambiguity behind "These Aren't the Best Four Years" being displayed next to my senior portrait brought me an immense (and likely unhealthy) happiness. The quote was always restricted to being exactly six words and the vibe of "does this mean high school sucks or does this mean even better times are ahead?" of my six words fit perfectly into how I was feeling about my high school journey coming to an end. Of course, the fact that I was still just bitter about having to move back into my family's house and tired of people questioning my sexuality on my behalf was going to stay with me. Seeing people trying to decipher my quote's meaning and what inspired it was just going to be part of the fun.

With final grades all but certified and finalized by now, the school prepared to hold the annual Top 25 Ceremony to announce the top students in academic order for the graduating class. As much as I wasn't willing to admit it verbally, my nerves had been all over the place for the last week surrounding this ceremony. Everyone in my class, especially my bubble of best friends, had worked incredibly hard on their work and their grades for the last four years. My grades had been pretty good, but my focus had been on my own social reputation, social media, and convincing everyone the dark cloud, tattoos, and ankle chain didn't exist. On top of that, I also had to keep a job since I turned 16 which made studying and homework that much harder to pull off. As we all gathered behind the curtains of the auditorium in no apparent order or fashion, I told myself that I was somewhere in the 11th and 15th spot to calm my nerves. They had sent out the invitations for the ceremony a few days ago but none of us knew what order we were going to be called out until it happened. With my own self-appointment in my brain, I let go of my nerves and tried to stifle my laughter backstage with all my friends and their jokes while name after name was called by the principal.

We were all caught up in the emotion and sentiment of the ceremony that we didn't even realize the name they just called was the eleventh spot. Everyone's mouth dropped open as our heart's all seemed to skip a beat. We were officially in the top ten of the whole class. Granted, the school wasn't that large but we still couldn't believe that this was really happening. All the small jokes and reminiscing stopped as we honed in on the microphone to wait for our names to be called out and our high school legacy solidified. Yes, we were nerds, how did you know?

Another name called that wasn't mine. Another one that wasn't mine. Another one of my friends walking out onto the stage. Another name that wasn't mine. My name. Wait. NO. There's no way. I awkwardly tried to put one foot in front of the other as the bright stage light hit my face and practically blinded me. A certificate was placed in my hand and I immediately started hugging everyone on stage from the principal to the guidance counselor who had kept me from drowning the past year and everyone in between. I stumbled over to my seat before falling into it as I tried to reach up and grab my heart and brain that were still floating up to the ceiling. The remaining three names were called out as our friend group was reunited once again on stage. Somehow four of my closest friends and I had landed the top five spots of our graduating class. By some stroke of luck or mistake, I was number 4 in the whole Senior class. Maybe these *were* the best four years after all.

The ceremony ended to open up the photography session with friends and family over the next half-hour as we all soaked in the feeling as much as we could. The five of us got told to expect an invitation soon for another ceremony and dinner in Knoxville for the top five from schools all around the area. One of the guest speakers at this event was apparently going to be the new football coach for the huge university in Knoxville, but that news went in one ear and out the other. Of course, Lilley was practically jumping for joy at the opportunity to be in the same room as him considering her obsession with football. As excited as she was, however, she still declined my request to help me out a little with the cost of dressing up for all of these fancy events. Thankfully, both Proms and this Top 5 Dinner fell within the same seven day time frame so I was able to rent all the necessary clothing in the cheapest, most efficient way possible. Not having to pay for three separate rentals was helpful, but my bank account was still in pain as the time finally arrived for the first event: Loudon's Senior Prom.

Staring in the mirror, I did my best to not even think about the forehead/body tattoos as I dried off from my shower. Only a few more weeks of time stood between today and my new life away from this school, town, and sinful, secret habit. I carefully put on the various layers of clothing associated with a tuxedo and double-checked myself in the mirror again to make sure my forehead and body tattoos couldn't be seen. I had rented one basic tux and just added a vest that matched my Lenoir City date's dress to save the most money. I didn't want to overdo it for the academic dinner in the middle of this week so I decided to just wear a dress shirt and the rented, bright red bow-tie that matched tonight's dress that also happened to be our school's color. Plus, I could add the red bow-tie to my silver vest next weekend and bring a little bit of Loudon into their Prom just for the fun of it. A few deep breaths in the bathroom gave me just enough reassurance and confidence to make my way out to my car and head over to my best friend/date/former stabbing victim's place.

Her sister was still putting up the final touches to her hair and makeup when I arrived, so I sat and talked with her mother in the living room while we waited. This was practically my hundredth time being at her house so I was her mother's unofficial son by this point. We sat on the couch, reminiscing over the memories her daughter and I had created together over the years. We were just covering the time I had to be taken by her to the emergency room the summer I spent all my free time jumping off of cliffs when her sister ran out to announce she was ready. The conversation about the amount of water pressure shooting into my sinuses causing me to have blurry vision and a headache that felt more like a sword inserted into my skull immediately ended. Our eyes shifted over to the landing as she stepped out in the most beautiful red dress I had ever seen. It's form looked like it was a dress made specifically for her figure and the shade of red matched the acne covering my face and the tuxedo vest perfectly. It took me a few moments to take in how perfect she looked before I remembered to tell my legs to stand up from the couch so I could ceremoniously place the corsage on her wrist.

We took a few pictures outside, my little sister even making an appearance in a pretty little red dress to match us. From there, we went down to the local fire station in town to meet her father, a man who terrified the hell out of me. More photos were snapped while I tried to say all the right things you're supposed to say to a prom date's intimidating father. Never having enough photo opportunities for memory's (and social media's) sake, we joined up with the group of friends from when I was able to go to church so consistently a year or two ago. A few more million photographs and a quick dinner later, we were pulling up to the same venue that was used the year before (and probably every year since the beginning of time). She had complimented the car as we hopped out, making me feel a lot better about not asking to borrow my grandfather's car again. After accidentally totaling my very first car on the way to the community college a few weeks ago (and having every high school faculty member ask *me* if my best friend in the passenger seat was okay instead of how I was doing), it felt more appropriate to just take the car I had just gotten instead. Poppop Luke had put his name as a cosigner on the bank loan, so it technically was still his car that I was using for Prom too though I guess.

The walk to the front door seemed to take an eternity as we all excitedly predicted how the next few hours were going to go. We finally made our official entrance and quickly filled out all the votes for this year's Prom Royalty. Of course, the thought of me winning Prom King crossed my mind, but honestly all I cared about at this point was having one last unforgettable night together with my close friends. As much as everyone was pretending the opposite, we were all about to have to say goodbye to one another so what does it really matter if you win a crown at a dance or not. It was fortunate that I came to this realization before I got there because shortly into the evening, a group of jocks decided to shout out that if I won King they were going to go out into the parking lot and blow their brains out. Realizing they'd have to have brains to blow out in the first place to even carry that out, I ignored them completely and continued dancing like an absolute moron with my best friend until it felt like my legs were going to collapse in on themselves. Once the slow song came on and all the high-school-sweetheart couples made their way out onto the floor, I seized the comedic opportunity of asking one of my favorite teachers who happened to be chaperoning the night if she'd have a dance with me.

Before I knew it, we were all grabbing one more snack before it was time to exit the venue and head home. After the disaster of last year, no one really made any significant after-party plans so we all just hung around the parking lot reflecting on how perfect the night had been. Sure, I didn't take home the crown, but at least that saved a group of massive success stories from ending their life in the parking lot. After we had soaked in every last drop of the emotional high, we parted ways and I carefully drove my best friend back home. Part of me still couldn't believe that my high school story was really approaching it's finale, but I couldn't have been happier to be ending it with the people I was fortunate enough to have befriended along the way. That being said, I had no idea how I was going to completely start from scratch again in a few months and put on the New Kid hat again at a new school again. Especially if the

189

stupid clou- actually never mind. That wasn't even a possibility. It was staying behind. Definitely. I dropped her back off at home before making my way back to my own house, the haunting memory of the nightmare I had from last year's prom following me the entire way.

I had no idea what I was expecting an academic celebratory banquet in Knoxville would be like, but it definitely wasn't this. The venue was massive and there were so many students from so many different schools that we all quickly felt like invisible, microscopic fish in an endless ocean. I pretended to know who the new football coach was as he made what was probably a motivational speech if I had paid more attention to it. The speech and dinner ended, giving the five of us the opportunity to flee and gather outside. Finally feeling like we could breathe again from the overwhelming crowd, we snapped pictures and told jokes until all five of us were practically in tears. Our principal came out and congratulated us once again and told us how proud she was of all of us before making her way to the parking lot. We grabbed a few more pictures while the sun was still out. With all the emotion of the last few weeks, I even asked my parents to take a few photos outside the venue, something I rarely ever did on a normal day. We all hugged each other goodbye as the reality set in that the last time we would all likely be in the same place again was on graduation day. Damn. This was really happening.

The metal clink and the snap of another tuxedo vest being adjusted snapped me back into reality as time continued to propel forward. My reflection in the mirror was staring back at me once again, my face a swirling pot of confusion, confidence, and uncertainty of what life would look like in a matter of months. The red bow-tie didn't quite look the way I thought it was going to look, but I didn't really have a back-up plan at this point. Plus, people would get that I'm just being facetious since I'm attending my rival school's dance. No one has to know this was one of the only ways I could manage to afford going to both Proms. In that moment, an eerie thought crept into my head that began to turn my stomach into an entanglement of knots. What if my oddly-sexual, heavily-male Prom dream from last year had been about tonight's event? I remember the venue being different from my Prom so what if that meant it was going to happen at Lenoir City's? I did my best to stifle these hypothetical concerns as best as I could as I put on the final pieces of my outfit. With a bundle of nerves following closely behind, and tattoos and shackle more prominent than ever in my mind, I made my way out the door.

I gave myself another mental pep talk as I put the car in park out on the street in front of my ex-girlfriend's house. I was still pretty good friends with the girl I dated for a week before breaking up without knowing she had her phone confiscated at a church camp so it wasn't awkward at all to be showing up here. Plus, between my date being her best friend and being one of the most consistent attendees of Lenoir City's Thursday Club, being awkward wasn't really an option for us. There were a few of us meeting together here before we went to take some official photographs and I immediately felt self-conscious of my outfit. It didn't match my date's dazzling silver dress as much as I hoped it would and the red tie felt like a giant tacky middle finger to everyone there the moment I stepped into the living room. Thankfully, the night moved forward quickly enough that I forgot the majority of my concerns and found my ranks within the crowd. I knew pretty much everyone in this group, but I still couldn't help but feel out of place for the first hour or so. However, a quick round of quirky picture poses and a nice dinner at the popular restaurant down by the river put me at ease just in time to arrive at the venue for the official start of the extravaganza.

Blowing my high school's allotted budget out of the water, their venue was a movie theater that had been rented out and completely transformed into an extravagant ballroom that looked like it was right out of an old-Hollywood classic film. The giant crystal chandelier, the velvet ropes, and the cascading levels that took you down to a shiny dance floor at the bottom of the room almost took my breath away. Every minute detail in the huge venue looked like it cost an entire year of my tips at the restaurant and took months of planning to execute. It took a few moments to catch my breath before my friends grabbed my arm and dragged me down to the dance floor immediately. To make the venue that much more insane, they projected the music video for whatever song was playing on the movie screen that overlooked the floor to add a whole other element into the mix. Somehow, quite unexpectedly, only knowing a small portion of the people in attendance made it all the more easy to throw caution to the wind and get lost in the dancing, music videos, selfies, snack breaks, and all the other details that made the night so unforgettable. By the time they had crowned their school's royalty and we were getting ready to make our exit, my mouth actually hurt from smiling so much over the last few hours. That smile left shortly afterwards as my friends demanded we spend our after-Prom time at an abandoned psych ward about 15 minutes away.

Pulling into my driveway around one in the morning came with another rush of surrealism. I quietly snuck in through the basement door and crept past my sleeping grandfather to get to my bedroom to try and process the fact that my last major event of high school (besides the actual graduation) was over. I wasn't sure if it was this disbelief or the fact that we had walked around a creepy, abandoned asylum for the last hour but I already knew I wasn't going to get much sleep tonight. Over and over again, the memories of every moment that lead me to this moment flashed across my mind all at once. Moving every year. Never learning how to make friends. The trial and error of social interaction in general. The teachers, schools, and towns I bonded with just to be forced to say goodbye once again. The damn cloud, psychological tattoos, and cumbersome ankle weight. Opening up to all the wrong people during the battles between my ankle and my keys. Everything was slowly coming to an end. A new era was getting ready to begin. Had I done everything right? Probably not, but that somehow doesn't matter that much anymore.

Just like that, we were all handing in our final essays and assignments to start getting ready for the big walk across the stage. Senior Project turned out to be a breeze once I realized one of my favorite teachers of all time was going to be a judge. With Seniors getting their grades and finals handed back a week or two earlier to ensure graduation requirements were met, we were all able to gather together one last time before the big day. In typical microscopic, Southern town style, we decided to use this opportunity to camp out in the field behind the school across from our football stands. While it wasn't necessarily a "Senior Prank" everyone seemed to make the most of it as we started a small fire, put some harmless graffiti on a few of the classroom windows, and soaked in the last remaining moments we had before it was time to receive our diplomas. One of the police officers in town eventually drove through and let us know we needed to head home, a request most of us obeyed.

Listening to my best friend deliver the valedictorian speech really drove home the reality that it really was all coming to an end faster than I could have ever imagined. Suddenly, I was lining up and hearing my name called to walk across the stage, stop, disrupt the flow of everything by hugging the principal and the guidance counselor, and heading back to my seat with my newfound piece of paper stating I had finished. The ceremony ended as quickly as it began as I found myself hugging every single friend I saw, even if we had only exchanged three total words together. Once I had shuffled through the crowds of students, I noticed Nana and Poppop standing in the hallway with my parents and my aunts and cousins. I had never seen my grandmother look quite as proud as she did as I walked up to give her a hug in my cap, gown, and strands of honor draped over my shoulders. Lilley immediately pulled out her phone and digital camera to capture any and every possible moment before we all eventually settled for taking one giant group photo. From there, it was time for all of my closest friends to dramatically walk out of the giant front doors of the main hallway one final time, with as many of the worst and best memories we could tuck into our pockets.

Of course, I made sure to update my profile picture to a selfie with my favorite English teacher from sophomore year the moment I got through the doors, honoring my promise that I'd wait until I was officially a former student.

Chapter Eleven

Remember When I Woke Up in a Washing Machine?

The summer after officially completing high school didn't feel quite as euphoric as I imagined it would. About a week into working nonstop trying to save up as much money and avoid the house as much as possible, I realized I genuinely had no idea what to do next. When do I sign up for classes? How do I sign up for classes? When do I move in? Where do I move into? How does a scholarship actually work? When do classes start? Not wanting to continue being a burden on the angel of a guidance counselor, I decided to send a blind email to the first email address I could find online to try and get an idea of what to expect. After a day or two of anxious patience, I was relieved to have gotten a response that laid out everything clearly. Now that I had an official room number/roommate, a date for a campus tour that included meeting with my advisor to sign up for classes, and a date that I should arrive to move in, I could put the worry to the back of my mind. With this weight lifted off my shoulders for a while, I could focus on what really mattered: having as much fun with my friends as possible for one final summer.

It took all of a week for me to start realizing that alcohol and weed had intertwined into pretty much every single social bubble I had created. I was typically pretty skilled at refusing to partake and laughing off any kind of peer pressure. However, with high school and all the religious/societal pressure quickly growing smaller and smaller in the rearview mirror, it was becoming more difficult. As it turns out, the idea that drinking alcohol makes you a terrible person, an idea that was drilled into my head for as long as I could remember, starts to make much less sense when all of your friends drink and/or smoke. To make the situation all the more complicated, every piece of social research I stumbled upon within social media and word-of-mouth methods pointed to partying and drinking as the main source of success in college environments. I'm 18 now, graduated from high school, and preparing to embark on a new journey into higher education for another four years. How was I supposed to make a name for myself and continue making new friends if I immediately present myself as someone who looks down upon kids drinking and having fun with each other? Day by day, the promises I made to Lilley when I was younger about avoiding alcohol were starting to feel more and more meaningless and silly, especially with our relationship being so complicated now.

One of my friend's birthdays turned out to be the perfect opportunity to finally tell some of my friends that I was willing to throw in the towel and go to a party. Pulling aside my best friends/former roommate aside at work, I quietly whispered that we should go to his birthday party that weekend and that I would drink as long as no one let it get out. I barely had time to get out the last word before she shrieked in excitement and almost ran to tell the whole restaurant, customers included, the breaking news. She quickly got the sense that I didn't want the news shared but the damage was already done. The seed of worry was already planted in my brain at this point. How was I supposed to keep my drinking decision a secret from the gossip factory of the small town I was forced to call home for the last few years? I quickly brainstormed how to keep it as low-key as possible until I was about to completely reconsider attending the party altogether. Then I remembered I didn't actually have to care about any of that shit anymore.

We walked up to the front door of the party, my mind refreshed with the mindset that I was allowed to have one night of fun. What was the worst thing that could happen? Someone snap a picture of me holding a drink and post it to the *Prayer Requests* feed? Half of the Thursday Club attendees regularly partied all through high school and they were still allowed to be Christians so I didn't care. I deserved one break. Our friend excitedly opened the door and brought us downstairs where there were already quite a few people gathered, all clutching a variety of different beverages. Music was coming from someone's phone connected wirelessly to a speaker that wasn't nearly powerful enough to play over everyone's conversations as I awkwardly made my way over to the first group of friends I recognized. Once they realized I had arrived, they erupted into claps and cheers. Everyone quickly gathered around as a drink was immediately placed in my hand, a sweet-tasting pink headache in the making. Not being one to disappoint the audience, I downed it all in one gulp, a feat that even impressed myself.

My friends, with impeccable pace, placed yet another drink in my hand the moment I was finished with the first. Then another. And another. I started to feel every ounce of stress and worry disappear almost as quickly as whatever sugary, boozy substance happened to be in my plastic cup. With every ounce down, another stress lifted off my shoulders and another muscle learned how to relax itself for what felt like the first time. Everything started to appear more and more amusing and the troubles that typically lived inside my brain started to seem sillier and sillier. Confidence that I had always had to pretend to possess suddenly crept into every part of my body until I felt like an unstoppable force. I walked up to someone from Lenoir City who was standing in the corner and bluntly asked him why he called me a faggot that one time. Taken aback, he stumbled over a few words before actually apologizing.

He even said we should hang out some more this summer if I planned on partying more. I grabbed another bottle of whatever out of the fridge as I tried to soak in this feeling. My problems didn't even exist anymore. My dysfunctional family didn't exist. I didn't have girlfriend problems. I've definitely had my first kiss. I've kissed lots of girls. Wait.

I saw one of my best friends shifting between resting her head on the wall and the counter and quickly approached. Without thinking, I asked her if she wanted to be my first kiss. Hearing a laugh, I quickly planted a peck on her and ran away. Wait. I just had my first kiss. Holy. Shit. She considered slapping me but then decided to laugh instead before grabbing another drink for herself. I knew that probably wasn't the best idea I could have come up with, flashbacks from the fast-food Promposal quickly flooding back to the surface of my mind, but oh well. Confidence was surging even more than before as I announced to the whole party that I had finally kissed a girl so that they could all shut the hell up about whether or not I liked women. Then I made out with another one who seemed happier than I was at my announcement, just to further squash any lingering suspicions. Everyone felt like my best friend. Everyone felt like my girlfriend. Everything was so happy and -

My eyes slowly opened as I immediately tried to figure out where the hell I was and what the hell was going on. Sunlight was beaming directly into my eyes from the window next to me as I sat up and realized I was still in my friend's basement. I had no idea how I got to this couch or this room or anything at all really. I wracked my brain trying to remember the night before but everything got super fuzzy after I called everyone's attention to my publicized first kiss(es). Speak of the devil, my best friend was on the couch across from me, already awake. She quickly let me know that my confusion and fuzzy recollections were because I blacked out due to all the drinks everyone kept putting in my hand(s). Oh good, so this was a normal thing if you drink too much. Panic quickly overwhelmed my brain as I started picturing myself punching someone or throwing up all over the place or any number of other things I've seen in TV shows and movies. After watching me squirm in agony for a few minutes, she quickly reassured me I had done nothing of the sort. Quite the contrary, I had stood up to a high school bully and secured my first kiss in front of everyone. Plus, I had avoided any kind of hangover which was apparently a huge accomplishment with the mixture of sugary drinks I had practically funneled.

We quickly finished waking up and gathering up our belongings and dignities and said our goodbyes to the birthday boy who naturally greeted us without any clothes on whatsoever. We walked out through the front door, leaving an old version of myself on the front porch as I realized just how much I already wanted to relive the night. I didn't care if it caused a scandal from everyone from high school. I didn't care that I still managed *Prayer Requests* and went to Thursday Club for four years. I didn't care if my parents found out that I got drunk (and plan to as often as possible from this point forward). The only thing that mattered is how free I felt and how much fun I was lucky enough to have had last night. Throughout the duration of the party, nothing mattered in the best way. Not my dysfunctional family. Not the dark cloud, my internet search history, and the countless times they both made me cry myself to sleep. Not the assholes who called me those things in front of me and behind my back. Nothing. If this freedom and release meant losing some friends from high school, then so be it. We got to my car and I quickly changed into my work uniform to head to the restaurant. Before driving off, however, I asked if they wanted to rinse and repeat last night the moment I got to clock out later that night.

As it turns out, working in a restaurant made it incredibly easy to supply yourself with alcohol. My coworkers felt like my family (in the good way) by this point so it wasn't awkward or tense whatsoever to ask them to run by the liquor store or gas station to pick up a bottle of whatever sweetened liquor or sugary beer they could find. The idea of going to any and every house party I caught wind of would have petrified the person I was a month ago. However, this new alcohol adventure felt more and more freeing with every random couch (and even that one washing machine) I woke up in. Something about finally finding an emotional off-switch for my brain convinced me that everything was going to be alright for once. You don't have a dark cloud following you or a family that is falling apart at the seams when you're absolutely sloshed on boozy sweet tea and/or raspberry-infused vodka. While I was closing the door on my original plan of working to save money for college with all these alcohol purchases, I was opening another door into new social research. College culture, dance music, parties, finally having the liquid courage to kiss girls, access to a whole new bank of potential friends and popularity, and everything in between was unlocking a whole new perspective on life just in time for me to move onto my next academic chapter of life.

Much to no one's surprise, the whispers around town and the rumor mill began to echo that Chase had fallen off the wagon, made a deal with the devil, and was officially just another fake Christian by the time summer was halfway over. What *was* surprising, however, was how little I cared once I heard. The whole town drinks so why was it such a monumental occasion when I started? Plus, for every friend who made their dramatic exit, there were five more to take their place at every new place I found myself every night. Before long, I was already branding myself as East Tennessee's newest Party Kid across all of Loudon, Knoxville, and the entire collective internet. To be honest, I couldn't have been happier to hear the disdain and disgust around my decision to finally allow myself to have fun. While I would have thrown up from the pure nausea of my name being passed around town in infamy before, my newfound outlook on life let me find the joy in the gossip. Thankfully, by the time this gossip started making its way back to my parents, I had already secured my graduation/full-scholarship gift from them.

With a tank full of gas, a nearly empty wallet, and an unhealthy amount of excitement, my best friend (who was coincidentally now my first kiss) hopped onto the interstate as quickly as possible towards Nashville. With some heavy negotiating on my part, my parents had hesitantly agreed to buy me a last-minute ticket to see my favorite singer that I had watched win the singing competition all those years ago. Not knowing how to buy concert tickets whatsoever, I searched the internet and grabbed the first (and best) one I could find on some third-party website. After two-and-a-half hours on the road, I could have kissed her again out of excitement once we saw the first sign welcoming us to Music City. We made a quick detour so that I could drop her off at her family's house that we were staying at (we couldn't afford to buy two tickets) before I made my way to the venue. Without an ounce of shame, I asked a stranger to take a picture of me awkwardly standing in front of the Grand Ole Opry sign and another one next to a mural of the very artist I was excited to be seeing in a few hours. Somehow satisfied with the awkward quality of the photos, I got my ticket out and headed inside the venue to try and find out where my seat actually was.

The usher took a glance at my ticket and began taking me towards it, my heart skipping a beat with each row closer to the stage we got. She stopped about four rows back from the stage itself and gestured toward the seat at the very end of the aisle. I didn't hesitate in case there was some kind of error and my seat was actually in the nosebleeds. I sat down in pure disbelief that in an hour or so I was going to be 10-15 feet away from the artist I had looked up to for so long. Not only was she the main person I would bring up and compliment in conversations so that everyone *knew* that I liked girls, but she was the first example I was shown of someone "normal" and "average" completely skyrocketing into fame and fortune. With a bit of time to kill, I daydreamed alone in my seat of somehow doing the same for myself. Of course, I'd probably need to learn how to play an instrument first and/or learn how to effectively autotune the animal-being-murdered noise that came out whenever I sang.

A microphone tap sounding through the various speakers interrupted the visions of myself performing on a stage or killing a talk show interview as the host for the evening started to let the crowd know the format for the show. Since this was the Opry, there were going to be a number of different artists and guests in 15 or 30 minute intervals with Carrie's set being the finale. Surprisingly, everyone's performances seemed to fly by as the night kicked off despite the fact that anything I ever looked forward to seemed to drag by in slow motion. As the more current, well-known artists started to make their appearances on the sacred circle by the microphone, I nervously leaned forward to ask the two girls in front of me if they wanted to run up close to the stage right before she was about to come on. The last man finished the last few twangs on his guitar strings before making his exit off the stage. My two new friends and I quickly took this opportunity to run up and get as close as we possibly could to the stage. The employees seemed upset at first but quickly gave up as the rest of the crowd followed in our footsteps. A few moments later, we were seeing her step out with a floral dress and heels as high as the heavens.

As she gracefully sang out the first note into the microphone, I knew it was the best decision possible that I attended this show by myself. I had no idea what possible explanation I could have given to justify how embarrassing my reactions to seeing Carrie up close and personal were. My phone couldn't snap pictures and videos fast enough for my own liking and quickly filled up my entire phone's capacity. I did everything I could to extend my phone out as close as possible in an attempt to record her voice instead of the loud screams and cheers until I realized the screams and cheers were coming from my own mouth. But that didn't matter. Nothing mattered. The only thing that mattered was that I was finally getting to enjoy a concert from my favorite singer who was standing mere feet away from me. She walked closer to our side of the stage, giving out a smile and a wave that I convinced myself was intended for me specifically. The eye contact and wave caused me to completely jump and scream all the more like a small child for the hundredth time that night. A quick glance at the crowd behind me would bring more eye contact with a very attractive person a few rows of people back. Caught up in the whirlwind of euphoric emotions, I didn't even realize that the eye contact was with a guy.

I quickly broke eye contact and regained my composure, telling myself that the last few seconds of life hadn't actually occurred. We didn't stare at each other and smile for what felt like an hour in those few seconds. My brain hadn't told me that he was attractive whatsoever. Staring straight ahead of me again, I caught the last few words of another favorite song before the stage was adjusted. Before she (or any of us) could realize, a dazzling bouquet of flowers and a plaque was being presented to her in honor of her Opry anniversary. A heartfelt speech of thanks and a final song later, I was grabbing my things from my seat and heading out of the venue. I told my newfound friends goodbye, forced myself to keep my head down so I didn't make eye contact with that guy again, and headed to the gift shop. After buying a couple of things that I definitely didn't need and definitely couldn't afford, it was time to head back to my best friend's family's house.

I floated from the car to their living room on a cloud with the sudden realization of just how much I loved music and concerts. I had no idea how, but I knew that this couldn't be the last time I experienced hearing my favorite songs performed live or feeling the connection to an artist from the front row. My friend and her family couldn't wait to hear all about it as I pulled out my phone to go through the million-and-a-half photos and videos I had taken to preserve the memories as much as possible. We all talked about concerts and music and Nashville and laughed and laughed and laughed some more until we eventually all headed up to our beds for the night. I told my best friend how thankful I was that she came with me and let me meet her closest family members before laying down, more happiness washing over me than I could take. That happiness, however, was quickly extinguished when I noticed the eerie presence of the cloud hovering up in the corner of the ceiling. There was a faint laughing sound coming from it as I squinted to try and see it through the darkness of the room. I leaned up in bed and could almost make out a video replaying inside of it while it was still emitting the chilling laughter. The closer I got, the more I started to realize it was replaying the eye contact memory from the concert over and over again as I accidentally let out a gasp that was just loud enough for my friend to hear. I quickly fell back onto the bed and told her I had woken up from a bad dream, rolling over so that my eyes couldn't see the ceiling anymore until I was able to drift off into a painfully restless sleep.

Naturally, I decided to blast the same songs I had heard on stage the night before for the entire car ride home the next morning. The return home was pretty bittersweet because each mile marker back to East Tennessee was another mile closer to reality now that the summer was almost over. Just in time for another reminder, I got an email whenever I pulled back into Poppop Luke's house. It came from a woman who was apparently the Housing Director for Wesleyan and she was letting me know that I had officially been matched with my roommate. I wasn't sure how, but apparently I was lucky enough to have been selected to live with a Resident Advisor in the nicest dorm building on campus. Basically, she went on to explain, an RA was the person on each floor of a dorm building who was in charge of making everyone feel connected and safe but also made sure no one was smoking weed, playing music too loud, and/or drinking. While this wasn't the best news for someone who had just discovered a passion for partying, all I was reading over and over again was how I was going to be getting my own private bedroom, bathroom, a full kitchen, and a huge living room. Say no more.

We exchanged numbers through email and got through the awkward "hey I'm a stranger who's going to be living with you in a confined space for a while" texts and started casually getting to know each other a little bit. He quickly let me know that living with an RA is much different than living with a random student and that I'd be held to a higher standard and expected to follow the rules more than anyone. Once again, I assured myself I was willing to keep my partying habits outside of my room if it meant getting my own bedroom and bathroom all to myself. After our introductions were made and the virtual ice was broken, I decided to hop on social media to see what kind of independent research I could do on him. Scrolling through all the posts, I quickly figured out that his parents lived in a huge lake house about 15 minutes down the road from me. I also noticed another thing pretty quickly. He was gay.

Suddenly, the dark cloud manifested itself once again, this time twice the size and cackling above my bed. A small wave of panic struck me as my mind quickly started manufacturing every worst-case scenario and hypothetical experience it could put me through. If you live with a gay person, does that mean you're gay? Will everyone think we're dating? Is he going to meet me and be able to see the cloud, tattoos, and ankle chain even though no one else seemed to be able to? Was this going to impact the start of my new journey? Would there be an Athens, Tennessee Rumor Factory built the very first step I take onto my new campus? Was I going to have to worry about more whispers throughout the hallways once again? What if he liked me? Should I look into getting a different room?

Forcing a dam to be constructed inside my mind, I eventually stopped the hypotheticals from flooding in. There was no reason to be thinking all of these things. I know I'm not gay. I've not even been watching those videos *that* often this summer. I was changing. People would know I wasn't gay. This wouldn't be a repeat of the last four years. This wasn't going to be the first time I have a gay friend. I reached out to a couple of people that I knew on campus and they mentioned he was one of the nicest people on campus and someone you definitely wanted in your corner, so that was that. I had a gay roommate and a room that's nice as hell for my very first semesters of school that I'm apparently not even having to pay for. Everything was going to be absolutely fine. Epic. Phenomenal. College was going to be amazing. And free.

With the minor emotional spiral suppressed and contained as much as possible, I jumped right back into any and every house party I saw and social media. At every social gathering, I was learning more and more about what each liquor was and what to mix it with so that I couldn't taste the alcohol. When there wasn't a party, or any tables to cater to at work, I dove further and further into social media trends trying to figure out how to make people laugh while still being myself (a very challenging task). One way to somewhat accomplish this, I found, was to throw compliment after compliment to various celebrities so that everyone could laugh at how thirsty I was while also seeing how much I clearly loved women! What I wasn't expecting, however, was for Carrie to respond back after the hundredth time to say that she was not "unaware of my existence" and that instead she was "just playing hard-to-get" with a winking emoji. Having to almost leave work from the heart attack I had, I soaked in every ounce of attention and happiness that I could. My favorite singer that I had seen a month or so ago just tweeted me back with a wink. And the whole world was able to see it. Take that, dark cloud.

Unfortunately, I couldn't soak in the moment of virtual celebrity interactions and alcohol-induced euphoria forever. Well before I was mentally prepared to do so, I was packing up everything I could from my secluded basement bedroom and stuffing it into my car. My parents suggested just taking a few things since home was less than a 30 minute drive away but that advice went in one ear and out the other. It didn't matter if my grandfather's house was two doors down, I was not going to be one of those students who went home every weekend. This was the start of my new journey and I wanted, actually *needed*, to be as distanced as possible from my family for it. Far away from the eggshells, landmines, emotional manipulation, and general warfare that saturated every square inch of any house we happened to reside in a given year. As I gave one last check around my room that now looked as empty as it felt, I knew I was ready. I wasn't nervous whatsoever about heading out and being a freshman. In fact, I was unusually excited for it. A fresh start and this new chapter was one that I had been preparing for over the last few months/years/lifetimes.

I left the dark cloud hovering in the basement, pried off the ankle shackle, and washed the tattoos off my skin one last time before hopping into my car. My parents were following close behind to help me unload everything, but I still watched the town shrink smaller and smaller in my rearview and couldn't help but feel like I was never going to return. I was shedding my skin, a vessel I had been trapped in for the last four years that I was finally free from. I rolled the windows down and breathed in the fresh air of a new beginning with the radio blaring as high as it could go the entire drive. My sister wasted no time running into my arms the moment I got out of my car in the parking lot of my new home for the next few months. After only one trip with all the extra hands, I quickly rushed along the theatrical goodbye hugs with my parents and little sister before sprinting back inside to my new life. Meeting a practical stranger that you're going to be sharing a living space with is never not awkward, but the fact that we had texted off-and-on this summer made it a little bit more bearable than I had imagined. It only took about an hour or two before we were taking turns shuffling the songs playing on my new speakers while I unpacked and rearranged everything in my room.

Against my will, I was told to make my way out into the Commons Lawn for a weekend full of icebreakers for the incoming freshman class that could be categorized in the same bracket as traumatizing CIA interrogation/torture methods. My confidence completely diminished within minutes as my brain suddenly forgot how to communicate with people I didn't know. Each activity I was forced to partake in was another step backward for my social confidence. My heart started to increase its pace as I experienced flashback after flashback of my middle school friendship failures until I thought I was going to pass out on the grass in front of everyone. I closed my eyes, took a few deep breaths, and tried to remember that I had this. I knew how to make friends. It's all I had focused on for the last four years. I was just having normal nerves. Everything was fine. I opened my eyes again and took a few more stabs at trying to learn everything I could about my fellow peers. I regained my footing by the end of the weekend as the rest of the student body made their way onto campus in time for the semester to officially begin.

I'm not sure if it was the fact that I spent the last three months constantly drinking hazardous amounts of alcohol, but waking up for an 8 am class in college was somehow ten times more challenging than showing up to high school at 7:30 every morning. After barely making it to my first class ever, I was immediately made aware that I arrived unprepared. Apparently I was supposed to have already purchased the Psychology textbook and finished the first two end-of-chapter assignments. Of course, I chose to sit on the very front row next to one of my close friends from high school (the valedictorian herself) without realizing how truly unprepared I was. Keeping with the theme, I found out the Biology course right after this class was one that was intended to be taken by Biology and/or Pre-Med majors instead of the normal prerequisite one. Immediately, I was a freshly-anointed high school senior again telling the guidance office that I was not going to be taking the dual-credit Biology class that would have completely saved me from this. Why did no one tell me that college was like this? Why did no one tell me I was supposed to log into the student portal to see that I already had assignments due and required textbooks that needed to be read for the very first day of the very first year? What else did I not know?

In true spoiled-kid fashion, I sprinted to the financial aid office the moment I had a bit of free time on this horrible first day of classes. Not knowing even what I was needing to ask them, I just vented about the fact that I couldn't really afford a whole roster of textbooks right now and if using my scholarship money was an option. To make the day all the more cheerful, one of the employees I was venting with decided to let me in on a secret. Not only did my scholarship not include a voucher for the on-campus bookstore, but my scholarships also didn't cover my dorm room and meal plan expenses either. I could feel the tears beginning to form in my eyes so I quickly made a break for it and sprinted to my room. Once I made it back to the solace of my four walls, I completely lost it. Apparently this wasn't a full-ride scholarship like it had been disguised as. My grades were somehow already bad within the first week, a struggle I had never experienced in my entire 18 years of life so far. And there was nothing I could do about it. Oh, and the cloud came back thanks to my private bathroom.

It took a few rounds of phone calls between Poppop Luke, Nana and Poppop, and my dad/stepmother before I felt able to stand back up on my own two feet again. Between the three separate groups, my books for that semester were taken care of and I was able to at least attempt to catch myself up on the semester's assignments. I asked Lilley and My Other Dad if they might be able to help, but they said they had already helped me enough as it was with the various dorm items we had gotten on move-in day. Lilley suggested getting a part-time job again to be able to sustain myself, unable to understand just how much more demanding college work was than high school work. Around a week later, however, I received a letter in the mail letting me know that I had been rejected from my credit card application. Panic shooting through me due to the fact that I had never applied for a credit card in my entire life, I called Mom to see what I was supposed to do. She let me know, in far too casual of a tone, that my identity hadn't been stolen. Instead, she had applied for a credit card using my name and Social Security number without telling me simply to "help with the textbook situation" which sent a fiery rage through my body similar to the one when I saw my bank account had been emptied into hers while we were all 7 hours away from home.

After making a mental note to never complain about anything finance-related to my mother, I did my best to get adjusted to this semester's routine (after making sure to check my Social Security number for any credit requests every now and then). After a few weeks of feeling like I was hanging on for dear life, I finally started to feel like I had hoisted myself back into the roller coaster seat and even fastened one of the three seatbelts. The only comfort I felt was the fact that no one else seemed to have a single damn clue what was going on either. I had never really taught myself the best ways to study or take notes during lectures because I never had to in the past. Whatever preconceived notions I had for the level of difficulty that college would be were completely thrown out the window by the end of the third week. Waking up from a nap or waking up in the morning quickly became synonymous with routine panic attacks as I pondered what was next. Was there an exam today? Wait, what classes did I even have today? Was something due? What day was it? Does anyone think I'm gay? What the hell was APA format?

Of course, I was able to find lifeboats in between the overwhelming spells of feeling like I was completely drowning under these new routines. A spontaneous trip to the movies at 10 pm with friends upstairs just because. A life talk with Nana on her new smartphone she bought just so she could FaceTime with me. She somehow always knew the right moment to call when I was feeling hopeless, even when I thought I was doing an Oscar-worthy job of hiding it from her. A house party at one of the popular student or athlete's house(s). Finding more and more friends online while I tried to figure out how to be funny and likable on the internet. Getting drunk and convincing a girl to kiss me in front of everyone to try to extinguish any of *those* rumors before they had a chance to start. Somehow convincing my roommate to pretend he couldn't hear me stumbling in at all hours of the night so he didn't have to deal with the awkward tension of writing me up and possibly having to kick me out of my beloved room. Successfully convincing the manager of the restaurant here in Athens to transfer me to their location during the semesters and back to Lenoir City's location between semesters so that I could attempt to keep my bank account from sinking underwater with me. I briefly considered trying to talk my various, disconnected family bubbles into giving me an allowance until I realized how much I would truly hate myself for it (especially with so much of my money going to vodka by this point).

Even with the overwhelming sense of dread and disappointment that came with transitioning from Smart Kid to Train Wreck, I fell in love with living away from home. No more worrying about hiding my newfound love for booze and parties. No more worrying about asking permission to see my friends at any given point. No more worrying about having to confirm that I was still making straight A's. No more worrying about the guidance office calling you to see if you and your friends were secretly planning on killing each other based on a single email or text message. The most notable, however, was the fact it just further confirmed what I had been thinking all along for the last couple of years: maybe everything I was taught growing up was wrong. I always knew something was off with the dynamics of my household based on how other families interacted with their kids whenever I was sleeping over, but actually being taught something outside of my own household (and public school curriculum) was a totally different story and experience. From politics to history to society in general, I quickly began to feel misled and misinformed with every lecture.

In the same breath, however, it allowed me to realize that the person I was led and informed to be didn't *have* to be the person I am. Being away from home provided me an environment to question all of this and the freedom to start breaking down those ideas and mindsets. With every new friend, both online in person, that came to be in my friendship circle to every lecture on who says what society/the brain/politics/history is or isn't, I felt a shift happening. Social media became a place where I continued learning more and more about this shift as my feed began to feature more and more theories and ideas that people were sharing from all over the country/world. While absolutely nothing felt like it made sense and no one had a grasp or understanding on what was happening, not everything felt bad in this way. We all seemed to be shedding the small-town high school skins that we had been forced to wear the last four years. We were all finally away from such extensive adult supervision and were actually creating our own little society on this small campus where it was okay to talk about these shifts and how much better life seemed to be while simultaneously feeling so chaotic and overwhelming.

As I continued riding the unicycle on a thin wire suspended between two massive skyscrapers, I started to get better and better at pretending like I knew what was going on and feigning intelligence for classroom discussions and exams. For a moment, I considered trying to find some study groups and actually learn how to college. Then that moment passed when I realized that would take up too much time and interfere with more important matters like my social life, social media, vodka, and definitely not still watching those kinds of videos on the internet in the privacy of my new bathroom. I decided to attend one of the Greek Life mixers to see what exactly a fraternity/sorority was and whether or not it would be able to help me put myself on the social map of campus. There didn't seem to be many other people interested, if any, but I agreed to come to the first few meetings to learn more about it. All the TV shows and movies show the popular people in them, so why not give it a shot, right? When I wasn't working, semi-pledging with the only fraternity, waking up in a dorm hallway/staircase after a night out, fleeing to Knoxville every chance I could for parties/overall escapism, or any combination of the above, I could study and worry about my actual academic performance.

After a few meetings and general hangouts, they decided to ask the pledges to participate in the Homecoming Lip Sync performance. The pledges were me and the dark cloud that was still hovering over my head and continuing to grow by the day. No one else that attended the mixer came back for another meeting but I was pretty much down for anything that would elevate my social status so I stuck around. They were apparently going to be teaming up with the softball team for a joint performance in the event this year. I had no idea what Lip Sync (or Homecoming Week in general) was but I wasn't about to decline any social opportunity. Of course, my excitement started to change slightly once I found myself learning choreography and lyrics to that popular acapella movie with the entire fraternity (8 members plus me) and the entire softball team (quite a bit more than 8 members). If no one was able to see the cloud and all the other terrors that followed me here from high school before, they probably could once I stepped foot on stage with a bunch of girls to lip sync and dance around. Of all the movies we could have chosen to collaborate on, why did the two groups decide on this one? Why couldn't we do a fun little skip and dance to some kind of gruesome, heteronormative war film?

I quickly found out through small talk between dance/lyric practices that Homecoming Week was pretty much the most popular event of the entire academic year except for Graduation itself. Every weeknight was a different activity or contest for every participating organization to win points that lead up to the final night with Lip Sync being the last challenge. After they announced the winners of Lip Sync and the overall Homecoming competition, they apparently also crowned the Homecoming King and Queen of the Senior Class with each class's two Homecoming Court winners behind them. I tried to calm my nerves about being on stage in front of the entire student body, faculty, staff, parents and family of the students, and pretty much anyone and everyone from the whole town but it was hopeless. Each practice brought more and more nerves right up until it was suddenly the day of the show. I barely remembered classes this week or any of the activities leading up to today. The thought of the performance tonight made me almost skip out on all of my classes but I finally pushed through and started downing airplane bottles every thirty minutes until it was time to get ready and head to the auditorium.

Surprisingly, my parents decided to come watch the performance to support my potential new fraternity but Nana and Poppop were unfortunately unable to. Realizing that might have been a blessing in disguise with how many shots I had taken to calm my nerves, I quickly said hi and bye to my parents and headed up to the reserved seats at the front to watch the show begin. Act after act started to perform and I started to think we might not be able to pull off a win until I noticed everyone around me shifting through the small archway to the backstage area. Oh god. It was time. I awkwardly shuffled in behind them as the act before ours began. I watched through the small opening in the curtains and immediately started imagining everything that could go wrong and how I could single handedly ruin the entire competition for everyone. What if I forgot all the moves and words the moment the blinding lights hit my eyes? What if I passed out? What if I threw up? What if I had *too* much fun with it and the cloud showed up for everyone to see? What if somehow-I felt a sharp, firm tap on my shoulder before it was quickly followed by a shove as I fell forward through the curtains and the painfully-familiar music began to play.

By some miracle of god, I remembered the choreography while keeping my mouth moving to the words. Between the blinding lights making it impossible to see the crowd and the vodka shots coursing through my veins, I was able to let the nerves go. I even had fun once I forgot what I was so stressed and worried about for the last month. But not too much. Not a questionable, suspicious amount of fun. The right amount so that no one in the crowd could raise any eyebrows. I even made sure to miss a couple of the steps on purpose so that I didn't seem "passionate about choreography" or anything feminine or homoerotic like that. I firmly planted the last step into the stage as we all froze in place to end the performance and immediately heard the crowd erupt into cheers, a euphoria I hadn't felt in so long. I soaked in the excitement before we were herded off the stage for the rest of the event to resume. All of the hesitation that almost developed into regret immediately lifted off my shoulders to be replaced with accomplishment and gratitude that I had signed onto this team (even if we only snagged second place instead of first). As I headed back to my room to change into something for the after parties, the only thing I wanted to change was Nana being there to witness it.

A few days after the buzz from the second place win and the unholy amount of alcohol we all consumed after had worn off, I got news that I was being kicked out of the fraternity. Thinking this was some kind of hazing, especially with it being done over text message, I played along and tried to call the guys to get ahead of the joke. My jaw dropped as I quickly realized it wasn't a joke and they actually just kicked out the only pledge they had managed to recruit and convince to get on stage in front of everyone. While they said it was due to the fact that I had said some sort of inappropriate jokes to the fraternity alumni after Lip Sync, I just *knew* it was because one of the main guys didn't like me. I wasn't so upset by the rejection from the fraternity itself but more so the fact that it gave me one less opportunity to climb the social ladder and one less pathway into parties. That being said, it only took one pep talk from one of my new friends who quickly reminded me it was a local fraternity with like eight total members before I was feeling back to normal again. By normal, I mean drunk.

My methods of pretending like I had a single ounce of understanding in all of my classes continued until a phone call from Lilley quickly interrupted my rhythm and peace one Thursday afternoon. My mother quickly started screaming a mile a minute the moment I accepted the call and started demanding that I skip the rest of my classes that week and come to Nashville immediately. Laughing off her bizarre request, I told her I would hang up if she didn't slow down and start explaining what the hell was going on. After almost hanging up three more times, she finally said a few words that immediately caused my stomach to turn inward on itself: Nana was in the hospital. I almost dropped the phone and passed out on the spot as I tried to find the right words to say. A few deep breaths later, I asked her how serious it was. As horrible as that sounds on the surface level, Nana had fallen before in the past and Lilley had the tendency to exaggerate anything and everything that happened to Nana and pretty much anyone else in the family. Plus, I had never skipped a single class so far and had no idea how to go about doing so. I was so far behind and clueless as it was, I could only imagine how much further that would plunge me into *D* and *F* territory.

About an hour later, my best friend sent me a text that she had called Lilley and even spoke to the hospital staff. Being a student at MTSU, she was already pretty close to Nana's hospital. My stomach continued to constrict itself into a complex network of intertwining knots as she confirmed that this was just as serious as Lilley was describing it, for once. With it being such a small campus, I immediately texted all of my professors to tell them that my beloved grandmother had suffered a sudden, very serious accident. Much to my surprise, I got their responses in about two minutes. They all urged me to get in the car and go see her and not to worry about anything related to classwork until I had things figured out with my family. My Psych professor, who I would be seeing a lot of if I was to continue my pursuit of being a counselor, even included that he'd lower my grade if he saw me on campus at any point the rest of the week. A couple of emotional spirals later, I was on the interstate with a duffel bag stuffed with the first clothes my hands could grab.

With two and half hours of a drive to go, my mind immediately started creating the best and worst scenarios possible. About 30 minutes into the drive, I had a full spectrum of possible situations and how I was going to react to each one once I parked my car at the hospital. My worst case scenario featured her having to have some kind of brain surgery or missing a limb. The best case scenario showed her being checked into the facility as a precautionary measure and Lilley overreacting as usual. Every other hypothetical fell between those two extremes and regardless, this was just going to be a weekend away from campus and then everything would go back to normal. Catching up on school couldn't be *that* hard especially if the professors already knew that I couldn't avoid something like this. Nana was a fighter. She beat cancer and an excruciating spinal issue for the last decade or so. I sped up a little bit, eager to get there so that she could scold me for skipping class for something so silly.

Rob met me at the front entrance after I intentionally spent 15 minutes finding the best parking spot to avoid going in right away. We gave each other a hug in that awkward way that only brothers who aren't actually that close can do. I tried to make a joke to break the silence once we were in the elevator but his face stared sternly back at me without even the slightest smirk. He told me that I needed to prepare for the worst before I see what I'm about to see. The knots in my stomach twisted even further inward on themselves and I thought I was about to hurl all over the elevator shaft. I could swear that the shaft was spinning a hundred miles an hour as it inched upwards on the ten-hour-long journey until the doors finally opened again with a ding that was way too cheerful to be in the ICU wing of a hospital. We rounded corner after corner, each foot feeling like it weighed a metric ton. My vision seemed to shift into slow vision as my Nana's room slowly crept into view as we rounded the final corner.

I saw breathing tubes and a million beeping machines and her eyes completely closed and completely lost control of my entire body. I collapsed into a crumpled heap on the icy linoleum tiles, wails and sobs already pouring out of my body. Rob and the rest of the family who were gathered around her bed rushed over to me, but I didn't care. I didn't care who heard all the random noises I was making or who saw how much I was crying. Nothing mattered. My Nana was unconscious and barely being kept alive by a machine. Eventually, I managed to pull myself back up onto my feet and quietly hovered over to her bedside. I took her hand in mine, hoping that somehow she would be able to tell I was here and wake up. I finally looked around the room to see who all was here, a warmth rushing over me as I saw that my best friend had come. Lilley was sitting on the other side of the bed with Poppop beside her. Dad was here, although I had no idea if they were even still married or not. Rob and his wife were standing in the doorway. My aunt, Poppop's daughter, was also here and looked like she had just got done crying too. Everyone in the room did, actually. Even Dad, who I had rarely ever seen express any kind of major emotion other than anger.

With my hand trick not working, I found the nearest empty chair and collapsed into it as Poppop started to explain what had happened, Lilley forcing herself into the explanation every other sentence. Painfully against my will, a haunting visual of Nana going outside early in the morning to let their beloved toy Australian Shepherd outside in the backyard. As she walked back up the stairs, her mind left her body in a seizure-like episode that had happened a few times before. With no one there to help, she fell backwards until her body collided into the concrete of their back patio area. Tears were once again welling up in my eyes as Poppop finished the story as he found her there. Unfortunately, even with the urgent emergency services that were there right away, there wasn't much that could be done to help. An eerie beep from one of the machines sounded again to interrupt the visual in my mind, a dark reminder that it was the only thing keeping my favorite person in the entire world alive right now. I walked over to the bed and held her hand once again, wishing more than anything that I could trade places with her right now.

The next few hours consisted of going back and forth with the stories about Nana the way you do when there's an unexpected accident. Every other story, someone or everyone would start sobbing uncontrollably and even pleaded out loud for her to wake up. From there, my family decided it was time to head back to Nana and Poppop's house now that visiting hours were technically over. We made our way into the house, Nana's absence immediately feeling like a dense fog weighing down inside. Nothing felt right. I shouldn't be here under these circumstances. Rob and his wife were living here, so I headed upstairs to the bonus room to get away from everyone a few minutes after arriving. Sleep was not even on the spectrum of possibilities as I tried to comprehend waking up the next morning without hearing her singing or the smell of whatever breakfast she had decided to make everyone. I turned off the lights, closed the blinds, and laid down on the couch to stare up at the ceiling in the darkness. The only slight ounce of comfort I could find came from replaying every single memory I possibly could. From my very first memory of life to the warmth I felt the first time she FaceTimed me on her new cell phone, the ceiling turned into a theater screen that my mind projected all of these memories onto until I saw the early rays of sunlight coming through the blinds the next morning.

The walk downstairs felt like an hour-long trek as I braced myself to walk into a kitchen where she wasn't whipping something up with a smile. I walked past everyone without a word and stepped out onto the back porch. It took all of thirty seconds before I was breaking down on the steps as I tried to comprehend that Nana had been hurt in this very spot 24 hours ago while I was probably waking up in a hallway, stairway, or lawn somewhere near campus still drunk from the night before. I should have been here somehow. I should have been here to catch her before she fell. I could have, and should have, been here to do something before she got to the state she's in now. It should have been me that fell. This wasn't right. This isn't how anything is supposed to be. I quickly ran inside before anyone saw me having yet another breakdown. I took a deep breath and stared at myself in the mirror before telling myself it was going to get better. She's going to fight this like she fought through every other hurdle in her life. She's going to wake up today. She's going to see me graduate college. She's going to see me get married. She's going to be okay.

Chapter Twelve

Remember When Nothing Mattered?

Taking a look at myself in the mirror, I adjusted my bow-tie (she loved bow-ties) for what felt like the millionth time that morning. The tie (and jacket, shoes, pants, shirt, and belt) that I had to quickly convince Dad to buy me from some random department store didn't look right no matter how many times I readjusted. Then again, I don't guess there's really a "right" way to look at the funeral you never imagined having to attend. No matter how long I looked in the mirror in her, well Poppop's I guess, guest bathroom, I couldn't wrap my mind around how my life had turned upside down in a span of like 48 hours. The beginning of the week featured me waking up in random locations as a drunk college student who didn't try nearly hard enough in his classes and now I'm getting dolled up for a funeral for the only person I loved more than myself. Nothing fucking mattered.

After convincing myself that I didn't look *too* devastated and depressed to go stand next to my favorite person in the entire world and listen to people lie and say how they knew exactly what I was feeling, I made my way out of the bathroom. My little sister ran up and jumped up on my leg, demanding I throw her up in the air and play the cheerleader game she loved so much. I did my best to not explode in anger as I told myself she wasn't old enough to know what was going on. I mustered up the motivation to throw her into the air above me a couple of times before heading upstairs to cry again. I dried my eyes for the millionth time, a burning sensation immediately surging through my eyes as I realized I didn't have any tears left inside me. Lilley or my aunt or a stranger yelled from downstairs that it was time to go and I did yet another check at my reflection. I quietly trudged downstairs, trying to convince myself not to break down again with every step. I wasn't sure what car I stepped into but the ten minute drive to the funeral home took several hours before we were parking outside the building that I wished didn't even exist.

For whatever reason, we stood in front of the open casket in front of my beautiful grandmother for the next hour. The line of people seemed to wrap around the entire building as they passed by each one of us, assuring us they definitely know how difficult this time was for us. Sympathetic face after sympathetic face, each one pretending they could comprehend how close I was with her and how it felt to have my entire heart ripped out of my chest overnight. Why the hell were the closest family members expected to stand up in front of a crowded room of people during the absolute lowest point of their life? Why was I supposed to smile and nod at all of these people who may or may not have even spoken to her in the last five years? Ten years? 30 years? How have this many people fit into this room? Why was this happening? How was this real? This was because of me. God's punishing me for all the-

I almost lost all semblance of my composure when I glanced over and noticed Poppop Luke walk into the room. In all my years of life, I had known him to leave a 50 mile radius of Loudon three or four times at most, yet he made the drive all the way to Murfreesboro to give his final goodbye to her. A snide comment from Lilley brought my focus back to the grim reality of where I was and what I was doing. She had been arguing aggressively with Poppop and my aunt for the last 24 hours straight it seemed. I wasn't even sure what the topics of the arguments really were because I pretty much tuned out the entire world once I realized the life support machine had been turned off. Although going off of historical references, I could only venture to assume that it had something to do with money and/or the funeral plans. Poppop had called me in to help earlier that morning I think but I stopped listening whenever my request to play her favorite performance of her favorite song had been denied. There was some disappointment, but the last thing I was about to do was make snide remarks or start arguments. Apparently not everyone thought that way.

Eventually, I stopped pretending to smile and hug everyone back who made their way through the line. Instead, I stared at a spot on the wall and kept pinching my leg through my pants pocket hoping it would wake me up from this unimaginable nightmare. A random preacher must have been speaking for fifteen minutes already before I looked around and realized we had moved inside for the service already. Her casket had been closed, moved up to the front of this huge funeral home, and adorned with some of the millions of floral arrangements that were sent in from god knows who and god knows where. What were we supposed to do with so many flowers? Why were flowers the thing that was supposed to magically make all of this okay? The low-quality, scratchy sounds of the songs that had been selected started playing through the building speakers and it took everything in me not to break down, scream, or both. This was not the service she deserves. Then again, no service in the world could honor her the way she deserved.

I took another glance around to notice we were now at the cemetery despite the fact I could barely remember the rest of the service or who I rode here with or what anyone had tried to say about her life and how perfect she made everyone feel. Nothing anyone was saying at the burial service entered my mind. None of the words mattered. Nothing was going to make this nightmare go away or bring back the woman who was now hovering above her final resting place. People eventually started filing out of the cemetery property, leaving the small handful of us to sit in somber silence. Lilley went back and forth from arguing about everything she would have done differently and posing my sister next to the grave site for photos until I felt like I was going to vomit. Without a word, I walked back over to the few cars that were left and waited for someone to offer me a ride back to Poppop's house so I could get in my car and flee. The thought of sticking around while Lilley reflected on losing control of the funeral planning or asking about her inheritance was not in the realm of possibilities for me. Did they think I'm on her side? Are there "sides" to this already? What was "this" exactly?

More arguments started to erupt the moment we got back to their house as Lilley began going through all of Nana's belongings and staking her claim to anything and everything. Without a moment's hesitation, I hugged everyone and got in my car and headed back to campus. I went back and forth from blaring the music up as loud as it could go to suffering through the drive in complete silence as I tried to make sense of what had just happened this weekend. Questioning the events of a weekend was not a first by any means but typically it involved a very different set of questions. What did I do last night? Why did I wake up in a washing machine? Who did I make out with? Was she pretty? Did I make sure to get a picture of it so I could post it online and show everyone? I would give anything to have those questions flashing through my mind instead of the ones on this gloomy, rainy return home. Why did she have to die? Why didn't I get the chance to say goodbye to her while she was still herself? What if I just ran off the road going 95? Should I just drop out of college now? Was there vodka in my dorm?

After driving through the tormenting thoughts about flying through the guardrail and/or wrapping my car around a tree, I arrived back on campus in one piece. I sat in the car for a moment or fifty, watching all the students bopping in and out of the various buildings and pondering how the hell I was supposed to go back to normal. How do I just turn on my brain switch again and show up for the rollercoaster known as a college semester again? Thinking back to *Prayer Requests*, Thursday Club, church, and the thousands of hours I had committed to all of the above only to have the most important person in my life stolen from me overnight without hesitation made me almost puke the second I stepped out onto the damp asphalt. If god was real, this was not how any of this would have happened. I took a few steps forward, contemplated getting back in my car and driving to California or somewhere and starting a new life, and then continued onward to my bedroom. Some of my friends were hanging out in my living room and immediately fell silent when they noticed me walk in. The thought of answering anyone's "how are you feeling" made me almost collapse on the spot. I kept my head down and walked straight to my room, firmly closing and locking the door behind me. Thank god there was still vodka in here.

A dismal grey film cast itself over the entire campus as I forced myself to somewhat maintain a presence within my classes over the next few weeks. Sure, all of the professors knew what happened and were sympathetic. But at the same time, I could just sense that they could only do so much for me without it becoming some kind of ethical issue. About every week or so, for the briefest of moments, I could hear a small voice in the back of my head. Nana's voice. She would tell me to keep going and not to give up. She would show up in my dreams almost every night and I'd wake up in tears every morning. Being able to hear her for what felt like a millisecond and see her while I was tossing and turning at night was painful but in the most beautiful way. Between breakdowns, I would stare at the ceiling of my bedroom. Stare at the linoleum tile of whatever class I could talk myself into going to. Stare at the shower wall in front of me as I turned the dial as hot as it could go in hopes of feeling something through the grey film of numbness. Then came the thoughts about grabbing my keys again. The thoughts of filling the tub and somehow trapping myself underneath the surface. Every now and then there came the thoughts of wrapping my car around a telephone pole again. Then her voice would pop back in again just long enough to dispel these thoughts for a few more hours.

Drinking by myself had never really been much of a problem but my evenings quickly started to become two or five glasses of some kind of vodka concoction. Part of me knew this was not a wise nor a healthy habit but it helped keep *those* thoughts at bay. Every now and then, a knock from one friend or another at my bedroom door would interrupt my blank stares at the wall and thoughtless sips from my cup. They would sit on my dorm bed with me and within seconds I would be in tears before they could finish asking how I was doing. A small handful of them got to witness these breakdowns and took me in their arms until I was finally able to gather myself again. A couple of them even got to listen to some of the last voicemails, text messages, and voicemails I had from her until that got to be too unbearable of a task. The more of these breakdowns that occurred in the passing days, the less grey everything slowly started to seem. With each drunken sob session that I arrived at, the more pixels began to fill with color in my vision. My relationship with alcohol quickly transitioned from a way to socialize and kiss girls into the only way I could trick myself into expressing and letting go of the immense dread and grief I was feeling all the way to my very core.

Fake smiles and feigned laughter became my favorite accessories as I started to put myself back together enough to keep up with my grades and try to maintain my friendships. Sometimes, this involved

214

going to my dorm between classes to make a boozy concoction to hide in my water bottle to get myself through the day. I realized it became easier and easier to keep those lethal thoughts at the back of my mind if I filled my head with classwork, making my professors like me as much as possible, and inviting myself to parties again. When there wasn't a party going on within the confines of our tiny campus or within the social network of my coworkers at the restaurant, I started inviting friends over for movie nights or random hangout sessions. Having friends around me more often made the constant drink that was within an arm's reach at any given time seem much less concerning somehow. Stumbling around, slurring your words, and showing up to class with a hidden bottle of booze wasn't a problem if you were still smiling and hanging out with friends. As long as you weren't drinking alone in an empty bar or downing a bottle in the corner of your empty house, it wasn't alcoholism, right?

Halloween and my birthday passed by in a meaningless blur with all the other occasions I invented to justify my constant consumption. It gave me a reason to start getting back on social media, however, despite how strange it felt following up a memorial post with a celebratory birthday one. Somewhere in a mindless scroll across my timeline one afternoon, through some kind of joke from the universe, I stumbled across the profile of someone who looked familiar. It took me a few moments before I realized it was the same person I had seen at the Carrie show in Nashville this summer. With a couple of glasses of alcohol already coursing through my veins, I sent a request to follow his account and sent him a message asking if he happened to love Carrie and attend a show back in June. Part of me started to panic and tell myself that wasn't very hetero of me to have done, but the rest of me just didn't care anymore. About anything.

In a matter of minutes, the mystery person from my first concert experience was no longer such a mystery. He suddenly had a name, a social media account, and actually replied to my out-of-nowhere message confirming he was in fact at that show. Not only was I suddenly online friends with the mystery person, but he apparently was going to school just 20 minutes away from me and his home was in the Knoxville area. Before too long, we were sending messages and snaps back and forth until it felt like we were best friends. We made plans to hang out as Thanksgiving Break flew by and Winter Break quickly approached. Thanksgiving felt empty and meaningless now that Nana was gone and Lilley had pretty much wrecked any hopes of a remaining relationship with Poppop and the aunts/cousins on his side. She kept sending me updates about how she was screwed out of money and belongings but I had quickly stopped paying attention once I was given a pair of diamond earrings that were meant to be passed down to me. It didn't help that I never felt like I really belonged at Grams and Gramps' place with how Lilley always talked about them and that I wasn't sure quite where I fit in on my biological father's side of the family yet. Signing up for a double shift at the restaurant seemed to be the easiest and most painless way to spend the holiday, especially with how much money there was to be made from families eating together at this particular restaurant.

Waking up one morning sent me into a panic as I realized I wasn't in my familiar dorm room setting until I realized that the semester had already ended. I hardly remembered submitting any final exams or assignments but it's not like I was in a rush to check my final grades to begin with, even before the tragedy of losing Nana. I still wasn't used to this auto-pilot mode that my body and mind seemed to operate under to push me through all the lectures, quizzes, tests, and, most importantly, parties to keep my mind off of death. However, the good thing about the auto-pilot feature was that it didn't let me go into too much panic over my newfound best friend being a man I've yet to meet in real life outside of a moment of meaningful, yet restrained, eye contact at a Carrie Underwood concert. We were texting back and forth every day at this point and were going to meet up for the first time and grab dinner before heading to this country bar in Knoxville for a college night special. Plus, with the semester and its million-and-a-half academic obligations out of the way, I could sneak twice as many airplane bottles through my waistband since I could sleep in tomorrow.

I got my timing completely wrong on dinner and he ended up having to meet my parents and me at a restaurant they had stopped at instead of just the two of us meeting somewhere. With him meeting Lilley and Dad, who might have been still together but it's unclear, I was pretty certain this was going to be the first and last time I'd ever see this new friend. However, he surprisingly followed our car back to the house instead of fleeing back towards Knoxville having to meet them. Once I started changing into whatever outfit I was going to wear the rest of the night back in my bedroom, I realized how easily we were able to carry conversation despite this being our first time meeting. However, a few moments later this pleasant observation turned into panic as I started wondering why it was that I was enjoying the conversation with him so much. Time for vodka.

We headed over to meet some of my high school friends to start pregaming as much as possible while they finished getting ready since it was always a wait-and-see game of whether or not you could sneakily drink once inside. He might as well have been someone who went to our high school with how easily he got along and blended in with the group. We danced around to whatever songs were playing out of the cheap Bluetooth speaker until they had put the final touches on their hair and makeup. Once we made it up to Knoxville and into line, it was time to do our absolute best to make sure they didn't check my waistband or pick up on the fact that we were definitely already drunk. Once we accomplished that pinnacle moment, the rest was in the clear. Once we got inside, we started line dancing (or attempted to), snapping a million or two photos to preserve the start of a wonderful winter break, and even sneaking the occasional sip or two of someone's beer and/or mixed drink. For the first time since October, I started to actually feel happy without it just being a mask to make sure no one was concerned about how drunk I was all the time. I was with friends who were making me happy, and a new one at that. I hadn't lost my ability to socialize after all, I suppose. My family may have fallen apart completely, but at least I still had my family of friends that I had chosen for myself with plenty of room for more.

The ceiling lights came on after what felt like fifteen minutes to remind us the bar was closing and it was time to make our way home. I walked through the doorway of the country bar and into the doorway of my basement bedroom before throwing myself onto the bed. My friend asked if it was fine to just stay the night so he didn't have to worry about driving home drunk and sneaking into his house. I happily accepted the request, maybe a tad bit too happily and quickly. I walked over and pulled out my hidden stash of alcohol and ran upstairs to grab a couple of glasses, ice, and whatever was in the fridge that sounded decent enough to mix with. We sipped between topics ranging from how ridiculous college was compared to high school to Carrie to how fun the night had been. We sat up talking and laughing for what felt like hours while we slipped more and more into a drunk euphoria until I felt an icy chill settle over the room. He didn't seem to notice it but I still glanced over to see what was going on and froze for a moment in total fear. The dismal, dark cloud that I hadn't noticed for months was hovering a few feet away from where we were sitting in bed, a faint yet eerie laughter emitting from its core.

Fear quickly rushed over me as my heart started pounding in my chest while I watched it grow larger and larger, the laughter becoming all the more prominent. He didn't seem to be seeing it whatsoever so I tried to seem cool and natural until I started to notice it creeping closer and closer to the bed in my peripheral vision. Right as it got a few inches away, I cut my newfound best friend off in the middle of whatever story he was sharing by saying it was time for bed before all this vodka made us sick. I jumped out of bed, through the cloud which shot an icy shiver down my spine, and cut off the light before he even had a chance to respond. The cloud disappeared suddenly as darkness cast itself over my bedroom. I emotionally exhaled as I fell backwards onto my pillows and felt my friend lay down next to me. What a close call.

We felt sleep start to creep closer and closer as we exchanged a few drunken pillow words, as heteronormative best bros do. My heart was still pounding in fear after so narrowly avoiding whatever the cloud's intentions were. My eyelids finally started to drift closer towards one another until I heard a deafening clap. My eyes snapped open again just in time to see the cloud hovering above my head until it quickly descended down into me. Without knowing what was happening, I felt it shift my body and roll towards the left and lift my arm. In what felt like horrific slow motion, my arm draped over my friend's back next to me. Oh god. Fuck. A million-and-a-half ideas rebounded off the walls of my mind as my heart felt like it was beating so fast it was about to explode. The cloud had finally succeeded in its mission of ruining my life and finally revealed to someone the thoughts that too often clouded my mind. The thoughts were no longer kept in the privacy of my mind. I wanted nothing more than to just remove my arm and roll back over to my previous position, but I knew that would definitely wake him up and make it ten times worse. But then again, leaving it here would also be disastrous once he eventually notices and freaks out. I could already hear the words he would call me before storming out and never speaking to me again. Then he'd tell all of Knoxville who would tell all of the world.

But then he didn't. Instead, I felt him slide a few inches closer towards me in the bed while he was still seemingly asleep. I accidentally let out a sigh of relief once I realized I didn't have a black eye and he wasn't driving back home at 100 miles an hour at 3 am. But that feeling of relief lasted only a few moments as it was replaced by more panic. What was going on? Did he just not mind a guy's arm touching him while he's sleeping? Did he enjoy it? What the fuck was going on? The chilling, eerie laughter filled the whole room and I felt my body slide even closer to him on its own until my entire body was pushed up against his. The cloud wasn't done. Great. Here's the part where he's going to inevitably wake up, freak out, beat the hell out of me, and bounce. Fear was filling my entire body like a dense fog as I begged the cloud to release me from its grip so I could roll back over and try to plan out my damage control plan. Instead, I felt his legs become intertwined with mine and our hands joined one another. Fuck.

I felt him suddenly roll over and realized we were now facing each other in the private darkness of my basement bedroom. What the hell was happening? Was this just alcohol? The cloud? Both? Did he have the same cloud following him around and using him like a puppet right now? My heart suddenly felt like it was being powered by rocket fuel with the cinder block of anxiety in my stomach suddenly evolving into a gigantic mansion until it felt like I was going to pass out, puke, or a combination of both. Beads of sweat began to form on my forehead as my breathing grew deeper and deeper until all of a sudden, he leaned forward and our lips touched. Then I just...surrendered.

Fireworks began to shoot off one by one inside my body until all of a sudden the euphoric feeling I often searched for was coursing through every single vein of my body. I had kissed countless girls at parties but compared to this, it felt like I had just been kissing a wall or my hand. This was almost-indescribably different. Fireworks. Another kiss. More fireworks. Deeper kissing. Five fireworks. Even deeper kiss of the French variety. Whole damn explosion of a fireworks factory. In the quiet stillness of the dark, our hands began to confidently navigate across the unknown waters of each other's body. The farther my hands roamed, the more fireworks and meteor showers began to appear on the ceiling of my bedroom. We shed our clothes and panic off to be entangled with the sheets at the end of the bed. I had absolutely no idea what I was doing or what it meant, but I did know two things for certain. I've never felt anything like this whatsoever and I definitely didn't want it to stop.

The bright morning light piercing through the bedroom window might as well have been a scalding hot iron striking the side of my face the next day. My eyes slowly opened and the mansion of anxiety immediately rebuilt itself in the pits of my stomach as I realized I was still cuddling with a man who was technically a stranger 24 hours ago. Each memory from the early hours of the morning began to swarm back over my mind like an army of angry ants after its colony had been stepped on. Did I really make out and feel up a guy I met online after one second of eye contact at a concert? Why did we do that? Where are my clothes? Neither one of us is gay so why was last night a real thing that happened? Was it real? Was he going to remember everything? Was he going to remember anything? Shit. He's waking up. Fuck.

He sat up in bed in silence for a few moments until he brought up how much fun the bar and line dancing and drink stealing had been with my friends. I happily agreed, eager to talk about *anything* other than what had happened a few hours ago. He glanced at his phone and said there were a million missed calls from his parents so he had to get back home before they legally reported him missing. I nodded and he got up to put on his clothes, not mentioning anything about the fact they were at the bottom of the bed instead of on his body. He grabbed his keys, told me he'd text me later after he got home, and stepped through the French doors of my room and slipped past Poppop Luke's couch/bed without a word. I sat in silent confusion for a few minutes and tried to figure out if he remembered anything from the night before or if he just didn't care that it had happened. Maybe it wasn't the first time it had happened with him? Nonetheless, I was just happy that I survived the night without a black eye and apparently the friendship had survived too.

It took all of 30 minutes before I sent him a disappearing snap asking if he remembered everything from last night or if he had blacked out. Considering how composed he acted, I was shocked when he said he did. From there, I sent multiple snaps (you could only fit so many words in the text bar at one time) explaining that it was just something that happened because we were so drunk and that it definitely couldn't, and wouldn't, ever happen again because we both knew we were straight. It was something we were never going to speak about again, with each other or anyone else in the entire world. We were just incredibly drunk and lonely and I wasn't myself with the whole Nana tragedy and everything. He assured me that he felt the same way, that he had never done any of that with a guy before either, and that we would never have to worry about it again. Furthermore, he said he'd like to still text and hang out and that he was glad we could still be friends. Crisis averted.

With the haunting void of Nana this holiday season, I tried to pick up as many shifts as possible but the restaurant in Lenoir City would not return my calls to put me back on their schedule since I returned home. Lilley was becoming more and more of an emotional wreck with each passing day as we approached Christmas and we all realized how empty the season now felt. Before I could even process what was happening, she was discussing a new plan to make the holiday as special as possible after such a devastating blow this year. My mother had always been somewhat of a spontaneous character, but as we talked about travelling to New York City to watch the New Year's ball drop in Times Square, I started to feel a bit concerned. However, when she mentioned funding the trip herself, all caution blew away in the wind. Without hesitation, I invited my best friend who was my roommate for that brief period in high school and the finalized plan was made. This plan literally came out of nowhere and made absolutely no sense, but then again nothing really did anymore. But at least this way we could all *try* to forget about the immense sadness and grief that had been presented to us in a gift box with a pretty pink bow.

My mind immediately surged with excitement as I pictured my best friend and I (and Lilley too I guess) wandering around the city that never sleeps. Buildings taller than I'd ever seen in person on every corner. People everywhere. Central Park. Celebrities everywhere you look. Times Square. New Year's Eve and all the ceremonies and performances we'd get to see live in front of our eyes. Pizza. PIZZA. That giant tree and ice skating rink that I'd seen in *Elf*. However, about a day before we were supposed to set off on the trip of a lifetime, my mother called us into her room that she hibernated in all day. Without warning, she told us she was planning on cancelling the trip altogether because of the second thoughts she was having about such an extensive trip. At this point in our relationship, if you could call it that, I didn't really hesitate when it came to retaliating against my mother's decisions. I wasn't going to take no for an answer considering how excited I was to see the city for the first time and finally take a break from my own internal misery since October. After what felt like hours of back-and-forth arguments, she caved. However, while she somehow agreed to fund the majority of the trip, she was not going to be attending with us. I almost left right then and there to go buy a lottery ticket with how much gold I had just struck.

Without a moment's hesitation, having just found a golden ticket in our chocolate bar, we reached out to a friend we had both met once to ask if he wanted to go to New York with us so that we could offset the cost. Before we knew it, we were loading up my car to make the 13-hour drive from my grandfather's house with my best friend and a stranger because that's what millennial children do. Between our combined, yet still miniscule, savings and the money my mother had provided us, we knew we wouldn't have much money for touristy fun after we booked a few nights at a hotel outside the city. But that didn't stop us from hopping in the car and going for it whatsoever. In fact, it somehow motivated us to go even more just for the memories and the experience alone. Even the drive seemed short in the way that only a road trip with your best friend can really explain. Inventing games to go along with all the unusual, random beeps and messages from my car's dashboard system also helped to pass the time.

After quickly booking a room and unpacking everything, we set out for the city and tried to teach ourselves what a toll system was. I quickly learned that driving was a vastly different experience in this city compared with driving in Tennessee and suffered through approximately seven panic attacks before we eventually found a street to park on. The chilly air somehow managed to pierce through the four layers of clothing we were wearing and went straight to our bones as we began to take everything in. A few sips of cinnamon whisky and the splendor of a literal concrete jungle helped take our minds off the cold just enough to enjoy everything. We powerwalked from corner to corner and avenue to avenue, taking in all the skyscrapers and laughing along at the fact that a bunch of kids had just jumped in the car and driven to New York City for New Year's Eve just because. After a few hours of literally just walking around and having the time of our lives with that, we made our way back to the hotel to laugh about the audacity of ourselves and talk about life and college and death and memories until the early hours of the morning.

I woke up the next morning horrified to see that I had drunkenly sent messages and snaps to the friend of mine that I had accidentally made out with the other night. They appeared to range anywhere from "I miss you" to "wish you were here" until I forced myself to stop reading. Seeing his reciprocated responses horrified me even further as I stared at myself in the hotel bathroom mirror, the tattoos quickly returning to my forehead and forearms bolder than ever. What the hell was going on? This had to stop. A sudden knock on the bathroom door brought me back down to earth from the rabbit hole of my existential crisis. I confirmed I was almost ready, splashed cold water on my face to wash off the ink for the millionth time, and threw on my three coats to head out the door for another day of exploration. Despite being our first full day, it felt as if we'd been there for weeks taking in all the wonders we had never been able to see before without spending a penny. Somewhere through the blur of hours that felt like weeks, we were hopping off at the stop closest to Times Square that wasn't blocked off to watch the ball drop to ring in 2014.

The energy coursing through every single street was something I had never seen nor felt at any house party I had ever been to. Thousands of people were flooding into the streets and sidewalks. A cloud of electric euphoria seemed to wash over every single person in the entire city as we were met with smiles, cheers, and even the occasional shot of any and every kind of liquor. For another precious few hours, nothing mattered in the world as we took in the lights, energy, and beauty of the night. While not attending a single actual event, we managed to have the time of our lives simply walking around and exploring the various parts of this foreign environment. We managed to find an escapism that we never thought was possible in the endless avenues and buildings. However, that escapism could only last so long before we found ourselves cleaning up the room, throwing away all the empty airplane bottles, and packing up our bags to head back to our dismal, grey realities. Oh, and I already had plans to hang out with my new best bro again once I got back home. But *that* wasn't going to happen again. It couldn't.

Seeing the city's skyline of skyscrapers getting smaller and smaller in my rearview mirror almost made me cry. I couldn't believe we pulled this spontaneous trip off but I couldn't be happier that we did. The 13-hour drive seemed a bit longer than the ride up, but that was only because of the fact that I veered off an exit in Virginia going too fast and totaled my car into a ditch at the ramp exit. Feeling the car slam to a halt, I tried my best to gather myself after all the screams and cries had settled down inside the car. I took a few deep breaths, made sure I had all my limbs, and hopped out of the car. I already heard sirens coming in the distance as I checked in on my two friends to make sure they were okay. Fuck. Tears were already welling up in my eyes as I noticed my car lying in a crumpled heap on the side of an interstate, a road sign that it had taken with it in several pieces in the grass next to it. What was I going to do? What if I had hurt someone? How were we going to get home? Why did we come on this trip? What the hell was I supposed to do now?

Sirens began to blur into one another and I lost track of whether I was talking to a police officer or an ambulance worker or a firefighter. No, this was definitely an ambulance. Why was I in an ambulance? Why was I holding onto some kind of traffic ticket? Was totaling my car and almost hurting my friends not difficult enough without the added stress of a damn ticket? Why was a solo car accident such a prime opportunity for this county to earn money? The inside of the ambulance quickly dissolved into a hospital room as they checked my vitals before it dissolved into a hotel room that my mother and best friend's mother got for us after driving all the way to us. I gave my best attempt at resting but it was a hopeless cause as my mind kept replaying the possible scenarios over and over again in my head. My best friend's funeral. The practical stranger's funeral. My funeral. Tonight could have gone so much worse and it would have completely been my fault. I didn't even notice that it was a new day and that we were all in some gas station fast food lobby until my best friend's mother's screams forced me back down to earth. Wait. The screams were aimed directly at me. Everything is my fault and I should be ashamed. Well, yeah. What do you think I've been telling myself for the last 12 hours in my head? We should have never gone on this trip. Well, my mother funded it. What teenagers *wouldn't* take the opportunity to go on a free trip to New York City? I glanced over at Lilley who was calmly sitting next to me as her mother launched word after word in my direction. My mind flashed back to her stepfather calling me gay and how I wasn't fooling anyone, another insult my mother sat back and watched occur without a word. Awesome.

The scene dissolved once again and I was quietly unpacking my things into my dorm room for another semester. The rest of winter break had passed by in an uneventful blur. Well, I hung out with my friend again and we ended up making out and messing around again but that was just because of the alcohol. I was just sad and lonely from losing my Nana and now my car. That's all it was. I'll be normal again once I'm not sad. I sat down on my twin bed, a mattress that was oddly more comfortable than my actual bed at home, and stared up at the ceiling to reflect on what my life had suddenly turned into. This wasn't who I was. I'm supposed to have a car, a ton of friends, a girlfriend, and Nana. Instead, I was now stranded on campus with no vehicle, a new list of classes to start worrying about, and a new bestie that I kept accidentally getting naked with. It would be pretty easy to hang out since he didn't go to school far from here, but how could I risk my roommate walking in to see me making out with him and risk more rumors starting around campus. We would just have to stop doing that. We aren't gay so that'll be easy. It's not gay unless we go all the way which we had no issue with whatsoever. My roommate is gay, but I'm not. We're not. We're just depressed, lonely, and always drunk. That's all.

As it turns out, the car crash took away more than just my car itself. Lilley had to hire an attorney to get the ticket taken care of since I had no way of appearing in court back in Virginia (a debt she was quick to remind me of the moment the ticket got dismissed). However, more importantly, it put a strain on the relationship between my best friend and me that didn't show any signs of being remedied anytime soon. Between her mother screaming at me and the medical bills that were going to come from the ambulance/hospital, we were pretty much forced to stop speaking to each other for the first time in our 5 year bestfriendship. My apathy began to grow more and more as I became comfortable with my Nana's absence and loss/disconnection seemed to surround me more and more with every passing day. Thankfully, my second semester provided the perfect escape from these realizations and gave me an excuse to focus on anything that wasn't my own disappointing phase of life I had found myself in now. My new classes all seemed to blend together as I was thrown into another ocean of stress with the hope of being able to keep my head above water seeming more and more impossible. Speech blended into Sociology which dissolved into Art Appreciation which might have been on the same day as History which could have been before or after Algebra but I wasn't quite sure yet.

By the time I felt like I had my schedule memorized, it was time to start pregaming for a house party and drink myself into forgetfulness until Monday came back around. My special friend came up one of the first weekends and I got to introduce him to college house parties since his school seemed to be a bit more strict than mine. My friends here liked him as much as my high school friends had despite the fact that a small part of my brain couldn't help but convince myself everyone could see the *we make out when we get drunk!!!* tattoos on both of our foreheads. After a million rounds of beer pong and selfies, we stumbled into my room trying not to make a sound in case we woke up my roommate and got caught with alcohol. Then I accidentally started sobbing about how depressed I was and how awful my life had become overnight. He sat on the floor with me and told me everything was going to be fine. I stopped crying after what felt like an eternity. Then we made out and took our clothes off, constantly checking and double-checking that the door was locked and the blinds were closed. The only thing left to do next was wake up mortified and promise that it was the last time we'd do anything like that. Jesus, we need girlfriends or something so this could finally stop.

The dark cloud's eerie laughter seemed to follow me around everywhere I went. All around campus. All around the restaurant during every shift. All around my dorm. All around my dreams and nightmares. It became inescapable. Eventually, I either became numb and/or apathetic to it or I just finally managed to tune it out so it didn't become too much of a distraction from my everyday life and all its wonderful glory. When I wasn't able to ignore or expel it with my own willpower, vodka always seemed to do the trick. When it got so loud shouting the events of the night before with my friend and I was certain everyone in class around me could hear it, all I had to do was take a few gulps from my water bottle to make it go away. The more gulps I took, the more *everything* seemed to go away. Nana's tragedy. Being all but cut off from the family because of my mother's demands and accusations. My car crash. My best friend not speaking to me. My mother being my mother in general. Not knowing how to suddenly be a good son to my biological father and stepmother. My grades and whatever they happened to be because I was too scared to check. Feeling like a disappointment. Everything and anything bad. Numb and hollow might not feel amazing, but at least it didn't feel sad. Drinking myself silly was better than attacking my ankles again, right? Neutral was better than negative, right?

Drinking the cloud (and everything) away worked wonderfully well until it didn't. I was sipping and scrolling social media in my living room while the vodka began to settle into its home. With a loud spark, the cloud suddenly appeared once again and immediately descended into my arms and hands. Before I could stop it or realize what was happening, I was messaging a friend of my special friend who went to the same school. I knew it was weird, but I suddenly wasn't strong enough to fight off the cloud while it pursued its antics. Weird messaging became weird flirting until I saw myself sending messages for him to come hang out and watch a movie here at my dorm. I started to panic and think of ways to cancel or claim that my phone had been stolen until I felt a vibrate and saw an "on my way" message splashed across my screen. I blinked and suddenly he was sitting on the armchair across from where I was sitting on the couch. We were chatting and laughing back and forth like new friends do until I saw the corners of my vision start to blur as the alcohol worked its magic in my veins. The cloud's chilling laughter sounded off the walls of the living room until I saw it appear again, this time shoving me over into the same armchair he was in.

My arm naturally fell over his shoulders and my lips naturally fell into his as electricity and panic both rushed over me like a tsunami of a thousand emotions. The euphoric fireworks as I felt his lips press against mine in reciprocation was more intoxicating than any therapeutic cocktail I could create. Nausea and pure joy mixed together in the most confusing way as I confirmed that this kind of kissing was in an entire league of its own compared to the countless times I'd kissed a girl at a party. What the hell was going on? What was I doing? Did I care? I should've cared. I did care, but was I going to stop? Hell no. Wait. I should stop. Each question bounced off of one another in the confines of my mind as I felt his hands start to roam over the new territory while mine did the same. More fireworks appeared on the ceiling of my dorm living room as I gave up all hope of stopping whatever was happening once again. This felt nice, to say the least, so why stop and worry about it now?

The main door of my room shut, the sound jolting me back to reality as I tried to process that I had just made out with a practical stranger with minimal clothing in the middle of the night. As if one guy/friend wasn't complicated enough, the cloud managed to drag another person into the mix. Nausea formed once again as I realized he was definitely going to tell my best friend what just happened. Why couldn't the cloud have picked an actual stranger to do this with instead of someone directly linked to the friend I had already done stuff with? Shit. Wait. Why didn't that guy want to just sleep over instead of heading back to his school at like two in the morning? Oh no. I was a bad kisser. My body sucked. I was ugly in person. Before I knew it, I felt tears forming in my eyes as I rushed into the bathroom. My reflection stared back at me, my eyes bloodshot from a combination of all the alcohol in my system and the anxiety tears streaming down my face. I could hardly recognize the person I was looking at. What was happening to me? Who the fuck was I? I brushed the tears off my phase, told myself this phase would be over once I found the right girl who made those same fireworks appear, took one more shot, and flung myself in bed.

After somehow avoiding a hangover, both physically and emotionally, my semester continued to skyrocket forward in a series of blurs outside of my control. Lectures about people and how they think and why they behave the way they do in society captured my interest each day while historical analyses made me want to bang my head into my desk every morning. I'd blink and suddenly I was at a house party again. Another blink and I'd be in my bedroom making out with one male friend or the other in what felt like alternating shifts. Another blink and I'd be having a complete emotional spiral wondering whether or not they had spoken with each other about me yet. Another blink and I'd be waking up on a random garden or staircase on campus before sprinting back to my room, narrowly avoiding campus security, to make it to whatever class I'd almost overslept for. An additional blink and I was running circles around the restaurant trying to make every customer happy enough to leave me a nice tip to help with my dwindling bank account and then having a breakdown in the employee bathroom whenever they left fifty cents or nothing. Everything was fine. This was just what college is. For everyone.

Talks of Spring Break began to find their way into every single prominent social bubble across campus as everyone tried to plan out the best trip possible. Without hesitation, I agreed to go with a group of girls to Panama City and paid my deposit despite the fact that I had just had an emotional breakdown about my bank account the week prior. I had no idea what to expect for Spring Break or

Panama City Beach, but honestly that didn't matter. All I was hearing was that I was going to get a weeklong break from thinking about my life and the friends I would take turns making out with and the perils of a college education. I'm going no matter what, even if it costs a million dollars at this point. I'll just take a credit card out in my mother's name using *her* Social Security number to turn the tables for once. A few more extra shifts at the restaurant later, I was packing up a duffel bag and hopping in my friend's car to start the seven-or-so hour drive to the beach. I had no idea how I was fortunate enough as a freshman to land a spot in their condo for Spring Break but I wasn't about to question it and risk being told to stay behind. What's the worst that could happen, anyway?

After what felt like a 30 minute drive, we were frantically unloading all of our things into the room, grabbing the first swimwear pieces we could get our hands on, and throwing ourselves into the ocean. We were there pretty early, but the sands were already filling up with masses upon masses of college students from all around the country. With the realization that this was definitely not about to be like any of the house parties I was accustomed to, the hours passed by in blurs. Crowded beaches turned into random makeout sessions that were posted on social media to continue convincing the general public of my heterosexuality which turned into pre-games at the condo (is it still a pregame if you had already started drinking at 9 am that same morning?) which turned into flashing lights at whatever clubs allowed 18-year-olds. Every morning began by waking up with my face against the cold tile floor in the kitchen or living room without a single memory of how/when we got home or what we had done the night before. By the time I got myself back up on my own two feet, another drink and/or shot was put in my hand and it was time to rinse and repeat the whole process all over again. For once, I was having so much fun with my friends that I didn't spend one moment thinking about Nana, the cloud, my slipping grades, work, or my chaotic family system that had all but completely crumbled.

Waking up in the bathtub of the room for whatever reason, I started to realize it was our last full day of Spring Break. I checked my phone to see that the girl I had been online friends with for years was already making her way to our place, an invite I apparently sent sometime yesterday. I threw on the best outfit I could construct from the various clothes from everyone's suitcases that all appeared to have blended into one gigantic pile, plugged in my phone for probably the second time the whole week, and took a shot to prevent my body from starting a hangover before she arrived. She walked through the door and I immediately put my arm around her to let the room know that not only was she gorgeous but she was here with ME. No clouds or tattoos here. Nope. Within a few moments, she already felt right at home as we all started playing drinking games and taking shots, a totally normal thing to do at

10:30 in the morning. By the time we made it out onto the beach, my vision was already blurry and I had already posted two photos of us kissing just to make certain the entire internet knew I was with a hot girl.

A few moments later, everything went black. When my eyes eventually opened again, I felt two metal rings tightly clenching both of my wrists.

Chapter Thirteen

Remember When I Became a Criminal?

Shit. Fuck. What the hell was I doing in the back of a police car? Why was I in handcuffs? Why was I the only one in the car? Panic surged through my entire body in a way I had never experienced before and I started banging my head against the window next to me, hoping to make enough noise to get someone's attention nearby. The last clear memory that kept flashing across my mind was taking photos on the beach with her and having a chugging contest with the group. Now I'm apparently being arrested for...something? Oh god. Did I kill someone? Did I try to drive somewhere and crash? Suddenly, the door I was banging my head into opened. My mouth opened to start asking questions only to have it fill with gravel as I was dragged out of the backseat and onto the ground below. Unable to hoist myself back up with the cuffs, I remained face-down in the gravel until an officer eventually picked me up and put me back in the car, telling me to shut up and not to mess with the window again. He didn't say what would happen if I didn't shut up or if I didn't stop banging my head, but his tone told me it would be bad. So I sat down and shut up as he got into the front seat and started driving to wherever it was we were about to go.

At the next stop, I was taken out of the car and placed on a sidewalk with a few other handcuffed people from other cars. Seeing another cop, I shifted my weight until I was able to stand up to try and ask him what the hell was happening and if he knew what I had done. I managed to get one word out of my mouth before his hands gripped my shoulders and shoved me backwards, the combination of concrete and a set of wooden stairs painfully breaking my fall. Okay, so it wasn't just *my* cop who hated the concept of questions and curiosity. Noted. Trying to catch my breath and regain some ounce of composure and dignity, I remained a crumpled heap on the sidewalk until I was placed back in line. My friends were nowhere to be found. I had no idea what day it was. Were my friends even still here? My life was over.

It felt like a literal week passed before I found myself being walked into a building to be told I was being arrested for underage possession of alcohol. Relief was sprinkled into the melting pot of confusion and fear as I tried to comprehend what I possibly could have done to get the attention of a cop enough to make him question the contents of a water bottle I was holding. At least it wasn't murder or burglarly or something else my mind had conjured up within the last few hours while I sat and suffered in silence. Before I could simmer too much longer on this new wave of information, I was being stripped down in front of five or six other people and was forced to shower in front of them before being dressed in jail clothes and rubber sandals. After I had showered myself to their liking, I was told I had a phone call if I wanted to make one. By some form of miracle, I convinced the employee behind the desk to let me use my cell phone to get the phone number since I didn't have one memorized.

I stared up at the ceiling in the darkness of my cell, my mother's screams still ringing in my ears before agreeing to call all of my friends to figure out what to do next. The man in the bunk below me didn't like small talk or introductions, but I'm pretty sure he was caught driving drunk without a license. Sobbing came a few moments later as I imagined what Nana would have done if she found out I got myself arrested. I tried to stifle the noises and tears because the last thing I needed was an angry cellmate tonight. Without any windows or clocks, I had absolutely no clue what time it was or even what "today" meant. My mind became a cluster of "you're a piece of shit" and "you're going to get kicked out of school" until I eventually fell asleep for either 30 seconds or three hours. An alarm caused me to jolt awake on the cold metal bed to apparently signal it was time for everyone to eat. The attempt of a meal placed in front of me suggested it was breakfast. Dammit. We were supposed to go home today. Were my friends already halfway back to campus?

It took all of 15 minutes for me to throw up my breakfast before I was escorted into a line for whatever the hell an arraignment meeting was. The line moved forward after a few minutes (and after I threw up again) and I was placed in a dirty waiting room with a few other men. I made small talk with one of them as we compared our similar stories. I glanced down at his wrist bracelet, made a mental note to befriend him online once we both got out (because that's totally normal), and then found myself face-to-face with a judge through a television screen. In a flash, I tried to reflect on all the crime shows and movies I had watched with Mom over the years to come up with a trial defense to declare my innocence. However, the judge simply asked my name, looked at my file, and said my bail was $300 and I had to come back for a court appearance next week. I opened my mouth to kindly inform him that would be impossible since I live in Tennessee and go to school, but the screen quickly turned to black as the connection was severed. Great. Awesome. Dammit. Wonderful.

I was taken back to the cell area after the arraignment where I immediately retreated back to my cell to reflect on how my life was completely ruined. I was stuck. I was going to lose my job. I was never going to get out of here. I was going to get kicked out of school for sure. Nana was going to come back to life just to scream at me the way Lilley already had. Ryan and my stepmom were going to cut ties with me. Everything was over. Sometime between two minutes or two hours or two years, one of the random guards approached me and said to gather my things. This was it. I'm getting transferred to a maximum security prison or directly to an electric chair or something. My stomach instinctively turned into a complex network of nauseating knots for what felt like the millionth time in my life as tears once again poured out of my eyes. However, after being taken down a creepy, long hallway the sobs turned into tears of joy as I was handed a plastic bag containing my phone and the swim trunks/tank top combination I had been arrested in. Before I could process anything, I was taken down another long hallway with the guard gesturing toward a doorway with the most beautiful exit sign above it.

The direct sunlight completely blinded me as I stepped outside of the jail for the first time in what felt like a month. Halfway expecting to see my mother and the ghost of Nana herself, I prepared for a barrage of insults and screams. However, when my eyes finally adjusted to the sun in time to see my friends waiting there with open arms, I almost collapsed on the spot. The embrace lasted a minute or so before I was rushed to get in the car since we were already so far behind schedule on the return to campus. They let me know on the way home that I had gotten absolutely obliterated, split up from the group with my online-turned-real-life girlfriend, accepted a silly little dare to jump in front of one of the cop cars, then naturally got arrested. Apparently the cop asked her if she knew who I was or if we were close to home but she had said no out of fear before crossing the street and heading up to the condo. My friends quickly asked why I wasn't with her and promptly kicked her out of the room when she casually mentioned she accidentally told the cop she didn't know who I was instead of assuring him we were 100 feet from the condo. It took Lilley all of five minutes before she had found the girl's info online to call her parents before she even had time to drunkenly drive back to her house an hour or so away from Panama City Beach. Needless to say, I decided not to reach out to check in on her.

I tried to stay under the radar whenever we got back to campus, narrowly avoiding all the paparazzi and journalists waiting to interrogate me about my time in jail. My roommate wasn't sure if they could kick me out of school or not so it was best to pretend it didn't happen. Lilley got in touch with a random attorney in Florida who managed to appear on my behalf since I didn't have any feasible way of returning to Florida even if I wanted to. After draining my entire bank account for educational courses and fees, I narrowly avoided having the event on my record while also not having to leave the state at all. While it might have taken a toll on my emotional well-being (or what was left of it, at least) and reputation, it seemed like I was through the worst of it. I took a day or two to reflect on how I had allowed myself to

231

get so drunk that I listened to a practical stranger's dare to hop in front of a police car. I needed to get my shit together and stop drinking every single day. Sure, it made me stop thinking about Nana and that I've kinda hooked up with guys before, but a criminal record isn't worth that temporary peace. This whole fiasco really taught me a lesson in how to put the bottle down and really take a look in the mirror.

A week passed before I was doing a keg stand followed by a vodka funnel at one of the soccer houses. After I realized I dreamt of Nana less when I was sober and the cloud showed up twice as much to follow my every move, I was convincing one of my coworkers to go to the liquor store for me. One of my managers found out I missed one of my shifts because I had been in jail, but she called me into the office one day to let me know she wasn't going to share the news with any of the other bosses because she knew the tough time I was going through. I wasn't sure how she knew everything that was going on, but I wasn't about to question her empathy and generosity especially considering I had about nine total dollars to my name. Instead, I found myself giving her a hug and asking if I could pick up more shifts to get myself back on my feet (and keep my alcohol stash intact). Yet another crisis averted somehow.

The semester barreled along in more blurs as I gave my semi-best attempt at keeping my head above academic waters. While I was genuinely more interested in the courses this semester, especially Sociology, I couldn't find the motivation to actually teach myself how to take notes during lectures or how to study for exams. Alcohol quickly became the only catalyst I could use to access the creative parts of my brain that were necessary for pretending like I knew what I was talking about. Whether it was essay questions on an exam or a five-page paper, my water bottle that was always full of a hidden vodka concoction became my best friend this semester. Outside of class, I was falling deeper and deeper down the rabbit hole of house parties, social media obsession, and trying to keep my two best friends from knowing that I messed around with them both anytime we got drunk together. However, after spending a couple of weekends on their campus, I quickly started to get the feeling that they knew the entire time. Part of me wanted to just clear the air, but I knew that would be a violation of the unspoken-but-fully-understood secret code of whatever the hell this situation was. None of us were gay. None of us made out with each other or felt each other up in the privacy of our dorm rooms. It never happened. Never.

That being said, not speaking about it out loud didn't stop the cloud from popping into my head at various points throughout every single day to whisper that everyone around me knew. Was it obvious? Were the *I've made out with two guys* tattoos becoming more and more visible to everyone around me in my classes or at parties? No. Surely not. I still had my reputation as the party kid who made out with girls and occasionally (always) posted it on social media. Everything's fine. At least it was fine until it happened again and I spent the entire next morning convincing myself that my roommate had heard us outside my door or someone had managed to see through my bedroom window and told everyone. At that point, booze was the only thing that could silence the cloud inside my head or at least shift my focus away from it for a while. Plus, getting unnecessarily drunk also meant I could fall asleep that much faster and wait for Nana to show up in my dreams again. It also meant another night away from my bathroom, staring at the tub and wondering if it was humanly possible to drown myself.

In the midst of one of my drunken spirals, I called a tattoo parlor in town and set up a consultation appointment. Something in my soul told me that I needed to get a memorial for Nana that also represented her Christianity (the kind of Christianity that loves everyone not the kind that wants people to burn in hell or control women's bodies). The next thing I knew, I had booked my actual appointment a few days later. Waking up and walking down to the tattoo parlor by myself didn't feel like a great start to the journey, but I knew I wasn't about to reschedule it just because none of my friends felt like coming with me to get ink injected into my shoulder blade. Plus, a small part of me knew that if I had a memorial, especially one that featured a cross, I would be that much closer to god healing me and actually putting the cloud and those drunken mistakes behind me. Then I could meet the right girl, actually get my shit together, graduate, and move on from this hellhole of a first year in college.

My name was called, yanking me back down to reality from my imaginary future that didn't feature looking up those videos or feeling up my guy friends in secret. The guy immediately sensed how nervous I was to get my first tattoo and said the quicker we got started the better it would be. When that didn't seem to calm my nerves, he rolled over to his desk station and grabbed a stress ball for me to squeeze through the pain with. After giving me about three seconds to emotionally prepare myself, I heard the eerie buzzing sound from the tattoo gun and then an immense burning/stinging sensation shooting through my upper body. Knowing I couldn't move without potentially ruining his work (and my skin) made the experience all the more torturous. After about an hour or so later and a few moments where I thought I was going to completely faint, the work was done. I apologized for ripping the stress ball into a million pieces before taking a look at the finished product in the mirror across from the table. My eyes widened as I saw how red and swollen my entire shoulder had become but he quickly let me know it would heal up just fine if I took proper care of it. A million questions later, I walked back out the door and made my way back to campus alone and on foot, each footstep sending more pain through my shoulder the entire way back.

Something about having this symbolic piece of Nana permanently on my skin made me realize this wasn't some nightmare that I would eventually wake up from. That being said, having a small part of her with me somehow conjured up a light at the end of this tunnel. The light might have been a dim one, but it still told me I could heal and start processing everything that happened. As the swelling started to subside and the ink settled in, I felt other parts of me start to heal as well. Of course, that all changed anytime I got a little too drunk by myself and decided to scroll through my last texts with her or listen to some of her old voicemails. Nothing could prevent me from completely breaking down even if I *did* have this memorial of her with me forever. As a last resort, I would send texts or online messages out to pretty much anyone that would listen, too often being random guys across campus or across the internet that just happened to be conventionally attractive (coincidence). Hearing a knock at my door during one of these unsolicited venting sessions at 1:30 am sent me into another spiral, one of panic this time. Seeing the very concerned face of a staff member on the other side of the bedroom door didn't help with that panic. I did my best to assure her that I wasn't planning on harming myself like my messages to someone had seemed while simultaneously doing my best to appear sober so that my room didn't end up getting searched. As I threw myself back onto my bed, I made a mental note to at least try and be careful who I vent to next time.

As another semester came to a close, I started packing up my room and checking the online portal for my final grades to start being posted. I started pondering which items I could leave behind until the next semester until I remembered I hadn't even signed up for classes. In the craziness and overall apathy, I completely forgot that I decided to transfer to the university up in Knoxville that I often escaped to for parties on the weekend. I had no idea if I had communicated the intent to transfer with the proper networks of people, but all I knew is I couldn't come back to this small campus where everyone knew everyone and their problems and secrets. Plus, my roommate pretty much hated me by this point so there was no way in hell I'd get the nice dorm room next year even if I *did* want to come back. Luckily, he only hated me for how reckless and drunk I always was and he hadn't found out yet that I started secretly making out with one of his crushes. My make out count was now up to a lot of girls and three guys but that was just what college was. It wasn't gay if you didn't go all the way. Now that I have a cross and I'm moving to a new school, this phase would be over soon.

I got right to work the moment I unpacked my things back into my basement bedroom at Poppop Luke's house. After 15 or so phone calls, I was finally able to get put back on the schedule at the Lenoir City restaurant and even convinced my grandfather to let me borrow his car anytime I needed to go into work so I could start saving up for one of my own. Without a single thought, I signed a lease with one of my friends in Knoxville for next semester and then decided to blindly reach out to the first email address I saw on the university website. I threw myself onto the bed once I became overwhelmed with how behind I felt on this transition but was then flooded with flashbacks to when I had messed around with a guy for the first time a few months ago right in this very spot. Who does that? Sure, my parents were pretty much divorced in every way except legally, but my friends didn't seem to have any problems hooking up or settling down with girls the way I seemed to. Hell, even my chaotic brother managed to get married and was getting ready to have his first kid. Why was I still malfunctioning?

The university emailed me back to let me know that just because I had a full tuition scholarship at my last school doesn't mean I had the same opportunities once I transfer. Not only was I going to have to worry about taking out enough student loans to pay for everything, but a vast majority of my credits weren't going to transfer over since I was moving from a private school to a public university or something like that. Amazing. So all I got out of the last academic year was the loss of my grandmother and a secret hobby of making out with a varying three guys whenever I'd get too drunk. Oh well. My plans were still the same. Even if I had to go into an evil amount of debt the size of Everest it would be worth it to leave the last year completely behind me. I responded back to the email with my official request to continue with the transfer and booked an appointment a few weeks away to sign up for classes even if that meant taking the same classes all over again. In honor of the momentous occasion, I grabbed a last-minute ticket to an EDM show with a couple of my close friends from high school.

I talked one of my work friends into grabbing me a bottle of whatever after rushing through my shift as quickly as possible. After she hesitantly agreed, I made my way down the road from the restaurant to meet my friends in a random grocery store parking lot to leave my grandfather's car and hop in theirs to head to the show at a random bar in Knoxville. We started drinking on the drive up and then some more in the parking lot since we weren't old enough to get drinks inside for the rest of the night. After drinking enough to keep an elephant buzzed for a while, I had the marvelous idea to sneak the rest in my waistband as we walked up to stand in line. Somehow, I managed to successfully sneak it in without being caught and before we knew it we were all jumping up and down to the DJ's set. Halfway out of fear of being caught and halfway out of realization that I needed to drive home in the next two hours, I finished off my hidden stash very quickly before tossing it in a nearby trash can. The next thing I knew, the DJ was finished, we were all dripping with sweat, and the lights came on above us to let us know it was time to hit the road.

The ride back to my car passed by in a blur of lights and music from one of their phones as I kept my head out the window trying to maintain the serotonin boost the concert had provided. I sent a few texts and snaps to some of my friends who lived a town over from where we were. The cloud had popped up again out of nowhere and was telling me that one of the friends was putting out *those* vibes and that I should head over to their bonfire and just see if anything happened. My count was already up to three so it's not like making it four would be a huge deal, right? My friends double-checked that I felt fine enough to hop into my own car. I paused, decided I did feel fine, and started making my way to the bonfire about 20 minutes away. I plugged in my phone to start shuffling a playlist when I noticed the triggering red-and-blue lights invading the entire interior of my car and bouncing off of the rearview mirror. Shit.

Having not had anything to drink in the last two or three hours, I felt confident that I was fine to drive but if there was anything I'd learned by now it was to fear the police. The footsteps got louder and louder as the officer approached the side of my car and I rolled down the window. He said something but all I could see or hear was the memory of being dragged out of the car and thrown face-first into the street again. I pulled myself out of the flashback in time to acknowledge the officer's requests to see my license. He asked if I knew I had been speeding and I tried to force a laugh and point out that I hadn't really noticed since I was the only one on the road this late. He didn't think it was as funny as I did. Next came the question about drinking which sent my stomach into that same nauseating network of knots. Taking a leap of faith, I admitted to drinking before a concert in Knoxville but that it had been quite a few hours since then. The officer stood in silence for a moment before asking me, in what seemed to be painful slow-motion, to step out of the car.

I considered dropping to the ground and pleading for mercy for a moment before realizing it would definitely land me in a set of handcuffs again. A few deep breaths gave me a little bit of confidence to go through the various field sobriety tests he started giving me. An incomprehensible wave of emotions and adrenaline were pumping through my veins as I stood on one foot, then the other, then followed his finger with my eyes without moving my head, then fifteen other insane tasks that didn't really make any sense. The tests finally stopped and he instructed me to take a seat on the bumper of his car while he went over and talked to a few more officers that had pulled up since the initial traffic stop. Between their distance and the cars that were flying by on the highway next to me, trying to eavesdrop on their conversation was impossible. After an eternity of silent suffering on the hood of his police car, he approached me and told me to place my hands behind my back.

I lost all composure in that moment, sobbing for mercy and begging him to reconsider the decision. Seeing the tow truck pull up next to my grandfather's car told me that it was no use whatsoever and that I was simply fucked. If I thought my life had been ruined when I got taken in for holding a bottle of vodka and cranberry juice, it *definitely* was over now that I was getting some form of DUI. Who knew losing Nana meant losing any hope of having a successful life or knowing who I was altogether. The crying continued in the back seat of his car on the way to Loudon's jail and I didn't even try to pull myself together. What was the use? It's not like I had any dignity to cling to or any ounce of self-respect to muster up anymore. I couldn't stop drinking. I couldn't stop sneaking away in the dark of night with my best guy friends. I apparently couldn't avoid the police. Might as well lean into this new life and criminal identity now. By the time we pulled into the jail, I was staring blankly ahead like an empty shell of a human being. I wasn't scared anymore. I wasn't panicking. I wasn't feeling anything at all. I was just numb.

One foot went in front of the other behind the officer who pulled me over. They took me through a number of doors until I was sitting in an office area waiting to breathe into a device and process my fingerprints. They told me I definitely didn't pass the breathalyzer, especially for someone who was under the age of 21. Wonderful. I started mentally preparing to spend the next week, month, or year in a cell here. I had no idea how the justice system actually worked, but failing a breathalyzer didn't sound like it was going to work out very well in my favor. Goodbye to the job I was definitely going to lose because of this. Goodbye to my family's already-minimal support after tonight. Goodbye to any hopes of finishing college or even returning for my second year. No one would hire someone who got arrested twice before the age of 21. I literally ruined my life in a little over half a year's time. I was a surviving college student in September. Nana died in October. My life was over by June. Suddenly, my imaginary bathtub plan seemed more and more possible with every second that passed in this icy jail lobby area. Were there even tubs here that I could use?

Seeing one of my old high school friend's mother walk through a door across the room reignited all the emotions I thought I had disposed of. I went from being a numb, empty shell to a sobbing mess in front of her in a matter of seconds. From her perspective, the kid who helped her daughter through some tough times and created *Prayer Requests* had somehow found himself in the same jail she was working at as a nurse. Without hesitation, she was instructing the guards not to process me into a cell and told me she'd call the restaurant and say that I was too sick to come into my shift. Angel wings sprouted from her shoulders and a halo appeared delicately above her head as she got them to remove me from the handcuffs and put me in a separate, more peaceful part of the building. I quickly thanked her between sobs while simultaneously warning her that I definitely wouldn't have the money for whatever bail amount they were inevitably place over a dumb kid who got drunk at the age of 19 and hopped behind the wheel of his grandfather's car. Without a word, she retreated behind another set of doors while I continued to sob an awkward blend of regret but spontaneous relief tears.

She came back into the room a few moments later, bringing with her another calming aura that filled the room. Apparently, the friend I worked with and went to the beach with one summer also had a parent working in the building. After reaching out to her, she somehow convinced them to let me go without paying an actual bail amount in good faith that I'd return for my court date. Not that I was thankful to be sitting in a jail right now, but I could not have been more grateful that I had at least been arrested at the same time as this guardian angel was about to get off from her shift. Bewildered and amazed, I collapsed into her arms and thanked her a million times over. Then I thanked her a million more. From there, I made my way to a jail's exit doorway for the second time that year. Then the sense of relief started to vanish and be replaced with the overwhelming dread that can only come from being arrested. Sure, I didn't have to sleep in a cell, but I still had the whole arrest thing to worry about. Shit.

Despite how much I wanted to retreat to my bedroom the moment I walked through the front door at Poppop Luke's house, everyone was waiting for me in the living room with stern expressions. Real Dad and Erin, Mom and Dad, and Poppop Luke could not have looked more upset and disappointed as I stepped into the living room and took my obvious assigned seat on the couch across from them all. They each took a turn explaining to me what I had already been telling myself for the last few months: I'm becoming a disappointment and I need to get my shit together. I deflected away from their words, not trying to justify my actions but simply explain them but it was no use. There was no way to explain that I already knew everything they were saying and it was nowhere near the same caliber of things I had been telling myself already. Part of me felt like shouting at the top of my lungs that I had been considering taking my keys to my ankle or taking a nap underwater but I knew that would just land me in some asylum somewhere based on Lilley's past reactions to anything I've ever told her. So I just sat there and absorbed all of their words until they stopped. Poppop Luke looked upset, but basically told me to pay the tow bill and he'd make some calls about the legal issues.

The conversation shifted away from pointing out the severity of my situation to following up on my progress for next semester. Had I gotten my scholarship information figured out? Were my credits going to transfer? Why was I going through the trouble to start all over again as a freshman? How was I planning to pay for tuition, food, vodka (my own mental question), *and* the rent for the apartment lease I rushed into signing? With the fall semester quickly creeping up, the overwhelming pressure flooded into the living room until it felt like I was completely submerged and unable to breathe. Tears started to form in my eyes as I realized how idiotic, once again, I had been to think I could just start over at a huge university with ease. Right before I thought I was going to pass out from the rush of emotion, I knew what I had to do. Swallowing my stubborn pride, I reached out to everyone I knew at the college I had just tried to flee from. By some generous gift from above, I was able to get signed up for more classes, resume my same scholarship, and move back onto campus in August even though that meant moving to the not-so-luxurious male dorm building.

After convincing one of my friends to loan me the money to get my grandfather's car back from the tow lot, I tried to accept the fact that my vision for my new future had gone up in flames all around me overnight. The only small comfort I could find was that I was at least returning to school instead of dropping out altogether. Poppop Luke had gotten in touch with a family friend who worked in a law firm down the road from the house who said he would take on my case and see what we could do to prevent any significant damage. Part of me felt a little bit of relief, but the majority of my mind was dreading how much this was all going to cost. There weren't enough shifts in the world for me to be able to afford all of this. But I was still going to try either way. In quite the unfamiliar fashion, I actually decided to take a small break from parties and drank in the privacy of my basement bedroom (with the occasional visit from *those* friends) after work shifts until it was time to start packing up my things to head back to school. There was only one more isolated, totally normal incident where the police were called to my house for a suicide scare after I vented to another stranger online about how meaningless my life was feeling before I was packing up my grandfather's car to head back to campus.

I did my best to avoid eye contact with anyone I had hugged goodbye under the assumption I wasn't returning back to this campus ever again. My new dorm room was on the other side of campus in a building that looked like it could fall apart at any given moment but I guess beggars can't be choosers. Instead of my luxurious private room and bathroom I had been so fortunate to have last year, I now had one single room that I was sharing with an Australian and a community bathroom I was sharing with the entire floor. Any ounce of privacy I was hoping to get was extinguished within the first day of moving back. To make matters worse, I was drastically unprepared for the level of hygiene (or lack thereof) from the vast majority of everyone on the floor. Note to self: never walk barefoot on any square inch of any floor within this entire building. To make those unfortunate matters even worse, I had to go with any courses I could get since I waited so long to sign up for the semester. Hey kids, college is fun!

Although I still felt like I was constantly struggling to tread water within every single course, something about this semester felt slightly more manageable now that I knew the inner workings and rhythms of campus a bit more. Or maybe I just felt more stable now that I had finally distanced myself from the toxic cycle of hanging out with those two guys I used to take turns making out with every other weekend now that I had no privacy. Or maybe it was just me starting to learn how to college, who's to say? Part of me missed the connection and the fireworks, but honestly I welcomed the small sense of peace that came with not worrying what everyone thought at parties and not worrying about someone walking in on us. That being said, my brain literally couldn't stop creating scenarios in my thoughts and my nightmares that depicted them telling the whole world what we spent the last 8 months or so doing in private. Those thoughts were pretty easy to dismiss once I realized they had just as much to lose as I did. Plus, I had the worst assortment of courses possible to distract and stress my mind enough as it is.

Two core Psychology courses within the same semester was enough to make me want to drop out after the first month. Environmental Science and the additional lab course that accompanied it brought forth enough balance to make me reconsider. That peace only lasted until I was forced to take a Christianity course, a concept I had actually started to distance myself from and reject the more I thought about how Nana was tragically taken away and the cloud was stronger than ever. The tattoo on my shoulder didn't help me get rid of anything whatsoever, so maybe none of it was real after all? Maybe all those years I spent begging and crying at night, attending every Thursday Club meeting against all odds, and joining any church small group I could were all for nothing. To add literal confusion to emotional confusion, I had an in-depth Spanish course that my high school training had hardly prepared me for whatsoever. Thankfully, I always had vodka to help me when all the stress got to be too overwhelming.

Through the sheer brilliance and uncomfortable privilege of having an attorney as a family friend, my charge was reduced to a traffic charge. There was a massive amount in fines and fees, required courses, and even an official alcoholism examination by a professional but I was getting to keep my license and keep a DUI off my official public record. While it only took me a few weeks to slip and fall back into the routine of house parties to avoid mental breakdowns, I made sure to be much more cautious of how and where I acted reckless. Also, I started walking to house parties even if they were across town just so I didn't have to worry about police interaction. That being said, the task of trekking across town (and campus for that matter) was becoming more and more cumbersome with the dense weight of the "I think everyone knows I've fooled around with guys before" chain attached to my ankle. College was amazing in so many ways but with it being such a small school, many parts of it felt like high school all over again.

To try and alleviate this stress, I started going to the gym for the first time with a new friend I made in one of my Psych classes. Being on the basketball team, she was far more advanced and knowledgeable in her techniques but she was incredibly patient with me as she tried to teach me the basics. While it felt nice to physically relieve some of my mind's stress the more often I kept going, I also felt like I was on the verge of a breakdown every time I convinced myself that everyone in the gym was staring at me and making fun of how much I sucked. It didn't help that this gym membership came free with tuition so the vast majority of the gym population were athletes, other students, and the exact people I was worried about thinking I'm a homo. The body in the mirror in front of me still looked like the same thin build that had somehow carried me throughout life, but it was still helpful to have some kind of outlet. The more time we spent together in the gym, semi-studying for Psych, and laughing about everything and nothing, the closer I felt with her. Caught up in the closeness one night, I almost shared with her that I had *done stuff* with some guys until I realized it was far too much of a risk to take.

As the semester barreled along at the speed of light, my roommate came in one afternoon to let me know he was interviewing for an open RA position on the first floor of our dorm building. The next afternoon, he shared that he had been offered the role. Being an Australian student, his opportunities for work were pretty limited so he accepted the offer immediately. It took me forever to realize that this now meant he would be moving from our floor down to the bottom which meant I now had a private room. I got an email from the residence office that confirmed I would be spending the rest of the semester in the room by myself and didn't have to worry about paying the extra fees that typically came along with that since I played no role in his decision to become an RA. That being said, that was one more person I would have to worry about finding my booze stash and writing me up to the Dean. Of course, that's a risk I was always willing to take. I helped him move the last box of stuff down to the first floor before making my way back up to my newly-expanded spacious bedroom. I did my best to ignore the fact that the cloud had reappeared in the corner of the room, the eerie laughter already filling the empty space.

It took all of a week living by myself before I had reconnected with *those* friends and invited them over to a party near campus. After drinking an unhealthy, but typical, number of mixed drinks in a surprising-but-not-really amount of time, all caution was thrown to the wind. Without a second thought,

I whispered to ask them if they wanted to head back to the room. Thirty minutes later, the cloud had entered both my brain and body as I started making out with both of them on the bed I had created by pushing both bed frames together. If there was any shred of doubt on whether or not they were aware of the secret situation I separately had with them, that was now extinguished. The fireworks were exploding in my body and across my ceiling in a way they never had before as my hands tried to figure out which person's chest I was feeling while I switched from one set of lips to the other and back again. However, the energy quickly diminished as one of them started to get visibly uncomfortable. In a flash, they were both walking out of my room, the slamming door feeling like a slap against my face. Shit.

Tears were streaming down my face before I could even figure out what they were for. Was I the one who caused them to leave? Had I screw something up? Did I care what they actually thought at this point? Did I just care that I'm so willing to make out with guys without a care? Why was I like this? Why won't God fix me if Christianity was so real? How could I make myself disappear permanently? I heard the chilling laughter from the cloud get louder and louder in my head and in my room. I looked over to see it hovering, larger than ever, in the corner of my room. I glanced down at my desk where my keys were laying and then back up to the cloud. Suddenly, it was shifting around in the air until it became a dismal, grey screen of some sort with a video montage from high school inside. I saw a younger version of myself, crying the same way I was now, with my keys in my hand and blood on my ankle. I forced myself to look away, throwing myself back down on my bed with more tears forming. I was still that same kid. Nothing had changed except my age and my drinking habits. That kid was crying about thoughts he was having about guys at school and videos he was watching on the internet and now here I was crying about actually doing things with guys sometimes even though I wasn't gay.

The cloud darted from the corner of the room to directly above my head, projecting more and more memories in its core and forcing me to look back over at my keys. Tears still pouring from my eyes, I walked over and picked them up from the desk. I ran my fingers across the jagged edges and felt the cloud right behind my ear, whispering encouragements. *One more time won't hurt. It'll make it all stop. Why stop at just the keys?* I paused for a moment, heavily considering falling backwards into the rabbit hole of my past behaviors. Realistically, however, even if I had wanted to go to the extremes that my mind/cloud was conjuring, it's not like I could drown myself in a dorm's communal shower. I didn't have any pills to take a fatal dose of. The top floor of the dorm building wasn't tall enough. I didn't own a gun or know where I could get one if I wanted to. No. I had made it this far without relapsing. If losing Nana didn't bring me back down this road, making out with guys definitely wasn't going to. I turned around, threw my keys across the room and through the cloud which finally made it evaporate into the air once again. Feeling accomplished yet defeated at the same time, I fell onto the bed one last time before slipping into a painfully restless sleep.

After narrowly relapsing into a darker headspace than ever before, I tried to keep my mind focused on my classes as much as I could. Homecoming Week came and went much more casually now that I was just an audience member instead of an active participant. The whole FOMO emotions were strong during Lip Sync but not nearly as strong as the drink I had brought with me to watch it. As it turns out, Environmental Science was a pretty interesting class with the lab portion allowing us to actually go out into a field next to some woods to build our own small-scale wetland to try and fortify the water and soil. As for the other classes, especially the one focused on a religion that I barely believed in now, not so much fun. Those two friends and I never made any other plans to hang out again after they stormed out of my dorm and we pretty much stopped talking altogether. My mind couldn't decide whether I felt sad or relieved so I chose to just drink nonstop to try and distract myself from figuring it out. Instead, I wandered around house party after house party secretly wondering if anyone else here had a dark cloud of their own. Of course, I'd never have the guts to actually risk making a move even if I did happen to catch a vibe that the guy on the other side of the beer pong table might have made out with a guy before too.

To add another layer of chaos to my semester, a text message woke me up in the quiet stillness of my dorm room. My best friend I had gone to high school with solemnly shared that her father passed away from his battle with cancer. I stared at the text on my phone for several minutes trying to process the words and figure out if this was real or another nightmare. Tears formed in my eyes as my mind flashed back through all the conversations we had, all the times I made him mad for making his daughter late for no reason, and everything else he did that made me both terrified and immensely respectful of him. He was the most important person in my best friend's life and she just had to say goodbye to him the same way I had to do with Nana. Once I found out the funeral info, I borrowed the first friend's car I could find since Poppop Luke had taken his car back for a few days and headed down the road to Loudon. I had no idea how to make her feel any better because nothing really could, but the least I could do was be there.

Pulling into a parking spot outside of one of the two million churches in my microscopic high school town brought forth an overwhelming feeling of dread. The last time I was at a funeral was for Nana. I got out of the car, stared at the building, and heavily considered getting back in and driving back to campus. Something about the double doors in front of me brought back all the sadness and hopelessness that I felt the last time I attended any kind of service. Then I thought of my best friend and the flood of memories that came with that and knew I had to go in. One foot forward. Another foot. Another foot. Another. Smile and say thank you to the man who opened the door for you. Get in line. Wait in line. Head down. Another foot. Once I made it up to the front and reached out my arms, my friend all but collapsed into them. My anxiety from being here suddenly vanished and the only thing that mattered was us in this moment. I could feel her grief pouring out onto my shoulder as I hugged her tighter, signaling that I knew that same hollow hopelessness she was feeling right now. The embrace lasted either a minute or an hour, I wasn't sure, until I continued through the line and found my way to an empty pew to await the service. We met up in the parking lot afterwards, alternating between tears of grief and laughter about all the fun times we'd had those four years. By the time it was time to head back to campus, I almost missed this tiny town and all the memories I'd made in it. Almost.

The first morning back on campus after fighting through my traumatic phobia of funerals, my Psych professor decided to let me know that his high opinion of me from freshman year had drastically changed for some reason. I walked into class to him saying I would have my own assigned seat in the back of both of the classes I had him for this semester. Assuming he was joking because no one assigns seats in college, I took my usual spot next to my gym friend. Except he wasn't joking. He refused to begin class until I packed up my things and moved to an isolated seat he picked for me in the back of the class. When I stopped by his desk after class, he told me that I was being a distraction to others in class so an assigned seat was necessary. Knowing I showed up to class halfway-asleep every morning, I knew this was some kind of twisted power dynamic he was exercising. However, he was tenured and practically owned half the town so there wasn't much I could do in protest. After a snarky remark, however, he grabbed the strings of my hoodie and pulled them down quickly, forcing me to lean in closer to him. Through gritted teeth, he told me I needed to learn how to respect figures of authority before releasing his grip on my hoodie. All of a sudden, psychology vanished from all thoughts I had for my future.

Halloween/Birthday season quickly crept up as quickly as everything else seemed to creep up nowadays. Thankfully, it gave me justification for drinking copious amounts of alcohol in celebration as opposed to just attempting to drown out the fact that I hated my professor and my life. In familiar fashion, I didn't start thinking about what kind of costume I was going to wear until about a week away from the occasion itself. My friend who I was separated from in class and I scrambled together for one of the parties and went as Jack & Coke with the elaborate, complex costume of corresponding t-shirts. Feeling the underwhelmed response, I decided to hit the drawing board to find something more memorable for the actual party weekend. The idea then shot into my brain to take my rock bottom phase and turn it into something positive. So I got a prisoner costume, printed out my mugshot from Panama City, and attached it to the costume. Problem solved. Except for the fact that the first party was an on-campus one that was chaperoned by a faculty member. Oh well!

After adorning the mugshot costume with Birthday Boy pins and ribbons for the party the following night, I got completely trashed and drunk-called my mother for some reason. I remember telling her I was out-of-my-mind drunk before deciding that was enough conversation with Lilley, hanging up, and passing out in the backseat of a random car parked in the front yard of the house party. To add a little lemon juice on the wound, I ignored all the follow-up calls and texts from her the next morning while I nursed the brutal hangover that comes from taking shots of Everclear. Leaning into the meaningless void that comes after a birthday has passed, I passed through a few weeks of classes (and more drinking) until I found myself in another tattoo shop watching my first kiss pass out from the needle as she got an abstract eye inked onto her wrist. In solidarity of her fainting spell, I decided I *must* get one too once she finally finished up in the chair. Without a moment's hesitation, I got my baby sister's birthdate stamped onto my chest in Roman numerals for the rest of my life. I knew I wanted something meaningful that I wouldn't ever regret and her birthdate fit nicer on my chest than a glass of vodka or a mugshot would.

Through another miracle provided to me by the universe, one of my friends in the nice dorm building wanted to switch to a cheaper living situation. I jumped on the opportunity immediately and was suddenly packing up my bags and moving across the street to the other part of campus. While I would have loved to move back into my private room, I was very content with any room that got me out of the all-male dorm building. In the span of only an hour or so, I had traded in my private room for a suite-style arrangement. While there was only a thin wall separating my private bedroom with the bedroom next to mine, I could only think of the fact that I was only sharing a nice bathroom with one person as opposed to an entire floor of residents with questionable hygiene (or none at all). Plus, I didn't really have to worry about having a thin wall between the rooms since I had completely stopped hanging out with *those* friends. I couldn't help but feel ecstatic about my new living situation and, naturally, celebrated immediately. Everything felt perfect, or at least as perfect as you can feel while you're constantly drowning in dread, until I stumbled back into the building that night holding a bottle of whatever mixed drink I had taken to the party. This would have been a totally normal experience except for the fact that the RA on the floor, my former roommate who now hated me, was staring at me holding said mixed drink from the end of the hallway.

Perfect. Not only had I been arrested twice already, but now it seemed like I would be adding a dorm write-up added to the list of my fuck-ups too. The usual punishment for having alcohol on campus was a fine and a quick meeting with the dean, but I just *knew* this was about to be a revenge plot and my former roommate was going to somehow use this to get me expelled. In desperation, I let a few jumbled words come out of my mouth just to break the tense silence that filled the entire hallway between us. Plans of which things to start packing up first in my room started to flood my mind until I noticed a slight smile form on his face. "Love your water bottle! Where'd you get it?" came out of his mouth in reference to his favorite movie. Another smile crept onto his face before he turned around, stuck his key in the door, and went inside the room we used to share. Part of me was consumed with relief while the rest of me was flooded with shock at the olive branch he seemed to have extended in my direction.

After the initial shock wore off that night and the weeks began to soar by once more, we started saying hello to each other in passing until we were actually hanging out in the room pretty regularly. I'm not sure if it was just maturity, the fact that we weren't living feet away from each other at all times, or some combination of the two but I wasn't about to question it too much in case he changed his mind. By the time I started sharing about the chaos of my life and how my family had completely fallen apart even further, my enemy had transitioned into one of my best friends here on campus. He had no idea how to relate or respond to hearing how most of my family didn't talk to me because of how Lilley acted after the funeral or how my parents were getting divorced now, but it was still nice to have someone to vent to. Once I opened up to him, I started opening up a little more to some of the other close friends I had managed to make here in the last year or two. Before too long, it became a pretty standard joke to reference my "crazy mom" or the overall chaos of my family dynamics and my life in general on a regular basis. However, while my relationship with Ryan and Erin was still growing stronger and stronger by the year, they lived too far away to have much of a meeting schedule, especially since I only had a temporary car at the moment.

Having my entire inner circle aware and supportive of my family situation(s) made it all the easier to request a double shift on Thanksgiving at the restaurant once again. The potential money I could make coupled with avoiding the "we're still one big happy family" dinner was enough to motivate me. That being said, I definitely started to notice Dad and I having more and more communication once their divorce decision was made. He was reaching out more and more often to check in on me, something that I was not used to but wasn't upset about either. The last time I recalled having this kind of close contact was when we were both playing the online video game together when I was in middle school so it took a little bit of time to get used to. Nonetheless, I was happy that he was happier and willing to work on things instead of letting ourselves totally drift apart. Of course, that also meant I had to get more and more used to the concept of having two dads and hoping they both weren't ever in the same room together with me to avoid that awkwardness. With every conversation that passed, he started sharing more and more of the behind-the-scenes details that sparked the countless arguments we always heard growing up. These new stories started to align with my own experiences with Lilley until I began questioning my entire childhood and my entire relationship with her altogether. The more things started to make sense, the less anything made sense.

After Thanksgiving flew by in a blur of customer chaos from 8 am to 10 pm, the semester began to wrap itself up. I could not have been more nervous to turn in my final assignments and exams now that I had somewhat made it through the worst (academically speaking) semester of all time. My lab partner never showed up to any of the planned writing sessions so I had to write our entire lab report on the wetland project alone. Throwing him under the bus to the professor scored me one or two brownie points but I still wasn't confident they would make much of a difference. The Psych professor clearly did not think very highly of me based on the hoodie pulling and the assigned seats so who knows what grades he would deem appropriate. The Christian history course made about as much sense as my standing on religion altogether. Thankfully, vodka was stashed in my clothes I brought back home to my grandfather's house for the holidays. You can't stress about holidays and final grades when there's vodka in your veins. That's just science. Not environmental science, but science nonetheless.

Vodka can't, however, stop the anger surging through your body once you see your Psych professor submit final grades that turn your GPA completely upside down. I refreshed the online student portal over and over again thinking it must have been some kind of mistake but the letters remained. My mind shot me back to the beginning of the semester when I told him how worried I was to take two of the core classes during the same semester and how he assured me everything would be fine as long as I gave it my best effort. I didn't miss a class this semester when half the class rarely ever showed up to begin with. Every single assignment was turned in on time or early. My participation during the lectures was just the right amount to seem engaged but not over the top. Yet I was still staring at two of the worst letter grades I had ever made in my entire academic career. The other class grades could have been better, but at least they weren't anywhere close to as devastating as the ones he gave me.

After reaching out to a few of my friends, particularly the girls, who shared the class with me, I found out they all had made A's or B's. Even the ones who showed up for maybe two or three total classes all semester made a better grade than I had. A few more venting sessions later, I was informed this was just how he ran all of his courses. The objective grades you receive on assignments, participation, and exams were practically scribbled out at the end of the semester and replaced with the letter grade he felt you deserved. People had complained about it, along with a variety of vastly inappropriate behaviors, for years but nothing had ever really been done about it. The man had taught there for decades and had a notable status around town so he was practically invincible. My eyes were clouded with a fiery crimson rage and I leaned into it for a change instead of trying to calm it down. There's no way in hell I was going to survive another two years with this man. And I wasn't about to try. Before I could talk myself out of it, I grabbed my phone and sent an email to the administrative office to let them know that my major was changing, effective immediately. The raging red filter over my vision faded almost instantly.

With sudden flashbacks of some of the shows and films I watched with Mom growing up, long before the vast distance had begun to form between us, I made the decision to switch to Criminal Justice. Something about the idea of me solving deeply-complex crimes or cases that had been cold for decades as a detective felt reasonable and right. Or maybe this would be my gateway into law school where I could inevitably solve the major case dressed in a stylish suit, fancy shoes, and a Chihuahua in my satchel. Or maybe a part of me thought this would be the life decision that would balance out the fact that I had been arrested twice. A rebirth. The start of a new era and a new version of myself that *didn't* wake up in handcuffs or cry myself to sleep in a cell.

With my newfound freedom from Psychology, I floated through another holiday break as I embraced the excitement of my new beginning. Sure, the weight of the cloud and my dysfunctional family was still pressing down on me but I had learned how to somewhat ignore that in order to get through my days. Some of the rush that came with a new beginning inspired me to even buy my parents a Christmas present, a gesture I had always avoided over the last few years. Leaving Grams and Gramps's house after a quick holiday dinner found us parking in front of the graveyard where it felt like we had left Nana only yesterday. Staring at the gravestone in front of me, I couldn't help but start speaking. I told her all about my life and all its changes, even including the instances where I started making out with two of my best bros. But I was going to get it figured out. I stood up, a sense of relief washing over me as I hoped that my words had somehow landed on her ears. I kissed my hand, pressed it against the cold stone, and made my way back to my parents car before heading back to my basement bedroom to pack it up once again. Time for another semester. An exciting semester. The semester that I died.

I don't remember the last time I was genuinely excited for school, but something about unpacking my boxes and looking at my newly-drafted list of courses generated a head rush that I couldn't shake. Suddenly, for a brief moment again, the cloud didn't follow my every thought, my parents weren't divorced or crazy, my grandfather wasn't starting to get sick again from his drinking/smoking, and none of the other million stresses existed. I was just a college kid eager to step foot into a new semester in hopes this new course list could help me repair the GPA damage that a toxic, yet protected, professor had unnecessarily inflicted. I heard rumors that the Criminal Justice major was the least stressful academic pathway on this campus but that *definitely* didn't influence my decision to join it whatsoever. I was doing this for all the right reasons. I couldn't help it that I'm passionate about society and correcting everything about it. That being said, I was only able to snag one vaguely-related CJ course this semester since I changed so last-minute. Instead, I got a social work course, an analysis course on physical education, the second part of Spanish, and a Pop Culture class that seemed right up my alley.

Taking one last deep breath, I performed a swan dive into the newness by pretending to know what I was doing with a foreign language, talking about celebrities and why society is society, how to research within a behavioral science, and analyzing physical education. Our first assignment within that course, which was taught by an absolute gem of an instructor, was to present the origin of a popular sport of our choosing. Naturally, thanks to a desperate request, I decided to present the history of beer pong and somehow landed an A on the essay. With my next project being the social hierarchy within the system of celebrity, I started to find out what it felt like to actually feel on top of my grades and not fear failing. For the first time since I started, my head felt like it was comfortably above water in the ocean that was collegiate dread. Maybe this whole college thing wasn't so hard after all.

Thanks to the encouragement of some of my close friends on campus, I started to apply to be a part of some extracurriculars. My newfound optimism about my classes and the fact that I had mentally moved on from the two-or-three attempts to transfer to a new school made me realize I needed to start improving myself. While my professional resume was full of restaurant work experience, my academic resume merely showed that I attended (most of) my classes and was only drunk *half* the time in class. I know my degree alone was going to guarantee me a nice, high-salary job like all our teachers and parents promised us our whole lives, but I was going to need some cosmetic work to help distract from my not-so-glamorous grade point average attached to that degree. After applications and brief interviews that flashed by in a blur, I was being awarded my new status as both a Student Activities Board member and a Student Ambassador. Long story short, I was sitting in on meetings for the planning of social events on campus and giving prospective students and their families tours around campus in hopes to inspire them to enroll.

As excited as I was for all the new ventures I was taking, a part of my brain couldn't help but feel angry at how necessary they were. I had no choice but to take on a job while I was also attempting to balance my schoolwork. If I had no job, I would have absolutely no money for any form of necessities or social life whatsoever. Why was that work experience alone not enough to make myself a worthy candidate for a shiny employment opportunity. Over half the peers I knew got an allowance of some sort from their family so they never had to worry about a job distracting from their classes/sports/life. Yet here I was, taking on more responsibilities onto my schedule because I knew I had to in order to best succeed after graduation. I let the anger simmer for a few minutes before sending it down the river toward the depths of my mind before getting back to work planning a daily schedule. If I wanted to maintain any kind of social life and keep attending parties, I was going to have to actually (gag) manage my time in a more effective way for once. Who was this new person I was becoming?

Clinging to anything that still made me feel a little bit like myself in this new wave of responsibility, I secured my spot for another Spring Break at the infamous Panama City Beach. My former roommate turned enemy turned best friend quickly advised me against it, but I felt it necessary to stick to *some* of my roots. The closer friends we became, the more I realized what a wealth of knowledge he was and while we were polar opposites in life and personality, we meshed incredibly well together. He seemed to have a cunning common sense and a close-knit family system that offered endless love and support whereas I seemed to be a reckless train wreck plummeting full speed ahead without any guidance at all. Yet where I seemed to lack, he was there to fill the void and offer some perspective and vice versa. For each lesson he was teaching me, or at least attempting to, about stocks and travel or something called discipline, I was there to teach him about painful loss, being super straight, having a crazy mother, and unfortunate ignorance of the world altogether.

One afternoon, I casually brought up that my brother called me to let me know Lilley had taken a credit card out in their name together only to run up about $15,000 of debt that was now tied to his name. I spoke casually, completely unsurprised as this was not one of her wildest antics, but seeing how shocked my best friend's face looked let me know just how different our words really were. His family's lake house in the nicer part of my high school town quickly became a second home to me. A place I could always escape to anytime I needed to, whether that be an emotional need or a literal need when I was forced out of the dorm for any extended semester breaks. By the second or third weekend visit, they treated me like a part of their family. It felt nice, to say the absolute least. All of a sudden, I had a support system that felt genuine instead of the usual "I'm asking you how you are because I gave birth to you so I guess I have to" vibe I was so used to. The sudden wave of positivity and wealth of life knowledge felt almost too good to be true. However, it wasn't enough to say no to another beautiful disaster known as Spring Break.

Halfway skipping, halfway stumbling through the semester was cut short whenever I started to notice the rumors start to creep their way across campus. Apparently, the general population and paparazzi was becoming skeptical of my tired explanation of saving myself for marriage. By this point in time, hookup culture had become a societal norm, especially within a college campus. After two years of "I'm just a Christian" and "I promised my Nana I'd be abstinent and I have to honor that because she's dead now", people were starting to have doubts. Party culture and hookup culture are so closely intertwined, how could I possibly be so passionate about one and be so completely absent within the other? Sure, I was still actively flirting and posting photos online of make out sessions with girls at parties, but that wasn't enough anymore. I could start to see the apprehension from guys on campus whenever I'd approach them or try to be their friend a little too much. Shit. This was about to be high school all over again. The eerie laughter from the cloud started to follow my every footstep until it consumed the entire campus at all times. Instead of invisible to all but me, it was now painfully translucent.

Okay. It was time to kick up the flirting, both online and public, and come to the realization that the only way to end the rumors is to do the deed. Maybe once I finally find the right one and finally go all the way, I'll feel those same fireworks. Or maybe I'll just get it over with one night in Panama City, make sure everyone is aware of it, expel the rumors, and get back to normal. Hearing my boss yell my name interrupted my thoughts as he motioned to come over to his office for a meeting. Meetings as a server, unless they were hastily thrown together last-minute in the kitchen walkway, were very unusual so panic immediately set in. Hearing him tell me that I was spending too much time flirting with "his" waitresses and hostesses and not enough time making him money set a fire inside of me that was nearly impossible to contain. Don't explode. Don't complain about how you constantly hear about his excessive groping and inappropriate touches from the women here. Don't tell him you know about those little late-night meetings and arrangements with that other server. Stay calm. Shake his hand. Everything is fine.

Without a moment of thought, I picked up a double shift for the upcoming Valentine's Day weekend since it was going to be busy. Then I decided not to show up for those shifts. Or any other shifts. I ignored every single call from the entire staff. The thought of walking back into the restaurant that the gross man was operating was unbearable. While I had no idea what I was going to do for income, I knew I was certain of this decision to leave. There were restaurants everywhere to work at, I didn't have to work for him. I didn't have to do anything.

With my miniscule savings pretty much extinct, I somehow managed to convince my mother to give me $100 to take with me to Spring Break so that I could at least afford to eat (and drink cheap liquor but she didn't need to know that). Part of my mind knew it was completely ridiculous to still go on this trip after quitting my job, but the majority of my mind viewed it as a necessity. How was I supposed to risk the impact to my social reputation by *not* being at one of the most popular college spots in the most popular week of Spring Break? How could I possibly endure the FOMO of seeing everyone's stories and posts detailing how amazing of a time they were having. Plus, I couldn't get my deposit back on the condo so part of it made logical sense. The cloud's laughter started getting louder as I tried to give every explanation in the book to avoid mentioning the fact that the beach was going to be flooded with shirtless men who looked as if they hadn't missed a single day in the gym in over five years. That wasn't why I was going. I wasn't even going to stare- I mean look. I wasn't going to even look. For too long. With the volume of alcohol flowing all over the city, would anyone notice if I looked? I should look.

As expected, the week flew by in a blur of euphoric bliss, recklessness, and chaos. I found myself passing through beach concerts, taking shots with elderly women, dancing in clubs that we had no business being allowed inside of, posting more pictures with girls so people might stop circulating those rumors and acting weird whenever I was around, and meeting more and more random social media friends. While I had made the decision to finally move past my purity ring phase, I hadn't managed to get past first base with anyone on this trip in the way that most of my friends always did. All I had accomplished was more meaningless make out sessions with girls on the beach or in a club. Packing up my things at the end of the week that felt like it had lasted both months and moments at the same time, I couldn't help but feel disappointed with myself. This week was supposed to be a formative moment in my life where I finally met the right girl and moved past the fog that had tormented me every single day for the last five or six or ten years. Okay sure, it was great that I had managed to snag a few social media posts that showed me kissing a few girls. However, looking back over the pictures in the backseat on the ride home, I could almost *feel* my followers saying to themselves, "I can just tell he isn't enjoying this. You can tell it feels like he might as well be kissing a brick wall or his own hand."

After a long drive back, I arrived on campus with a newfound determination to forget any remaining strands of religion and its silly promises, go all the way, and eradicate the cloud or fog or demon or ghost or whatever it was once and for all. A few weeks of house parties and the other college things that weren't important, like finding a job or keeping my grades up, flew by in a flash until I found myself lying on the couch with her. This wasn't the first time we had cuddled or even made out before, but something about it felt different. It might have been my newfound motivation or perhaps the fact that we were alone instead of doing this in front of everyone at a party, but it was just *different.* Before I could even comprehend what was going on, I was being led away from the couch and toward the twin bed of my room. The make out continued there, picking up in its intensity until I was certain we were both comfortable with moving a little bit forward.

About two minutes into kissing and putting my hands where I felt like they were supposed to go, the horror set in that something was wrong. The woman in my bed was objectively attractive, that was just a scientific fact, and the interest was clearly there. However, there wasn't a single fireworks show happening above my bed or inside my body. The certain part that was vital in crossing over this formative bridge of adulthood was completely malfunctioning. She clearly noticed my panic, not that it was difficult to notice considering I had completely frozen on top of her. She leaned up to kiss me again, asking me what's wrong as I hovered there petrified, barely even able to return the kiss.

"Sorry, I guess I've just had too much to drink haha," I said, voice trembling.

"Chase, I've been with you all day and we haven't drank anything," she returned.

The panic that was already bubbling inside of me tripled in volume as I realized there really wasn't a way to explain my way out of this one. We had been making out, started inching closer towards second/third base, and nothing about my body gave the signal that I was enjoying the experience whatsoever. I already knew the thoughts that were probably forming in her head, thoughts that were inevitably going to be discussed in the soccer team group text or across all the house parties in the coming weeks. She was either going to let everyone know that I probably liked guys and/or that she hadn't been hot enough to arouse me. Everything is going to be downhill from this point forward. It'll be high school all over again, except much worse. Without knowing how else to respond, I retreated to the bathroom. I told her I was getting a shower and that I'd see her in class or at the next party. She left without a word.

After diagnosing myself with anything and everything I could find on the internet to explain my sexual ineptitude, I started considering transferring once again. Another fresh start, even if it meant bankrupting myself for the next 40 years under the weight of crippling student loan debt. The dark cloud stopped appearing in phases and instead followed my every single footstep of every single day. It would be there when I opened my eyes in the morning and would remain hovering over me when my head hit the pillow each night. Icy, bone-chilling laughter filled the room at all times until it began to shift into eerie screams. Everywhere I went, no matter how quickly I walked or how much I drank, the cloud went too. It was no longer ignorable or avoidable whatsoever. It's only a matter of time before everyone else is finally going to be able to see and hear it as well. See it and what I did in secret with the small handful of guys and my porn history dating all the way back to middle school. It took two full weeks after my failed sexual encounter for it to finally take a break from piercing my eardrums from sunrise to sunset.

Finally able to focus on something other than the evil entity, I looked around at my surroundings and tried to figure out what was going on. I knew I was in my dorm room bed that I had turned into a fort with the mattress on the floor covered by a large blanket over the raised bed frame. However, I wasn't alone. I was on the brink of my next chance at finally losing the V-Card that had been hindering my social reputation for so many years. Without giving myself a chance to seem weird, I leaned in to start the make out session that the auto-pilot version of myself had initiated. Fireworks immediately sounded off in my dorm bedroom, silencing the cloud before it could make a single sound. Our hands began exploring as the intensity kicked in, adrenaline rushing through every vein. I paused for a moment as our clothes magically drifted off our bodies into the floor. The moment passed as I decided I was finished second-guessing everything. I took a deep breath before diving into the unknown waters ahead of me, soaking in every firework and every feeling I was experiencing for the first time.

His head fell onto my chest as I stared up at the various metal parts of the bed frame above my mattress, going over everything that happened a few moments ago. Eventually, he put his clothes back on and made his way back to his school, leaving me to further process the million thoughts bouncing around inside my skull. I tried to convince myself that I did not remember how he ended up in my dorm room or the various snaps we had sent to each other leading up to that moment, but it was no use. The plunge into the ocean of uncharted waters was undeniable, and the happiness of his head resting on my chest afterwards was a feeling I already missed dearly. I knew he was going to come over and I knew things were going to happen, whether I wanted to admit it or not. More so, everything worked this time around, both anatomically and emotionally. To add even more to the pile of confusion that was cluttering my mind, the cloud was nowhere to be seen. It hadn't been there whatsoever during the make out session or the events that transpired afterward. All of this had been me. I was in the pilot seat for everything.

The cloud didn't come back the next day. For the first time in weeks, I went to class and work without a single screech or laughter following my every step. An ounce of clarity started to creep into my thoughts as I continued to process the fact that I had lost my societal innocence to someone with the same parts as me. However, the worst part about this process was realizing I couldn't tell a single soul about it. Every single thought, stress, worry, confusion that was rebounding in my head was a risk of total social suicide that would probably lead to actual suicide. Not only was my social reputation at risk, but there was also the risk of potential academic consequences if anyone found out. I know there's some kind of religious affiliation with my college, but did that mean they can kick someone out for being gay?

The moment the final word of that fleeting thought sounded in my mind, I heard the familiar popping noise of the cloud as it reappeared in my bedroom. However, this was not the same ominous presence that had been painfully stalking me for so many years. Instead of the sinister grey and black aura, this cloud was emitting a soft, warm orange glow that quickly began to fill the room. Tears began to fill my eyes as the small ounce of clarity became an ocean of realization. The cloud grew closer and closer until it absorbed into my chest, causing me to rush over to my bathroom sink. Looking back at me was a version of myself that I had never seen before, tears still streaming down my face. Everything made sense now.

I'm gay. I've always been gay. It's literally who I am. And that's okay. My body didn't "work" a couple of weeks ago and it never will because I wasn't straight. I never was. Fireworks were never going to form whenever I kissed a girl at a party the way they formed in the private moments with those guys. There was no dark cloud forcing me to make out with guys in private or occasionally take their clothes off. I *am* the cloud and not an evil, sinister one. It was never evil or sinister to begin with. The church, my parents, my brother, the kids at school, and society made it seem like an evil burden following me around but that's just not the case. If it was so wrong, religion could have healed it but it wasn't wrong. It's just me. My identity. The tattoos and the shackle around my ankle were created by them. It was their shame and guilt, not mine. The epiphany was almost too much for me to comprehend as I started crying even more happy tears. I had been waiting for this moment for so many years even when I didn't realize it.

The overwhelming warmth of acceptance lasted all of about an hour. It was then replaced with an overwhelming pressure and wave of anxiety. How the hell was I supposed to tell other people about this?

Chapter Fourteen

Remember When I Became a Gay?

The vodka concoction sitting on the counter that used to be mine during freshman year stared back at me with a glimmer of encouragement reflecting off the lightly-tinted glass. Tonight was the night. Or at least I think it was. I skimmed back over the scribbled list of pros and cons for making the announcement across all of my social media accounts. I was finally going to reveal my deepest, darkest secret to the world all at once. Maybe. Over the last two weeks or so since the Great Epiphany of Homo, I told three or four of my close friends and their reactions could not have been more supportive. From the confession on the dock of my former-enemy-turned-bestie's lake house to the snap I sent to my best friend that said "I think I might be bi but I'm definitely not straight", I had received all the encouragement I could have asked for. It was the perfect encouraging set-up to take me to this exact moment. Having a drink or two or five while I crafted the perfect Notes App message to come out to the entire internet just felt right. Or did it? Yes. No. Yes.

After one more round of reassurance from two of my best friends in the room, I took a breath before hitting send on all social media platforms. From there, I immediately silenced my phone, turned it face-down on the counter, took a shot, and cheered as loudly as I could. I walked over to the front door and shouted, "I'M GAY!" out into the hallway. A few people clapped as they walked by. One guy yelled "finally" from his doorway. It felt nice. Music started playing from inside the room, a playlist my former roommate put together for the occasion, and I started dancing around without a single care. I couldn't think of a time in my life where I felt more overwhelmed with fear and euphoria at the same exact time. I knew I wanted to check my phone and see what kind of response my big announcement was garnering, but I couldn't. All I wanted to do was dance around with my best friends right now in this brief moment of naive joy without knowing whether or not I was losing friends, gaining fame, and/or being expelled. A cloud carried me around the living room for the next hour or so to the beat of whatever pop song was playing until I decided it was time to take a peek.

Stunned was an understatement for the state of mind I was in once I witnessed the tidal wave of encouragement, love, and support I was receiving. My accounts were getting more likes and comments than ever which is obviously the most important part of anyone's life. There were two or three guys who decided they couldn't bear the thought of following their gay friend online who promptly unfollowed me, but there were a dozen or so new followers and friends who quickly filled their place. Even the people I had already emotionally prepared to respond horribly gave a "good for you, man" or a "proud of you, bro" underneath the posts, transforming me into the happiest emotional heap ever. I swam in the excitement of acceptance for the next 30 minutes as I tried to message everyone back until something dawned on me. I still had to tell my family.

While I had considered having one of those heartfelt, emotional meetings in a living room where I would spill my heart out, I knew that was never going to happen. The moment I considered picking up the phone and calling Lilley, I remembered. The way she forced me to stop hanging out with my first set of best friends because it would make me seem gay being the only boy in the group. The little jokes that Dad and her would say about a seemingly-gay man on the sidewalk or on television. The way Rob would always call me that one little word anytime I did something annoying or when he found out I had messed up another first kiss opportunity in middle school. The way Lilley almost tried to have me committed to some kind of psych ward whenever I revealed my secret of self-harm without even trying to listen to me. The possibility of having one of those cinematic coming out scenes where the parents immediately embraced me and assured me they loved me no matter what was simply never going to be my reality. For all I knew, coming out in person meant they would try to physically force me into some facility that would "fix" me and I was not about to risk that. Social media was the main reason I broke out of my shell and started learning how to be myself and speak to other people so it just felt right to come out as myself there. I knew I should have at least picked up the phone to call my father and stepmother, but a small part of me was scared of how they would react. If my own mother reacted so harshly to confessions, anything was possible.

Taking a few deep breaths that did nothing to calm my nerves, I sent everyone in my family a text simply asking that they check my social media. It was already pretty late at this point and I had already gulped down a countless number of celebratory drinks. I put my phone down, collapsed into the comfort of my bed and my own skin, and slipped off into the most peaceful sleep of my entire life. Making my gay debut out of my dorm building and onto campus filled my stomach with butterflies of both the nervous and excited variety. While I had absorbed all of the positive feedback from my grand escape from the closet, I couldn't help but imagine someone showing up to kick my ass or everyone in my classes to scoot their desks far away from mine in an attempt to avoid catching the gay. Instead, every other person I walked past congratulated me or told me they were proud of me. My professors somehow already caught wind of my announcement and stopped me before class to show their support and let me know they were here to help me or congratulate me in any way on my journey. One of the popular jocks in my class even went out of his way to walk across the room and hug me before the professor started her lecture. Out of the million scenarios I had created in my mind for how this formative moment could have gone, not a single one of them was as perfect as this reality was. But then I got a notification on my phone after all of my classes. It was a call from Lilley.

I wasn't sure if I was ready or not to answer the call, completely unsure of what was going to come through from the other line. Hesitantly, I slid the dial to answer, and was immediately met with an onslaught of questions and comments regarding my posts. My grandfather, Dad, and Lilley were all in the room with her phone on speaker mode. Disappointment, anger, and overall disgust were so heavily laced into every single word that it was almost tangible through the phone. She was shocked that I didn't tell her first before anyone else. She was confused because I said I was a Christian. I've kissed girls before on social media so how was I suddenly gay? I was not allowed to have any boys over to the house during school breaks. Even if they were just my straight friends, they were not allowed to be in the house with me. Was I not worried about going to hell? There are facilities I could go to and try to fix this. Nana was rolling in her grave.

Eventually hanging up the phone, I passed through the following days in a gloomy haze as I tried to process the words from my own mother. She continued with her rants online, posting statuses explaining how she would always love me but she couldn't understand why I would announce something like this without trying to heal first. To follow my mother's social media behavior, the Loudon County Baptist Association, an account run by my friend-at-that-time's mother who put together one of those youth groups, reached out as well. She proceeded to tell me that she had seen my post and felt obligated to reach out and let me know that god had also seen my post. They were both disappointed because there were so many good plans for my life but I had just thrown it away for a life of evil. There were links to prayer groups and programs to help me whip myself back into shape. After ignoring most of her messages, she concluded by stating it wasn't a sin to have gay thoughts, only to have gay actions. I should just pray more (six years of prayer and sobs weren't enough) and force myself to have sex with women. Religion, am I right?

Reflecting over everything that was spoken to me over the next week took me on a rollercoaster of varying emotions. However, the final conclusion at the end of each of these mental pathways was that I needed to be done. Done trying to make my parents proud to call me their son even if he's gay. Done keeping parts of myself locked away in a prison cell in my brain. Finished telling myself it's my fault that my childhood and family structure in general were so dysfunctional. Finished with this idea that just because they attempted to raise me that they deserved 100 percent of my respect and loyalty when it was never even remotely reciprocated. I was finally going to be myself for the first time and if they weren't on board with that, then so be it. I had already been so distant due to the chaos of our relationship so it only made sense for this to be the final straw. If I didn't already consider my network of other family members, my friends, and their families to be my actual family, I definitely did now.

Happiness crept back into my mind as I ignored the calls and texts from Lilley and paid more attention to the texts, calls, and online messages from both friends and strangers. I wanted to take the next step in the journey of my new identity and downloaded two of The Apps. Online dating platforms had already kicked off and intertwined itself into society overnight in the way that social media had in middle school so it was only natural that I update my profile. Not only did I update my "searching for" section to men on the main dating app, I also downloaded that one app that's specifically designed for my new community. Discretion was a common theme for users of this app, but I was bound and determined to find my first love somewhere within the grid of headless torsos and anonymous solicitations.

Quickly realizing that I was one of maybe three homos on campus in a small town in the middle of nowhere, I updated my distance range on The Apps to the maximum in my search for Prince Charming. Without knowing anything about gay dating or whether I even wanted to partake in it, I basically swiped right on anyone I was even slightly attracted to. I got lost in the messages and flaky plans to meet up and nauseating pickup lines. Even with the moderate amount of matches I was making, I very rarely came across anyone who was willing to make the travel plans to actually meet me in person to see if we had a spark. Therefore, I had to start relying on the app that was typically reserved for discreet hookups whenever I was craving attention and validation. Shallow conversations quickly turned into one night stand after one night stand as my ideas of Prince Charming quickly began to dissolve into thin air like the dark cloud had. Maybe gay dating didn't actually exist. Before I realized it, my desire to actually connect with another man in a way that was more meaningful than casual nighttime (and the occasional afternoon) intimacy had been almost entirely replaced. My body and sexuality quickly became the only thing I presented to anyone in exchange for validation and acceptance. Parts of my mind were concerned, but I quickly told myself this was a new phase of life and seemed to be the normal factors of this new community I had announced my entrance to.

With the hectic adjustment to a new life, I barely realized that the semester was coming to an end quicker than I could imagine. Standing out on the Commons Lawn watching my friends, especially my former roommate turned enemy turned best friend turned gay guide, walk across the stage and grab their diploma felt surreal. I wasn't sure what I was supposed to do without his constant guidance. However, seeing the accomplishment on his face as he took in the fact that he had survived four years as one of the only gay kids on campus made me realize I could do it too. I may not have had the support and encouragement from my immediate family, but I had my friends and all their families in my corner to help me along the way. Everything was going to be okay. It had to be. There wasn't really a back-up plan at this point.

Unpacking my things back into my basement bedroom in my grandfather's house could not have been more awkward and tense. There were a million more eggshells and landmines scattered around the floor and a million more sets of eyes watching my every move despite the fact that no one had really spoken to me at all yet. No one had even really acknowledged the fact that I had returned home, not that I was complaining. I had already secured a job for the summer at the local restaurant down the road from my house. While the idea of money after scraping by for the last couple of months seemed amazing, I was more thankful for the opportunity to keep borrowing Poppop Luke's SUV whether I was actually using it to go to work or not. Not only that, but I desperately needed any excuse to flee the house as much as possible given the feedback from my sinful, homoerotic coming out post. Maybe I could take up church again and ask them to perform an exorcism or something in front of the whole town while I was back.

Working, hanging out with literally any friend who would give me the time of day, parties at bestie's lake house, and isolating myself in the basement quickly became my routine as I forced myself through the tension at home. His family's home quickly became a second home and common hideaway as his family became more and more aware of my situation. I reached out to a guy who I knew from Lenoir City's Thursday Club now that I was comfortably out of the closet and started hanging out with his roommate and him on the weekends. We liked each other enough in high school but considering we were both constant residents of the They Are Probably Gay Rumor Mill, we had to keep a safe distance. Now, we were able to freely spend our weekends playing drinking games, talking about the competitive cheer gym they owned, and sneaking me into the country bar every Sunday whenever they would forget I was supposed to be banned until I turned 21. Somewhere in the first month of the summer, a batch of good news finally arrived in my lap.

Unsure of what he was going to do now that he had his diploma, my best friend decided to accept a position within the domestic version of the Peace Corps. Basically, he was going to be managing a new food bank program that would run alongside the main food bank program that had been in place for a while. The best part of this news was that the food bank program was conveniently located on campus which meant I didn't have to worry whatsoever about what I was going to do without his constant encouragement, support, and gay guidance. Naturally, I committed to any and all volunteering opportunities to help my best friend *and* start putting my name on the map of campus. While it was great that I started to have my extracurricular activities added to my academic resume, a healthy appetite for volunteer service would help propel me all the more further into adulthood after I finally crossed that stage and snagged my diploma. With the stress of the unforeseeable future off my shoulders, the only thing left to do now was rally together a group of friends, pregame, and hop around a trampoline park drunk before I retreated back to the lake house to insert myself into whatever house party the family had thrown together.

After what felt like the millionth right-swipe on the millionth boy who lived a million miles away from Loudon and/or Athens, Tennessee, I made my millionth match. He seemed charming and I was immediately entranced within the first scroll through his dating profile photos and was shocked to receive the first message from him. Typically, the process was right-swipe, possibly match, radio silence, drink too much, send the first message. However, he seemed to shockingly be just as into me as I was into him and we immediately fell into message after message. Messages quickly turned into texts which evolved into phone calls and FaceTimes until I was completely head over heels. Although it didn't take too much convincing, I was able to talk him into making the three-or-so hour drive up to visit me one weekend so that we could finally meet in person after what felt like endless years of agonizing distance.

My fears about relationships being an extinct concept seemed to fade away as quickly as they appeared as the weekend passed by in a blur of aquarium and restaurant dates, walking around Chattanooga, and pillow talk. It seemed like a rare occurrence, but maybe I had finally found the right person. My heart fluttered as we talked late into the night about anything and everything, particularly about how quickly our feelings were developing. Devastation came pretty quickly when I tried to have him stay the night at home only for both of us to be kicked out of the house by Lilley and Dad because they weren't going to have "that" in their house (even though it wasn't their house). Even then, he seemed to know exactly what to say as we made our way to my friend's house in Knoxville so we didn't have to sleep in a car. But then came the part where we had to discuss the fact that he was planning on attending an art school up in New York City while I was still stuck in this small Southern town in the middle of nowhere. A few weeks later after the magical first visit brought forth our very first fight and the sinking feeling I got in my stomach hearing the harsh words he carelessly threw my way. To add salt to the wound, I found out he had been messaging my best friend behind my back a few days after he had told me how much he was starting to care about me during one of those pillow talks. The flames of romance were extinguished as quickly as they sparked up as I told myself in the mirror through teary eyes that dating probably wasn't for me whatsoever. At least not while I was stranded in the middle of Southern society.

With how small and inconveniently located the restaurant I was working at this summer was, I barely had any money at any given point. Therefore, I said yes to every single social gathering I was invited to and even said yes to a beach trip with my Knoxville best friends and another boy I had developed a crush on. Things seemed great until they weren't within the first 8 hours of the trip. The crush and I sat in the backseat talking about how much of a crush we had on each other (gag) and how it would be nice to think about dating since Knoxville was relatively close to campus only for him to match with someone online before we had even checked into our room. In familiar fashion, I took my frustration and sadness out with vodka and bonding life talk sessions with my two best friends while ex-crush practically dated someone else in front of me the entire week. An unfortunate side-effect of this totally healthy amount of drinking was dropping my phone in the ocean in the first couple of days of the trip. Bad omens everywhere. The vibes were *off*.

Just in time to continue the distractions from my family abandonment, I decided to throw my own house party for the first time with another close friend of mine in Lenoir City. Planning out all the details, making sure his parents would be out of town, and inviting everyone I came in contact with quickly took my mind off the fact that I had no idea how to date or if I deserved love. It seemed as if any time I ventured any further out into this new world, bad vibes surrounded me. I'd match with someone new, start to feel things, and then they'd call me a whore or snap my best friend behind my back. I'd find someone closer to home and then they'd bring someone new around mere hours after confessing their like for me in the back seat. Part of me even considered reaching out to those former friends I had shared so many secret moments with until I realized that would be *begging* demons back into my life. Even the person I had given my "first time" away to that afternoon had pretty much disappeared a week or so after that formative moment. Putting all my focus and energy into planning a huge party seemed like a much better way to spend my time. That was, of course, until the party got busted by the cops within the first two hours resulting in 27 cars being towed away from the neighborhood. Turns out it wasn't the best idea to use social media to advertise a huge house party.

As I was about to make my millionth stealthy exit from the basement sliding door, Poppop Luke called for me to wait and talk with him for a moment. Shit. This was the moment. He hadn't said a word to me directly about the whole burning in hell thing whatsoever and we had adopted this Don't Ask Don't Tell policy in the house but I guess he was finally ready to confront me. I started preparing to return the car keys to him and probably start packing up my things to go find some place to live from now on, but instead he asked me if I had a minute to talk about something important. Willing to talk about anything other than being a homo with my elderly, likely-homophobic grandfather, I nodded. Instead of diving into the train wreck of the conversation I was emotionally preparing for, he asked me how I felt about signing on to be the executor of his estate.

I accepted his request without having a single clue what he was talking about, mainly because I was still terrified of the hypothetical conversation I had created in my head right before. Seeing the confusion on my face, he clarified that the executor of an estate is the person legally designated to enforce someone's will and final wishes (particularly the financial ones) whenever someone passes away. My face must have shown horror as I prepared for him to tell me his cancer had returned because he immediately started reassuring me there wasn't anything to worry about. He said that he had made updates to the will and that Nana was originally going to be the one carrying out his final wishes and he didn't trust Lilley to handle anything related to finances in a fair way. From there, he showed me his online banking information, the copy of the new will with all the details listed in case I ever needed it, and made an appointment for us the following week at the law office down the road to sign all the necessary paperwork. Not thinking anything of it considering he seemed normal and healthy (all drinking/smoking habits considered), I launched it to the back of my mind almost immediately.

As I went to pack my final box up to head back to campus after a summer break that passed by far too quickly, I realized something was missing. Something important. Between the stuff that was already packed in my car and my bedroom, I tore everything apart in search of them. No matter how feverishly I searched for the pair of diamond earrings that Nana had left me, I couldn't find them anywhere. I always kept them in the same place along with a number of other sentimental items, all of which were still there. That's when the spark of rage ignited into a bonfire inside my body as I realized what was going on. Before I could pause and think anything through, I was storming upstairs and shouting at the top of my lungs to my parents in the living room. Lilley didn't even turn away from whatever she was watching on TV to address my accusations that she had stolen my heirloom. In fact, there was even a slight grin slithering across her face with every word that slid out of my mouth.

"Your dad is the one who technically took them out of your drawer and you're not getting them back. Nana would not have wanted them to be made into a ring for a man instead of a woman. You'll get them back when you get your shit together, son."

The words struck me like a baseball bat to the stomach. Scenes of my mother with the earrings that were passed down to me, taking them into a pawn shop somewhere or selling them online, were enough to make me almost throw up on the living room floor. Angry tears started to well up in the corners of my eyes as my vision turned crimson. The venomous look on her face was still burned in my memory as I sped off towards campus. Once I made it back to my dorm for the start of Junior year, I sent a simple text to Lilley stating that if she didn't return the earrings to me, I would report them to the local police station as stolen items. Considering they likely weren't cheap, they would probably pursue and charge her for the theft. The jewelry showed up in my school mailbox a few days later. While I couldn't have been happier to have them back, any ounce of respect I still had for my mother was not returned with them.

To fully finalize this loss of all respect, she stole my car that my grandfather was still letting me use about a week or so later. She lied and told me that he had instructed her to grab the car and take it to a place down the road from campus to get new tires and some other maintenance work done on it. When she stopped responding to my texts and calls 12 hours later, I realized I had walked right into yet another one of her traps because she had apparently wrecked her car and wanted to use his in the meantime. While this normally would have just been a minor inconvenience, I had just snagged a new job at one of the nicer restaurants in my college town that I obviously needed to be able to drive to within the next two days. A quick phone call to my grandfather brought the vehicle back along with a dramatic, angry scene from my mother in the dorm parking lot. Thankfully, one of my best friend's parents were there to emotionally protect me and simultaneously see for themselves that I wasn't kidding or exaggerating my chaotic family situation. Staring up at my ceiling later that evening, I couldn't help but feel jealous and angry at all my friends who had such seemingly normal parents.

Who was this woman? Was it the whole divorce somehow being projected onto me? Why was she suddenly the villain of my story? Shouldn't I have been able to hang out with that first group of girls who were so nice to me? Shouldn't I have been able to come clean about the cutting without feeling like I was being sent off and punished? Shouldn't I have been comfortable enough to come out to her instead of letting her read it online? Furthermore, shouldn't I have been able to come out without her saying my grandmother was rolling in her grave? Shouldn't I not have to worry about her stealing my family heirloom and the only mode of transportation to my new job? Shouldn't I have been able to stay in one town/school for more than a year at a time? Shouldn't things have been so, so much different? She couldn't be the same person I clung so closely to growing up. Surely, this wasn't the same person I saw when I was so much younger, the decent daughter of the best woman I've ever known? Yet here I was staring up at the ceiling crying about the person she apparently had always been.

The piercing alarm noise from my phone jolted me awake from a restless slumber to let me know it was time to officially start yet another semester. Something about jumping back into a new routine made it all the more easy to ignore the mental crisis I was stressing over. With that crisis sailing off to the back of my mind, I could focus on the new job, new classes, new and old friends, my resume-building extravaganza, and the relationships with family members I actually wanted to work on. Despite the random act of theft, I was starting to grow closer and closer with Dad now that he was finally separated away from Lilley. Ryan and Erin were always in my corner and we were starting to see each other more and more often despite the distance. I'd also come in contact with Poppop Luke's brother and his wife who just so happened to live a few minutes down the road. Within a few weeks of connecting, my Great Aunt had even managed to contact the school's financial office to start subtracting my semester's books from my account thanks to all her connections from their time at the school. This would continue each semester as long as I kept up the GPA requirement for my scholarship, which I was still somehow pulling off.

Since I changed my major so late into my collegiate journey, I had to take any and every class I could in order to graduate in time. This meant having another semester taking a core class and then an hour later taking the course that was supposed to be its sequel. Breathing through the traumatic flashbacks of Psychology, I met with the professor to seek any and all advice for avoiding crumbling under the weight of the Criminal Justice curriculum. He laughed at my fears and told me to show up and do the work and everything would work out the way it's meant to. I couldn't be further reassured based on my past experiences, but I figured it was best to play it cool. Thankfully, I found myself able to absorb the material that was being taught in class and actually enjoyed it which was a very new albeit welcome experience for me. An introductory course into Social Work was another requirement which made my best friend's job at the food bank I was still volunteering regularly with make all the more sense. Between this and the Racial/Ethnic Identity course with my favorite Sociology professor, my thoughts I had been raised on in regards to the socioeconomic systems of the country began to dissolve all around me. What part of my childhood *was* real and accurate at this point?

With social media being intertwined with my identity since middle school, I was vastly unprepared for the dramatic shift in social media whenever you publicly come out. It was almost as if there was this underground network of social connections where everyone who's gay knows each other. Even if they *don't* know each other, they follow each other. Some of them were out, some of them weren't, but a quick glance at the socials and you knew if they were gay or not. But you never, under any circumstances, discussed it with anyone else. While this new phase of my online life was overwhelming, I quickly took it as another form of the social research that had been so vital to my development back in my early teen years. Then again, I was pretty happy with any kind of gay online research that didn't involve nosediving into the grid of headless nude torsos in search of any ounce of validation I could wrap my hands around since I was stuck in the middle of heterosexual nowhere.

With so much going on at any given point this semester, I didn't really have any time to stress about everything from the summer. Whenever I started to think about how sinister my mother had become, I remembered there was a campus tour to give. When I started thinking about Nana being gone, I remembered there was an essay to write that I was actually excited to get started on. The moment I thought about stolen cars or heirlooms, I hopped in the car to go work a shift at the restaurant or volunteer at the Service and Leadership House. Looking in the mirror one night, I could almost hear freshman-year me laughing at how responsible I had so quickly become. I went from the party kid who fell asleep in the crosswalk during a snow week to the gay party kid who was passing all of his classes, planning Homecoming Week and other campus events, and keeping his bank account in somewhat decent shape all on his own. Of course, this wouldn't have been nearly as possible without all my friends who were helping to keep me afloat during all the madness. The partying helped me stay afloat too, of course.

I wasn't sure exactly what I was expecting to change now that I was comfortably out on campus with my One of the Only Gay People ribbons on. However, every party that I entered felt almost the same as every other one from my past, if not better. No matter which athlete was hosting an event, they always welcomed me with open arms. Drunk talks in the kitchen would always shift whenever I would walk in. "I'm like really proud of you, bro. That took some balls!" and "You don't even act gay so it's cool. You're not like a fairy, ya know?" quickly became a constant weekend conversation. Endlessly. With how many scenarios I had created in my head before coming out, however, I was happy with any kind of acceptance even if it felt like some kind of betrayal to this new community. I didn't want to be treated any differently so I welcomed these conversations. I didn't know any better and the last thing I needed to do was piss off anyone and burn the bridges connecting all my straight friends on campus with almost two more years here. If that means being the straight-acting gay guy, so be it.

To go along with our addiction to responsibility, my best friend and I decided to rescue a dog who barricaded herself in the food bank during a bad rain storm. He had an apartment on campus that was reserved for staff members and I secretly stayed there 90 percent of the time, so co-parenting seemed like the most reasonable solution. We both fell in love with her the moment we saw how scared and soaking wet she was in the Service and Leadership House so it was only a matter of days before she was running around our apartment with her new collar, the name *Reina* delicately etched into it. We both knew it was insane to go into raising a dog together but it somehow didn't matter. It felt right and we loved her. Our afternoons and nights quickly became walks around campus to keep her energy levels normal enough. Naturally, the rumors started circulating that we were practically a married gay couple now that it was legal but I got pretty good at ignoring them. Now that I relinquished the power that one secret used to have over me for so many years, not a single silly rumor could affect me now.

With how hectic my life had become, I didn't even realize Homecoming Week was only a couple of days away. I panicked and texted my boss to explain I needed quite a few days off only to have her laugh in response and say I had already cleared it with her two months ago. There was another meeting with the board where we went over all the events I helped throw together and I immediately started wondering if anyone was going to actually show up for them. I quickly jumped at the opportunity to open up Lip Sync night on behalf of our board despite the fact that I knew I would panic all the way up to the moment I stepped in front of the microphone. In another fun turn of events, I received enough nominations to be selected as the Junior Male Homecoming Honoree. While I had to deal with the whispers of "that was rigged" from a few people on campus since I was technically part of the planning committee of Homecoming, I was still ecstatic to have won. It's not my fault I was so beloved and popular!

The week's festivities passed by in a blur as the smile on my face grew wider with each event once I saw people were actually attending. Before I could even attempt to keep up, I found myself walking through the curtains to a packed house the night of Lip Sync, pausing in front of the mic stand. While I was seeing crowds and crowds of people, I was also seeing all the hard work that went into pulling off this week. I was seeing a full auditorium of people but also a handful of contracts that we had negotiated for the entertainment and the various arrangements we had to make with the facilities department. My mouth opened to address the crowd and officially begin the night, but I had no idea what words came out. All I knew was I was smiling and filled with euphoria as I realized I had succeeded against all odds. The more my personal life seemed to fall apart, the more it seemed to patch itself together in a brand new way that couldn't feel more right. I had best friends, a dog, a resume full of responsibilities and then some, an evergreen social life that I had created all by myself, and a happiness that I had never felt before.

The night concluded shortly after I walked across the stage to represent the Junior Class in the Homecoming portion of the event. From there, I exited out of the auditorium like I was the lead actor leaving the premiere of his new hit movie, a band of my best friends close to my side. In familiar fashion, I spent the remainder of the celebratory weekend hopping around from house party to house party on my victory press tour. With Homecoming Week officially coming to an end, I had that much more free time in my schedule since it was my main responsibility within the Student Activities Board. Now I had all the more time available for shifts at work, keeping myself ahead of my assignments and exams, and learning more and more about the gay networks within the various social media platforms. I even started spending more and more time with the family members I felt like I could actually trust by this point.

The more stories I started hearing about Lilley started to confirm every gut instinct I felt before reaching the decision to distance myself as far away from her as possible. Now that I was getting to know Dad quite a bit more outside the confines of their marriage, his explanation for the countless arguments and emotional absence from my brother and me began to make all the more sense. On top of those, I listened to stories from Other Dad/Erin and my Great Aunt/Uncle that really put things into perspective. Whether they were stories from before I was born, too young to recall or comprehend, or even as recently as a couple of years ago, one thing was certain: I was right to question whether or not she had ever been the person I thought she was. It seemed as if she had even predicted an epiphany like this happening at some point which explained why she always seemed to paint a picture of Dad, Grams/Gramps, Ryan/Erin, and my Great Aunt/Uncle being the villains of the family right before we would see them at any point in our childhood. Yet here I was receiving more support and encouragement from these "villains" and receiving zero from her.

Halloween and my birthday crept up just in time to provide the perfect distraction from these formative realizations. Not only was it a reason to celebrate, but it was also the most important birthday in a college student's entire scholastic journey: 21. In just a few days, I could officially (and legally) purchase alcohol from stores and restaurants. I would finally be allowed back in the country bar in

Knoxville for College Night Sundays. It had to be the best. A night to remember (or not remember) for the rest of my life. With only a few days to plan, I threw together some ideas for Halloween parties, a birthday brunch, and my fateful return to the country bar that Sunday night. I sent out what felt like thousands of texts to try and get all my various friend bubbles to join together until it was time to officially begin the excursion. The first party began on a Thursday night close to campus where I decided to dress up as a Roman soldier in a maroon costume I made out of a bedsheet. It didn't make much sense next to my date who had decided to dress up last-minute as a blind mouse but oh well. Naturally, after that I decided to leave campus for the weekend and celebrate as much as possible in Knoxville.

In an attempt to merge all my high school friends with my college friends, I invited anyone and everyone to attend the Halloween pregame and house party. I arrived, appropriately dressed as a red plastic cup with a giant inflatable ping-pong ball, to an apartment with some of my Lenoir City friends to start downing a questionable amount of alcohol before heading out to the most crowded basement of a house I had ever fucking seen. From there, the night quickly turned into actual games of beer pong, way too many drunk selfies, and various early birthday posts. Once the clock got close to striking midnight, I grabbed the first friend I saw in the basement to give me a ride to the closest gas station to complete the ceremonial, traditional transaction. Cementing the moment in real time, I snapped a picture of myself holding my first case of legally-purchased beer at 12:02 am while still wearing a giant beer pong costume with the cashier grinning from ear-to-ear in the background. I felt unstoppable.

Realizing toward the end of the night that my best friend had left me behind in Knoxville to drive a guy she was interested in back to campus rapidly extinguished the "unstoppable" feeling. After stomping around the block a few times, my anger at being stranded on my birthday started to slowly subside. I found a ride back to campus with a random party friend I somewhat recognized back inside. He wasn't a student but he was always at all the local parties in town so I knew he was a pretty safe way back. Stumbling back into my best friend's campus apartment, I did my best to put my frustrations to the back of my mind before passing out. Somehow, I woke up feeling refreshed and actually ready to take on my first full day of being 21 and downing any and every drink that was passed my way. Instead, I glanced at my phone to see a slew of texts from a number of my friends officially bailing on all the birthday plans I had thrown together.

Not even giving me time to become devastated by my close friends' actions, my best friend and secret roommate threw me into the car. Before I knew it, we were pulling into Market Square in Knoxville for my very first boozy brunch. We hopped around from restaurant to restaurant without a care in the world.

One of my high school friends tagged along for a portion of the afternoon, making special care to point out that his long hair was longer than mine (I was embarking on a long hair phase for some reason) before he had to leave us and head to his job. By the time I had fully soaked in the euphoric feeling of freely ordering a drink at a bar without worry of getting kicked out, it was time to head back to campus. For some reason (probably the nine mimosas in my system) I even decided to accept Lilley's offer to have a birthday dinner at the restaurant I work at. Careful to avoid giving her too much of a benefit of the doubt, I came equipped with two of my best friends who were painfully aware of my maternal situation and who hadn't flaked on the weekend plans.

The liquid courage from the eventful afternoon helped dispel much of the awkward tension that filled the entirety of the beautiful Ruby Tuesday. The conversation I created was light and airy and the moment it started to shift toward "healing" the strained relationship, I deflected away to another topic. With two of my friends there, it was easy to quickly ask them if they remembered the time we did this thing or the night we did that thing until Lilley gave up on her attempts to reel me back into the chaos. Even though I desperately wanted to hash things out and cause a dramatic scene, I knew it wouldn't have changed anything. It wouldn't take away the pain she had caused me through her words and actions and she was never going to understand the things that she had done, even *if* she presented the slightest desire to. It wouldn't heal anything because there wasn't anything left standing *to* heal. Therefore, I did my best to enjoy the birthday dinner and all the free drinks that my favorite server was sneaking my way (we had plenty of heart-to-hearts about Lilley throughout the last couple of months). Eventually, it was time to stand up, awkwardly hug, and say goodbye. I quickly offered to cover half the check even after my employee discount was applied once I noticed the pained look on her face when it arrived. The feeling of my sister's little arms gripping my neck was enough to get me through the rest of the awkward goodbye.

Having mostly processed the fact that the remainder of my birthday plans had been met with flakey texts or no response whatsoever, I decided to call it a night after dinner. Naturally, this lasted about ten minutes or so before I was going door-to-door in my dorm building rallying together any friends I could find to go on the traditional Sunday night country bar adventure. An hour later, I was floating through the entrance, finally able to veer toward the right for 21-and-ups. A drink stayed in my hand the remainder of the night as I reunited with some of my friends from middle and high school, took a thousand-and-a-half pictures, gave my best attempt at learning all the line dances, and let myself hop onto cloud nine. I couldn't help but reflect on the time I had hung out with the first guy I ever kissed right on this floor and now I was happily out of the closet having a better time than ever. The lights suddenly coming on to interrupt my cinematic, emotional flashbacks was the only thing that was able to push me off the euphoric cloud and send me flailing back down to reality/campus.

A few days later, my best friend and sometimes-roommate decided to surprise me with a last-minute weekend trip to Nashville after he saw how upset I had been over my other friends bailing on my plans. Without me knowing, he had thrown together a hotel booking, a birthday lunch that my mother ended up crashing simply so I could see my sister, and a couple of nights of bar hopping around the touristy spots in the city. Neither of us knew anything about Nashville, but we made the absolute most of it and by the time we were stumbling back into our hotel room the last night, I didn't even remember my other friends had all bailed on me last meet or left me stranded in Knoxville whatsoever. We spent the early hours of the morning talking about how far we had come together since those first days living together. Story after story, I felt prouder and prouder of the people we were starting to become while still holding on to the parts that made us fun. All of a sudden, the invasive sunlight was beaming through the window to remind us it was time to head back to reality once again.

The semester continued to surge forward until it was time for another break from classes for Thanksgiving. I started preparing to pick up a few shifts to keep my mind off of Nana and the overall dysfunction of my family until my best friend let me know he'd already texted the manager to let me have the couple of days. He already added us to his family's reservation for a nice brunch buffet at a restaurant by the lake. Part of me started to feel upset that he texted her, but he assured me Thanksgiving was not a profitable shift at this restaurant the way it had been at my last Southern-style one. Plus, this gave me the opportunity to let Lilley know that I was still doing just fine even with her emotional abandonment on my conscience. The brunch couldn't have been more perfect and we all went to one of their docks afterward to hang out for a few hours. From there, the day turned into a big house party with all the different family members hugging it out, talking about how great life was, and spontaneous drinking games. Eventually, I couldn't help but accidentally open the floodgates in front of them as I became so overwhelmed with how quickly and lovingly they had taken me into their family and accepted me right away. Between them and the handful of other parents that had been supporting me emotionally, life felt too good to be true. I was the happiest I had been since before Nana had been taken away from me.

I rode the emotional high from that embrace with one of my chosen families until I found myself suddenly at the end of another semester. It was a strange sensation to suddenly not be constantly panicked about my final grades being calculated when you spent the entire semester actually enjoying the material you were learning. Confidence in my final grades before they were even presented to me was a feeling I hadn't felt since high school but I welcomed it back with the widest of open arms. Just in time to celebrate actually having a grip on my collegiate performance for a change, two of my friends and I packed up the car and set sail for Atlanta. There, we checked into one of the nicest hotels we had ever seen at this point in our lives and started mentally preparing to see one of our favorite up-and-coming musical artists.

Social media had always played a significant role in my social development and everyday life in general so it only made sense that I kept up with my favorite musicians through the various platforms. To make my relationship with the internet all the more enjoyable, I had a few lucky interactions with some of my favorites like Carrie Underwood and various Vine stars. Niykee was included among those, having both responded to several tweets and followed me back on the platform. Groundbreaking, I know. Now that she had finally amassed a cult following through her acoustic covers of rap songs and a collection of her own original music, a tour was the only sensible next step for her career. Therefore, even if it meant travelling all the way to Atlanta, I knew I couldn't miss it. Plus, I had somewhat used my connection with her and her manager to ensure that we'd be able to meet her backstage once her show had finished. I was finally going to meet the stunning celebrity that had helped me convince so many people on campus that I was definitely not a homosexual. How could I not be a hetero when I was internet pals with such a beautiful, talented young woman?

After networking with people in the crowd, I stocked up on drinks from the bar and passed them around to everyone else who were *definitely* old enough to consume them. What felt like three seconds later, the lights cut out. Niykee slowly stepped out to a booming bass that shook the whole venue. There were screams all around me until I realized I was the main one emitting the screams. I was finally in the same room as my internet bestie and was watching her kill it on stage while she made eye contact with me and occasionally held my hand during a chorus, excitedly shouting my name into the microphone between songs. I blinked a couple of times and was suddenly cutting past the VIP pass line backstage to hug her before the official meet-and-greets began. I tried my best to tell her everything I had planned on saying since I first discovered her in high school but my brain couldn't spew out all the words in time. She gave me one final hug and snapped a few more pictures for social media (duh) before the venue security team forced us to leave.

We all floated from Atlanta back to campus on a cloud as we talked over and over about how perfect the concert experience had been. Wrapping up the semester to a handful of *A*s from my courses was the sweetest cherry on top of such a formative year. With my job at the restaurant and the uncertainty of when Lilley was going to move out of my grandfather's house following the divorce and overall ability to get along with anyone, I made the decision to stay on campus this winter break. While the typical student was rarely ever allowed to stay on campus during these break times, the typical student rarely had a close friendship with a staff member with an on-campus apartment that just so happened to already have most of his stuff inside. In the same breath, I also assigned my name to a dorm room in the all-male building with a roommate so that my living expenses would be cheaper while deciding to *actually* move into the staff apartment full-time. With co-parenting the dog and being such close friends, it just made sense. Plus, having a cheaper dorm room would secure me a more substantial refund check and I was in no position to turn away any kind of additional income at this point.

My routine quickly became nights at the lake house with his family, walks around campus with Reina, shifts at the restaurant, and endless movie nights in the apartment with endless amounts of wine. I picked up even more volunteer shifts at the Service and Leadership House, building my volunteer hours in the system as well as building relationships with the various staff members whose offices were housed within the old home. After deciding to re-download The Apps for the millionth time, I somehow matched with one of the most attractive guys I had ever spoken to. I wasn't sure how we managed to match considering He lived near Atlanta, but I wasn't about to question it or complain. With distance involved, I put our wedding plans to the back of my mind in order to avoid getting my hopes up too high. Instead, I stressed about what I was going to do for the holidays this year.

Spending a few drunken nights with my second family at the lake house was a given, but I wasn't sure how to go about planning to see other family members. Even if I was okay with using my grandfather's car to travel the distance to see Ryan/Erin and Grams/Gramps, it was a gas guzzler and I didn't have the extra cash on hand to support that narrative. Therefore, I decided to do it anyway and spent a couple of days at my biological father's house with my stepmother and their combined families and just kept it a secret from my grandfather. Once I got back from that heartwarming trip, I made a my way down the road from campus to have a nice dinner with my Great Aunt/Uncle who had been showing so much encouragement and support for me. As much as I wanted to avoid it, I even decided to return back to Loudon for dinner to see my immediate family. Of course, this decision was pretty easy to make considering Lilley had threatened to keep my sister as far away from me for as long as possible if I declined the invite.

My best friend decided to tag along for moral support so we spent the first few minutes sitting in the car outside my grandfather's house mentally preparing for the worst things that could possibly happen. After that, we hopped out of his car (we took his car instead of mine in case Lilley tried to steal it again) and headed inside with Reina happily trotting along between us. I tried to hide the enjoyment on my face once I noticed the obvious discomfort on everyone's face to have not one but two homosexuals inside the home. Rob must have noticed it as well because he immediately let me know that he had brought some liquor with him to help ease the tension. We took a shot (or four) in the kitchen before making our way out to awkwardly mingle with the rest of the family while pretending everything was sunshine and rainbows (but not the gay kind). After a painfully silent dinner, we decided to break out the booze publicly and turn the entire evening into a drinking game to make things less uncomfortable. This worked wonders until Lilley had one too many shots and decided to start screaming. From hearing how I was a train wreck that was ruining the family with my "lifestyle choice" to how Dad was the sole reason their marriage ended, we decided to make our swift exit from the house back to campus.

It took a day or two to process the scene that had unfolded at Poppop Luke's house and talk myself out of being embarrassed that my best friend had been there to see/hear it all. Thankfully, after texting and video-chatting for a couple of weeks, I had convinced my recent online match to make the trip to visit me in person to help take my mind off of everything. While I was attempting to not get my hopes too high for once, our chemistry had been undeniable from the very first video call and I could not have been more ecstatic to meet Him in person. My secret roommate was going to be out of town for the weekend so it could not have been the more perfect scenario for an out-of-town romantic visitor. I could already hear the wedding bells chiming in my head as He pulled up to campus in a massive truck. Wedding. Bells.

Fireworks immediately erupted all around the living room of the apartment the moment He walked in and wrapped me in His arms. These were almost like the fireworks I felt during my first gay kiss, except these were a million times prettier and more intense. All hopes of not getting too emotionally attached to this new prospect flew out the window the moment we were face-to-face. Conversation immediately poured out of both of our mouths without an ounce of effort until the chemistry was figuratively flooding the entire apartment. Trying to keep a little bit of distance between us so I didn't come off too clingy lasted all of ten minutes before I was trying to get as close as humanly possible to Him on the couch, the kitchen, the bedroom, and everywhere in between. Wherever He walked, I wanted to be close behind. When He spoke, all I wanted to do was listen. As if the chemistry and conversation wasn't enough, the raw physical attraction and sexual longing was almost tangible. Do I make a move? Is it too soon? I had no idea how to navigate this new connection, but I did know I couldn't fathom messing it up so soon. This was fucking terrifying.

The weekend passed by a million times too quickly as we laughed, cuddled, explored campus, snapped pictures when we thought the other wasn't looking, took sappy selfies, and "other things" every now and then. Seeing Him pack up His things back into a duffel bag immediately turned my stomach into the knots I hadn't felt in so long. A tsunami of darkness replaced the euphoric fireworks as I watched His truck pull out of the parking lot back to His family's home in Georgia. Tears filled my eyes as I sat like an empty shell on the cold laminate of the bathroom floor trying to talk myself out of the fact that I was already so deeply attached to Him. A ding from my phone in the other room brought me out of the melancholic episode that I had been dwelling in for god knows how long on the cold floor. A smile cracked through the stoic mask that my face had become once I realized He was already texting me about how amazing the weekend had been. He was already trying to plan out the next visit before He had even made it back home. He was feeling the same things I was feeling. Pure happiness mixed with fear erupted inside of me as I tried to imagine how this could possibly work while knowing I was willing to do whatever it took to *make* it work.

Thoughts of my newfound infatuation quickly filled every moment of every day as I gave up trying to focus on anything else. Autopilot mode kicked in the moment I set foot inside the restaurant, the Service and Leadership House, the apartment, or anywhere else on the planet. After constant texts and FaceTimes, we decided to hang out again on New Year's Eve. I knew there was absolutely zero logic behind trying to form a relationship out of whatever this was, but I didn't care. He lived in Georgia, went to school a million miles away, and wasn't out to anyone (especially His family) but none of that mattered. The only thing that mattered was the feelings I got the moment we met in person for the first time. I had never connected so deeply and so quickly with anyone before and I wasn't about to give it up without trying.

In a random turn of events, I agreed to babysit my little sister for a couple of days. While I avoided the small talk whenever Lilley arrived for the exchange, I paid special attention to make sure my sister knew that she was a very special part of my life. Lilley was having to do something divorce-related so I tried my best to turn the apartment into a fun circus to take her mind off of our parents and the divorce debauchery. While she was still very young, I knew she was old enough to start being impacted by the various events unfolding around her the same way that I had been. She'd already been moved around a bunch of times the same way we were as kids so the least I could do was try to reverse some of the potential damage. That being said, there's no telling what Lilley has already said about me when my sister was around so who knows if this effort was even worthwhile. The next two days passed by in a haze of walking around campus, playing with Reina, braiding each other's hair (which I was still growing for some reason), and talking about how much we loved each other.

While having Lilley and my sister at the dinner I was making for my roommate and my potential new husband wasn't originally a part of the plan, I couldn't seem to give them the boot from the apartment in time to avoid it. Meeting my mother was the last thing I wanted, but He didn't seem to mind too much once he arrived. In fact, He immediately started playing with my sister upon arrival which sent a special kind of butterflies throughout my body. Suddenly, having my sister and mother here wasn't the worst thing that could happen which is something I never imagined saying. Of course, all of that changed the moment I noticed her asking question after question about His weight-lifting and His football stories with such interest and pride that I had never felt from her in my entire life. She was looking at the son that she wished I would have been. Sure, He was still gay, but He was muscular and masculine and played the sports she loved. Suddenly, I couldn't wait for her to leave us alone as my stomach started to turn inward.

After rushing my mother out the door, I packed a quick bag before we set sail for Knoxville. He booked a hotel room down the road from my friend's house so that His parents wouldn't possibly get suspicious of where He may be sleeping. Already behind schedule, we checked in and changed as quickly as possible. Of course, one glance at each other and our outfits in the mirror quickly turned into a contest of who could take their clothes off quicker. After winning that contest and ignoring the million dings from my phone for a while, it was time to quickly throw the outfits back on and head to my friend's pregame down the road. The romantic fireworks followed me from the room to the car to the living room of the pregame and showed absolutely no signs of letting up anytime soon. Seeing how quickly my friends approved of Him in between shots and drinking games only amplified them that much more.

With every small moment, the fireworks grew more and more as the night progressed into the bar hopping phase. The random eye contact we would make in the middle of a story or a game. Casually and gracefully sliding closer towards me on the couch. Resting His hand on my leg in the back of the car that was driving us towards Downtown Knoxville. One of my friends leaning in to whisper "y'all are so cute" or "He's perfect" in my ear. This was already one of the happiest nights I've had in so long and the night was just beginning. Once we were in the bars, it didn't even matter that there were crowds and crowds of sweaty people because the only ones I saw were my two close friends and Him. Everyone else may as well have not even existed the entire night.

With all caution thrown to the sweat-laden wind, I took turns dancing with the group and dancing with Him as the night swung into full effect. While I had never been one to risk public displays of affection, I didn't care anymore. I threw my arms around Him and even kissed Him without a single ounce of care for who might see. We took turns buying each other drinks from the bar as if the establishment was somehow going to run out of alcohol until the clock got closer and closer to midnight. To seal this night as unforgettable as possible, I threw my arms around Him once again and planted my lips onto His face just in time for my friends to snap a photo. With the confidence of a drunk gay who was falling faster than ever for the first time, I posted the photo with the cliché "new year, new me" caption without a worry in the world for how anyone might or might not react to it. An hour or so later, we both decided it was time to make our exit back to the hotel to spend the rest of the holiday alone. It took all of 15 seconds in the car home for us to tell each other at almost the exact same time just how special this all felt. The rest of the night dissolved into intimate pillow talk that sent the fireworks spiraling all over the room.

The light shone through the poorly-drawn curtains and hit my face like a sack of bricks that were also forming in my stomach the moment my eyes opened. He had to leave today. Sure, we still had several hours with each other but how was I supposed to tell Him goodbye after *another* perfect weekend? We scurried out of the hotel as quickly as we could in order to avoid the late checkout fee and within five minutes of the drive back to campus, I was spewing out ideas as quickly as my brain could construct them on how He could lie to his parents or come out to them to make this all easier. I knew He had to go back to school in a week or two which would all but extinguish this flame we had created together and I couldn't bear the thought of just standing by and letting that happen. But every single idea that came out of my mouth fell on deaf ears as He stared forward at the road without a word. We stopped once on the way home to grab something to eat and tried to laugh through the inevitable depressive wave that was about to crash over both of us in the next few hours.

As predicted, this goodbye felt even worse than the first one as if it were literally a knife going into my stomach. Sad music filled the apartment as I sat down in the shower letting the hot pellets of water strike my skin, the bathroom lights off to reflect my mood. With no idea what was happening or why, I couldn't help but tell myself that I might have just seen Him for the last time. One of the most important people I've crossed paths with and there's a solid chance that I'd never see Him again because of how

278

impossible the whole situation seemed. He would return home to His parents who didn't have a clue, return back to His college a million miles away, and never think about me ever again.

By the time He made it back to school and I forced myself out of my Sad Shower, we immediately decided it would be best to make our hazardous situation all the more chaotic by officially becoming exclusive. I knew there was nothing but turmoil ahead on this road, but I still couldn't help a gigantic grin from forming once I realized I secured my very first boyfriend. And He was perfect. While I didn't really have to worry about taking myself off the miniscule market here in the middle of nowhere, I was terrified to embark on this journey with so much distance between us and His family not knowing anything about Him or knowing of my existence whatsoever. But it didn't matter. Nothing mattered when it came to Him. I knew what I was about to get into was nothing but trouble, but I was willing to do it if it meant occasionally experiencing those fireworks whenever He would pull me into His chest. Plus, I was already practically dating Him from the moment He first stepped into the living room so it's not like it was that much of a transition or adjustment.

Another semester began as I tried my best to ignore the stabbing pain that came with knowing He was going back to school and we didn't have any set plans to see each other again anytime soon. I carefully wove "text Him and FaceTime Him" in between every new class I was starting. Except the Serial Killers course. I paid full attention during that one. My thoughts were quickly crowded with daydreaming about the next time I'd get to see Him or hug Him or why He hadn't texted me back yet or wondering if He still liked me as much as I liked Him. When it wasn't focused on my newfound relationship, my mind was absorbing all the new material in my classes and realizing how great of an idea it had been to change my major. It was almost surreal to be getting along so well with my professors and actually enjoying school for the first time in so long. Part of me kept waiting for all of this to be some kind of dream and to wake up in my freshman year dorm, still stuck in Psychology and the closet. When I wasn't second-guessing my boyfriend's decision to be my boyfriend or focusing on class and all my extracurriculars, I was busy convincing my manager to let me start training as a bartender for the restaurant. When I wasn't doing that, I was playing with the dog, maintaining my social status via house parties, and/or crying.

It only took a few weeks of constant texts and video calls before He managed to visit again. As always, the fireworks I had been craving exploded into view the moment He walked back into the apartment. We went to dinner after I made sure to ask Him 53 times if He still liked me, sitting with my favorite coworker at the restaurant so I could show Him off to everyone there. From there, we watched a movie back at the apartment, my head resting on His chest the whole time as I tried to think of a way to freeze time in this exact moment before the inevitable sadness had a chance to hit me when He left in a couple days. To distract myself, I decided it was time to show Him off to all of my college friends. I whipped up a few pregame drinks before we made our way across the street to an apartment complex to make our official debut as a couple to the press and paparazzi.

Within moments of walking in, I started to get nervous for how everyone was going to perceive us and whether or not I should even tell anyone since He wasn't out to anyone. However, within seconds He was hitting it off with everyone inside and introducing Himself as my boyfriend to anyone He spoke to. I whispered in His ear a few minutes later wondering if He was worried at all but before I could even finish the sentence He kissed me and said to stop worrying. Looking at the puzzled expression on my face, He elaborated and said He wasn't worried about anyone here finding out and He was proud to claim me as His, especially to all my friends. Cue the emotional fireworks show in the most extravagant way yet. We lasted about an hour or two at the party before I decided it was time to sneak off back to the apartment for alone time, scrapbooking, meditating, and bible studies of course.

Just as expected, the sharp pain hit my stomach the moment my eyes opened the next morning as I realized I was going to have to say goodbye once again. However, the pain was even deeper than normal because we had absolutely no idea when He'd be able to visit after this. Visiting Him was out of the question considering I was perpetually too broke to travel and His school was 250 times stricter than mine *and* no one knew about His identity there. Watching Him sleep for a few moments before His eyes slowly started to open with a smile immediately forming on His face when He saw me somehow settled all of my uneasiness. This was going to be fine. Everything was going to be fine. Even if I only got to experience this overwhelming euphoria in small intervals, it was worth it. I'd rather deal with the paralyzing sadness that came with Him leaving me for unknown periods of time than deal with the unthinkable feelings that would inevitably come from discarding the relationship because of the various challenges. Still, I'd drop anything and everything to be able to pause time and soak in these fireworks as long as I could.

As if to mock the recent acceptance I felt, the universe decided to shake things up in the passing weeks of volunteering, taking food orders and training behind the bar, classroom lecture after lecture, dog walking, and lonely drinking. Slowly but surely, I started to feel the distance grow from literal distance between us to emotional distance as well. He started removing Himself further and further from our text conversations. FaceTime dates started to become less and less frequent. Even when He was replying consistently to my messages and calls, I could just tell He wasn't as "in it" as He had been before this sudden shift. Naturally, I blamed myself for this sudden, apparent disinterest by deciding I had been too annoying at various points or that He had found someone better looking and more interesting at His school to focus on instead. While I didn't speak up about these concerns at first, the bricks of anxiety and nausea began multiplying in my stomach until I felt like I was seconds away from vomiting and/or collapsing at any given point on any given day.

Reading the breakup text that came through when He knew I was about to walk into work immediately paralyzed me for several minutes. It felt like the rug had been pulled out from under me and the entire universe I had created for Us in my head was demolished into rubble all around me. I couldn't tell if I wanted to cry, vomit, pass out, or some dramatic combination of all the above as I tried to calm my thoughts as best as I could. While we had just talked about potential plans to see each other for Valentine's Day, it wasn't enough. I wasn't enough. I no longer had a boyfriend. I read over the text messages one final time before I had applied enough emotional pressure to stop the bleeding enough to walk into work without replying to a single one of the messages. Once I was inside, it would be easier to put this sudden turn of events to the back of my mind long enough for it to heal enough.

Walking up to my first table, I pushed away every thought of him. I dropped off the first round of drinks and ignored thoughts of him. The plates of food took an eternity to prepare as I stood around thinking of everything in the world except him. The tables of guests and plates of food became the only lifeboat to keep myself afloat in the ocean of sadness I was trying to escape. I went back to the computer system to print out the first check of the night when I felt my manager's finger tap me on the shoulder. With an eager smile, she casually asked me how everything was going. She saw straight through my hollow response and quickly followed up to ask what was wrong and if everything was okay with my boyfriend. The lifeboat suddenly vanished into thin air as my head was plunged underneath the icy waters. Without a word, I sprinted to the bathroom and barely made it to the stall before collapsing into sobs I tried to stifle as much as possible.

I'm not sure how much time I spent letting out all the sadness I spent the last hour trying to compress but enough time had passed for my best friend to drive to the restaurant. He was catching up with my manager by the host stand since they hadn't seen each other much since he switched to his new job. She must have texted him the moment she watched me break down and I didn't even need to ask to know my tables were covered and taken care of, along with the remainder of this shift. Half a second later, I was sprawled out on the living room couch cuddling with Reina, wine glass filled to the brim in hand, trying to verbalize everything I was feeling inside. How had I fallen in love with someone so quickly? Why had I convinced myself it was going to somehow work? When did I expect to actually see him for Valentine's Day or any occasion for that matter? How much of it was my fault? Did he really end both of our first relationships through a fucking text?

Without much of a choice, I continued along the roller coaster tracks of this semester as I tried my best to look past the grey film that draped itself over everything. My close network of friends surrounded me with love and support but a part of me couldn't help but feel embarrassed that I was so far behind all of them. They'd all had their first loves and these heartbreaks back in middle school and/or high school and here I was as a Junior in college finally getting the joyful opportunity to feel mine. Thankfully, I had plenty of things on my plate to keep my mind distracted while it started to slowly mend itself from my first relationship, as short-lived as it may have been. This was the one time where the long distance actually came in handy since I didn't have to worry about seeing him anywhere or ever speaking to him throughout the aftermath. Instead, I could focus on the important things in life right now: Parties, Spring Break planning, classes, volunteering, bartending/serving, and silently staring at the wall for hours at a time.

When my phone randomly stopped working one afternoon, I quickly made my way down to the store in town. Once there, I was informed that my account had an unpaid balance of like $3,000 that would need to be paid in order to have my service reinstated. While I didn't know that much about cell phone plans, I knew this number was an outrageous amount of money to charge an account that only had my mother's phone and mine on it. Standing in shock in the middle of the store, the employee began to explain that my mother had added Rob and his wife to our plan without letting me know, stopped paying the balance over a number of months, racked up the unpaid balance, then removed herself from the plan. However, before removing herself from the plan, she made sure to pass the ownership of the account to my name and Social Security number without paying a cent towards the remaining debt. I managed to get a hold of Rob using the store's Wi-Fi only to find out that he and his wife had been sending money to Lilley for the bill each month the entire time.

Without a single one of us being in any kind of position to fork over three or four thousand dollars or anything even remotely close to that, it seemed as if I was about to be without a phone for quite some time. With the amount of interest that would likely accrue while I picked up every single available shift in an attempt to save up the necessary funds, there's no telling when I'd even be close to having a phone again. However, at some point in my emotional spiral of hopelessness and despair, my angelic Great

Aunt showed up and saved the day. Without even running it by me (she knew I wouldn't let her), she paid the balance and put the account in her name. From there, she locked Rob's family's phones until they paid her back and put my phone number onto her own personal plan for me to pay for each month. Not wanting to continue being a burden on my Aunt/Uncle, I swiftly moved my phone number onto my best friend's phone plan so I could just pay him each month instead of my actual family that had already done so much to help me out. Totally normal situations all around for me. Very normal stuff.

With the chaos of my sudden phone plan disaster still fresh on my mind along with my breakup, my best friend and I decided to take a trip to Louisville to see his best friend from high school. While we were there, we spent a magical night in an arena seeing Carrie perform on her new album's tour which further solidified my friendship with him. He somehow always knew exactly what to do/say whenever I was faced with yet another disaster. Not only did this long weekend confirm that he was one of the most genuine friends I've ever had, but it also confirmed my love for music and live performances. While I was still floating on a cloud outside the arena, I couldn't help but feel slightly angry at my parents for never trying to get me to experience anything even remotely close to concerts, plays, or any other various form of artistic entertainment other than romantic comedies at the local movie theater and dinners at Applebee's. As we got to the car, he suggested we make a trip out to one of the gay bars there, but I quickly shut the idea down. Something about making my way to my first gay bar with drag queens and whatnot didn't feel right yet. I had clung to the "I'm not like the other gays" banner that all the guys on campus had adorned me with too much to risk doing anything to potentially lose it. I could tell he was disappointed in my apprehension (as was I) but he didn't pursue it any further as we made our way to the main strip of the city.

Upon our return home, my best friend decided to drop the news on me that he was going to start looking into other possible employment opportunities. Apparently, while the food bank position was emotionally rewarding, the salary was next to nothing. The federal government decided that the role needed to be paid at the poverty line of whatever state you were in so that you were able to "more accurately connect with your clients" which basically meant they wanted you to do this great work but they didn't want to actually pay you for it. Therefore, it was practically impossible for him to make a living for himself or build his savings whatsoever even though he had a college degree now. Wanting the best for him, I obviously encouraged him to seek out whatever role he thought best even if it put me in a sticky situation since I lived in the apartment that he was given in exchange for taking on this position. A couple weeks later, I was hopping in the car with him to go interview with a company all the way in

Charlotte, North Carolina. He seemed pretty stoked about how well the interview went but we wouldn't know anything for a while. To put the stress of the vast unknown behind us in familiar fashion, we went bar hopping around the city neither of us had ever visited before.

Before I could even get my feet back on the solid ground of a consistent life schedule, I was packing my bags and getting ready to head out on yet another Spring Break trip to Panama City. My first Spring Break where I actually felt financially stable enough to attend. My first Spring Break where I was able to legally drink. My first Spring Break where I wasn't trapped inside a heterosexual mind prison. However, only about 30 minutes passed after we first glanced at the waves and sandy beaches before I could tell something was off. Once we unloaded the car and figured out the sleeping arrangements in the room, I noticed there were two or three guys from campus that were awkwardly hanging around the room from the moment we got there. Upon pulling some of my friends aside to ask why they were here, I was informed they were going to be staying in our room for the week as well. Pulling out the vodka for the first round of shots, I tried to put my annoyance to the back of my mind and not think about the fact that I'd probably have to share a bed or share the couch with one of them now that they were apparently part of the group. Of course, I made a mental note to bring up some form of reimbursement plan since we had all paid such a huge deposit for the room while they hadn't paid a penny.

The next few days passed by in a frenzied blur of clubs, stumbling around the beach, gawking at all the men and women who looked like they just stepped off the set of a Sports Illustrated shoot, skipping way too many meals, and taking way too many shots. After finally opening up The Apps for the first time since the break-up, I managed to match with someone new who became a boyfriend for the week. Something about the spontaneity mixed with salt in the air made me realize that I had finally seemed to get over the first big heartbreak. I was heading to dinner/drinks with my beach boyfriend and fully leaning into the make out sessions at clubs and cuddle sessions at either of the hotel rooms all week. However, the small annoyance that formed in my brain at the beginning of the week had constantly been growing larger and larger with each passing day. The handful of guys were clearly getting a free place to stay for the week simply because they were decent looking and liked to party while we had to actually save up for the room *and* constantly worry about whether or not the hotel staff was going to catch us and kick us out of the room or charge us a huge fee.

Saying goodbye to my Spring Break fling towards the end of the week only opened the door for that frustration to grow all the more massive now that there was one less distraction. Thankfully, today's plan was to go to the beach and immediately to the bars right afterwards so I wouldn't be sober long enough to let my anger get the best of me. However, once we made our way back into the room from the crowded beach, one of my friends and I noticed everyone starting to shower and put on nice outfits. Outfits that definitely weren't the vibe for bar hopping. Confused, we both asked the group why everyone was getting so dolled up only to be told that they were planning on going on a nice dinner together instead of a night of drunken debauchery. While it wasn't being spoken aloud, we could tell that this was more of a romantic dinner with some of the guys who were staying in our room for free and who were now directly responsible for changing all of the plans last-minute. The frustration inside me grew from an annoying spark to an intense wildfire within two-to-three seconds.

The absurd amount of alcohol in my system completely took over my body as I hovered above my body watching myself screaming at the entire room. Scream after scream about how ridiculous it was to have your close friends pay a huge deposit but let random campus friends and potential one-night-stands stay in the same room for free without even contributing to food or alcohol the entire week. From there, I launched missiles all around the room from my mouth as I relayed how annoying and frustrating it was to completely change plans last-minute without any form of communication. However, the words might as well have fallen on deaf ears as my group of friends looked back at me with a facial expression of either confusion or complete apathy. They didn't care. For most of them, it hadn't even been their own money they put forth towards the room fees. All they cared about was what/who they were wanting to do. Somehow, the fire inside me grew even further, shooting out of my nostrils and ears. Then they all simply left for dinner without the two of us.

Watching the anger rage inside my body from above, I felt powerless to the alcohol coursing through my mind and body. I watched as I turned around, scrambling for the right words to scream that would properly describe the fiery rage that was billowing inside. I saw my fist rise up and slam into the pantry door next to the refrigerator before I fell back down into my body to regain control. But it was too late. My drunken fist had already gone straight through the door, leaving a sizable hole that was definitely not going to go unnoticed by the owners of the condo. Shit. I'm a Chad. The painful reality that I was definitely going to have to pay a repair fee for a hole that was punched in anger at a situation involving room fees was almost unbearable to think about. My other friend who they had also left behind took me in her arms, whispering that everything would be okay as I started to sob into her shoulder.

Waking up the next morning, one of the girls said that she was cutting her trip short and heading back to campus early. I promptly reserved a spot in her car and decided not to try and bear the awkward tension that had quickly polluted the entire room for the remainder of the trip. The palm trees, beautiful waves, and salt air quickly dissipated from the rearview mirror as we made our way back to the comfort and sanctuary of our dorm rooms. Part of me was still angry at what a disaster this Spring Break had transformed into but another, smaller part of my mind was somehow happy that this shroud of doubt had been draped over so many of my friends. Maybe I had been putting way too much of my energy and self into friendships that didn't actually matter as much as I had thought. If my network of close friends were willing to chase after random guys at the expense of my perpetually-empty wallet and birthday plans and rides home and everything else, what else would they be willing to do?

The quiet, stable comfort of settling back into the controlled chaos of the semester only lasted for a few more weeks before I walked into the apartment and immediately sensed something wrong. My best friend was sitting on the couch, Reina cuddled up next to him, with a tense expression painted across his face. He didn't even need to say a word for me to know what was about to come next. He got the position in Charlotte. A swarm of pride and excitement for him dissolved into fear and anxiety for myself as he spoke the words out loud that I had already seen coming. I immediately congratulated him and went in for a hug which gave my face the opportunity to express how terrified I was at how this was going to impact me. No more seeing him every single day. No more Reina. No more secret apartment. No more instant volunteer hours anytime I needed/wanted some. The hug seemed to last forever which allowed me to swallow as much of my fears as possible. As much as I wanted to be selfish, I knew he couldn't turn down a huge opportunity like this just so he could wait around and help me get *my* shit together.

We started packing up some of his things right away, each piece of tape on a box sealing another fear in my mind as we crept closer and closer to his final day on campus. With his early departure, he would not be completing the annual term of the Food Bank role which meant the Service and Leadership House started seeking a replacement right away. He casually suggested that I look into applying for it but I tossed the idea aside almost right away. I had seen how stressful it could be and the thought of trying to add that onto my plate for my final two semesters of college was enough to make me almost hurl. How could I possibly throw a full-time federal job on top of the restaurant, Senior classes, Senior Seminar, Student Activities, campus tours, a required internship, a social life, and a mediocre fitness routine? I was good at juggling, but that would just be overkill.

A couple of weeks before his last day on campus, I got a text from his boss asking if I would be willing to come in and at least discuss the opportunity with the both of them. After making her promise the discussion wouldn't require any commitment by the end of it, I hesitantly walked into her office. She knew she didn't have to explain the job description itself, but instead went into explaining that she knew I had what it took to keep the program on its feet. However, she also knew it would mean taking the role of a staff member on campus despite being a student at the same time. Therefore, while I would be granted a lot of responsibility, she knew at the end of the day my classes and various Senior responsibilities would have to come first. I'd be expected to be in my office during normal business hours anytime I wasn't having lunch or sitting in a classroom while orchestrating the monthly Mobile Food Bank event. Something about the way she was explaining everything to me, coupled with her confidence in me, made it seem ten times more possible than I had imagined it being an hour before.

Putting the lengths of my hair up into a tight knot at the back of my head, I absorbed the rest of her words as I approached the fork in the road inside my mind. The path on the left would take me on a familiar, safe routine that I knew I could accomplish blindfolded. The alternative road to the right would take me on a challenge that I'd never faced before. While the left was definitely guaranteed to be more enjoyable and leisurely, the path on the right would enhance my professional resume more than anything else possibly could before my graduation date. I would have two full years of extracurriculars on top of a year of full-time federal employment under my belt by the time I had my degree in hand before embarking into the real world. The freshman-year version of myself was screaming from whatever cage he was trapped in at the back of my mind, urging me to pick the party path. However, I knew before I even stood up to head back to the room that I was going to officially apply for the position by the end of the night. Worst case scenario, I could always just quit if it got to be too overwhelming, right?

Staring at the empty apartment, the reality that life was about to get dramatically different started to really set in. It had taken us the whole weekend to pack up all of my things into Poppop Luke's car (that I was still somehow getting to use) and the moving truck that was about to send my best friend on the way to his new life. We took another quick scan of the place to make sure we hadn't missed any belongings before walking out the doorway for a final time, our keys and all the memories left lying on the windowsill inside. I wish I knew the right words to say during these cinematic goodbye moments, but instead all I could manage to do was hug him and Reina both for what felt like hours outside on the sidewalk. It took everything in me not to have a horrific breakdown on the sidewalk as I watched my former enemy turned best friend turned brother turned roommate turned former roommate hop up into the moving truck and make his final exit from campus. All I could do was keep telling myself that this was going to be a great thing for both of us and try my best not to think about how much this was going to actually impact our friendship.

I unpacked the car into another friend's place down the road as I tried my absolute best to accept and appreciate my new reality without my mentor/bestie being close by anymore. My final exams and projects passed by in a blur now without much stress as I started emotionally preparing to begin my new role now that my application had officially been processed and approved. Almost as if to confirm that I had picked the right path, I even snagged a handful of awards during the annual Awards Day ceremony on campus. It was a surreal experience to hear my name called out over the speaker for a change and even more bizarre to actually see my name emblazoned on a fancy plaque for what had to be the first time in my entire life. Most Outstanding Male Junior. Volunteer Service Award. Who's Who Among Colleges recognition. Who was this new person I had apparently become? However, these recognitions didn't stop me from celebrating them in a way that the former version(s) of myself would appreciate as I hopped around house party to house party all weekend to signify the end of yet another semester.

The best part was not feeling the slightest desire nor need to let Lilley know about these accomplishments and feeling all the necessary pride all by myself instead.

Chapter Fifteen

Remember When Everything Went Straight to Hell (Again)?

As it turns out, it wasn't the worst thing to have moved in with another close friend for the summer until I was allowed to move back to campus. However, after the fourth consecutive house party for anyone else who was sticking around for the summer, I needed a break. Of course, this "break" merely involved going to a different house party back in Loudon just for a change of scenery. This totally-necessary escapism took the form of a bonfire with some high school friends that I still kept up with that I couldn't resist making an appearance at simply to honor the version of myself that used to throw the same genre of party back in the day. While a fifth night of drinking might have been questionable, I wasn't sure how much free time I would have once I got back from the federal training trip and settled into my new role within the Service and Leadership House. The bonfire passed by in a blur of lethal drinks in plastic cups, selfies, old stories about high school, and random nonsense until there were only a handful of people left.

Two of my high school best bros were part of the handful that stuck around, mainly because we were all way too intoxicated to leave anywhere and ride services were definitely not a thing in Loudon. Somehow, we all got to chatting about my new identity and how happy they were for me to have announced it. From there, they went on to drunkenly express their support until this somehow turned into a contest between the two of them. Turning back and forth from one of them to the other, I watched and listened as they battled each other on who supported my homosexuality more. I stared in silence as the battle somehow concluded with a kissing contest to prove just how unbothered they were that I was now a gay. I had no idea how kissing me was going to prove their allyship, but at the same time I wasn't complaining about it. I kissed one, then the other, repeated the process a couple of times, declared an official winner, and went inside with the rest of the party as we all laughed hysterically at the absurdity of the whole experience.

A terrifying crashing sound interrupted our movie night as we rushed upstairs to see what happened. Laughing at the bottom of the stairs, one of the friends I had somehow just made out with was covered in blood and shattered pieces of glass. He had attempted to step over the dog gate at the bottom of the stairs, completely tripped, and collided with a glass shelf. A quick trip to the emergency room would bring about a number of stitches and a story to tell our grandkids one day before we were back at the house. From there, we took another round of shots to celebrate the craziness of our first reunion since graduation before passing out in the basement in a failed attempt to finish the movie we had started.

The summer continued to fly by in a series of these random parties as my training trip crept closer and closer. I managed to grab tickets to the university in Knoxville's version of a music festival. After pregaming a dangerous amount with my friends at their place, we made our way to the festival in time to get a good spot to see Niykee's set. In a random stroke of luck, she managed to make eye contact with me in the crowd. Since she still followed me online for whatever reason despite how annoying I was, she messaged me and had her manager get me and a friend backstage to hangout after she was finished. We stood around, took way too many pictures, caught each other up on life, and then gave a final goodbye hug and swore to keep up with each other until the next tour came around. From there, I spent the remainder of the weekend name-dropping her and showing our pictures to anyone who would give me the time of day until it was time to head back to my place down the road from campus.

I managed to talk the Dean into letting me move into the dorms before my staff job officially started in exchange for checking in/monitoring a random group of kids that were attending a basketball camp on campus. While I loved living with one of my close party friends, I had grown tired of sleeping on an air mattress and never knowing if the house was going to be full of 25-50 people every time I walked in from another shift at the restaurant. Once I had unloaded all my things into one of the random empty rooms and checked in all the kids, I took a deep breath and did my best to plan out the upcoming training trip. They had already emailed me my flight information but I couldn't remember the last time I stepped foot in an airport or how to even navigate the experience. Thankfully, one of my friends offered to let me stay at his apartment the night before. From there, his girlfriend was able to explain how to find my gate and board the flight since she was a normal, functional member of society unlike myself.

I had no idea what gave the federal government the idea to have a training trip for their domestic version of the Peace Corps in Miami but I wasn't about to question it and risk being reassigned or fired. I did my best to keep my anxiety under control as the plane took off and landed before making friends with some strangers who appeared just as confused as I was trying to find out where to go next. We managed to locate the shuttle that would take us to the hotel and conference center where we barely had enough time to check in, find our room, throw everything down, and head to orientation. Feeling like a tiny needle in a gigantic haystack of poverty-fighters, I found my seat and listened to the speaker talk through the various training sessions we would take part in this weekend. While I was going to be the supervisor of the Mobile Food Bank program, the person in front of me might be teaching art to underprivileged people within their community while the person to my left might be a researcher analyzing the specific complexities of homelessness for a city board. My mind drifted off in order to avoid feeling completely overwhelmed as I remembered my new boss's words of affirmation that I could overcome this new phase of my development. Everything was fine. Plus, the hotel had a bar.

My first friend at this training conference came in the form of a woman who seemed my age in our first break-out session group. Once we sat down at the same small table, she carefully asked if I knew where the closest liquor store was which practically sealed the deal for our friendship. We spent the entire weekend by each other's side through the various training sessions that were incredibly detailed and informative albeit a tad unnecessary. While we didn't have very many large gaps in our itineraries, we managed to sneak away for the occasional fresh seafood and sandy beach explorations together with a few other like-minded friends. We heavily considered sneaking away the final night to explore the nightlife in the area until we realized a ride from the conference to the closest clubs and back to the hotel would cost each of us around $150 alone *and* we all had early flights home. Therefore, we naturally decided to drink an intense amount of alcohol by the hotel pool until it was time to oversleep our alarms the next morning. Scrambling around my room, I threw on a random outfit and shoved the rest of my stuff into my suitcase before sprinting downstairs to the official graduation program.

After barely making it in time to receive my pin and papers that officially declared me a federal employee, I hopped on the shuttle back to the airport. A nauseating number of layovers and flight delays later, I was sprinting through the Knoxville airport trying to find my friends again. Once I finally located them, I threw my bags into the trunk of their car and hopped in the backseat to officially begin our road trip to a music festival in Tampa, Florida. I wasn't sure how I managed to convince my boss to delay the start day of my new job simply so I could make it to a festival I had bought last-minute tickets to, but why not?! I took full advantage of being a passenger and slept for the majority of the drive to my friend's grandmother's house where we were planning to stay and relax until it was time to make the rest of the drive to our motel in Tampa.

Much to no one's surprise, I was lucky if I could name one single artist on the festival's lineup let alone one of their songs. However, I didn't let that stop me from having the time of my life as we made our way into the festival grounds each afternoon. From trying not to stare at the countless chiseled torsos walking around to paying an unholy amount of money on drinks to keep the vibes flowing, I felt on top of the world. My best friend and his girlfriend decided to try acid to enhance their festival experience, but I was just as content as could be with my overpriced vodka soda and eye candy all around me. Dancing around like maniacs, I even managed to forget about the new tidal wave of responsibility that was getting ready to crash into my daily life. Well, I managed to forget about it until it was time to pack up our bags, leave the motel, and make my hesitant return to the dorms on campus the night before I was to make my grand entrance into my new world.

Sleep was nearly impossible as I tried to do whatever I could to emotionally prepare for the busiest summer of my life. In order to stay in the dorms despite the fact that students weren't technically allowed to, I agreed to supervise any children's camp for the rest of the summer. I had my brand new role of Mobile Food Bank Supervisor to try to understand and navigate. I was still working as a server and bartender at the restaurant since the federal government didn't deem this job to be worth more than whatever Tennessee's official "poverty line" was. The thought of balancing it all was enough to increase my heartrate to a concerning level as I stared up at my bedroom ceiling in the dark. I forced myself to take a couple shots of vodka and a couple of melatonin tablets before I could start imagining juggling all of this *and* a full course load once the actual Senior semester started in August. They barely helped me fall asleep without waking up in a panic every 30-45 minutes.

Standing outside the brick pathway in front of the house I was going to be spending the next 12 months inside felt insanely surreal. In a span of what felt like 24 hours, I had gone from helping my best friend as a consistent volunteer to the overtaker of the position without any kind of training or adjustment period. Sure, I had attended the conference in Miami but that wasn't actually tailored to the role itself but the concept of American poverty overall. I had no idea what was going to happen after I took my first steps through the doorway for the first time. Was my name going to be hanging above the office doorway? Did I have a staff email already? How do I use a staff email account? Does everyone on campus know that I'm staff *and* student now? Do I sign clients up for the next food bank event today? How do I do that? Wait. When is the next event? How do I plan it? How do I recruit volunteers, especially during the summer? I took a few deep breaths, tried to silence all the paralyzing questions ricocheting through my brain, and followed the pathway into the house.

My boss glided down the staircase when she heard the door open, immediately greeting me with a hug and asking how Miami and Tampa were. From there, she jokingly gave me a tour of the house that I could probably navigate blindfolded. She pointed out my name plate delicately hovering over the office I'd be sharing with the employee who covered the on-campus food bank system. Something about seeing my actual name over the office sliced through the idea that this all might still be just some dream I was stuck in. I had actually changed. I went from trainwreck freshman to a staff employee/Senior student. She let me take in the experience because she knew me well enough to know I needed a few seconds to absorb...everything. From there, she introduced me to the new Career Services employee next to my office before ending the tour at the two Associate Dean offices. It was hard to keep track of how many hats my boss wore, but her main title was Associate Dean of Students for now. The other **ADS** in the office next to hers just so happened to the same person who had knocked on my door at 2 am freshman year to make sure I wasn't going to kill myself. Believe it or not, we actually became pretty decent friends between then and now. Good times.

Sitting down across from her desk, I began to feel even more overwhelmed as she gave me the full rundown of the expectations for the next 12 months. Pick a Saturday each month to host the event. Pick a location to host said event. Recruit 20-30 volunteers to make sure the event ran smoothly. Confirm the food truck can deliver the food on that Saturday from the massive food bank in Chattanooga that we partnered with. Sign up 100 or so families within the community to show up and receive their 75 pounds of free food from the event. Keep track of every family who actually shows up and every volunteer who shows up for recordkeeping and analysis. Work on improving current processes. Work on developing marketing so we can have more of an impact on the county we are serving. Don't post myself partying all over social media with other students now that I was going to be shown on the school's online directory as a staff member. The most difficult challenge of them all.

I spent the first couple of weeks staring at my computer screen entirely unsure of how to actually *start* doing my job and being too intimidated to ask. Then one day I found the ability to suddenly take all the million-and-a-half stresses surrounding this new phase of life and file them away into various little folders and cabinets in my mind. With all the mental organization taking place, I started to realize that I could condense all these worries into smaller, more approachable questions and challenges in a way that I had never been able to do before. If I didn't need to immediately answer/stress about something, I filed it away to deal with at a later date. From there, I started bringing the various questions to my boss in an organized fashion until I had actually started to develop a decent daily routine to start getting closer and closer to all the tasks and goals I had been assigned. Maybe I really did have what it takes to balance all of this.

Do these Saturdays work for us? Do they work for Chattanooga's food bank? What are their emails and phone numbers to confirm? Perfect. Can I change the design of our t-shirt that we hand out to volunteers? I want to make it look more like a trendy, fashionable shirt so that people actually want to wear it more often. If it's a more fashionable shirt instead of one that emits a "I got this for free doing something random in college" vibe, more people will see it and potentially ask them where they got it which would bring even more awareness to our program. Awesome. How do I get in touch with our marketing/graphic design team on campus to try and put something together. Great. What business do we use in town to print out and purchase these shirts from? How many do we usually keep in stock in the house? Suddenly, the insurmountable task of running a full-blown food bank program seemed more and more possible as I began to settle into the role and cross things off the list.

The random serving/bartending shifts at night helped my wallet and also my mind during this overwhelming adjustment period. The last thing I knew I needed to be doing was leaving the office to sit alone in the empty dorm building with my own thoughts (when there wasn't a random camp of children running all over the place). Whenever I wasn't able to snag a shift, I started hanging out with whoever happened to still be in town for the summer or whoever I could convince to come down to campus to visit me. Dating apps were still a regular part of my routine, but it was pretty difficult to match with anyone living in the middle of nowhere with the closest city being an hour away. It was even more difficult to locate anyone I was into using the location-focused hookup app that had seemingly intertwined itself into my identity. I was still struggling to realize whether or not one-night stands were healthy for my mentality but I had resolved that it was just part of being gay and there wasn't anything I could do about it, especially considering where I lived. Being an isolated gay in a small town pretty much meant you had to find intimacy, validation, and attention however you could.

Once June had made its grand entrance, I finally decided I was ready to attend my first Pride festival once I heard about the one happening up in Knoxville. However, I only got to make it for the last 15 minutes of the actual festival since one of my friends took so many hours to get ready. Sure, this made me angry and added even more doubt to my idea of friendships but I did my best to ignore all of that. Instead, I drowned the stress in more alcohol until I was comfortable with the idea of hopping into my first gay bar. I wasn't sure what to expect whenever we all walked in, but I wasn't really coherent enough to even form an opinion of the experience with the amount of alcohol I was drinking to avoid my own anger and doubt. Nonetheless, I was proud of myself for finally feeling comfortable enough in my own new-ish skin to theoretically attend a Pride festival and enter a gay bar for the first time. New level of gay unlocked!

Staring at the first orders of my new volunteer t-shirts shot a feeling of immense pride throughout my entire body. Within my first month, I had already secured my legacy with the best logo our program had seen yet. The first couple of Saturdays had been booked and confirmed with Chattanooga. I had already talked a vast number of my friends, from both the student body and faculty/staff, into signing up to volunteer. Following in my best friend's footsteps, I booked the downtown pavilion down the road from campus to host my very first event. However, I started to start brainstorming a way I could improve our normal process and came up with the idea of branching outside of Athens. We served the entire county which had a total of six cities/towns within its borders so why not start networking and hosting the mobile food bank events at a different town each month? From there, we could expand our clientele and reach many more families that could really use a grocery cart full of free food each month.

Fully leaning into this new tidal wave of responsibility, I took up my friend's offer to browse through the parking lot of the car dealership he had started working at. Something about the feeling of having my own car again instead of the perpetual state of borrowing my grandfather's felt right. Before I knew it, I was staring at a stack of paperwork in front of me to potentially own a brand new white hatchback. Part of me knew it was a reckless, spontaneous decision but the rest of me didn't care. Between the food bank job and bartending shifts, I knew I could afford the monthly payments at least for the next 12 months. From there, I'd have a shiny new college degree that would secure me a fancy high-paying career just like we'd all been promised throughout our entire lives. What could possibly go wrong? Without giving myself any time to talk myself out of the decision, I signed my name and took the keys to my new car. Pearl was the name I gave her before I even climbed into the driver's seat to leave the dealership in honor of Nana and the fact that it also happened to be the name of the paint color.

My friend who sold me the car returned Poppop Luke's SUV to the parking lot on campus shortly after as I poured us both a drink to celebrate his first sale and my first brand new car. This was also another way to keep my mind off of having a car payment and car insurance bill added onto my list of responsibilities. The night wrapped itself up and suddenly the piercing noise of my phone's alarm was letting me know it was time to check all the kids out of the dorm and make my way to my office despite the fact that I was painfully hungover. I was coming in from the checkout to throw on some sort of professional-ish outfit to head into my office when I glanced down to see Lilley's name pop up on my phone. My stomach instinctively turned in on itself seeing her call after not speaking whatsoever for the last several months. As always, I decided to ignore it and tried to focus on picking out an outfit since I was already running behind. She immediately called back three times and I couldn't help but imagine my sister being in some form of immediate danger or something similar. I hesitated a few moments before finally answering.

I put the phone down onto the kitchen counter and tried to process the hysteric, theatrical dialogue she had spewed into my ear. Poppop Luke, who I was just contemplating visiting to officially return his vehicle, was in the hospital. It wasn't looking good. He's apparently on a ventilator and mostly unconscious. My knees almost buckled underneath me as I flashed back to the eerily similar phone call I received about Nana freshman year. However, there was something different about the tone of her voice in this call compared to that one. Sure, the dialogue delivery was roughly the same, but there was a disturbing calmness to the way she told me my grandfather was potentially on his deathbed. It sounded almost calculated, as if she had rehearsed the phone call in her head before dialing. Regardless, this was clearly not a situation to contemplate and tiptoe around. I called my boss, quickly packed a duffel bag, and hopped into my car to make my way to the hospital in Nashville.

After a quick phone call with my brother (who she had also called), I tried to piece together a timeline in my head of the situation based on the details she had shared with us. Even though my brother and I had both spoken to him on the phone within the last two weeks, Lilley had apparently stopped by his house on her way to work (she travelled all over Tennessee for her job) and found him "in bad shape" after apparently drinking too much the night before. From there, she felt an obligation to drop her work and take him to get help. However, that apparently meant driving him all the way from Loudon to a hospital two-and-a-half hours away near Murfreesboro coincidentally close to her own place. Still not considering calling any of us, she admitted him into the hospital where he remained for several days without any way to contact anyone. After that, he was apparently transferred to some form of rehabilitation center where he had his phone officially confiscated before his treatment plan began. After that, he took another turn for the worst which landed him in the intensive care unit where I was now headed after I was finally given a phone call two weeks after she "found" him. Made total sense.

I waited for Rob to pull into the parking lot next to me before hopping out of my car to walk towards the hospital. My nephew ran up to me and leapt into a hug which helped cut through the stress and anxiety of the situation at hand, even if just for a brief moment. We heard the doors of the hospital open to reveal Lilley already meeting us at the front entrance, immediately forcing us both into a hug. Neither of us returned it. Without a moment's pause, she began another clearly-rehearsed speech about how we need to restore our family back to its former glory for the sake of this tragedy, a tragedy that we were *definitely* more skeptical than ever of. We assured her that the only reason we had come was to see our grandfather and we headed towards the elevators up to whatever floor she was leading us to.

The similarities of Nana's situation continued as we rounded the corner to be struck with the sight of our grandfather unconscious in a hospital bed connected to a million machines, the sight immediately turning our stomachs inward. The longer I stared at the various things keeping our grandfather alive, the more rage I felt billowing inside me. How the hell was she okay with letting him get to this state without letting a single family member know? What was the reason? What was the goal here? The only thing I could think of was that she had somehow played a major role in this entire situation and needed him to get to the worst phase of it so that he couldn't tell us what she had done. When the fury felt as if it was about to outwardly explode inside his room, I turned and made my way to the nurse's station a few feet away to ask for any kind of information on my grandfather. There was a sympathetic look on the woman's face, as if to almost say "I know this sucks but..." before telling me that there had been a layer of password protection placed over all of my grandfather's medical information.

It took everything in me not to combust right then and there and start punching the walls and/or the cold linoleum tiles. Not only had she kept all of this away from us, but my mother had gone through the court systems to get a temporary, medical conservatorship filed. She now legally had the authority to keep any and all information away from anyone who didn't know the password she had stored up in her evil head. If she hadn't done anything wrong or suspicious, what was the reason for going through all of these hoops to keep us out of everything? Testing the waters, I walked back to the room and politely asked for the patient password. A sinister smirk slithered across her face as she stood, as if feeling triumphant, with her arms crossed. She declined the request, her words dripping with a competitive tone that made me sick to my stomach. Somehow, the health and fate of my grandfather had been turned into some kind of competition that she wanted to be the frontrunner for.

Over the next couple of days, as my grandfather laid helpless on his bed connected to a factory, each discovery brought tidal wave after tidal wave of rage and nausea. Lilley had taken him from his home all the way to her area of town. She had taken his credit card and debit card and used them both on the very same day she had "rescued" him. He had called his brother, the same Great Uncle and Great Aunt who lived near campus, to say that Lilley had managed to pull some strings and get him checked into the same rehab center he went to when I was in fourth grade. However, after a quick phone call, I was able to convince the employee on the other line to tell me without *actually* telling me that my grandfather had not step foot in that facility since I was in elementary school. Suspicion, anger, confusion, nausea, and an abundance of other emotions swirled inside as I kept awaiting the next update in whatever the hell this situation was turning into.

Seeing Dad's name pop up on my phone screen created another layer of knots in my stomach as I tried to prepare for what could possibly be coming next. He had a spare key to Poppop Luke's home since he made a habit to check in on him sometimes and mow the yard. However, after showing up to see if there were any kind of clues there, he opened the door to a completely empty house. Realizing how much more serious this situation was quickly becoming, I began to see fiery crimson. My mother had literally stolen his credit card, hired a moving company and god knows what else, and emptied his entire house into some unknown location all while he was laying helpless in a hospital bed. Essentially, she had kidnapped him. She manipulated him into thinking he was going to a particular treatment center and then checked him into a random hospital only to move all of his things without his knowledge. With his condition remaining the same, I decided to return to campus before letting the rage get the best of me. I hugged Rob goodbye and made him promise to relay any updates here the moment they occurred.

Only a day after attempting to calm my mind by settling back into my routines, I got a call from one of my grandfather's attorney friends. Apparently, there was another court hearing that had been scheduled on my grandfather's behalf regarding the medical conservatorship in a county not too far away from me. Since she clearly was keeping this info away from the rest of us, the attorney friend and I decided to show up the morning of. The look of shock and rage on Lilley's face as she ascended the stairs of the court house only deepened my loathing and disdain. We sat on opposite sides of the lobby until the doors finally opened. Once inside, we positioned ourselves only a few rows apart as we impatiently awaited my grandfather's case to be called out. A millisecond after his name was spoken by the judge, Lilley was on her feet and rambling uncontrollably for the whole planet to hear. The conservatorship needed to be made permanent. Her father was unable to make any decision on his own now. He's taking a turn for the worst and she's the only one in the world who cared. His other family members weren't by his side when he got sick. No one visited him until this week. Suddenly, her plot became apparent and so painfully obvious that it took everything in me not to throw up right there on the courthouse floor.

Unable to stop herself from speaking, the judge eventually instructed her to take her seat and stop speaking so he could think. At that point, the family friend stood up and, while he wasn't a legal representative of my grandfather, stated that he felt morally obligated to speak. A moral and ethical obligation to make him aware that my grandfather's condition was being kept away from those very family members she was claiming to be absent. Conditions that were still being kept away through password protections and complete isolation. Choosing his words very carefully, he even pointed out that his credit cards and checking account had been used without his consent to completely empty out his entire home while he was hooked up to a ventilator in a lonely hospital room. The judge took a few moments to mull over everything he had just heard before speaking. He expressed his apprehension but acknowledged the lack of legal grounds for suspending the conservatorship given that Lilley was the next of kin. However, he gave a stern warning to Lilley about the gravity of the situation at hand and the way her actions could come back to haunt her.

It was nearly impossible to focus the next couple of days at the office. My boss kept asking for updates and could tell things were getting rough but she knew there wasn't anything she could do to suddenly make my mother's antics less extreme or painful. Another phone call from Rob sent my stomach turning once again, something I didn't even think was possible at this point. I packed another quick duffel bag and made my way to Nashville once again immediately after hearing that my grandfather was being released from the hospital. However, the tears streaming down my face on the drive were far from the happy kind. My grandfather was being released from the isolation of the hospital room directly into the isolation of Lilley's living room. To make matters even worse, hospice was also being called in to visit him several times a day. My grandfather was dying. Not only was he dying, but he was being forced to die in the last place he'd want to, hours away from the comfort of his own home.

I dropped my bag off at my friend's house in Murfreesboro before making my way over to Lilley's place to begin to assess the situation. Like I did at the hospital, I waited for Rob to arrive before braving the walk inside. Seeing my grandfather forced to lay on his couch that had been forcibly placed in Lilley's living room was almost unbearable. I wanted nothing more than to run rampant around the house screaming at her and telling her how evil this entire situation was and how everything was bullshit but I knew I couldn't. That's all she wanted was for me to lose my composure, somehow record it, and present it to the courts to make the conservatorship permanent and/or take away my right as his executor. Oh shit. I'm the executor. If this hospice decision ends up being the case and my grandfather passed away, I'm the one that has to manage his estate. On top of everything. With a conniving Lilley to throw into the mix. Shit.

Just in time to take my mind off of my own rage for a moment, a random woman walked through the front door with my little sister by her side. I quickly assumed she was one of the random people my mother had convinced to be her friend aka babysitter-for-free. However, without the slightest hesitation, the woman stepped in between my brother, myself, and Lilley. Noticing our confusion at her placement, she sternly stated that she was "not going to tolerate any disrespect from us" toward our mother whatsoever. It took everything in me not to completely burst into laughter at the audacity of the stranger's message. Then again, it wasn't likely her fault. There was no telling what Lilley had told her before we arrived to make herself seem as much of a victim as possible. My mind quickly flashed back to freshman year after Nana had died where she befriended this random woman after convincing her that Poppop and my Aunts and cousins were all evil menaces out to get her. The funniest part of that situation was the way the woman actually ended up manipulating her instead and convinced her to give her almost all of the inheritance that Nana had left her instead of using it for, I don't know, her own debts, professional/personal future, or her own children. Good times.

Stepping away for the sake of my own sanity, I wandered throughout the house that Lilley was somehow affording to reside. It wasn't an extravagant mansion by any means, but it seemed too spacious for a single mother with a young child and unknown job to comfortably afford. However, that was pretty much my entire childhood with a small handful of exceptions (like the time we lived in a motel). Always packing up and moving into the next nice house that we probably couldn't afford so that we at least presented the aesthetic of financial stability. Walking through the poorly-decorated kitchen, I stumbled through the laundry room until I discovered a door leading to what I assumed to be a garage. However, upon opening the door, I faced my grandfather's belongings stacked like Tetris blocks from the floor to the ceiling filling 100 percent of the space typically reserved for cars. My jaw hit the floor as my brother walked up behind me to exhibit the same reaction. No swear word in the entire English language was potent enough for the rage were feeling inside. She never had any intention, whether he survived or not, of letting him go back to his home.

All caution for avoiding the eggshells and landmines scattered around her floors was thrown to the wind as we realized more and more that she had plotted this entire scenario. Once she finally took a nap somewhere in the house, we tiptoed back to the garage to investigate the stolen property further. However, we discovered she had already removed the entire doorknob system and replaced it with a single deadbolt lock that we obviously didn't have a key to. A few hours later, or maybe days, one of the hospice nurses approached us with a somber facial expression that said more than words ever could. He wasn't getting better. I saw her mouth moving, but not a single word was reaching my ears. The way that she was attempting to deliver the news that my grandfather was close to dying with positive body language and cheery tones somehow made the entire situation worse. She eventually finished the routine "hey, your cherished family member is dying soon just so you know" dialogue with a smile that was somehow supposed to make everything better. It doesn't. Stop doing that.

A few more hours that felt like an eternity in the abysmal prison of my mother's house would show my grandfather seemingly returning to a normal state of consciousness. Bewildered, I watched him blink his eyes and sit up a few inches on the couch, the first sign of life I'd seen whatsoever in the last couple of weeks. Was the overly-cheerful nurse wrong? Was he going to be okay? Was this the miracle I had been praying for? This was the first thing I'd ever prayed for since Nana's tragic fall. Was religion actually real after all? Was he finally going to be able to give us some answers to all of this chaos? Much to everyone's discomfort, Lilley immediately appeared to start lecturing him about how he was positioned and needing to take this pill or do this or do that. He put up a fight without any words but she shoved some unknown concoction into his mouth and urged him to try and swallow. She placed a cup of juice that might have had other medicines in it and told him he had no choice but to drink up if he wanted to feel any better. Rob and I hesitated a few moments before chiming in to try and drink it and see if he could still swallow normally.

"You two are too smart to be acting this damn stupid," he exclaimed with as much intensity and clarity that he could muster before eventually going back to sleep. For the first time in probably a month, we all cracked up laughing at this sudden return of the stubborn personality we were all too familiar with. I expected to show up the next morning and see him slowly walking around the house and complaining about being stuck there against his will, but that wasn't the case. Instead, I walked in to have the eager smile completely vanish from my face as I noticed he was somehow worse than he was before he had spontaneously awoken. The miraculous recovery that I thought had been graciously awarded to me had been yet another illusion. Doing my best to channel my favorite TV detective, I shifted my focus to finding any clues I could around the house to reveal my mother's wrongdoings. Dad eventually showed up to help watch my sister for a while just in time for Lilley's random friend to show up with her boyfriend (or husband? Cousin? Cousin-Husband?) and their child.

Why would you bring even more people into this house during these current circumstances? In order to avoid causing a scene, I made a swift exit out into the front yard to play with my sister and Dad until I could gather my composure again. Of course, the other child eventually made his way outside the moment he saw my sister having fun. His mother eventually walked out onto the porch to oversee them playing whatever game they had invented but kept an adequate distance away from us. A few moments later, her son kicked the ball into the road which prompted my sister to go retrieve it. I nervously watched my sister get closer and closer to the road and glanced over to see the boy's mother playing with her phone without a care in the world. When my baby sister was practically inches from the asphalt, I let out a scream to tell her to stop. I sprinted over to her, scooped her up into my arms, whispered into her ear to never run into the street no matter what the rules of the game were, and looked back to see Dad already storming towards Lilley's friend on the porch. Before a war could break out, I rushed my sister inside.

Dad was already shouting in her face to start paying more attention to the kids if she was going to continue being the one that watches her for free. Rob appeared behind him for support just as the woman's significant other had. The tension and anger from both sides immediately ignited into a paralyzing fire in front of my eyes. To add gasoline into the flames, Lilley stormed downstairs to throw her voice into the ring of shouts as everyone's volume continually increased with every passing second. Dad and the woman's partner eventually moved closer to each other which only triggered Rob's aggression until it seemed like the front yard was about to become a literal battlefield. My sister then stormed down the stairs, her eyes erupting rivers of tears, screaming for everyone to stop fighting and that she was terrified. Thankfully, her tears were enough to douse the flames in the front yard before they got too out of hand. I followed Dad and Rob to the driveway as everyone retreated to calm themselves down.

And then he died. Just like that. No warning. No cinematic farewell with the family gathered around his side. Instead, we had to find out via the bloodcurdling scream that erupted from Lilley inside the house. She didn't have to say a word for us to know what had happened. However, before we could rush inside to confirm the worst, she was sprinting outside into the yard swinging a stethoscope and a fist towards us. Between each swing of the medical tool as she got closer and closer to us, she belted out (for the entire neighborhood/county/state to hear) that her father had just died and that we had killed him with our fighting. She made it close enough to land a blow to Dad's side before collapsing onto the ground and hysterically wailing between sobs. Noticing some of the neighbors starting to come outside to stare at the scene playing out, I quickly fled into the house away from the uncomfortable display.

Seeing his body on the couch sent my stomach into the most uncomfortable entanglement of knots. Thinking of how the last thing he heard, if he was actually conscious in any way, before passing was a screaming match made me want to die. Wait. Lilley was the only one who was in the living room with him right before he passed. Had she...Never mind. Surely that wasn't a possibility despite the wickedness of her actions up to this point. Tears started to form in my eyes as I felt Dad and Rob's hands on my shoulder. More formed as I realized I was going to have to figure out what the hell an estate executor does sooner rather than later now. Was I allowed to be sad first or did I have to jump right into a suit and get to business? What was Lilley going to do to interfere with anything and everything? Why couldn't he have at least passed away in a more comfortable setting instead of trapped here and forced to hear fighting all around him? What the hell was I supposed to do now?

Nothing felt right. This wasn't how this was supposed to happen. This wasn't supposed to happen at all - not right now at least. He didn't die peacefully. He died surrounded by everyone yelling at each other. He died under the weight of everyone's tension. He didn't die in the comfort of his own home. He was taken from his home, manipulated into thinking he was going to his former rehab facility, cut off from all outside contact, thrown around random hospitals, and tossed into his daughter's own makeshift jail cell with all of his stolen belongings. No sense of peace. No closure. No sense or logic. No resolution. More tears began streaming down my face until Lilley stormed back into the house to continue accusing all of us of killing him. I wiped my face and stood in silence in the kitchen until she finally ended her vocal assault. We all stood in pained silence as we waited for the hospice staff to arrive to confirm what we were already attempting to process.

Seeing my grandfather eventually taken from the couch and transported to the back of some kind of van solidified the fact that this wasn't some nightmare I was once again caught in. Before I could even begin to let myself cry, a frail woman I had never seen before was standing in front of all of us in Lilley's driveway urging us to start praying. Confused, I joined the huddle she was urging us to form as she asked her god to place a healing hand over my family during this difficult time. Part of me wished I could find any kind of significance in her words, but they were words I had heard before. Words that had always found themselves woven into any tragedy that I've faced before. Words that didn't make me straight. Words that didn't make me not want to attack my own ankles. Words that didn't make me normal. Words that didn't bring Nana back. Words that won't bring Poppop Luke back. Words that never filled the holes they were leaving in their place. Just hollow, empty words.

I finished up the meal I had been preparing for most of the day to help take my mind off the sudden loss. To my surprise, I found enough matching dinner plates in Lilley's cabinet to place next to the crockpot now that it was finished. The last thing I wanted to do was force myself into the garage to try and find his stolen dinner plates. Taking a few deep breaths, I announced to the rest of the house that dinner was ready whenever anyone wanted it. Not even trying to hide the smugness on my face, I watched as everyone complimented the pot roast and vegetables I had prepared, a dish that Lilley had tried to master our entire childhood unsuccessfully. Somehow, the culinary skill of my grandparents had seemingly skipped a generation. However, the satisfaction only lasted a few seconds before reality reminded me of today's tragedy and suddenly being a better cook than my mother didn't matter at all. A few bites later, I started sharing a story or two that reminded everyone of some of the good times and memories with my grandfather. Pushing all the earlier chaos aside, we all started going around in circles doing the same until the water glasses next to our plates were replaced with a shot glass of whiskey. For old time's sake, I suppose. To Poppop Luke.

As I went to leave my plate in the sink, my eyes fell on the garage door that was now just a single deadbolt lock. The brief emotional peace quickly vanished as the reminder of everything Lilley had done, both to Rob and I and now our grandfather, came rushing to the front of my mind like a speeding train. Moving every year for no apparent reason. Not getting to know various family members because she didn't like them. Not getting to hang out with my first friends because it "seemed" gay. Getting thrown into therapy when I told her about my ankle. Charging my friends a fee for coming on vacation with us. Going on my social media friend list to ask people to babysit my sister only to never pay them. Applying for a credit card in my name without telling me. Asking my friends to cash a fraudulent check for her. Running up credit card debit in my brother's name. Telling me Nana was rolling in her grave whenever I came out of the closet. Stealing the jewelry she left me because "it was meant for my wife" and not my husband. Practically kidnapping our grandfather and stealing all of his things. Everything. All at once.

I quickly removed myself as quickly as possible instead of simmering in the spontaneous flashbacks. Walking out of her doorway almost felt like a weight had been lifted knowing I wasn't going to be forced to walk back through it again. While I would have killed to have my grandfather back already, at least he was free from her house too. It only took half the drive back to my friend's house before I was getting a call from Lilley. Hesitantly, I answered only for her to immediately ask me what I was planning for the estate. Assuring her I hadn't yet gotten that far in my head due to the fact that he passed mere hours ago, I tried to shift the conversation to my sister and how she was doing. Instead, Lilley drilled further. She said I needed to be reminded that during the colossal fraudulent check warzone against my grandfather I promised her the money from his will if she was written off. Not having a clue what she was talking about and wanting to stay as far away from this kind of a conversation as possible right now, I hung up without a word. Why and how the hell was this the thing she was already thinking about?

I pulled up to my friend's place in Murfreesboro and sat in my car for several moments as I started to piece together everything. So this really was her entire motivation all along. Money. His estate. His belongings. It wasn't enough that she emptied his house and started swiping his credit cards while he was trapped in various hospitals. No, she had to get more. Her father had passed away only hours ago and her first phone call was to ask her son what the dollar amount her portion of the inheritance was going to be. Crimson once again inching its way into the corners of my vision, I decided to head inside and ignore any call or text from Lilley for the foreseeable future. Once inside, my friend and I went over all of our fun high school memories to take my mind off of everything. From there, we moved onto all of our college adventures with only the slight mention of the time Lilley took our money each month for the phone bill only to spend it on something else until our service was cut off for a month. It might not have been as disastrous as the most recent phone plan chaos, but it still proved that money was the root of all the chaos in my mother's life. And I was finally done with it. I had reached my breaking point. She wasn't getting any more. No more manipulation. No more chaos.

I made my return to campus early the next morning but decided to reach out first and plan a quick stop to a couple of spots on the way. First, I stopped at my aunt's house to ensure that there weren't any hard feelings about Nana's funeral arrangements and that I was sorry Lilley had been so vengeful during that entire experience. From there, I stopped to see Grams and Gramps to basically let them know that I was sorry that Lilley had made it seem like they hated us from the moment we first started spending holidays there. Feeling reassured that I had made the right choices and mind full of hopeful new family relationships, I made my way back to campus. My boss forced me to take the next few days off to try and process the grief that I still hadn't allowed myself to start feeling. Instead, it was more of a stare-at-the-wall-and-wait-for-life-to-make-sense kind of vibe for minutes that might have been hours or days.

At some point, another phone call from Lilley interrupted the bleak silence, a call I ignored once again. The text that came through afterward let me know that she had been granted the authority as next-of-kin to fully arrange his funeral. Not wasting any time, she messaged my brother and me to let us know if we wanted any role in planning the funeral to show up to the funeral home in Loudon that afternoon. Not having much of a choice, I hopped in the car and made my way there. Walking into the same funeral home that had been used for MiMi and Nana's mother felt eerie and depressing, but the number of funeral home options in a small town was pretty limited. I could already hear Lilley's voice in a back room, every other word almost dripping with a venom of superiority now that she had secured her "power" to plan his funeral. She was still treating this entire experience like some kind of competition. Great.

Rob was seated across from her at a table so I grabbed a seat next to him, thankful to have someone else in my corner for whatever was about to happen. Lilley firmly expressed that she had a number of plans for her father's funeral but that she'd be "kind enough to consider" any suggestions we provided. Her nose practically remained pointed in the air in front of the funeral home director, my brother, and me as we all sat bewildered around the table. Tension quickly filled the room like a black smoke until the director had covered all the general information and details of the entire process, carefully including a deadline for payment. Lilley quickly rose from the table afterwards and let us know she would be going up the road to his house to pick out an outfit for him. Without thinking, I let out a snide remark wishing her luck considering his clothes were likely in her garage all the way in Middle Tennessee and that we had already changed the locks to his house. Rob and I assured her we were capable of going into his closet and picking out a suitable outfit from whatever her movers left behind but it was no use. Whether we liked it or not, she pulled up right behind us as we made our way inside. She immediately stormed into the house, threw together a tacky outfit, and made her swift exit leaving my brother and me to silently reminisce in the now-empty house that once vaguely felt like home.

I walked around the funeral home giving my best attempt at smiles for everyone I came face-to-face with. Lilley was nowhere to be found yet. A few awkward, forced conversations later, Dad let Rob and me know that she apparently tried speeding all the way here from her house in Middle Tennessee only to hydroplane off the road and total her car for the hundredth time. I kept my comments to myself as I noticed one of my close friends walk through the front door behind my best friend/former roommate's mother. Tears formed in my eyes before I made it over to give them a hug and thank them for showing up so unexpectedly. I continued making my way around the building, paying special attention to avoid looking directly at the casket delicately placed in the center of the main room. I'd decided that morning that if I laid eyes on my grandfather laying there in the casket, it would confirm that this nightmare was more than just that. Maybe if I kept up with this disastrous scenario that my brain was forming, I'd eventually wake up and none of it would be real. But then I accidentally looked. And I didn't wake up.

Lilley dramatically limped into the funeral, making sure to cast a fiery glance in my direction the moment I came into her view. Already making sure I found myself standing with various others at any given time, I avoided the glare and tried to focus on literally anything else. That was made a bit more difficult when she began mingling with whoever would speak to her and voicing her opinions of me loud enough for the entire county to hear. Thankfully, the service began shortly after due to her absence from the majority of the visitation time. However, the relief was quickly replaced with more tension and discomfort as she sat next to me in the front pew. The tense silence lasted for ages as I stared ahead taking in the fact that my grandfather was gone and this wasn't some kind of vivid hallucination or nightmare. The man's sermon began and immediately honed in on the concept of broken families and forgiveness. A deep knot formed in my stomach as I realized she had even tried to manipulate her father's funeral service into some kind of victimizing plan. She had to make sure everyone in the building knew she was devastated and her ex-husband and sons were the evil villains of the story despite the fact that she stole him from his own home using his own credit cards. The eye rolls from Dad, my Great Aunt/Uncle, Rob, various others within the pews, and myself could practically be seen around the world.

Once the stranger was finished with his random messages of the forgiveness and healing of a broken family and his direct eye contact with me, I found myself standing up to say a few words. Standing at the podium in front of his casket, I felt my legs start to shake from nerves and the overall reality hitting me that this was all real. My eyes scanned the various faces in the pews as I shakily started to voice my grievances. How much I was going to miss him. How much I valued the financial, culinary, and life lessons in general. After making accidental eye contact with Lilley in the front row, a scowl permanently etched onto her face, I almost paused my words. Part of me considered stopping the speech altogether and telling the entire room about everything she had done. Everything she had done when I was growing up all the way up to the point where she had stolen my grandfather away from us during his final weeks. Knowing this was far from the time or place to do so, I concluded my words with how much he meant to me and how much I was going to miss his support and guidance before returning to my seat.

I wanted nothing more than some kind of closure as I watched my grandfather's casket hover over the grave that it was to be lowered into forever. But there wasn't. There was no feeling of relief or acceptance that he was really gone. Instead, there was just an emptiness and fear lingering over my head as the final words of goodbye were spoken. An emptiness that came from feeling like this was not the plotline that was meant to occur in the timeline of my life. A feeling hovering over my head that there was something I could have done differently to prevent this particular reality from happening. Fear intertwined itself in the worst way as I started imagining what was going to happen next. For everyone else, they could leave this cemetery today, process and heal like a normal person, and resume their lives in the coming days and weeks. Instead, I get to continue dealing with Lilley as I start figuring out what it means to manage someone's estate and their final arrangements. Not wanting her to start harassing me with more questions while we were literally still at the gravesite, I made my way to a restaurant to meet the others as quickly as possible after the funeral ended.

Once I pulled into a parking spot in Lenoir City, I made my way to the table that my Aunt/Uncle were sitting at with Dad and Rob. Skipping the casual conversation that we had all had to endure all morning, they let me know they had gone ahead and set up a meeting for me with a lawyer down the road. He apparently had already been filled in on the particulars of this situation and adequately warned that Lilley was going to be coming at us full force in an attempt to obtain any and all possible funds from her father. However, I remember seeing his checking account back when he first asked me to be the estate executor. The number that stared back at me on the screen wasn't nearly enough to legally pursue, especially after I pay for the funeral. Plus, there's no telling how much she drained from it using his cards to move all of his things while he was hooked up to life support. I did my best to put all these possible scenarios to the back of my mind and enjoy the meal in front of me as much as one can do on the day of their grandfather's funeral. Much too soon, it was time to return to campus and start figuring out how I was going to balance...everything.

Both of my bosses could not have been more understanding despite the fact that I was *craving* a normal routine. They both assured me that they were in my corner and to take whatever time off that was needed throughout this next rocky phase of life. The first meeting with the estate lawyer who my Aunt and Uncle hired for me was here before I could even begin to emotionally prepare for it. His office was only about 20-30 minutes away from campus which made it even easier to juggle. I began our discussion by telling him everything that was going to be on my plate for at least the next 12 months, how my mother was going to likely make this particular process as difficult as possible, and the fact that I had no idea what an executor really does. He quickly put my mind at ease, explained what it would entail, and assured me that he had complete control of the steering wheel from here. He had already submitted the legal paperwork to officially create the estate and officially declare me the executor. However, he quietly told me that he had also directly reached out to Lilley to have his personal/legal documents returned as quickly as possible to keep the process rolling along smoothly.

My mother arrived shortly after this warning, aggressively stomping through the office and claiming the seat across from mine. I kept my head down but I could still feel the intensity of her glare striking me from across the table. The lawyer thanked her for coming and began to explain the estate process before she immediately interrupted him. With hardly a pause between each venom-soaked word, she demanded the executorship be examined and that her father was not competent enough at the time the decision was made to list her son instead of her. She went further and exclaimed that there were several things she was legally entitled to from her father including his home and his vehicle. When she had finally concluded her list of demands, the lawyer calmly told her that she was getting way too far ahead of herself and that there weren't any logical or legal reasons to justify her claims about his incompetence. He sensed the fire inside of her growing and quickly added that he'd look into the deed of the property to double-check the validity of her claims. Unsatisfied, she simply rose from the office chair and stormed out into the parking lot.

I quickly followed her outside and reminded her that she still needed to return the items I would need to begin the estate work. Practically growling, she reached inside a car I had never seen before and shoved two handfuls of items into my hands. Her face was still twisted into a snarling scowl as she spat more words in my direction. She warned that this was just the beginning and that she'd be hiring her own attorney to make sure I didn't get away with what I was stealing from her. I didn't have a chance to respond with any words of my own, not that I was going to in the first place, before she was getting into the car and speeding out of the parking lot and narrowly avoiding yet another wreck in the intersection outside the lawyer's office. I quietly walked back inside to give him my grandfather's wallet, ID, and car keys before making my way back to campus once again.

The music blaring out of my car speakers as I rolled along the highway hardly did anything to stop the million questions and thoughts bouncing around my brain. Could she really sue me over all of this? What would happen then? Could she afford an attorney of her own? Had she already taken more money out of his bank account somehow? Does the house and car belong to the estate or will those actually end up in her possession? Did my grandfather actually own other properties or have bank accounts hidden elsewhere like she claimed? How the hell was I supposed to figure all of this out? I pulled into the empty dorm parking lot without even realizing I had gotten off the highway and made my way here. I had an hour or so before I had to check-in another kid's camp into the dorms for the week and I don't think my boss would care if I took that hour to decompress in my room instead of the office. I needed to start taking phone calls to sign up my first set of families for my first food giveaway along with figuring out how to recruit volunteers for said event but that could wait for a bit.

Somewhere along the way of random bar shifts, begging people to volunteer at my next event, and signing up families into their allotted time slot, I got a random phone call. Apparently, my grandfather *did* have another account with money outside of the one at the bank down the road from his house. The investor working to manage this money called my Great Uncle to get in touch with whatever attorney was handling the estate to give him more insight. The interesting part of all of this was that my grandfather had not designated this account to roll over into the estate's bank account. He did not set it up to roll over into his brother's name. He did not list his daughter as the beneficiary upon his death. He legally designated it to me. Upon his death, this account would become mine to technically do whatever I wanted with it. Holy shit.

This is what she was after all along. She wanted the access to that specific account no matter what it took. That's where the claims about his medical incompetence were born from. If she could prove that he couldn't have made these decisions regarding his investment account and the estate executorship being of sound mind, everything would default to her since she was the next of kin. On the same note, this is why my grandfather had done this. He listed me as the executor so that I could effectively manage his final wishes while leaving the majority of his money in my name directly so that I didn't have to include it into the estate's bank account in case she got control of the executorship somehow. I could now essentially control how much money went into the estate's account to pay out final expenses and inheritances. The majority of my grandfather's money was now legally my money. Effective immediately. Once again, and I cannot stress this enough, holy shit.

I called my Aunt and Uncle to vent and think out loud to see if they shared the same thinking about the entire situation. They did. I knew I could only trust a small handful of people with this colossal update but it was nice to know they shared the same thoughts about why my grandfather had done everything the way he had. They invited me over for dinner later where they said they could share some old emails and documents that might make things a bit more clear from my perspective. After a quick catch-up and casual conversation, she went upstairs and came back down with a box of various folders. Scanning over some of the papers inside the folders she put in front of me, my stomach once again turned into knots.

This was far from the first time she had planned out something like this. Reading over the old emails in front of me, I was mortified seeing that Lilley had once reached out to a financial manager to ask if her father passed away from withdrawal symptoms in the rehabilitation program back in elementary school, would the government garnish her inheritance since she was about to file bankruptcy. She asked a similar question once again whenever he was diagnosed with cancer during my freshman year of high school. A quick phone call to Dad with this info suddenly shed light on why she went behind his back around those times to remove her name and other information from the bankruptcy documents altogether. Her father's money had always been at the top of her priority list from the very beginning.

Whether it was while he was alive through fraudulent check attempts or while he was unresponsive in a hospital bed, she was going to do everything in her power to get her hands on something that was never hers to begin with. I wanted to vomit. Wait. Actual vomit.

Wrestling with all of these updates that were seeming to come every other minute, I did my best to throw myself into my routines and schedule my stresses. Just in time for my lawyer to let me know that all the legal documents had been processed and I was officially the executor, we got a letter from a random lawyer in Middle Tennessee letting us know he was representing Lilley in contesting the estate based on her claims. It was official. My mother was suing me. Well, technically she was suing the estate but with me being the executor of that estate, it was basically the same thing. It was still a legal battle that was attached to my name and a legal battle that I would be having to participate in. During my Senior year of college. During my very first big boy job for the federal government. Panic began to swish around my entire body but it was mixing with a fiery rage at the same time. Uncertainty might have been thrown into the mix as well but I was incredibly certain of at least one thing: I was going to fight back like hell.

Chapter Sixteen

Remember When It Was All Okay?

Everything was going to be okay. It had to be. The court officially declared me the executor and I was finally able to set up a bank account on the estate's behalf. Yet here I was in the parking lot of my grandfather's bank near his house terrified to walk inside. Terrified to see what kind of state my mother left his checking account while he was literally dying. Terrified to have to show yet another person a death certificate to prove I wasn't somehow lying about my own grandfather's death. Terrified to pay the funeral home and further confirm that this entire nightmare was real and *still* happening. A few deep breaths and a phone call to one of my best friends later, I got out of my car and made my way inside.

The puzzled expression of the bank teller sent a shock to my entire system as I contemplated what could possibly have gone wrong with my request. She called over another woman who gave the same expression until the confused look was replaced with a mixture of fear and anxiety. Anticipating the worst, I showed all the legal documents that proved that I needed to empty his checking account to begin resolving his final expenses and wishes. However, she quietly relayed the message that the issue was not with my paperwork or my authority. Instead, the issue was the fact that the bank account had already been completely emptied a few days ago by his daughter. She had apparently created quite the emotional scene which, combined with a very new employee, caused the bank to accidentally overlook the fact that Lilley had not been the bank account's beneficiary for around 10 years now. I turned and left the bank building without a word, angry tears burning down my face by the time I got to my car.

As if draining his bank account illegally wasn't enough to make my vision turn red, the lawyer called soon after to let me know how many times she had used his credit card in the last month after having the company send him a final statement. Another call from the bank parking lot to Dad would further blind me with rage. Apparently, Lilley was on vacation with my little sister. It took everything in me not to snap my phone in half hearing all of these updates all at once. My mind immediately flashed back to the pristine lens I used to view my mother in back when I was so much younger. Before the lens had been shattered by each and every word. Each manipulation. Each insult. Each act of theft, both physical and emotional. As if stealing her father's money while he was helpless in a hospital wasn't enough, she had to continue stealing more of it after he was gone. Then to add even more insult to injury, she used it to go to some tacky beach weekend getaway right after threatening to sue her own son. There was no going back from this. There was no *healing* this. Not anymore.

The CEO of my grandfather's bank called me less than 24 hours after I had left their lobby without a word. She invited me into the office and met my stern expression with as sincere of an apology as she could muster. She then handed me a check for the full amount that was in my grandfather's account before it was illegally drained by Lilley. I quickly asked what actions were going to be taken in regards to my mother's activities but apparently the bank was not interested in pursuing anything whatsoever. Anger quickly surged through my body once again as I realized she was going to get away with yet another deceitful, shameful (and literally illegal?) act. Sure, I had the money to now deposit into the estate's account, but that wasn't enough. I wanted them to pursue her. I wanted her to be held accountable for once. Sure, now that I was being reimbursed this was all technically just an inconvenience, but her actions hurt. Emotionally. As if stealing all his things and swiping his cards while he was incapacitated wasn't damaging enough, she was continuing to get away with stealing from him even after his time here on Earth had come to an end. It was disgusting but all I could do was simmer in anger and resentment or swallow it and try to move on. I chose the latter.

The alarm could not have been a more jarring, painful way to wake up the morning of my very first Mobile Food Bank. The moment my eyes were forced open, I began to panic and tell myself I had somehow forgotten something monumental. The checklist in my brain had been reviewed three times in the last several days, but I couldn't shake the feeling that it, and I, were about to be a colossal failure. My best friend, who I had called a dozen times this week for reassurance and advice, made it seem so easy yet my brain felt fried. I signed up 150 families into various 30-minute time blocks and recruited 30-ish volunteers yet I was positive I had forgotten something. However, once I pulled up in the work van with the borrowed tables and grocery carts to a pavilion full of volunteers, my anxiety began to ease up. Maybe I really had pulled this off. We quickly organized all the tables in an efficient line around the pavilion and organized the sign-up table just in time for the truck from Chattanooga to drop off the huge shipment of food supplies for us to hand out.

Hearing my voice speaking to all 30 sets of ears in front of me brought a sense of confidence and accomplishment I had never felt before. The tables were organized. The carts were set up. The volunteers were assigned various roles ranging from the sign-up table to guiding families through the tables to keeping the tables stocked and pretty. The families were already starting to show up early for their designated time slots. Most of the volunteers were already putting on the new volunteer shirts once they saw the new logo I had designed. My anxiety had completely vanished as I wrapped up my introductory speech and dismissed everyone to their roles for the next few hours. My first Mobile Food Bank was about to be a success and I had even changed the process a little bit to allow any families who didn't get a chance to sign up to come at the end in case we had extra food. Everything was actually going smoothly despite the chaos that was happening in my personal world.

As I shut the door to the van and locked up the doors at the Service and Leadership House, I couldn't help but feel overwhelmed with euphoric pride. Throughout the event, we handed out 75 pounds of food to 150 or more different households, spread awareness of our program, packed up any leftover food to be handed out through the on-campus food bank, and many more accomplishments without a single mishap. For the rest of the day, I was ignoring the chaos of the summer and focusing only on the fact that I now knew that I could pull off this job despite all the reservations I had prior to accepting the role. The only challenges now were to network throughout the county to find other towns to host the future events each month, keep track of all the data for recordkeeping and reporting, and rinse/repeat the family sign-up and volunteer recruitment processes each month in as efficient a way as this month's. Oh yeah, and all this on top of the whole managing a lawsuit and a quickly-approaching Senior Year thing.

In what felt like a single blink, it was time to buy all my books and organize my binder tabs for one of the two final semesters of my collegiate career. I knew this was going to be the most challenging, unique year of my entire academic life but I was somehow confident as hell. I had my grandfather's estate and all the chaos that came with that thanks to my mother, a full-time government job, a full semester of classes, a restaurant job for nights and weekends, a required internship, and my role within the Student Activities Board. Oh, and of course the challenge of figuring out what the hell to do and where to go after graduation. Oh, and my social life. Oh, and adjusting to a new boss while my current one was preparing to go on maternity leave. Oh, and trying to balance all of these things without completely falling off the deep end. Everything was fine.

After settling into my final dorm room for the remainder of my time here, I found myself already drifting through the various classrooms hearing about the schedules and syllabi. Senior Seminar wasn't going to happen until next semester, along with Trial Practice which was another final milestone required to graduate, but the internship seemed just as stressful. Within my major, my options were basically sitting in a lawyer's office or riding along inside a police car. I chose the latter since it would at least be something different and interesting compared to filing away paperwork for various attorneys for hours on end. However, it was made much more difficult when the police chief let me know I was only allowed to ride along with an officer on weekdays between 8 am and 9 pm. When the requirement to pass the internship was 250 logged hours, this sounded like a death sentence to someone with such a chaotically-packed schedule. With all of the responsibilities on my plate, I found myself having to turn in my resignation at the restaurant, a necessary decision that made both my wallet and heart weep.

Starkly different from my previous years, I found every day to be planned down to the hour in order to pull off everything I was juggling. For what felt like the first time in my life, I was actually having to keep a constantly-updated calendar and list of obligations that I needed to be focusing on at any given time. When was my next exam? When was the next Mobile Food Bank? When was the next federal report from the food bank due? When was my next internship essay? When was my next assignment due? Dear god, when does my boss come back from maternity leave? When was the next Student Activities Board meeting? When was Homecoming this year? When was the next holiday break? Was I allowed to actually take that break too or am I required to be in the office as a staff member? When did I have time to stress about this? When did I have to stress about that? When was the next attorney meeting? When did I have time to cry?

My professors and I had a really great relationship by this point and they were all aware of my circumstances, but it still felt horrible (okay maybe only a little) anytime I'd have to miss class or come in late for one reason or another. The internship turned out to be pretty easy once I put the restaurant/bar job behind me out of necessity. I'd show up at the police department (ugh) around 5 or 5:30 after class and work and wait to be assigned to an officer's car for the next four hours or so. Naturally, I developed a crush within the first week and would do anything in my power to get paired with his car as often as possible. Once my assignment was relayed to me, I'd simply sit in the passenger seat and take in as many details as possible about the job so I could write a decent reflection essay every couple of weeks. 10 of the 250 hours were going to be spent observing courtroom proceedings for traffic violations but I quickly determined to save that for the final hours. With this internship and a required History course (my worst subject) aside, I could pretty much coast through all of my obligations on auto-pilot by the third or fourth week of the semester. That being said, it was still a challenge to adjust to this jam-packed schedule.

If I wasn't in a class, I was sitting in my office signing up families for whenever the next Mobile Food Bank was. If I wasn't in my office, I was driving around meeting with various organization/church/city leaders trying to secure a site in a new city to reach new clients. If I wasn't driving around to network, I was in someone else's classroom explaining our program and trying to encourage students to volunteer with us especially if their course came with a volunteer hour requirement on top of the regular student hour requirement. If I wasn't recruiting volunteers, I was meeting with my temporary boss discussing the food bank role or something about Homecoming. If I wasn't meeting about my Student Activities Board responsibilities, I was sitting in on the Student Government Association meetings to relay various volunteer opportunities for student organizations. If I wasn't in an SGA meeting, I was meeting with the estate lawyer to try to figure out the mess Lilley was creating. If I wasn't managing an estate and paying its bills and returning my grandfather's belongings, I was in the Dean's office checking in to make sure my mother was still banned from campus to ensure my own emotional and physical safety. If I wasn't dealing with Lilley's antics, I was somehow finding the motivation to work out, or at least attempt to, at the gym down the road from campus. If none of these other things were going on, I was trying my best to sleep, if you could really even call it that.

Two months into the semester and it felt like the estate was somehow even further away from being resolved than when my grandfather had passed. Lilley had recruited her second or third attorney, was sending angry texts and letters every other day, and even recruited other family members to try and attack the estate as well. Family members my grandfather hadn't heard from in years were reaching out to request this amount of money or that amount of money as quickly as possible. I'm sure there were various grounds to do so, but it somehow felt like a calculated attack motivated by my mother's words, a weapon she had mastered over the last few years. My grandfather had lived in the same house in the same town for so long without a single check-in from anyone yet it only took a month or two after his death for people to start knocking on the estate's door to see what they were possibly entitled to. Death sucks.

Thanks to the various responsibilities that I was juggling at any certain time, I started having to dodge texts and calls from Lilley that were growing more and more aggressive by the week. Even though I had stopped responding in any way since July or August, they would still regularly arrive on my phone almost daily in the form of texts, emails, or voicemails. Nana would be ashamed of me. I was the reason the family fell apart. I was never going to see my sister again. The Tennessee version of the FBI was alerted to this major theft of "her" money. I would never have a chance at any job after graduation. She was going to the media to let them know what I was doing. She was going to show up to campus soon. The whole family hated me. I was not going to see Heaven. I should be disgusted with myself. I was a failure of a son and a failure of a human being. I was the reason my sister didn't have anything to eat today. My grandfather didn't actually love me. These were all usually easy to dismiss, but receiving them in such frequent waves did make them pretty impossible to fully ignore. Part of me imagined how easy it would be to just give up and give into her demands, but I knew I couldn't let her continue manipulating everyone in her life to get what she wanted. She had already stolen so much from him by this point so I couldn't let her continue.

Eventually, my lawyer and I decided to sell my grandfather's SUV that I had borrowed for such an extensive period of time. The funeral had still not been paid for and after the second follow-up call we knew we had to act fact. Predictably, this upset Lilley as she was expecting to receive the vehicle as part of her inheritance. We explained that it wasn't going to work out that way considering the will was worded to "do anything needed" to resolve any outstanding balances before moving onto the inheritances but it might as well have gone into one of her ears and directly out the other. Another angry text and letter arrived shortly after I had secured a potential buyer that basically said we had to hand over the keys to her since she needed the vehicle "more" than the estate did. Without thinking, I quickly followed up that if she needed a vehicle that badly she should have used the bank account money she stole instead of heading straight to the beach. Needless to say, more angry words came.

In an attempt to once again ignore everything that was going on until I had the time to stress about it, I threw myself deeper into my responsibilities. Homecoming Week was pretty much planned by this point so I just had to wait for it to actually arrive to stress about it. Having to squeeze myself into the floorboard of a police car during an active shooter situation at a building in town gave me plenty to write about in a reflection essay compared to speeding tickets and the occasional spousal fight in a front yard. As I distanced myself even further away from my mother and started to realize I was no longer a captive of the restaurant industry, I started to make holiday plans with all the family members I still had a relationship with. Now that I had a car that didn't cost an arm and a leg to fill up every 100 miles, I could actually plan on seeing my biological father and stepmom which was more difficult in the past few years. Now just to figure out how to see them, my Great Aunt/Uncle, my other Aunts and cousins, Dad and my sister, Rob and his family, and Grams/Gramps. Totally easy.

Before I could even begin emotionally preparing myself for it, Homecoming Week and my final Lip Sync night were here. The week and all its festivities passed by in a blur as I successfully checked off everything on the list for my final reign on the Student Activities Board. All of a sudden, I was semi-tipsy and holding a microphone behind the curtain and trying to figure out what I was about to say to introduce the year's most popular event on campus. Thankfully, I only had to really speak for one brief moment before passing the microphone off to the talent we had booked to perform and host the event between everyone's performance slots. I had managed to book someone that had already been booked within the last year or two but I justified it by pointing out that the event had only a small handful of attendees so he deserved to come back and sing for a full crowd. Plus, I had a crush on him and Homecoming/Lip Sync was my job so I demanded no one else be booked in case he was the one who handed me the crown if I won.

Each group's performance was intoxicating but also brought me closer and closer to the realization that this was my final Lip Sync as a student. This time next year I'd be working at my fabulous job with a fabulous salary that was promised to me in exchange for an expensive college degree. I tried my best to remain present and enjoy everything happening in front of me on stage, but I couldn't ignore the intense bittersweet feelings swirling around inside my mind and body. However, I only had a few moments to analyze and try to process this emotional fondue before it was time to head backstage with the Homecoming winners of the lower classmen and the other nominees from the Senior class. One by one, the male and female winners of the Freshman, Sophomore, and Junior class walked out and took their place on stage with their sash and flowers. Suddenly, only the three male and three female nominees from our class were the only ones still positioned backstage.

I watched everyone walk out slowly as the host, the man of my hypothetical dreams, read aloud their hometown, parents, and major. Eventually, I heard my name being called out of the speakers and my feet somehow started moving forward. I heard Nana and Poppop Luke come through the speakers and my mind was suddenly at ease. Maybe I should be angsty and exclude my parents' name from special occasions more often. He decided to add that I was "one of the most popular kids he'd ever met from the internet" which was enough to melt me into a puddle on stage. The stage lights were intensely blinding but I anxiously glanced down and caught the eyes of my interim boss, actual boss, and the other Associate Dean of Students beaming up at me from the front row. Suddenly, time seemed to freeze in place as I saw the happiness and pride in their eyes which was enough to open the floodgates of memories from the last four years all at once.

I had survived college in one piece. In one-and-a-half more semesters I would be holding my college diploma. I was a student *and* staff member at the same time. My resume was full of extracurriculars, a 3.5 grade point average, and a full-time federal job along with various restaurant ones. The woman who nervously knocked on my door at 2 am freshman year to make sure I wasn't planning on killing myself in my drunken, depressive state after losing Nana was now smiling up at me with pride and joy before I

318

discovered whether or not I was voted Homecoming King. I had transformed myself from Train Wreck Party Kid to semi-responsible, mostly-mature Young Adult Who Still Knew How To Have Fun. Time kicked back into place after I skimmed through every flashback that shot across the screen in my brain as the drumroll ended and the Homecoming Queen was announced. Then came my name.

Frozen in place, my jaw dropped to the floor as I tried to determine whether or not I had hallucinated him saying my name for Homecoming King. All of a sudden, he was putting the crown that I had ordered several weeks ago onto my head. His hand patting me on the shoulder somehow brought my back to reality and I was finally able to move once again. Hearing the claps and cheers from the crowd somehow washed away everything from my mind that had been constantly cluttering it the entire semester. Somehow, winning this final popularity contest on campus was enough to finally make me forget, just for a moment, the fact that my grandfather had died, my mother was suing me, my family was a disconnected jumble of confusion, and I had no idea what my future was going to look like after graduation if I survived that long. The euphoric buzz had fizzled out by the next morning when I woke up with a hangover from hell and realized I already had to jump back into my routines if I wanted to stay afloat. But it was 100 percent worth it to feel like a normal, reckless college kid again.

To keep myself somewhat grounded, I decided to take my fall break and take a trip to see my best friend at his new place in North Carolina. Since I had to go by the staff schedule instead of the student schedule, I only had Thursday and Friday off instead of the full week but that was still more than enough time to pull it off. Now that I had a car that I could afford the gas for, I drove a million miles an hour Wednesday night, secured a spare key from one of our mutual friends who lived there, played with Reina, and hid in the kitchen until he walked in from work. Jumping up the moment he walked through the door almost gave him a complete heart attack, the only reaction I would have been content with. The rest of the weekend shot by in a blur of catching up, talking about life and the food bank, and hopping around to various bars and restaurants until it was suddenly the final night of the trip.

Being away from campus and all the apprehension that comes along with it, we decided it was finally time to go to a gay bar together. We walked into the two-story home that had been transformed into a bar and I was immediately met with an exciting feeling that comes from a bar where you feel a sense of belonging. I threw myself right into the rhythm of the house, fog machines, and drag queen performances while my best friend beamed from ear-to-ear at how much I was leaning into the moment. Everything about the night and the decision felt incredible as we watched lip sync after lip sync and music video after music video on the various screens on the wall. However, my vision suddenly started to get pretty blurry out of nowhere until it went completely black. What felt like a few seconds later, I was suddenly waking up in a complete stranger's bedroom in an apartment that definitely wasn't my best friend's. What the hell was happening?

Panic began surging through my body as I tried to take in my surroundings without waking up the complete stranger who was lying next to me in the bed. I had drank too much plenty of times over the last few years, but this was definitely not the same. I was only sipping my second drink of the night when everything went dark. Thankfully, I could tell I was still wearing my entire outfit from the night before so I don't think anything physical happened. However, I was still completely confused on how I ended up here, who the man next to me was, and how I was supposed to get myself back to my best friend's apartment. After a few moments of internal struggle, doubled by the amount of missed calls and texts I noticed on my phone, I woke up the stranger next to me and asked him to take me back. He leaned in to try and kiss me, his hands already touching my body, but I immediately turned away and got out of the bed. He seemed to notice my panic and discomfort and hopped out of bed too. We didn't say a word the entire drive back to my friend's place and I hopped out of the car without a goodbye.

My fist barely made a single knock on my best friend's door before it swung open. His face looked like he was having a difficult time figuring out if he wanted to yell at me or hug me. He went with the latter and I quietly walked into his living room and threw myself on the couch. I quickly explained that I was only on my second drink and didn't remember a single thing after that and he got incredibly quiet. Unsure what was going on in his mind, I urged him to say something. After what felt like an eternity, he said he was pretty sure I had been drugged. A sinking feeling came over me for a few minutes but I did my best to push it to the back of my mind. I took a few deep breaths, realized everything could have been ten times worse, and spent the remainder of the morning cuddling Reina in bed. My mind kept going a mile a minute but I finally managed to convince myself that waking up with my clothes still on meant that I hadn't been taken advantage of and that it hadn't been the man in the apartment who slipped something into my second drink somehow. I had no way of knowing if this explanation made sense but it had to be true if I didn't want my mind to create worse scenarios for the rest of eternity. Eventually it was time to make my return back to campus and leave my best friend, Reina, and the stress about the last 24 hours in my rearview mirror.

There was hardly any time for me to process anything that may or may not have happened in Charlotte before it was time for me to focus on the next global event of the semester: my birthday. I knew that following up 21 was virtually impossible, but at the same time I didn't want to abandon the fun of birthdays just because I could legally walk into a bar whenever I wanted. After a quick last-minute group text to a large handful of friends, I determined the best route to take was a weekend in Knoxville hopping around from bar to bar to ring in my Taylor Swift Year. In the spirit of a new birthday, coupled with the fact that I needed to start thinking about interviews and professionalism and whatnot, I decided to finally make a change to my appearance. After waking up one morning with the sudden inspiration, I made a phone call to my hair person and headed to his house. An hour or so later, the hair I had spent the last year and a half growing out was all on the floor around me. A new, polished reflection was staring back at me in the mirror and I couldn't help but feel on top of the world just in time for a nice birthday weekend. I couldn't wait to show the press.

Halloween shot past like a bullet considering I could only attend one party and secretly hope my boss didn't find out. Nonetheless, I showed up for a few drinks or 8 and then started preparing for my Knoxville weekend. To add a little spark to the occasion, I designed a filter that could be used for a few hours on the street where all the main bars were located. It may not have been as magical of a birthday as the monumental one from the year before, but I was just as excited to spend some time hopping around with some of my closest friends (or at least the ones who were allowed to enter bars now). The night seemed to be over in the span of 15 minutes of pure bliss before reality was sucking me right back down to earth. With my mind screaming to stay behind in Knoxville with my friends and just forget about the world, I dragged myself back to my life an hour away.

Realizing these random weekend trips were the only thing allowing my mind to escape reality in order to stay somewhat sane, I began planning as many as I could as often as possible. A few weeks after my birthday, I overheard some of my friends talking about a potential trip to Nashville and immediately invited myself by way of offering to drive since I was the only one in the group with a car and/or valid driver's license. By the time we had packed up the car and picked up our other friend at our rival college 30 minutes away, the excitement within the car was almost tangible for another fun weekend away from life. However, the first speed bump occurred the very first time I stopped for gas and realized the amount of weed my friend had brought along without asking. While weed wasn't really my thing, I still support it in any capacity. However, I don't really support it whenever I'm actively interning for a police department in which getting pulled over and inevitably arrested for marijuana would definitely be in jeopardy. Not only would it get my internship revoked, but I would no longer be eligible to pass the internship course and would therefore not be graduating, at least not next semester as planned.

After getting nothing but laughter and jokes in response when I tried to relay these concerns, I turned up the music and kept my eyes forward for the entirety of the drive there. My anger eventually fizzled out by the time we got to our friend's friend where we were going to be staying for the weekend. We were pouring rounds of drinks before we had all unloaded our things into the various rooms. From there, the weekend quickly turned into a game of how many different bars we could hop around and how many different sets of live music we could hear at the same time. Eventually, we collectively decided to make our way to the gay bar and see what the Nashville scene might be like since we had all only experienced the main tourist spots so far. I wasn't sure if I was more ecstatic to find their gay bar to be the most fun I've ever had in one or that I managed to make it back home in one piece without being drugged once again. Nonetheless, I knew immediately that I wanted to return to their gay bar as quickly as possible. Maybe one day our campus town would have its own gay bar. Okay, you're right. They won't.

Despite the debauchery we had put all of our bodies through, we still made it to brunch the final morning and continued the flow of alcohol via mimosas. We had made plans to return to campus once the brunch was over, but something about the amount of fun I was having in this city and the amount of mimosas made me want to stay for another hour or so. Another hour turned into another hour and another round of mimosas until I was definitely drunk once again. The next thing I knew, it was 5 or 6 pm and almost all of my friends were pissed that I was still drinking and that we were still in Nashville. However, with the support of just one of the friends, I let the stubborn side of my brain take full control and demanded we stay for another round before we head back. Another round turned into another two or three before I felt myself slipping further and further away from coherence. Part of me knew exactly what I was doing but the other parts of my brain knew I wanted to hold onto the escapism of the weekend trip for as long as humanly possible even if it meant facing dire circumstances afterward.

After making the spiteful decision to keep downing drinks just to piss my friends off and put off returning to my million obligations, my vision started to phase out for a few moments. Those few moments, or alleged hours, later I came back down to earth and realized it was now full-blown nighttime. My eyes quickly blinked a few times as I realized I had left my dreams and was in a car I definitely didn't recognize. Thankfully, no one else was with me. Wait. No one else was with me. Where was the one friend who was on my side? Where were the friends who were upset at me? I took out my phone to call my friend only to feel the buzzing coming from my own left pocket. Why did I have her phone? Shit. Panic rushed over me as I cautiously opened the back door of the car to step out, unsure of whether or not an alarm would go off. By some complete miracle from above or below or somewhere, my friend was rounding the corner of the building across the street. She was laughing with a man I didn't recognize and then immediately sprinted over once she saw me standing in the street.

She confirmed that my stubborn day-drinking had quickly gotten out of hand and turned into an all-out booze fest which did nothing but piss off my friends even more. This situation apparently turned into a tense, heated argument outside the gay bar that I didn't remember walking into. From there, after I declined their demands to go back to the house and head home, they decided to go back to her friend's place without us. Not only did they leave us there at the bar, but they grabbed my car keys from the kitchen counter, packed up their things, and headed back to campus without us. My friends stole my car. They stole my brand-new car. Not only did they literally steal my vehicle, but they left us stranded here in Nashville without a single way home. I immediately collapsed onto the sidewalk as I tried to process this sudden reality.

Sure, getting drunk on the day we were supposed to go home was reckless and irresponsible, but by no means was it justification for literal vehicular theft. My mind kept going over the possible ways that this decision would have been deemed acceptable in their minds but it kept drawing a blank. People, especially ones who you consider to be your close friends, don't just take your car and leave you stranded with no way home. No matter what. However, I knew that this was in fact a reality and getting pissed on a sidewalk in front of a gay bar wasn't going to solve anything. They had taken my car and gone home and clearly weren't going to come back now to get us home safely. My friend and I were stuck and that was just that. It's Sunday night and we both have things to do back on our campuses starting at 7:30 tomorrow morning and we're in Nashville stranded.

We made our way to the nearest fast food restaurant that happened to still be open and slid into one of the booths to try and brainstorm. One of the employees was kind enough to let us borrow his phone charger which at least solved *one* of our problems. We considered trying to use a ride service to take us all the way back to campus until we realized that it required something called money that we definitely didn't have. She called every single friend in her phone who lived within a 50 mile radius but every single one of them was asleep or had to be at work themselves within the next few hours. Shit. We both frantically searched for the greener grass or the light at the end of the dark tunnel we had woken up inside until a tiny lightbulb flickered on in my head. My brother.

After calling 23 times, I finally heard a voice answer on the other end, a voice that was clearly annoyed and exhausted. Feeling tears unexpectedly form in my eyes, I immediately started explaining my situation with a shaky voice and begged him to come rescue us. After pulling the fact that he had called me homophobic slurs for so much of my childhood, I was finally able to talk him into waking up his whole family and coming to the rescue. I had no idea how I was going to pay him back for this, but I couldn't help but bathe in the relief that I was going to make it back to campus and recover my stolen car in time for work/class. We did our best to ignore the tension that was filling the entirety of the car until it was time to drop her off at her campus and me at mine. Rob interrupted my thanks to let me know that I was not to call him again for a monumental favor like this for a very long time unless it was an absolute life-or-death situation. I agreed.

I was relieved to see my car parked in the dorm parking lot still in one piece although I immediately felt a surge of anger when I noticed it had been left with a completely empty gas tank. All guilt that I was feeling about drinking too much and risking whatever it was they were needing to be back on campus for had vanished. Whatever assignments or study session they had put off until last night didn't justify this. Anger quickly replaced the guilt that had formed on the ride back here. You'd think after stealing your alleged best friend's car you would at least fill the tank back up. I didn't have much time to simmer in this anger before I remembered I had to be in my office in approximately 15 minutes if I wanted to continue pretending that everything was fine and my weekend trip to Nashville hadn't been a disaster. Sitting in my office, I began to dwell in my thoughts and tried to process them all.

The main themes of this vast collection of thoughts and emotions were my identity and the effort I was putting into all of my friendships here. Something about the feeling I experienced whenever I walked into a gay bar in a different city knowing that I didn't have to worry about the guys on campus judging me or doing something worse made me question everything about myself. Was I being a different, almost censored, version of myself the last couple of years just because I was in a small town in the middle of nowhere? I thought coming out was all I had to worry about but apparently that was just the very beginning of his whole thing. And sure, it was awesome that I had built up this social network on campus since freshman year enough to even win Homecoming King, but was it really worth it? Was it worth it to be "popular" in college when the friends you think are your closest are fine with leaving you stranded in Knoxville on your 21st birthday, bail on the rest of the plans, and literally steal your car and leave it empty?

The end of the semester quickly approached as I began to put an emotional wall up against the vast majority of my friends on campus and began looking inward to figure out what the hell my "gay identity" really is. My internship hours were finally met once I sat in on a few court proceedings and watched everyone explain why they didn't deserve their speeding ticket for *only* going 35 miles over the speed limit in a school zone. Of course, I managed to snag the hot cop's phone number before my final meeting (for networking purposes, duh). I already had a pretty good expectation for what all of my Criminal Justice final grades were going to look like and even managed to snag a B- in the dreaded History class (that I actually ended up enjoying because of the professor but I'll never admit that). With the internship completed and my final obligations fulfilled with the Student Activities Board, I could focus some of my free time on figuring out what the hell I was going to do whenever I finally got my hands on my degree.

My collegiate career was ending in one more semester and I had no idea what I was going to do. My Food Bank position term ends two weeks after my graduation date. I'm going to be homeless and unemployed in approximately six months. The worst part of this sudden realization was the fact that I knew deep down I didn't want to dive into a Criminal Justice type of career. My internship had been full of excitement and, at times, adrenaline but I knew I didn't want to spend any part of my life being a cop. Part of me wanted to be a detective, but the short glimpse I had into that kind of role during my time within the police department building confirmed that it wasn't a route for me. Plus, the entire justice system in the country seemed so gross so I couldn't imagine being a contributing member for it. I knew law school was going to be virtually impossible to get into so last-minute even if I could somehow afford it. So basically I had no dream job, no passions to pursue, and no connections to help me figure out what my life might look like in a few months.

The ending of this semester was unlike any that I had faced in the past considering I still had the Mobile Food Bank to run and the estate to manage. I breezed through the monthly events this semester and even managed to network within other communities to land the locations for a few of next semester's events. Lilley was still practically banging on the estate's front door every single chance she could, demanding anything and everything under the sun. The threats were still coming pretty regularly and still included ruining my potential future careers and keeping my sister away from me for the rest of my life. Her words had lost their venom a long time ago so thankfully it was easy for me to ignore them and focus on my job, the upcoming final semester, and the million other things that seemed to be going on. Once I had wrapped up the remainder of the staff semester schedule that lasted a week or two after the student one, it was time for winter break and all its adventures.

I packed up a duffel bag or two and moved into my best friend's townhouse down the road since the Dean decided I could not remain in my dorm despite my circumstances of being homeless and an employee of the school. After a wine night or five with her, I decided to embark on my holiday adventures as quickly as possible. A dinner gathering at my Great Aunt and Uncles where I was served an abundance of delicious food after what felt like an entire semester of scraps when I had time to consume them. Another dinner at my other Aunt's house now that I had begun to remedy our relationship that was so strained during Lilley's spiral after Nana's passing. Poppop was there with his new wife among a crowd of other family members like my brother, sister, Dad, other aunts, and cousins. Part of me expected to feel some kind of discomfort or anger at his remarriage, but I was honestly just happy that he was happy and that I was back in this side of the family's good graces after so much turmoil. After dinner, the entire group reminisced on the good times and the not-so-good times from the last 20-or-so years. Each behind-the-scenes story involving Lilley that was shared continued to shed light on the woman we were so seemingly unfamiliar with for the majority of our lives.

These revealing stories continued as I made my way to my father and stepmother's house to celebrate the holidays. After a quick meal and fireside chat in the backyard, I decided to ask them for more insight into my creation and anything else they felt comfortable sharing with me. Lilley had apparently quit her job after a first date with my father and moved over an hour away to the same apartment building he was living in. From there, my creation was either an elaborate marriage trap plan gone wrong or a drunken mistake. Or maybe it was a little bit of both. Nonetheless, I came to be only for the marriage to be dissolved shortly after my birth. He then met Erin, fell in actual love, and got married with a consistent custody arrangement for me. Naturally, this update was a shock for a variety of reasons. It's difficult to hear that your creation was accidental and/or a tool of manipulation on top of all the other stories I had been hearing about my mother. Furthermore, my mother had always told me a vastly different story that involved her being devastatingly cheated on by my father which clearly was not the case.

From there, the stories moved along past my birth and into some of the antics that she had displayed over the first few years of my life. Forcing my father to watch me *and* my brother at times despite the fact that Rob was not his son. Not showing up for the drop-offs and pick-ups sometimes. Filing a false police report against him. Claiming that he hit her at some point and almost ruining his military career before a specialist proved that the wounds/bruises were either accidental or self-inflicted. With each chaotic story my ears were hearing, the version of my mother that once existed, or at least existed in my young mind, fell apart piece by piece. Hearing another batch of stories from Nana's brother during a quick holiday visit to their home, the version of Lilley from my childhood was nothing but a pile of shards. Eventually, I accepted the fact that she had never actually existed and that my mother was a deeply toxic, troubled person. Once the estate was finally settled, I could be completely free. A large part of my mind couldn't help but wonder what kind of damage she might be inflicting on my sister's young mind, though.

After somehow crossing off every holiday visit to my scattered family members, I had about two days of rest before it was time to go into party mode. Without a second of thought, I hopped in my car (alone this time just in case) and headed to Nashville for another Niykee show. I made friends in line, screamed every word to every song, and hung out for a little bit with her after the show before heading out to the gay bar once again. After a night of dancing in the mostly-empty club since it was a weeknight I somehow talked a new group of friends into letting me sleep in their hotel room so I didn't have to worry about driving. Waking up bright and early, I hopped back into my car and made my way to Knoxville to get ready for another New Year's Eve with my best friend. While this one would be missing the boyfriend aspect that made last year's so wonderful, I was excited for the escapism nonetheless.

Some of my best friends from campus merged with my Knoxville friends as we embarked on another New Year's throughout the Knoxville bar scene. Around the second bar of the night, I happened to cross paths with a tall, handsome man that I had seen earlier that day on one of The Apps. He recognized me and struck up a conversation and I was pleasantly swept off my feet with how easy it felt. One thing led to another and I found myself hopping into a car with him to head back to his place shortly after midnight struck. More things happened until I found myself waking up in a bed next to him. While I didn't regret a thing, a part of my brain started telling me that I should probably get up and make my way back to my friends before he woke up. Right as I was about to make the escape, however, he woke up with a smile. Suddenly, we were cuddling again and chatting back and forth for over an hour that felt as if it was only a few minutes. He noticed the number of times my concerned friends were texting and calling me and offered to drop me off at their place.

I kissed him one more time before hopping out of the car to head into the shopping mall that my friends were browsing in the same outfit I had on last night. Excitement filled my body as I found them and quickly filled them in on everything. I glanced down at my phone to see that he had already sent me a text about hanging out again sometime soon, a text I could not have replied faster to. The next week or so flew by in a flash until I found myself driving back up to Knoxville to have dinner with him. However, dinner quickly turned into a movie back at his apartment and the movie quickly turned into a sleepover. I knew I had to wake up really early to get to my office in time the next morning but it somehow didn't bother me whatsoever. Morning came as quickly as ever as I rushed to get ready to leave. However, whenever I walked out the door of his apartment, I didn't leave single.

The entire drive home I couldn't stop smiling. Part of my brain was telling me it was insane to think I could throw a relationship on top of everything else going on in my life, but I didn't care. He was attractive, charming, had a stable job, made me laugh, and didn't live 12+ hours away from me which was the most refreshing part. By this point, I could operate the Mobile Food Bank blindfolded and I knew my professors well enough to know I was going to be alright this semester so why not? Outside of those two obligations, all I had to really worry about was finding a job after graduation and continuing to ignore Lilley's threats until we figured out the home ownership and the remainder of the estate. The cherry on top was that I now had an official reason to leave campus on the weekends as often as possible.

Our weekends quickly became a back-and-forth routine. I'd drive up to Knoxville one weekend, explain more and more of my life, admit that I had no idea what life was going to be in six months, and laugh and laugh and laugh. The next weekend, he'd drive down to campus and I'd give him the official Student Ambassador tour before taking him to eat at the restaurant I used to work at. From there, I'd force him to go around to various house parties so I could show him off to my friends until we both agreed it was time to go back to my dorm room for bible studies and meditation. Somewhere between the apartment visits, he started to be one of the biggest encouragements for figuring out my life. Although I didn't give away many details about my mother and the estate situation, he was constantly eager to listen and offer any kind of feedback on what little he knew. He also offered free advice on applying for jobs and writing cover letters which was something I was starting to do every week now to any job posting I saw in Knoxville, Athens, and Nashville. He even tried to teach me how to drive his stick shift car. It didn't work.

Whether I was prepared for it or not, the final semester of my college journey arrived at my front door. Constitutional Law seemed like it was going to be easy enough. Trial Practice was definitely going to be the most fun considering the "final exam" was a mock trial in a courtroom downtown. Ethics in Society was going to mainly be classroom discussions on complex and popular societal issues which was practically a drug to me. Senior Seminar was definitely going to be the most challenging since it was nothing but writing a 30-page paper on a Criminal Justice topic of your choosing and presenting for 20 minutes. Panicking at the concept of my entire academic future riding on two classes, a mock trial, and one massive paper and presentation, I chose a random topic off the top of my head. Walking back to my dorm to take a much-needed nap, I had no idea how I was going to manage to tackle a massive project on the concept of homeland security alone. Oh well. Everything was fine. Everything was always fine.

The semester's routine quickly established itself over the next few weeks as I started juggling class lectures, being as vocal as possible in Ethics without being cringey, accepting the prestigious Lead Prosecutor position for the mock trial, and constructing a vague, general outline for my seminar paper. More importantly, however, I was figuring out the best ways to insert time with my boyfriend, my friends, the estate, and the food bank into this juggling act. Just in time to escape all of these realities, the school's trip to Washington, D.C. that I was lucky enough to be a part of arrived. I wasn't sure if my application from last year had been approved because I was a school employee and the chaperones of the trip were my boss and the other Associate Dean, but I wasn't about to question it either way. Considering my employment and the fact that I was already on the school's vehicle insurance roster because of the work van, I was chosen as one of the drivers of the two vans we were going to be taking.

After a painfully early wake-up time and a tragic nine-hour drive, we pulled into the city and found our way to the townhouse we had rented. Assuming I was going to sneak off to bars as often as possible, I grabbed the bedroom closest to the front door and began to unpack all of my things. While the trip was technically for that man's inauguration, I was choosing to view it as a travel opportunity since I had imagined a different person being inaugurated whenever I turned in the application. Thankfully, my boss had already assured all of us that we were going to be attending a number of incredible places including a walk within the Women's March the morning after his inauguration to balance out the toxic energy that was already filling the city.

The days passed by in a blur of museums, Arlington cemetery, Tomb of the Unknown Soldier ceremonies, nice restaurants, side-by-side videos at the Holocaust museum comparing Hitler's campaign strategies with a certain someone else's, and various other touristy sites. At night, I did my best to sneak away to hop around various bars that were close to the house, my "trip buddy" who happened to be my replacement after I completed my federal term joining me each time. He may or may not have been old enough to order drinks at the bar but with the chaos of the inaugural week there weren't very many bartenders who cared enough to check IDs. However, after watching him throw up outside the National Association of Realty building as well as puking inside the car home, we decided it probably was best that we not sneak away for bars anymore. After what felt like one single day instead of several, we were waking up at 4 am to head to that man's little ceremony.

We had to wait a couple of hours after we made it through security and found a spot for all of us. The crowd size kept growing and I quickly realized we were surrounded by red hats. Considering we were inside the official inauguration gates, I was certain the ceremony would run smoothly. However, as the screens lit up and the government officials began to step out as their names were called, I quickly realized that was not the case. Whenever a certain party representative would walk out, the crowd would roar. Whenever other certain party representatives walked out, they would lose what little composure they had to begin with. Swearing. Jeering. Holding their small children up towards the screens and instructing them to flip off certain people who walked out. Taking their shirts off to wave them around. What I thought was going to be an official, federal inauguration quickly began to feel like a rodeo party or country concert in the middle of a corn field. I did my best to ignore them as I proudly wore my favorite blue sweater in a sea of tacky red hats.

Their idol eventually made his way out onto the Capitol steps to accept his new job title as they cheered and practically threw their children up as sacrifices. After a terrifyingly unexpected cannon shot that gave me a heart attack, the ceremony wrapped up and the worst political era of my life officially began. As we all shuffled our way through the crowd trying to find our leaders, we all shared our thoughts about the crowd and the ceremony overall. Despite potential political differences, we all agreed that it couldn't have felt further from a respectful federal ceremony and instead felt like a rowdy concert. We finally spotted our leaders, who immediately shared the same thoughts we were all having, especially the cannon scare, before we made our way as far from the crowds as possible. The majority of us tried our best to hide our delight at the protest crowds that were already forming all over the city until we managed to get back to the house.

We all packed up most of our things that night except for whatever we were going to wear in the morning to the Women's March before heading back to campus. Morning came quickly although this time I was actually excited for the day's agenda. Within ten minutes of walking from the house to the meetup spot, we realized just how monumental of a moment this was. Despite it being the first official march, the streets were flooded with participants adorned with pink hats. In every direction, the crowds all seemed to merge together into one gigantic ocean of peaceful protests. However, the energy could not have felt more different than yesterday morning. From the signs to the people themselves, positivity and encouragement overcame the entire city until it was practically tangible in the air. While everyone's message and vibe were stern and rigid, their attitudes could not have been more welcoming and endearing. It was a peaceful protest, but everyone's message was still crystal clear.

Everyone quickly lost track of each other within the masses of people as we all got sucked further and further into the historical movement. Eventually, everyone was able to make it back to the vans after absorbing as much as we could from our first Women's March. Despite being an hour or two behind

330

schedule, everyone couldn't help but smile. As we made our way back towards campus via a nine hour drive, we apparently heard that the crowd for today's march was almost double the size of the ceremony the day before. I managed to talk my future replacement into driving the second half of the trip home so that I could peacefully text everyone in my phone to see if there were any parties happening by the time I got back. It's really important to focus on the important things in life. Within ten minutes of finally being home, I had thrown my bags into my dorm room, said hi to the three freshmen roommates I barely knew anything about, and headed out to the first party I could find before I had to fully return back to normal life once again.

The semester routine quickly returned full-speed until I could find the next distraction: Valentine's Day. Sitting across from him in a restaurant in Knoxville, I reflected on the last month or so since our relationship officially began. A smile hit my face as I retraced over our weekend trips to each other, my constant venting about my mother, his advice as I got a call from my best friend in Charlotte which ended our friendship completely so he could focus on a new boyfriend, and all the random experiences we had in such a short period of time. It felt nice to feel a sense of support, admiration, and encouragement but there was a tiny thought bubble in my brain that couldn't help but compare it to my first boyfriend. Damn it, Chase. Stop. Everything was going so well. Stop. It doesn't matter that you don't feel the same fiery passion and infatuation that you did back then. He's a great guy and you're happy. I'm happy. Maybe.

The thoughts were able to be pushed to the back of my mind for the remainder of the dinner, but they popped back up over the next few days after I got back to campus. Trying to force everything to go back to normal, I planned a fun weekend in Knoxville. I brought my best friend with me up to my boyfriend's apartment and invited my Knoxville best friends to come over and pregame for a fun night out on the town. We blew up the air mattress for my friend to use at the end of the night since we'd likely be too drunk to figure out the pump. Before we knew it, we were tossing back drinks and making our way downtown for yet another fun weekend away from reality. Somewhere between the third and fourth bar, my boyfriend had split off to hang out with his friends. He seemed somewhat worried but I assured him it was fine and that in the worst-case scenario we could just meet back up at his apartment at the end of the night.

My phone was controlling the music in my friend's car as we made our way closer and closer to my boyfriend's complex. As we pulled into the entrance, I kept getting call after call from him. Knowing we were about to walk through his door in less than two minutes and not wanting to miss the ending of the song, I ignored them. My best friend and I stumbled through the parking lot up to his apartment door, laughing about everything and nothing. However, before we got to the door, I noticed him standing in front of it with the most angry facial expression I had ever seen him wear. We stopped laughing.

We silently stepped into the apartment and were met with immediate shouts from my boyfriend who was more drunk than I'd ever seen. Apparently, ignoring his phone calls was not the best idea. The shouts continued as my best friend and I absorbed every word trying to make sense of them. His angry rants went from ignoring his phone calls to leaving Knoxville without telling him to getting food without asking what he wanted. The majority of the points didn't make any sense considering we never left Knoxville, never got food, and clearly hadn't gone back to campus considering we were literally standing in his apartment. He launched a finale of words into the room before storming off to his bedroom, leaving me with tears forming in the living room. A few seconds later, he came back out to inform my best friend that I was to sleep on the air mattress with her and to not even think about coming to his room. I turned to face her but she had already read my mind and was deflating the air mattress to head back to campus immediately.

He sent a string of apology texts the following morning and even drove down to campus to try and talk things out. I hesitated before accepting his apology although my mind couldn't stop thinking about how insane the whole night had become. Sure, he was clearly drunk but how does that translate into screaming at me (and my best friend of all people) for little to no reason whatsoever? As hard as I tried to convince myself that everything would be fine if I just moved along, I knew that wasn't the case. By the end of the week, I ended our relationship. Something about the spontaneous screaming had flipped a switch in my mind that made it clear how dumb it was to be getting into a serious relationship with graduation and whatever life was going to be afterwards approaching so quickly. Knowing that sitting down and actually processing the feelings about the breakup and life in general would just result in a full-blown spiral, I threw myself right back into the normal swing of things and drank away my stress and overall emotions as often as I could over the next few weeks.

After yet another trip to Nashville with some of my friends who I knew wouldn't steal my car, I started to realize something. Living in East Tennessee after graduation had never been an idea that sparked any joy since I had spent so much of my life here already. However, I had no idea where I could move to or how to even go about moving somewhere permanently. The last four years or so had been spent figuring out a place to stay for the next period of time. Dorm for this many months. This person's couch for this semester break. Back to the dorm for the next semester. This friend's apartment for a while.

Rinse and repeat. However, now that I was in my final stretch of college, the part of the timeline after I got my diploma was a gigantic blanket of unknown. No more having a scheduled, structured life. No more knowing exactly what the next phase was going to be. A stretch of blank opportunity. Until now.

Nashville sparked joy from the moment I first visited. Each time I visited after that, even with that terrible weekend of being stranded, had been more fun than the last. It was a city but not in the overwhelming way like New York or Los Angeles seemed to be. A city I could comfortably navigate. Plus, it was far away from "home" or whatever that meant but also close enough for my close friends to still be a part of my regular life. There was music everywhere. Concert venues everywhere. A gay bar that actually felt comfortable to exist within, an experience that was new and intoxicating. Plus, even if I didn't find a job right away, it seemed like I was going to be financially stable enough to survive for a bit. While I hadn't signed an apartment lease or anything, I knew where I was going to be moving to after graduation even though I only knew one or two people in the whole city. A fresh start. A new chapter.

With hardly any of the work done for my seminar paper, mock trial, or the next Mobile Food Bank event, I decided I should leave town once again for Spring Break. Since I only got three days off instead of the normal five due to my imprisonment, I mean employment, with the school, I managed to avoid any potential trips to Panama City Beach. Avoiding this was something that made my wallet and mental state pretty happy considering I was broke and still had no idea who my true friends were or what friendship even meant. In the meantime, I still wanted to get away so I snuck away to have a long weekend with a friend and her girlfriend. Since she lived at a semi-halfway point, we spent the weekend relaxing and exploring Chattanooga and Atlanta. While I wasn't on a beach surrounded by 100,000 shirtless men, it was nice to have such a fun weekend with people who seemed to genuinely enjoy and respect my company. However, as always, the break ended as quickly as it began before it was time to throw myself back into the twists and turns of whatever my life was turning into.

Leaning into anxiety, pressure, and insomnia one night, I ended up accidentally writing the majority of my seminar paper in one sitting. After hopping around a couple of study groups with friends before sitting in my dorm room completely restless, I noticed the sun coming up and a fully-finished piece of writing staring back at me from the computer screen. After a quick read-through, I submitted it online even though the first rough draft (only half the paper) wasn't due for several weeks. With that particular weight lifted off of my shoulders, I could focus my energy on the mock trial, another work event, and pretending like someone *hadn't* told me that my mother showed up on campus searching for me when I was away on Spring Break. She apparently stopped my food bank replacement of all people to ask about my whereabouts but I stopped listening after he mentioned her presence because I didn't want to know or imagine what her intentions may or may not have been if she found me. Instead, I let the Dean know that she had arrived on campus despite her ban letter but he brushed off my concern and let me know he had agreed to a brief meeting with her that same day.

The frustrations I was feeling towards the Dean and Lilley in general was enough to motivate me to throw myself even further into my obligations. I locked in the final dates and locations for the rest of the Mobile Food Banks I was responsible for. I started putting more time and energy into the trial preparations as my team dug deeper and deeper into how we were planning to prove the wife murdered him on purpose (she definitely did). I voiced my opinions louder than ever in Ethics as we dove into how slavery was still having impacts on society today and how women should be allowed to have control over their own bodies which was somehow a confusing, radical concept to a large portion of the students. However, try as I might, the estate still felt as stuck as ever although the house was now completely emptied and cleaned to perfection. Now we just had to figure out who had the authority to sell it and where those funds might be delegated. By now, Lilley was on her second or third separate attorney because they kept dropping her once they realized the insanity behind her claims.

Feeling accomplished enough with my spontaneous productivity, I decided to take another escape to Nashville just to see if I *really* felt that same spark. This time I drove up by myself to meet one of my friends from high school to stay with her and her girlfriend in Murfreesboro. On the first night, we decided to head to the gay bar in Nashville since this was one of the first times we'd gotten the chance to hang out since I came out. She could not have been more supportive or excited to see me so happy in the middle of an openly gay scene and got me drink after drink. Suddenly, everything started to feel euphoric and fuzzy once the drinks set in and a fairly attractive guy came up to us and started flirting with me. This was not something I was accustomed to whatsoever, but I wasn't about to question it. He was tall, muscular, and arguably one of the most attractive men I had ever seen face-to-face. Once I had determined this wasn't part of some prank show, I was on cloud nine. One thing led to another and suddenly we were back at my friend's apartment together.

She assured me it was fine to crash at her place because she was going to go stay with her girlfriend for the rest of the night. While I was pretty nervous to have been hit on at a bar for the first time and brought him home, my nerves dissipated as his hand started roaming over my body. Standing over by the bathroom counter, he took my face into his as our clothes floated off of our bodies. He laughed at something awkward I said in the heat of the moment before picking me up and setting me on the counter with such ease that I felt like I weighed ten pounds. We didn't make it too far with how much alcohol was coursing through our veins, but I was still overcome with intoxicating intimacy and confidence as we floated over to the bed to finish up whatever was happening, something we were figuring out as we went. My vision eventually faded out as the alcohol fully sunk in as my body hit the bed. Sleep wafted over me whether I wanted it to or not.

My eyes shot open and panic flooded over my body like a tsunami as I felt myself more and more unable to breathe. My throat became more and more constricted as the man's forearm pushed harder and harder into my neck. Even with adrenaline fueling coursing through every muscle, I was unable to move under the weight of his body. Not that my mind was having a lot of time to process, but I assumed I was being robbed or murdered or both. However, he slowly leaned in, kissed me, and whispered, "you don't get to sleep until I'm done too" directly into my ear. He then began trying to press inside me as tears quickly filled my eyes. Still unable to breathe or free myself, I immediately began struggling and scrambling as much as I could underneath him until I could catch little pockets of air whenever his arm would move slightly. He pressed more of his weight down and continued his attempts despite my pleas and sobs until I was sure I was about to become the subject of a tragic news story or documentary film special. Another surge of adrenaline shot through my body as I envisioned what might happen to me if I don't do something. By some miracle, I was able to move my leg upward enough to knee him in the groin, causing him to finally roll over off of me for a split second.

Not giving myself a single moment of hesitation, I scrambled and flailed around until I managed to get off the bed. I threw on my clothes, grabbed my keys, and sprinted out of the apartment while still coughing and trying to catch my breath. Even after I made it to my car and drove down the road to a gas station, I felt everything but safe. Visions in my mind kept flashing by of him sprinting out of the apartment, finding me here in the parking lot, and unleashing his wrath. Tears were streaming down my face as I envisioned what could have happened to me if I hadn't managed to muster the adrenaline to get him off of me. I had successfully fled the scene, but I could still feel his forearm crushing my neck and his unsuccessful attempts to push himself inside. His whispered words were still lingering and repeating themselves over and over as I pulled out my phone to call anyone who might possibly be awake.

After a quick therapy session with the first friend who was awake enough to answer my calls, I dialed 911. Through a shaky voice and a brain that couldn't function well enough to form the best words, the operator told me to return to the apartment complex and await the police even if I didn't feel comfortable walking back into the actual apartment yet. About 15 minutes later, I stepped out of my car to greet the two officers that had arrived. Tears were still in my eyes as I explained that I had been sexually assaulted and almost raped by the man who was still inside my friend's apartment. A brick formed in my stomach as they eventually closed their notebooks and made their way inside to talk to him while I remained outside. The brick doubled in size until I was certain I was going to vomit and/or pass out on the spot as they came back outside a few minutes later.

Their faces remained emotionless as they had been from the beginning of our conversation while they told me that there had been a misunderstanding. They explained that we had an altercation but that I had not been sexually assaulted. Seeing the confusion on my face, she followed up by saying I should be more careful with who I bring home and that I shouldn't drink so much next time. After confirming they weren't going to be filing any kind of report or taking any action whatsoever, they got in their car. Right before pulling out of the parking lot, they advised me to go back inside and discuss the situation with him, the man who had just woke me up by choking me and trying to shove his penis inside me.

I stood outside, frozen in shock, as I tried to process what just happened. Eventually, the thoughts and tears subsided and I felt completely numb inside. They didn't believe me. I had pleaded with the police to help me and they didn't believe me. Maybe they were right. Maybe this actually was my fault in a lot of ways. I wiped the tears off of my face and walked back into the apartment. Avoiding any and all eye contact and social interactions, I climbed into the bed. I positioned myself as far away from his presence on the other side of the bed, pulled the blankets over my entire face, and did my best to go back to sleep only to hope that he didn't try anything again. However, I found myself waking up every ten minutes or so in a panic until I was certain he was peacefully asleep, as if nothing had happened at all, next to me and wasn't going to try to forcefully have sex with me again or kill me.

Eventually, I heard the front door open as my friend rushed inside after reading all the texts and listening to the voicemails I left. From underneath the blankets, I heard him sit up and ask if he could catch a ride back to downtown Nashville so he could get back to his hotel. Hearing the frustration in her voice at his casual request, I felt more tears form once again. She sternly told him to get the hell out of her apartment and I finally felt the first ounce of peace all day as the door closed behind him. She came and sat down on the bed next to me as I wiped away the tears with the blankets that were still draped across my face. She asked me how I was feeling once I revealed my face but I told her I was fine and that I didn't want to talk about it. This wasn't a lie because I had already decided I wasn't going to talk about it ever again. Telling the police only to be told I was basically lying was difficult enough without thinking about trying to convince my friends that I was telling the truth. It had happened, it was over now, he wasn't going to face any consequences, there's nothing I could do about it, and that's all that mattered. I mindlessly drifted through the rest of the weekend before once again making my way back to campus, leaving the entire experience buried within the confines of that apartment and the officer's notebook.

Seeing my reflection in the mirror as I adjusted my suit that didn't quite fit right felt surreal as I prepared to head to our town's downtown courthouse. Something about our official mock trial being tonight didn't feel real. How the hell was my final semester so close to being completed? I made my way downtown, walked fast, faces passed, and entered the courtroom to find my spot at the head of my group's table in front of the judge's seat. We only had a few minutes to go over our strategy one last time before she made her entrance and the trial began. I glanced to my left to see Dad, my Great Aunt and Uncle, my best friends, and their various family members in the pews and suddenly felt a wave of happiness and motivation. Maybe I could invite them to the courthouse I'd have to share with Lilley later this summer to hopefully settle the estate for good.

The mock trial lasted 45 minutes as the professor floated between both sides and offered the occasional piece of advice. The judge retired to her chambers for a moment to consider the case she had just overseen in order to arrive at a verdict. I knew I had done my job to the best of my ability, or at least enough to pass the class, but deep down I really wanted a win. However, my dreams were crushed as the verdict was delivered about 15 minutes later. The wife was found not guilty despite the amount of incriminating statements we had obtained from all of their witnesses over the last hour or so. The professor and all my support systems still congratulated me on a job well done before I looked towards the courtroom exit and the final stretch of my college journey. My seminar paper was officially turned in, my take-home final for Constitutional Law was done, my seminar presentation finished and memorized, and my final Ethics paper was already submitted. For all intents and purposes, I was done.

Even with all my coursework completed and the final Mobile Food Bank planned, I wasn't able to fully soak in the happiness of being at the finish line. After a number of random interviews and countless rejection emails, I had no job lined up. Even if I had managed to impress any number of the hiring managers I had interviewed with, the salaries were all between $30,000-35,000 even with a college degree. How the hell was I supposed to live in Nashville, or anywhere for that matter, when that was the highest salary I could hope to obtain? What happened to the abundance of high-paying jobs that an expensive college degree was supposed to unlock for us? Briefly speaking with the majority of my friends who were getting ready to graduate alongside me confirmed I wasn't the only one experiencing this either. We were promised interviews, nice salaries, and overall stability if we did the right thing and went to college and yet we were being offered scraps in return. Yay!

Thankfully, I still had the lawsuit with my own mother to consume the parts of my brain that weren't focused on the fact that I was likely to be unemployed and homeless a month or so from now. The attorney and I spoke and met regularly, but we still weren't sure when the real estate issues were going to be figured out so that we could finally cross the finish line with my grandfather's estate and the separate account he had left for me. However, before I could spend much time trying to come up with a miracle solution for that (and everything else in my life at the moment), my eyes were opening to realize I had overslept for graduation line-up. I shot out of bed, silenced my phone alarm that had apparently been going off for the last hour-and-a-half, and tried my best to shake off the buzz I was still experiencing from last night's celebrations. With my favorite cat t-shirt, khaki shorts, cap, and gown on, I made it to my spot in the line-up just in time to head towards the stage and begin the ceremony.

As we took our seats in front of the stage, a sense of community washed over all of us. The majority of us had been with each other the last four years and we had made it to this final point together in one piece. Also, most of us didn't have a job lined up and had no idea what the rest of our life might look like after today. There's a certain peace that comes over you when you start to realize that no one really has their shit together and I wish I could bottle up that peace to carry forever. After smiling at everyone who made eye contact with me, I started to reflect on my own journey as the speakers began talking into the microphone. Somehow, mostly thanks to my select few family members and friends (and their families), I had turned myself from train wreck to Honors graduate with a year of full-time big boy job employment already under my belt even with a separate resume of hurdles within my personal life. More importantly, I had done so while maintaining my fun social life and personality (if you could call it that). My brain started flashing through memories over the last four years, both great and awful, until I suddenly heard my name called through the speakers.

Knowing it was hardly time to start walking across the stage and receiving diplomas, I was incredibly confused. I looked around before looking up at the president of the college on stage until I realized I had just won an award. They had already announced winners at the Awards Day Ceremony a few weeks ago, but apparently that didn't include some of them. My friend sitting next to me gave me a quick nudge and I awkwardly made my way up to the stage to shake hands. Once I got back to my seat, I looked down at the plague that read *Most Outstanding Male Senior: Chase Freeman* in gold letters in complete disbelief. How the hell did I manage to win Homecoming King and this all while dealing with a full-time government job, internship, seminar, mock trial, getting drunk at parties in semi-secret, and a 12 month long (so far) legal battle with my mother? A smile spread across my face and remained there for what felt like hours, or at least however much time had passed before the hired speaker decided it was appropriate and acceptable to imitate a child with Down Syndrome's voice during his commencement speech. Everyone's smile stopped then although his check probably still cleared.

The ceremony concluded after we all accepted our pieces of paper that cost anywhere from $5,000-$100,000 that we'd likely spend the rest of our lives paying off with salaries that hadn't been updated for generations. From there, it was time to take pictures with anyone and everyone all across the campus lawns before making our way to whatever dining arrangements we had made. After a joint celebratory meal with my best friend, we decided to go have another weekend escape in Knoxville after my father and stepmother (who was practically my real mother by this point) gifted us a nice room at a resort in Gatlinburg. We spent the rest of the weekend celebrating and relaxing, as if my liver hadn't been through enough the last four years, before it was time for yet another return to reality. While everyone else on campus was free to leave for good to whatever the rest of their life was going to be, I still had two or three weeks left of work at the Service and Leadership House.

I wanted nothing more than to take a deep breath and soak in the same newfound freedom everyone else was feeling but I couldn't. There was one final Mobile Food Bank I needed to accomplish in the next two weeks. I needed to find a place to live in Nashville before I was kicked off campus in two weeks. I needed to compile a huge report to submit to the government that showed my annual analytics from my entire term. I still needed to figure out a job in Nashville in the next few weeks just in case I somehow had my financial security blanket ripped out from under me. Deep down, I didn't feel like that was a risk whatsoever, but I knew better than to dip into any funds until the estate was officially resolved. Plus, by this point in all of this, the court costs and administrative fees were going to be massive with how extensively Lilley had drug all of this out.

My final food bank event wrapped up just as smoothly as the first one and I began working on the final report. Both Associate Deans had moved on to bigger and better opportunities, so the report had to be turned into the current Dean. With how unaware he was of our program's specifics, I knew the only way to get any questions answered was through the actual government so I hoped for the best and turned it in. Looking over the data for volunteer recruitment, household registrations, pounds of food distributed, and everything else brought forth another wave of pride and accomplishment. Somehow, I had been talked into taking this role and actually pulled it off. I hosted an event in various towns throughout the county and broadened our program's reach more than ever before. Despite the fact that my life felt like an illegally-built roller coaster for the last 12 months, I had accomplished everything. Except the whole job and apartment thing, of course. And the pending lawsuit from my mother.

Eventually, I was somehow able to figure out a roommate situation with a stranger at the last minute before I was about to awkwardly be kicked off campus for good. Packing up my office and my dorm room for a final time probably should have felt more emotional than it did, but I was craving the next chapter. The last four years were filled with great highs and deep lows, but they felt fulfilled nonetheless. Every journey has to end for others to begin and I could not have been more ready for this next one. After squeezing all of my belongings into the confinements of my car, I left campus in my rearview mirror. Since I had endured random roommates at various points during the last four years, I'm sure signing a 12-month lease with someone I barely knew wouldn't be any kind of issue. I was wrong, but that's life.

Trying to adjust from having every hour of your life planned to complete freedom from any kind of class or work schedule was nearly impossible in the best of ways. After withdrawing a small amount to survive on and furnish my new bedroom in the apartment, I kept at the job applications despite how hopeless the whole process seemed. I still wasn't sure how I convinced the apartment complex to let me move in without a secure job, but oh well. I was too busy absorbing the thrills of being in a new city and making new friends to care about anything negative. Having a luxurious pool in my apartment complex made it all the easier to relax for the first time in what felt like ages. However, I couldn't help but feel a tinge of guilt about living on the money that had been left to me even though I didn't really have any other choice. I did my best to push these thoughts to the back corner of my mind while I focused on the new life I had started to occupy and create overnight.

By the time August rolled around, the attorney called to bring me back down to reality by letting me know there was a court date in a couple of days. He warned me that Lilley would be there with whatever attorney she had managed to recruit this time and that it could likely be the last court date for the estate if we played our cards right. Therefore, I happily agreed to pack a quick bag and make my way down to my high school town once again. After spending the entire drive playing over every possible scenario in my head of how the day might go, I felt more ready than ever to get it over with. Even if there were some hurdles to leap over, I was willing to do whatever it took to settle the 14-month-long estate battle once and for all.

Walking into the icy courtroom building, I was pleased to see my Great Uncle and the attorney once I made it through the metal detectors. We quickly caught up on everything but the peace only lasted a few moments before Lilley stormed into the building, shooting a fiery glare in our direction. After making her way to the reception area and having a shouting match over some kind of ticket cost or court fee that was unrelated to today, she made her way over to a man that I assumed was her newest attorney. After what felt like the most tense hour, it was finally time to file into the courtroom and await our case to be called by the judge. A millisecond after he had finished calling out my grandfather's name, Lilley was on her feet practically shouting all the reasons why she was challenging the estate and why everything her father ever touched was rightfully owed to her. I found a quiet delight in watching the judge's facial expressions as she hurled her statements in his direction. He took a deep breath once she finally stopped, looked over a few papers in front of him, and glanced over in our direction.

After what felt like an eternity, he stated that he didn't see any legal reason or standing for her to continue pursuing anything that was purposefully left outside of the estate and final will. He continued by saying it was clear that he was not the first legal representative to inform her of this and that it would be best for everyone involved if this issue was resolved privately as opposed to legally within a courtroom setting. He concluded by suggesting we take advantage of one of the private meeting rooms within the building to work out a resolution before the court adjourned today. If not, we were just going to continue extending these court dates and wasting everyone's time, energy, and money for years.

Lilley filled the private room with insults and accusations the moment the door closed and we all found a seat at a table. Once she was finally finished, the attorney calmly explained that we needed to settle this. We weren't going to be caving into all of the insane demands she had been making for more than a year now. He explained that even if she continued with the legal battle against the estate (me), the portion she *might* receive would not be worth it in the end after the extensive legal fees. I decided to make stern eye contact with her as he continued to explain that if she continued fighting this battle, we would not stop returning for each one until she gave up and/or ran out of attorneys who would agree to represent her. To soften these tense explanations, he added that if I ever wanted to consider surrendering any or all of the money that had been left in my specific name that I could do so at any point in the future without any legal representation or courtroom fights needed. Not that I was considering that whatsoever at this point, I didn't deny his statement.

Everyone in the room went back and forth for a grueling hour in the private meeting room until we agreed to writing her a check. She immediately demanded more but we said that the offer was final and that the only way she'd even receive that smaller amount was if she agreed to never legally pursue the estate, my Great Uncle, anything related to either of them, or me ever again. Within a few moments, we had the draft of this agreement printed onto paper, signed, and notarized before making our way back into the court to have the estate issues finally resolved.

Hearing the judge read aloud that the agreement was valid and standing which made the matter officially resolved brought a tidal wave of relief that I had never felt before. It was over. Everything was over. My mother had spent the last 14 months attacking me, insulting my character, and making my life hell in an attempt to win what my grandfather had left me. But she lost. She had used every weapon she could think of to win and it didn't work. She used my sister, my potential future career(s), and even my grandmother's memory against me and none of it had worked in the end. On top of everything she had done throughout her entire life while he was alive, she had taken him from his home, kept him from everyone, emptied his house and bank account, and then sued me/the estate on top of it for over a year. Not only had she chosen to do all of this when our relationship was already strained to say the least, but she had done it during the most important year of my life. When life was already at its most chaotic without a legal battle involved with your own mother. But I won.

The judge adjourned the room and we all stood up to shake hands and go over any last-minute details about the official closing of the estate. After these brief conversations had ended, we all made our separate ways out of the courtroom and headed toward our cars. I had almost made it out of the building doors when Lilley stepped in front of my path. Her facial expression was smug and I thought for a moment she was about to ask me for a larger check and/or physically assault me. Instead, after an uncomfortable amount of silence, she crossed her arms and asked, "So that's it then? We're done? You just don't want anything to do with your own mother now?"

"No, I do not," I replied, stepping past her and out the courthouse doorway.

Lightning Source UK Ltd.
Milton Keynes UK
UKHW031810050922
408362UK00007B/1680

9 798886 801558